THEY WOULD NOT BE MOVED

THEY WOULD NOT BE MOVED

The Enduring Struggle of the Mille Lacs
Band of Ojibwe to Keep Their Reservation

BRUCE WHITE

MINNESOTA
HISTORICAL
SOCIETY

The publication of this book was supported with a gift from an anonymous donor.

mnhspress.org

The Minnesota Historical Society Press is a member of the Association of University Presses.

Manufactured in the United States of America

10 9 8 7 6 5 4 3 2 1

♾ The paper used in this publication meets the minimum requirements of the American National Standard for Information Sciences—Permanence for Printed Library Materials, ANSI Z39.48–1984.

International Standard Book Number
ISBN: 978-1-68134-296-2 (paperback)
ISBN: 978-1-68134-297-9 (e-book)

Library of Congress Control Number: 2024938108

On the cover: Tom Wind (Mayzhuckegwonabe), a Mille Lacs band member from Pine County, and Mary Pendegayaush (Wahbooze), whose family lived on the Mille Lacs Reservation near Vineland, c. 1920. See page 252. Cover design by Andrew Brozyna.

The text of this book has been set in Sirba, a typeface designed by Nicolien van der Keur. Interior text design by Wendy Holdman.

Contents

Foreword

Melanie Benjamin, Chief Executive,
Mille Lacs Band of Ojibwe, 2000–2024

I have had the great honor to serve as the Chief Executive (Chairwoman) of the Non-Removable Mille Lacs Band of Ojibwe since the election in the year 2000 and through the five subsequent elections. Writing this foreword to *They Would Not Be Moved* is one of my last acts as the chief executive of our tribe, as after so many years I chose to pass the baton to the next generation of leaders and did not run again for reelection. What a delightful project to work on in my last week of office.

The Mille Lacs Band of Ojibwe is comprised of three districts today, spread out by fairly significant distances across east-central Minnesota. District I encompasses a 61,000-acre reservation along the southwest side of Mille Lacs Lake, which is where our main government center is located. Nearly fifty miles to the north and east is District II, which includes Isle, East Lake, and Sandy Lake. District III is located about fifty miles east in the area of Hinckley, Minnesota, with our village of Lake Lena being farther east along the St. Croix River, some eighty miles from District I. We are three districts, but we are called one "band," or tribe, of Anishinaabeg.

Each district is equally important, and each has a unique history prior to being consolidated as the Mille Lacs Band of Ojibwe in 1936. This book by Bruce White is about the history of District I, our main Indian reservation established by the Treaty of 1855, where most of our citizens live and where we have experienced the most contentious battles over the past 170 years to preserve our homelands and our very existence.

Prior to taking office as the chief executive for the Mille Lacs Band in 2000, I had many years of service to the band in an administrative capacity. During these early years I was provided with leadership lessons by my two predecessors, Arthur Gahbow and Marge Anderson. Chief Executive Gahbow hired me as his commissioner of administration in 1989. Gahbow was a trailblazer, a man of great vision. In one of our first meetings, he told me that his vision included first securing our 1837 hunting, fishing, and gathering rights, and then certifying the boundary of our Indian reservation in District I.

Gahbow observed how the Wisconsin bands of Chippewa went about securing their hunting, fishing, and gathering rights, and he knew the importance of telling and documenting our history. In 1979 Chief Gahbow directed that our history be researched and published. This research resulted in a book, *Against the Tide of American History: The Story of the Mille Lacs Anishinaabe*, by W. Roger Buffalohead and Patricia Buffalohead. He was right about how important this history would eventually be for our lawsuit to require the State of Minnesota to recognize our right to hunt, fish, and gather without state interference in the territory we ceded to the United States in 1837. It was and is a wonderful book, but it was only the beginning of the much more extensive research we would eventually need to prove the existence of our rights.

Gahbow wanted to create a case to litigate the band's 1837 treaty rights. Our ancestors had signed the Treaty of 1837 in which we ceded a large swath of east-central Minnesota to the United States in exchange for the right to hunt, fish, and gather throughout that territory. The State of Minnesota enacted rules regarding hunting and fishing in ceded territory that were later found by courts to be contrary to treaties. Gahbow himself was cited by the Minnesota Department of Natural Resources. The promises of this treaty were made to us before Minnesota was even a state; there were no stipulations in the Treaty of 1837 that restricted our right to feed our families to only certain months of the year, by a future government that did not yet exist. In fact, a provision of the treaty stated that the signatories would retain their rights to hunt, fish, and gather.

During the late 1980s and early 1990s, other band members joined in carrying out this strategy, and were also cited for fishing violations. The state commissioner of natural resources was likely aware of the strength of our case and did not want to be forced to litigate it. Instead, he chose to drop the charges against Art and other band members. But these acts of defiance were a step toward justice, a cornerstone in our struggle to protect what was and is rightfully ours, and eventually formed the basis of our lawsuit against the State of Minnesota.

Finally, in August 1990, Chief Executive Gahbow's dream took a big step forward: our case against the State of Minnesota for interfering with our 1837 treaty rights was filed in federal court. This was a historic moment, a result of thirty years of struggle, advocacy, and unshakable determination.

Sadly, Art passed away in 1991. I had served as his commissioner of administration, the chief of staff position for the chief executive. Marge Anderson, who served as our elected secretary-treasurer/speaker of the Mille Lacs Band Assembly, took over the reins as chief executive. Anderson continued the work of securing our treaty-guaranteed rights to hunt, fish, and gather in the 1837 ceded territory. I continued as commissioner of administration throughout most of the 1990s.

As Art knew, winning our lawsuit would depend on unearthing and carefully documenting the facts of our history from over 150 years ago. Historians Charles Cleland and James McClurken were already on the case, and then historian and anthropologist Bruce White came into the picture. We first hired Bruce to conduct historical research for our lawsuit in 1992. I have a vivid recollection of meeting Bruce: he had a kindly face, but behind the white hair and the bushy beard was a brilliant scholar who could recite more historical facts about the band than anyone I had ever encountered.

It is impossible to overstate the importance of Bruce's testimony and written contributions to our legal battles. In federal Indian law, the US Supreme Court has developed "canons of construction," or rules, that the courts are required to follow whenever analyzing a treaty. One of these rules is that treaties must be interpreted as the Indians would have understood them at the time the treaty was signed.

Imagine owning a cabin or farm that has been in your family for many generations, and being told that in order to prove that you own the property today, you must provide historical evidence documenting what your ancestors were thinking over 150 years ago. And imagine that your ancestors did not speak or read English, so you had to depend on finding letters, journals, and reports from English-speaking witnesses from 150 years ago who might be able to provide first-person testimony as to what your ancestors were thinking about!

This painstaking effort is what Bruce White has undertaken for our people for over three decades. His research and testimony laid a critical foundation for all the litigation victories we would achieve in federal court over those years.

At one point in the middle of the 1837 Treaty litigation, in 1993, we had actually reached an out-of-court settlement with the State of Minnesota, which had to be ratified by the state legislature. This settlement only involved recognizing the rights of Mille Lacs band members (versus other tribes) and would limit them to fishing in one small zone of less than five acres on Mille Lacs Lake. Many band members felt we were conceding too much to the state, but the groups led by Mille Lacs County protested loudly against the settlement, demanding their day in court. So the state legislature killed the settlement, and the case moved forward.

In 1999 the US Supreme Court delivered a ruling that recognized the rights of not just Mille Lacs but thirteen other tribes in Minnesota and Wisconsin to fish the entire Mille Lacs Lake. The Supreme Court opinion was authored by Associate Justice Sandra Day O'Connor. She cited Bruce White's research.

◆ ◆ ◆

I was elected chief executive of our tribe in the year 2000. Having learned the critical importance of our history from Art and Marge, I made it a practice to learn as much as I could about the leaders who came before them and about our history more broadly. There was yet another legal battle on the horizon. After the US Supreme Court decision in 1999, the Mille Lacs County Board of Commissioners, private landowners, and small businesses that had financed the legal battle against the band vowed to continue the fight.

In 2002, my second year in office as chief executive, Mille Lacs County attempted to disestablish our reservation by suing us in federal court. It was a short-lived case, promptly dismissed for lack of standing, meaning those bringing suit could not prove that the existence of the reservation had caused them any harm. But we knew they wouldn't stop, because they publicly said they wouldn't. And they didn't.

Since our Supreme Court victory in 1999, Mille Lacs County has challenged nearly every action our tribe attempted to take on lands within our reservation boundary. The county has engaged in a multipronged legal, political, and administrative campaign in its effort to deny the existence of the Mille Lacs Reservation. Since the Supreme Court's 1999 decision, Mille Lacs County has, among other things: 1. Filed a multimillion-dollar lawsuit against band officials in federal court seeking a judicial declaration that the Mille Lacs Reservation no longer exists; 2. Repeatedly sought rulings from state courts that the reservation no longer exists in cases in which the band was not even a party; 3. Lobbied the US Department of the Interior and other federal agencies to withdraw their recognition of the reservation; 4. Challenged the issuance of federal permits to the band for projects on the reservation on the grounds that there is no reservation; 5. Repeatedly sought to regulate the band's use of its own lands on the reservation; 6. Pressured state officials and agencies to renounce the reservation's existence; and 7. Directed county officials and employees to purge all references to the reservation from county files and records.

With the exception of persuading some state elected officials to deny the existence of the reservation, the county's actions have failed. No court or federal agency has accepted the county's requests to conclude that the reservation no longer exists. The only thing the county seemed capable of accepting was our mutual aid cooperative law enforcement agreement, in which our officers shared concurrent jurisdiction with county officers to enforce state criminal law within the boundary of our original 61,000-acre reservation at the northernmost end of Mille Lacs County. This agreement benefited all citizens, Indian and non-Indian, because we were providing almost half of the law enforcement resources in all of Mille Lacs County. The arrangement worked well for nearly twenty-five years.

However, the issue of the history of the reservation and whether or not it had been disestablished was still at the core of a multitude of disputes we had with the county. One dispute in particular was the tipping point that would bring us back into federal court over whether or not our reservation as established by the Treaty of 1855 still existed.

In 2013 the Mille Lacs Band filed an application with the US Department of Justice to get federal help under a new program authorized by President Barack Obama called the Tribal Law and Order Act. Acceptance into the program would help deter crime because there could be federal prosecution of the most violent crimes on the reservation, with longer federal sentences that would be served in federal prison.

We believed the county would eventually sue us again. So we again enlisted James McClurken and Bruce White to begin researching the history of the creation of our Indian reservation. What we did not expect was that the band would eventually be the party to file a lawsuit that would result in litigation of our boundary.

Since the early 1990s we had a fully operational tribal police force employing approximately thirty Minnesota Peace Officers Standards and Training (POST) Board–certified police officers. But in 2016 the county unilaterally revoked our law enforcement agreement and falsely informed every county in Minnesota that our thirty-plus tribal police force of POST Board–certified police officers no longer had the powers of a police department and should be arrested for impersonating police officers if seen enforcing state law beyond a few acres held in trust by the federal government inside the reservation. County officials said they would reinstate the law enforcement agreement only if the band would agree that the reservation no longer existed. Never in a million years would we agree to give up our homelands.

The situation quickly became a life-and-death public safety crisis for our community between 2016 and 2018. Word spread among organized drug dealers in Minnesota and surrounding states that our reservation was a police-free zone. Our community was overrun by opioid dealers. Funerals due to overdose or violence became a weekly occurrence. To protect our community, we had no choice but to sue Mille Lacs County. In order to decide this case, the federal judge needed to first establish whether or not our reservation existed. The county remained adamant that the reservation did not exist. We needed our lawyers and we needed our historians.

Bruce White's and James McClurken's work again played a critical role in this district court battle. Bruce painstakingly documented the words of our great chiefs like Shaboshkung and Monzomonay. Bruce found the historical evidence that crystalized how exactly our ancestors viewed the various treaties, what they understood was being promised to them in meetings with President Abraham Lincoln, and the indescribable pain, suffering, and loss they felt when they saw squatters taking over their homes and lumber companies chopping down nearly all of their pine forest acre by acre, destroying the habitat on which our people had thrived for generations.

In 1855 our ancestors signed a treaty with the United States that created the Mille Lacs Reservation, as well as Leech Lake and other smaller reservations. In 1862, when the Dakota War took place, several Ojibwe bands from the north wanted to join the Dakota and fight the United States. The Mille Lacs chiefs refused to join the war and instead sent warning to Fort Ripley and tried to protect the fort and settlements. In 1863, after the Dakota War, in order to appease the white settlers, the United States wanted to remove several tribes with which it had made treaties in 1855. However, two articles in the Treaty of 1863 seemed to contradict each other. Article 1 seemed to say that Mille Lacs and other bands had to give up their homelands to the United States, but Article 12 said something different. Because of the Mille Lacs Band's good behavior during the Dakota War, Article 12 said we would never have to move, unless we caused harm to the settlers. Tribal leaders from Mille Lacs met with President Lincoln, who told them our people could stay on our reservation for a hundred years or a thousand years.

Despite these promises, squatters and others who wanted our valuable pine timber tried to take away our reservation. For twenty years band leaders like Shaboshkung and Monzomonay fought to preserve the reservation for band members. But federal officials wanted to send our kids to boarding schools and divide up our lands. The pressure to move all the Ojibwe to White Earth was intense.

The Indian commissioners reported back to Congress that the Mille Lacs and Fond du Lac bands would not accept removal to White Earth. Congress responded by passing the Nelson Act (1889), which authorized more negotiation with the Ojibwe to give up our reservations and take allotments. The Nelson Act commission came to Mille Lacs to negotiate. Our ancestors told the commission that they would remain on the reservation and take allotments at Mille Lacs. They understood that the allotments would allow them to stay on the reservation forever if they wanted. The Nelson Act commission promised that the band could receive allotments at Mille Lacs.

However, before the allotments were made, squatters again swarmed the reservation and claimed nearly all the reservation lands for themselves. Band members' homes were burned down by the county sheriff, and they were forced from their lands, sometimes at gunpoint.

But our ancestors fought to stay, even when the federal government withheld annuity payments unless they went to White Earth. Eventually a few allotments were granted on this reservation, and band members and the federal government also bought back some land when they could. But most of our land was taken by force. We went from about 61,000 acres down to just a few acres. Our leaders would spend the next 135 years gradually buying back a small part of our lost land, which we are still doing today.

The first year I worked for Chairman Arthur Gahbow, he made a speech about the Nelson Act. He said: "I see a people who stayed on their own land after the Nelson Act tried to move them. . . . I see a people who stayed on their land in spite of the burning of their houses by the County Sheriff. . . . I see a people who are proud and strong. . . . In your veins is the blood of Shaboshkung and Shagobay. In your hearts, there is the spirit of . . . warriors."

As mentioned above, in 2010 President Obama signed the Tribal Law and Order Act (TLOA) into law, making it possible for some of the worst crimes committed on a reservation to be prosecuted by the United States. If a person was found guilty, they could be sent to federal prison instead of county jail. We decided to apply for Tribal Law and Order Act status, to give the federal government concurrent criminal jurisdiction on our reservation, because it might make people think twice before committing terrible crimes. But the process slowed down after Mille Lacs County objected to our application. The county board told the federal government there was no reservation in their county.

In hindsight, the county probably should have kept still. Because of the county's objections, the US Department of Justice had no choice but to ask the Interior Department: Does the Mille Lacs Reservation exist? Interior had no choice but to answer the question, which involved intensive research about the county's claim.

After almost two years, Interior finally issued a thirty-seven-page opinion explaining how and why the Mille Lacs Reservation never went away—and continues to exist. With that opinion in writing, the US Department of Justice accepted our application and we gained TLOA status. And once again, historical research by Bruce White found its way into the opinion.

Finally, in March 2022 federal judge Susan Richard Nelson affirmed that our reservation did, indeed, exist. Later she ruled that we had law enforcement jurisdiction over the whole reservation. We won.

In her ruling Judge Nelson repeatedly cited and relied upon the historical narrative documented by Bruce White's research—evidence of how our people understood the Treaty of 1855 and subsequent federal actions as preserving our reservation within its original boundary. The historical evidence was overwhelming. Judge Nelson concluded her decision with this: "Over the course of more than 160 years, Congress has never clearly expressed an intention to disestablish or diminish the Mille Lacs Reservation. The Court therefore affirms what the Band has maintained for the better part of two centuries—the Mille Lacs Reservation's boundaries remain as they were under Article 2 of the Treaty of 1855." The band won its long struggle for its reservation.

◆ ◆ ◆

Thanks to Bruce's work, we also know that our ancestors were no pushovers. They fought back against infractions on their lands as best they could, demonstrating keen intelligence, strategy, and even sarcasm. In the early 1860s an Indian agent who was not very good at his job had a meeting in Crow Wing with several bands of Ojibwe from all over the region. He made this speech: "My red brothers, the winds of fifty-five winters have blown over my head and have silvered it with gray. In all that time I have never done wrong to a single human being. As the representative of the Great Father and as your friend, I advise you to sign this treaty at once."

As the story goes, Shaboshkung, who was head chief at Mille Lacs, stood up and replied: "My father, look at me. The winds of fifty-five winters have blown over my head and have silvered it with gray. But they haven't blown my brains away."

Over and above the value of recounting Bruce White's exceptionally well-documented history as it relates to our legal rights, this book also represents the potential to put an end to the intolerance and lack of understanding in our region that has been fueled by the misinformation and in some cases outright lies being spread by county officials and their attorneys. My predecessor, Chief Executive Marge Anderson, always said that ignorance breeds fear, because people fear what they do not understand. And fear often leads to hate.

Over the decades, fearmongering on the part of county officials has taken its toll. Mille Lacs band members and other Native people have experienced incidents of hostility and racism simply because of their real or perceived affiliation with the Mille Lacs Band. The county's campaign against the Mille Lacs Band and its reservation has provoked hostility toward the band and our citizens. In order to generate and maintain support for its lawsuit against band officials, some county commissioners falsely claimed that the band would tax, zone, and prosecute non-Indians living within the reservation boundaries (which the band has no authority or intention to do).

Leading up to and during the Treaty of 1837 litigation in the 1990s, several anti-Indian organizations formed around the Mille Lacs area, including the Citizens Equal Rights Alliance, the Mille Lacs Equal Rights Association (here "equal rights" means taking rights from Indians), and Proper Economic Resource Management (PERM), a group still fighting our Supreme Court win on hunting and fishing.

This book tells the truth by sharing facts that cannot be disputed. Truth and understanding are the most powerful forces against fear and hatred. This book will be required reading for students in our tribal school, but it should also be required reading for public schools. Only through mutual understanding can we undo the lies that have been spread about us and stop the fearmongering.

Throughout my years serving the band, I always asked our elders about our past. We have a rich oral history passed down from many generations of elders. This oral tradition is filled with stories of struggle, persistence, and steadfast refusal to give up our homelands in the midst of trickery and schemes financed by the rich and politically powerful. What I love about this book is that it affirms these stories that have lasted over many generations, adding fascinating details backed up by decades of Bruce White's careful research. His knowledge is wide-ranging and of great value: the number of times during my tenure as chief executive when someone has said, "Call Bruce White" are too many to count.

This book represents the promise of the continued survival of our people for the thousand years or more guaranteed by President Lincoln, because it will forever be an invaluable resource of documented history that our young people and those who have yet to be born can rely upon to continue protecting our homelands. Like their ancestors before them, they too will not be moved.

I write this foreword as we are awaiting a decision on the county's appeal of our reservation boundary case to the Eighth Circuit Court of Appeals. At all levels of this case, Bruce's research was indispensable. Lawyers prefer to call on Bruce because his writing and testimony is always objective and accurate. I appreciate that he can meet a band member and quickly explain the great deeds of one of their ancestors. He makes us proud to be members of the Mille Lacs Band of Ojibwe.

Bruce White was the only person who could write this book. Other excellent historians and attorneys have helped us over the decades, but Bruce combed through the archives and found truth. Eventually band members found justice because our historian uncovered the scandals, the false patents, and the schemes by politicians and timber barons. Band members know and trust Bruce, as do the band's elected officials, administrators, and attorneys. He is respected by the academic and legal communities. Bruce has conducted more than three decades of research on the ways land was taken from the band, and here, with this book, he puts it all in one place, but he goes beyond that to provide details about non-Indian politicians, the band leadership through many treaties, and the impact of oppression on band members throughout history. This story highlights the strength, stubbornness, and resiliency of the Mille Lacs Band, summed up in the appropriate title, *They Would Not Be Moved*.

From this book readers will gain some perspective on Indian treaty rights; on the greed of the lumber barons; on the complicity of federal officials in taking Indian land illegally; and about the stubbornness and grit of the Mille Lacs Band. Reading this book will provide any reader with a history of Minnesota they have not heard before. It will offer insights into Alexander Ramsey, Henry Rice, Senator Dwight Sabin, and Amherst Wilder that will require readers to reevaluate these men who are still viewed as great Minnesota leaders and pioneers. These men deliberately dismantled our reservation. We have spent one hundred and fifty years trying to get it back together.

As for the Mille Lacs Band today, we stand by the words of our great chief Shaboshkung, who fought removal in the 1880s when the United States sent a commission to negotiate with the Ojibwe of Minnesota. They wanted us to give up our reservations and take allotments at White Earth. Shaboshkung said to the commissioners he would "rather that his bones bleach out on the shores of Mille Lacs Lake than move." He reminded the officials about the 1863 Treaty and President Lincoln's promise of our right to stay on our reservation.

We did not move. In one thousand years, the Mille Lacs Band will remain here. Miigwech to Bruce White, our other historians, and our brilliant litigators!

Introduction

Is the one thousand years up that the Great Father sent you here?

—Mille Lacs leader Shaboshkung, 1886

They call themselves the nonremovable Mille Lacs Ojibwe (sometimes Chippewa or, in their own language, Anishinaabeg). From the beginning, members of the Mille Lacs Band of Ojibwe made clear to anyone who would listen that they would never leave their reservation, along the shores of, and including the waters of, Mille Lacs Lake. Despite all inducements suggesting they would be better off at another location in Minnesota, such as the White Earth Indian Reservation on the other side of the state, or elsewhere, members of the Mille Lacs Band asserted their connection to the reservation formed in their own previous history and in negotiations with the US government in 1855, in Washington, DC. In keeping with federal Indian policies of the time, this location was to be their "permanent home"—a place with access to many resources for survival, including game, fish, wild rice, maple sugar, and garden produce. When federal officials sought to negotiate a new agreement in 1863, Mille Lacs band leaders repeated their insistence that they were not interested in signing a treaty that would have them leave Mille Lacs. In the negotiation, their chief asserted, "We demand that we should be allowed to live on our Reserves." The treaty as written honored this request, transferring title to the lands in the reservation to the federal government but reserving the right of the Mille Lacs Band to live there indefinitely, into the future.

Up until that time, over many decades, the Mille Lacs Band of Ojibwe had had no reason to fear a forced removal by the federal government. Since American civil and military leaders had arrived to stay in the early nineteenth century, the Ojibwe had shown their peaceful intentions toward the Americans and even toward their Native neighbors, with whom they were sometimes drawn into war. The earliest Indian agent at Fort Snelling, Lawrence Taliaferro, who came there in 1820, recalled later that

Bezhig (Lone Man), a Mille Lacs and Snake River chief, was the first Indian leader who came to him, asking for help in negotiating peace between Ojibwe and Dakota people. Mille Lacs band members may have been more inclined to seek peace because of their own history. While Dakota and Ojibwe had fought many battles over more than a century, the actions of Bezhig made sense considering that he, like other members of the Ma'iingan or Wolf clan of the Ojibwe, could trace his ancestry to a marriage between a Dakota man and an Ojibwe woman at the time when his Ojibwe ancestors had first come into the Minnesota region a hundred or more years before. French government official Paul Marin recorded, in the 1750s, that one of the men working for him had traveled to the Rum River, where he encountered four "cabanes" or lodges of "demi-Sioux et demi-Sauteux," meaning "half-Dakota, half-Ojibwe." While the Ojibwe of the St. Croix and Mille Lacs bands fought against the Dakota, their story was not one of "implacable warfare," as some American officials would later write. When Ojibwe came to Fort Snelling, they met Dakota and engaged in ceremonies and peace treaties, which Taliaferro facilitated. When relationships between the two peoples broke down, the Ojibwe of Mille Lacs were not the cause.[1]

Even when Ojibwe signed their first treaty of cession with the US government, involving the area bordering Mille Lacs, at Fort Snelling in 1837, the agreement did not require their removal. Article 5 of the treaty stated: "the privilege of hunting, fishing, and gathering the wild rice, upon the lands, the rivers and the lakes included in the territory ceded, is guarantied to the Indians, during the pleasure of the President." While the treaty opened the region up to the southern shore of Mille Lacs Lake to lumbermen and other whites, the Ojibwe continued to reside in their homelands, coexisting with the newly arrived European Americans.

Pressure for the removal of Ojibwe from throughout the ceded territories of the 1837 and 1842 treaties came to a head in 1850 when President Zachary Taylor issued an order for the removal of Ojibwe in Wisconsin to the area around Big Sandy Lake in Minnesota Territory. During the next few years, the Mille Lacs Band was never subject to that order, which in any case was a failure and was soon rescinded. In the mid-1850s federal officials, led by Commissioner of Indian Affairs George W. Manypenny, abandoned the previous policy of removal of tribes throughout the country, determining instead to create reservations within territories ceded by tribes. This approach was the background for the Treaty of 1855.

Reservations consisted of land areas designed for the exclusive and permanent use of Native tribes. In Minnesota and elsewhere government officials found ways to compromise such areas over time, either by disestablishing them or by subverting Native land ownership within them, the latter of which did not actually disestablish reservations. By the late 1850s Minnesota officials, like Henry Mower Rice, who had helped negotiate the 1855 treaty, wavered in their support for all of those reservations. But no means was considered to attempt to disestablish the reservations created in the 1855 treaty until September 1862. At the same time that Dakota began to battle against Americans in southern Minnesota, it was rumored that the Gull Lakes chief Bagone-giizhig or Hole-in-the-Day the Younger (also known as Gwiiwisens or Kwiiwisens, meaning Boy) was going to raise a similar attack in the Upper Mississippi region. Messages were said to have been sent by Hole-in-the-Day to recruit Ojibwe leaders and warriors from throughout the region to join in such a fight.

Mille Lacs leaders were not tempted to lend support to Hole-in-the-Day's effort. They sent a message to Commissioner of Indian Affairs William P. Dole, who was in Minnesota to make a treaty with the Red Lake Band, informing him they would not participate in Hole-in-the-Day's plans. Episcopal minister Ezekiel G. Gear vouched for the peaceable nature of the Mille Lacs people: "They condemned the movements of Hole-in-the-Day in council and told their young men that if any of them joined, they would never be permitted to return to the band again."[2]

Because of the threat from Hole-in-the-Day, Commissioner Dole initiated a plan to remove all the Ojibwe in Minnesota to a single reservation, near Leech Lake, the better to manage any future trouble. However, Dole promised the Mille Lacs people that their fidelity would be rewarded. He would later say of the Mille Lacs Band: "They came and promised to keep the peace, they aided us, and I am determined to be their friend in all their troubles." At the time of the 1863 treaty negotiation, Mille Lacs leaders met with President Abraham Lincoln, who, it was reported in various newspapers at the time, "assured them of his good will and protection of the Government as long as they deserved it, and they promised good behavior in the future." For decades the Mille Lacs leaders would recall that the president promised they could remain on the reservation for a thousand years and more.

Henry M. Rice, a former trader and the soon-to-be former Minnesota senator, who had helped negotiate the 1855 treaty, became the main federal treaty negotiator of the 1863 treaty. While removal from the 1855 reservations was the purpose of the new agreement, Rice knew the Mille Lacs Band's leaders would not consent to sign a treaty that required removal. However, he apparently hoped that band members could be persuaded, eventually, to leave. He had boundless faith in his ability to convince Indian people to embrace policies against their own interest. In crafting the treaty Rice created a document that appeared, to some whites at least, to be ambiguous. But it was not so to the Mille Lacs Band, and Rice, who returned in 1889 to persuade them to sign another agreement, was forced to admit that they were right, that they had always been right about the meaning of the treaty. Even so, thirty more years of ambiguity and turmoil unfolded before band members could receive a few meager allotments due them on their reservation at Mille Lacs.

What happened in the following years, during that whole period from the time of the treaty until the 1920s, is a confusing story, which a Mille Lacs County newspaper, the *Princeton Union*, called, in part, "a tangled skein." The story is confusing not because of anything about the Treaty of 1863, but because of the way government officials, timber company businessmen, and so-called or real settlers sought to get around the provisions of the treaty, effectively stealing title to almost all of the land owned by the Mille Lacs Band on the reservation, but never disestablishing it. Band members were forced to share the space with lumbermen, settlers, and other whites who wished to have vacation homes at a beautiful lake.

One outside observer, S. M. Brosious, of the Indian Rights Association in Washington, DC, wrote in 1901 that throughout the 1890s, "the entire political machinery of the State seems to have set to work to force the Mille Lacs off their homes and to locate them on the White Earth Reservation." He believed the federal government had been "duty-bound" to protect the rights of Mille Lacs band members to the land, but that because of a "vacillating policy" nothing had been done.[3]

Despite such efforts, the Mille Lacs Band and its leaders did all they could to counter the efforts to make them leave Mille Lacs, using their traditional peaceful tactics. They sought alliances with nearby white residents, like the citizens of Little Falls on the Mississippi River. Various leaders went to Washington to meet with federal leaders and remind them of the promises made in 1863, and the words band members had heard from President Lincoln. At no point did they pick up arms to fight against whites, regardless of the threats, physical or otherwise, they faced. Aside from negotiation, their main weapon was their stubborn resistance to removal.

A Multipronged Approach

Studying the complex and sometimes confusing interactions between Native people and Euro-Americans in the story of treaty making and the creation and maintenance of Indian reservations can benefit from the multiple approaches to history I have pursued in my work in the last forty years. This kind of history, which is sometimes called ethnohistory, or ethnographic history, combines a determined effort to gather historical information from available sources, whether written or not, along with an analysis based on an understanding of social, cultural, and geographical patterns in the history of the people described and their interactions with others.

In the case of reservations, spaces created by treaties but often including within them areas of long historical use prior to such agreements, it is necessary to consider not simply the events that took place within the boundaries of the reservation but also the participants' points of view, the nature of their tenure of the land, and the patterns of their use of the reservation. Reservations are human spaces, with specific histories and a specific meaning for those who live there.

My own interest in the history of the Mille Lacs Reservation may have begun on my thirteenth birthday, when my mother, who was a historian, did an oral history interview with her father, my grandfather, Rev. Edward McCann. He had been a Methodist minister some fifty years earlier along the south shore of Mille Lacs Lake in the towns of Onamia and Wahkon. That day he told of meeting and inviting to dinner at his bachelor parsonage two great leaders of the Mille Lacs Band, Migizi (or Megesee) and Wadena (or Wadiina). I did not know then the role of the two chiefs in the struggle to keep the Mille Lacs Reservation, but I would encounter their names later on in my research.

My grandfather did not know or remember all that the Mille Lacs Band of Ojibwe were undergoing on the Mille Lacs Reservation in those years. He did recall that an Indian agent at Mille Lacs had been attempting to get the band members to agree to move to another reservation. He did not remember that it was the White Earth Reservation, but he did recall that one of their chiefs, named Wadena, was a leader of those resisting removal. He said: "Wadena was a keen fellow, he was bright, he was intelligent, and he had a mind of his own and he was [a] big obstacle in the way of getting those Indians to go off to the reservation up there. He did everything he could to keep them right there around Mille Lac Lake, and you can see that that was a very desirable place for those Indians. They could fish there, you know, and they lived off the land pretty much—picked berries, fished—in every way. They were trying to be self-supporting."

He told of meeting Wadena and his fellow leader Migizi through the intercession of his good friend Rev. Frank Pequette, a French-Ojibwe Methodist minister who had a church at Sawyer, on the Fond du Lac Reservation. Pequette arranged for him to meet Migizi and Wadena, and for the two leaders to visit him at the parsonage where he lived. McCann himself served up a meal of steak, mashed potatoes, and peas, which seemed to please the men.

I don't recall exactly what impression I received from this story, but apparently it did stick in my mind. Around 1985 I began to do research and fieldwork prior to and during my graduate work in anthropology at the University of Minnesota. Perhaps as a result of this research I was invited to assist the Mille Lacs Band of Ojibwe in their lawsuit concerning hunting, fishing, and gathering rights under the Treaty of 1837. I wrote a report on President Zachary Taylor's Removal Order of 1850 and testified at a trial in federal court in Minneapolis in June 1994. I did further research for the Mille Lacs Band in the later phases of the 1837 treaty case, concerning the enforcement of game and fish laws in Minnesota in the nineteenth and twentieth centuries.[4]

After the conclusion of the 1837 treaty case, I began, for my own scholarly interest, to study the history of particular communities and families of Mille Lacs band members located in specific areas of the four partial townships contained in their reservation. I was interested in the ways tribal members lived on reservations, not as an undifferentiated group of people but as specific families and groups arranged in relation to the natural resources found in such places. Early on, some of this research was supported as part of a project paid for by the Minnesota Department of Transportation, which examined the possible effect of expanding Minnesota Highway 169 in the area of the town of Onamia and nearby South Harbor Township. Coincidentally this research involved the history of a piece of land at Cove where Wadena had once lived, as will be discussed in more detail in this book.[5]

In 2002 the Mille Lacs Band was sued over the issue of the status of the Mille Lacs Reservation, and the band asked me to expand upon the research I had done on particular Mille Lacs communities and their locations. I wrote the report "Ojibwe-White Conflicts over Land and Resources on the Mille Lacs Reservation, 1855–1923" and provided testimony in depositions in early 2003.

Because of the possibility for further litigation and the need for historical research to facilitate band decision-making about cultural resources,
the Mille Lacs Band asked me to continue my research for various purposes over the next fifteen years. In 2008 I wrote a report for the band in
a project funded by the US Army Corps of Engineers to study the possible
effects of changing levels of rivers and reservoirs in the Mississippi River
watershed on Mille Lacs Band cultural areas. Starting in 2012 I worked
with the band's Department of Natural Resources to help with a survey of
resources in their traditional cultural areas. In this research I collaborated
with Mille Lacs band member and Tribal Preservation Officer Natalie
Weyaus to study important cultural sites and to interview band elders.
And I was hired in 2014 by the University of Minnesota Duluth as coor-
dinator of a project to study the history of the Mille Lacs Band, under a
Legacy grant from the Minnesota Historical Society.[6]

Most recently, in 2018 the Mille Lacs Band asked me to update my 2003
report, including new research done in the previous fifteen years, for the
lawsuit that began in 2017, on the continuing existence of the Mille Lacs
Reservation. From all these many research and writing efforts, this book
has come to be.

Research Materials

To prepare this book, I have expanded on my earlier work, making use of
the many kinds of sources that can shed light on the full, rich history, culture, and geography of the Mille Lacs Reservation, combining the disci-
plines of history and anthropology.

A major resource for the study of the process of treaty making is the
correspondence of the US Office of Indian Affairs, now called the Bureau
of Indian Affairs. Letters back and forth between Indian agents in the field
and officials in Washington provide a varying understanding of Indian
policies and how they were carried out. However, they do not always give
a sense of the points of view of Indian people about federal Indian policies,
unless officials made a concerted effort to include such perspectives.

It is possible to write a history of treaty making using federal correspondence and other records as a primary resource, making little reference to the points of view of the Native tribes, leaders, or bands. This
approach would, of course, be remarkably one-sided and would miss out
on an important and necessary feature of treaty research in a legal context: the understanding of such documents by their Native signers.

Found occasionally in federal records are petitions signed by tribal leaders and sent on to Washington by Indian agents or tribal leaders themselves. Such documents provide a window on interpretations and understandings about treaties and key federal policies. The occasional petitions from Mille Lacs leaders, received in Minnesota and sent on to Washington, DC, are often revealing, even recording the memories of Mille Lacs leaders over the decades about the key 1863 treaty and the events surrounding it.

Mille Lacs leaders were vehement—though peaceable—in emphasizing their understanding that in signing the 1863 treaty they had agreed to cede title to land while retaining the right to remain on the reservation into the indefinite future. Their understanding of this fact was allied with their memory of having met President Lincoln at the time of the treaty and being told that they could remain for a thousand years or more, providing they behaved well toward their white neighbors.

An 1867 petition recorded the memories of Mille Lacs leaders: "[We] have remembered the words of our great father that he said to us six [sic] years ago when we went down to Washington if we would behave ourselves as we have done before that we should be let alone on the land we had before occupied [sic] for one hundred years or a thousand years or as long as we do not commit any depredations."[7]

Such events were also recorded in newspaper articles, at the time of the 1863 treaty and later. Using newspapers from that time is easier now that websites like Newspapers.com allow for text searching in digitized newspapers throughout the country for relevant material. In this case, the fact that so many newspapers recorded the visit of the Ojibwe bands to Washington that year, frequently called the "Chippewa mission," provides a relevant source of information, parallel to the memories Mille Lacs tribal leaders recorded in their petitions. And, as will be shown, later accounts in the *Princeton Union*, for many years the major newspaper in Mille Lacs County, provide an invaluable record not only about what was happening on the shores of Mille Lacs Lake but also about the activities of whites and Indian people alike.

Weighing the Evidence

When reconstructing the story of past events, it is important to gather, with no preconceptions, all the information available, with no prejudices about form or content. The many rich sources of information to be used in telling the story of the creation and later history of the Mille

Lacs Reservation can be interpreted using all the basic tools of historical research and writing. To begin with, it is important in doing history to be detailed both in research and in writing. The historian, whether working in the context of anthropology or not, must gather as much information as possible, from as many sources as possible, and start by taking into account the point of view of the apparent authors of documents found. A letter from a timber company making claims about the thinking of Ojibwe leaders or band members cannot be viewed as equally reliable as one recorded by a friend of the community such as the missionary John Johnson (Enmegahbowh). However, if the writer seems to be furthering an aim to advance the departure of the Mille Lacs Band to White Earth, a point of view supported by the Episcopal bishop Henry Whipple, then even the evidence of friendly missionaries must be used carefully.

In addition to taking into account the point of view of individuals who provide the evidence, it is important to look for patterns in the picture the information presents. In the case of the Mille Lacs Reservation, the way band leaders talked of the promise contained in the 1863 treaty is an example of such a pattern, especially in light of Henry Rice's later acknowledgment that they were right in what they had believed about their reservation.

From an anthropological point of view, the ways the Mille Lacs Ojibwe made use of the natural resources available to them, following the seasonal round, is another important pattern, because it aids in understanding why the Mille Lacs people were so attached to their permanent home at the lake.

Understanding the Mille Lacs people's connection to Mille Lacs Lake helps answer the question asked in the February 4, 1880, *Princeton Union*: "Of what earthly use is the Mille Lac reservation to the Chippewas? They do not reside on their reservation. There is not an acre of it under cultivation. Why not throw it open to settlers? It contains valuable pine lands and we are informed that there are many excellent farming sections."[8]

In fact the Mille Lacs Ojibwe did live on the reservation, as documented in numerous accounts both before and after that time, and while they did not farm in the manner of Europeans, they grew a variety of crops and made use of the resources on the reservation and, with the reserved rights they had under the Treaty of 1837, in the region surrounding the reservation. The pine mentioned in the article would of course be what many non-Indians sought to take, and would in fact be a wedge used in the continuing effort to drive the Mille Lacs Ojibwe from their homes.

Beyond these facts probably nothing could have been said to the author of the question about the value of the Mille Lacs Reservation to the Ojibwe, simply because the cultural gap between the writer and the Ojibwe was too great to cross. Such divergent points of view are a major part of the story of the origin and later history of the Mille Lacs Reservation.

Ojibwe Names

Recording the names of Ojibwe people in this book has been a special challenge because of the many variations in the way the names have been recorded. When the meanings of names are known, the John Nichols and Earl Nyholm dictionary of Anishinaabemowin, the Ojibwe language, has been used as a standard source. For example, the name of one chief, Minogiizhig, is a compound word which means Fine Day in English, and the spelling can be taken from that of the two words in Ojibwe. When names appear to be more ambiguous, the spellings in historical documents have been retained. Place names have been treated in a similar fashion. For aid in spellings related to the Mille Lacs area, I have used *Gidakiiminaan (Our Earth)*, an Anishinaabe atlas of place names distributed by the Great Lakes Indian Fish and Wildlife Commission. The atlas authors note the variation in spelling and pronunciation of Anishinaabe place names as given in various dialects. They state, "Anishinaabemowin is a dynamic language and the dialect differences should be celebrated rather than denigrated."[9]

Acknowledgments

In the many years since hearing my grandfather talk about his encounter with Wadena and Migizi, I have had the opportunity and honor to meet, talk, and work with Mille Lacs band members from all parts of the reservation and in other communities where band members live. I never met Wadena and Migizi, or even Art Gahbow, the great leader of the band in the 1970s and 1980s, but I have had the opportunity to know and appreciate the leadership of their successors Marge Anderson and Melanie Benjamin.

As usual in any project like this, one person leads to another. When I began to do the research among Mille Lacs band members in the 1980s, I was pleased to get the help of Betty Kegg at Mille Lacs and John and Marion Dunkley, and their daughter Geri Germann, and Dave and Alvina Matrious at the Aazhoomog (Lake Lena) community in Pine County. From them I met Doris Boswell, Jim Clark, Bernida Humetewa, and others in that district of the Mille Lacs Band. In my research at Aazhoomog I learned that the history of the Mille Lacs band members who live in communities apart from the reservation has many parallels to the history of the reservation I have set out to tell in this book. The story of those communities could fill many more books.

Later on, when I began to do historical research on the history of the reservation at Mille Lacs, I met and had the opportunity to work with Elisse Aune, Curt and Brad Kalk, and Melvin Pewaush, who was living on the land at Cove where Wadena had been for so many years. Later I worked with tribal historic preservation officer Natalie Weyaus on culturally important places for the band, and I got to meet many band members for the first time.

Don Wedll, who was the Mille Lacs Band commissioner of natural resources, was instrumental in hiring me to be a witness in several lawsuits involving the band. As a result I got to know the attorneys Marc Slonim, John Arum, Jim Genia, Beth Baldwin, and Tadd Johnson. I also worked with the ethnohistorians Charles Cleland and James McClurken, whose efforts in the 1837 treaty case set an example for me on how to be a historical witness in court. Later, James McClurken and I worked together on the two reservation-boundary cases. He has been a good friend and an invaluable colleague.

It may seem odd to say so, but I have also appreciated the opportunity to test my own research and writing while competing with other expert witnesses in the contest of ideas that occurs in such court cases, as we each explain and justify our own research and interpretation. These intellectual battles help to improve the quality of historical work.

Over the years I have been privileged to know and learn from many colleagues in the field of Ojibwe history and culture in the Midwest, including Brenda Child, Jon De Ment, Rebecca Kugel, David Mather, Cary Miller, Michael McNally, John D. Nichols, Chantal Norrgard, Laura Peers, Tami K. Plank, Anton Treuer, and Mary Warner. Colleagues from my time as a staff member at the Minnesota Historical Society, including Virginia Martin and Deborah Miller, have been helpful in reading my work and suggesting improvements. Colleagues from the University of Minnesota Duluth project on the history of the Mille Lacs Band of Ojibwe, including Joseph Bauerkemper, Ed Minnema, and Erik Redix, have provided many insights in the spirited conversations we shared. Over the years Charles J. Lippert, an air quality specialist with the Mille Lacs Band, who was one of the contributors to *Gidakiiminaan (Our Earth)*, the Anishinaabe atlas of place names, has been helpful to me on many questions concerning names in Ojibwe and English. Many thanks to my editor, Shannon Pennefeather, with whom it is always a pleasure to work.

Finally, I am thankful to my wife, Ann Regan, for helping and inspiring me for so many years. We first met when we were fledgling editorial assistants at the Minnesota Historical Society Press. After a few years of our working together I left to do graduate work in history and anthropology. Ann stayed on at MNHS Press, eventually becoming editor in chief. Ann's influence has been not on the press to put my work in print (unfortunately), but on me to be a better writer and historian, and a better person.

CHAPTER 1

The Mysterious Lake

In December 2014, at home in Cove, Mille Lacs band member Dorothy (Clark) Sam spoke about the sacred importance of Mille Lacs Lake for Mille Lacs band members. It was, she said, a relative, and like the animals that inhabited the water and the land, it was treated with special respect.

> Our value is this, and it's mainly out there, you know, in teaching . . . the *aadizookaan*, the legends, you know, that we're told in the winter-time. . . . A lot of it is dealing with the animals out there. And you could almost tell where we learned how we're like the trees, because the trees have limbs and it sheds like we do, but we keep growing when we got limbs, call them limbs. And then they talk about the animals out there, the four-leggeds—so do we when we crawl on our hands and knees, you know. And then we're like the fish—you know, we could swim out there. And then we get up, we're like the ducks, you know, the wild ducks out there. All that was where our names come from there. Those are our relatives. They were here first, and we always acknowledge that.

When going out on the frozen lake in the winter her family members were careful to bring their sage and tobacco to offer to the lake and to the spirits that were there.[1]

Sam's words resonated with the commitment of the Mille Lacs Band to the lake, and the history of the Native people who had resided there long before her.

The Geographical Context of Mille Lacs Lake

Mille Lacs Lake, located in north-central Minnesota, has a surface area of 132,516 acres or slightly more than 207 square miles. The lake is surrounded on three sides by glacial moraine, a deposit of rock and sediment left by the last glaciers to cover the region. The lake has a maximum depth of only forty-two feet and a watershed of 240,000 acres, consisting of twenty small streams. The lake's only outlet is through the Rum River, which flows from the southwest corner of the lake, through three smaller lakes, before taking a circuitous 148-mile route to its outlet on the Mississippi, within twenty miles of the Twin Cities.[2]

Though Mille Lacs has only a few short tributaries and a lengthy outlet, the lake is in close proximity to many other rivers flowing through wetlands to the east, north, and west, through which early inhabitants had access by portage and river passage to the Platte, Nokasippi, Muddy, and other rivers, which provided a faster route to the Upper Mississippi, St. Croix, and St. Louis Rivers.[3]

As indicated by historical accounts and archaeological evidence, inhabitants around the shores of Mille Lacs Lake found abundant resources for survival, including wildlife and plants of many kinds, fish, wild rice, maple sugar, cranberries, and other berries in a region with soil and weather conducive to cultivating gardens.[4]

These resources and the habitat of the Mille Lacs region were reflected in the experiences of Dakota and other Siouan-language speakers who lived in the region for generations before the arrival of the Ojibwe in the seventeenth and eighteenth centuries. James R. Walker, an agent among the Lakota people of South Dakota in the late nineteenth century, recorded a myth of the time "long ago when the Lakotas lived in the region of the pines" and "had but one chief." In the lake was an underwater spirit, known as an Unktehi, one of many powerful spirits who appear in Lakota and Dakota beliefs. The Unktehi decided he wanted the chief's daughter for his own wife. He said, "I have nothing to give you but if you will put the seed of things that are good in the water and in the earth, they will grow and you can have plenty to eat."[5]

The Lakota chief agreed and thus the Unktehi taught the Lakota how to grow things on the shore of the lake: "When I push the ice from the waters, then I will appear to you. When I do [this], then the next moon, put the seed in the earth and I will put the seed into the water."

So when the ice was on the water, the chief watched it and he saw the *Unktehi* push it upon the lake and he watched for the *Unktehi* but he did not see him.

In the moon when the grass begins to grow, the *Unktehi* pushed the ice from the waters and the chief saw him.

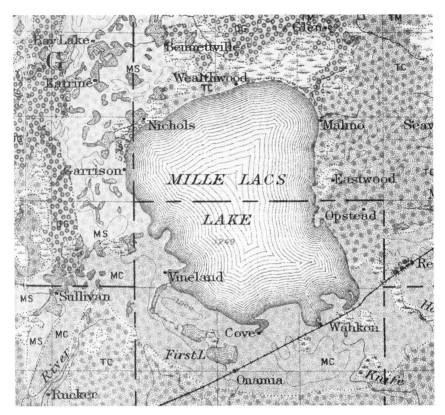

A detail from a 1916 Minnesota Geological Survey map of Minnesota shows the position of Mille Lacs Lake in an area filled with lakes, rivers, and wetlands, to which the big lake has few direct connections except for a couple of small streams and rivers and the Rum River, which exits the lake to the south. Color coding on the original map shows various soils resulting from the glacial history of the region. The areas to the west labeled MS and MC show the glacial moraine deposits that created the lake in the last ice age.

Then the chief put the seed into the ground (the *wamnu*, pumpkin, *wamnahaza*, corn, *omnica*, beans) and they grew so that there was food in the camp.

Ever afterward, when the *Unktehi* was seen in the lake, the people planted and things grew well. But if the *Unktehi* was not seen, then the things planted did not grow.

So the people made sacrifices to the *Unktehi* to please him that he might appear in this lake. . . .

The *Unktehi* planted the seed in the water (*psa*, rush; *psin* wild rice), and he also planted some seed near the waters (*psin ca*, water turnip; *psin cala ca* or *timpsila*, turnip). And he taught that these were good to eat. . . .

For this reason the Lakota called Mille Lacs "The Mysterious Lake."

Many aspects of Mille Lacs Lake described in the Lakota story would resonate for later residents. For example, the movement of ice on the lake and onto its shore has been observed and photographed by current and former residents. For the Ojibwe and those who have shared the region with them, Mille Lacs Lake has many timeless and enduring qualities.[6]

CHAPTER 2

People of the Lake

Allied Dakota and Lakota peoples were living in the Mille Lacs region when the first French people arrived in the seventeenth century. According to French maps from the late 1600s and early 1700s, Lakota and Dakota lived in scattered "nations," actually villages or bands located around Mille Lacs Lake and along the Upper Mississippi and St. Croix Rivers. Jean Baptiste Louis Franquelin's 1697 map of the Upper Mississippi locates a rich assortment of named Dakota groups described by the French term *nations*. The map places the "Mendaoucanton" or Mdewakantons at the eastern edge of the lake, near the headwaters of the Snake River. It also shows the Matantons or "the people of the large rock" near a rock marked on the western or southwestern side of the lake. The Matantons were also called "the people of a large lake that flows into a smaller one," which could refer to the outlet of Mille Lacs Lake through present-day lakes Ogechie, Shakopee, and Onamia, at the headwaters of the Rum River.[1]

In between these groups on a peninsula that seems to stretch out into the lake, Franquelin locates the Quiocpeton or nation renfermé, meaning secretive, or refermé, meaning enclosed in some way. Mille Lacs Lake does have several peninsulas along the south shore that were the locations of Ojibwe villages in the nineteenth century. Another name given for the Quiocpeton was "nation of a lake that discharges into a river," possibly Lake Onamia, which is the first of the small lakes leading into the Rum River. In the nineteenth century the village located on Mozomonie (also Mazomonie) Point in South Harbor Township just north of the present town of Onamia made use of both the point on Mille Lacs Lake and Lake Onamia.

According to the book *Mni Sota Makoce*, a study of the relationship of Dakota people to the lands of Minnesota, one possibility to explain these so-called nations associated in some way with Mille Lacs Lake is that they represented a series of bands that resided in village sites along the south shore of the lake and in the nearby rivers and lakes. Their names, then, would have referred to the characteristics of very specific locations. The distribution of such bands would have been similar to that of the Ojibwe in that same region in the nineteenth century, consisting of around a hundred people each and under the leadership of particular chiefs and headmen. For example, as shown in Table 4 (page 81), there were six bands of Ojibwe living in the region of the south shore of Mille Lacs Lake within the Mille Lacs Reservation in 1881, including 653 people.

Some historical accounts of the various Dakota peoples who lived around Mille Lacs Lake suggest that they did not start cultivating corn until their departure from the big lake, though archaeologists have found traces of corn kernels in pottery recovered in the Mille Lacs region. However, in other ways the story of the Unktehi in the lake does hold true as a description of the seasonal markers in the region and the favorable plant resources found there. Plentiful plant and animal resources meant that inhabitants could spend both summer and winter near the lake, although trapping and buffalo hunting could take them away from the region at certain times of year.[2]

When Father Louis Hennepin spent the late winter and spring of 1680 in the region of Mille Lacs Lake, he did not witness all the people's subsistence activities, though he mentions being fed wild rice seasoned with dried blueberries and smoked fish eggs cooked in an earthen pot. Hennepin also noted that the people trapped beavers and in the spring and summer left Mille Lacs to hunt buffalo to the south, along the Mississippi River. Hennepin accompanied them on one such journey, describing deer hunting and the killing of turtles, catfish, and paddlefish or sturgeon for food along the way. Some of these seasonal subsistence practices of the Dakota at Mille Lacs shared features with those of the later Ojibwe in the region. For example, though the Dakota would later be described as using only dugout canoes, when living at Mille Lacs they made canoes of birch.[3]

The Ojibwe first entered the Minnesota region in the seventeenth century, coming from the east, particularly the area around Sault Ste. Marie. Early French maps of the Upper Mississippi even give Ojibwe names for some of the rivers and lakes in the region, despite the continuing presence of the Dakota there. For example, Franquelin's 1697 map names Mille Lacs Misizagaigan, a version of the Ojibwe name meaning, according to Ojibwe historian William Warren, "the lake that spreads all over."[4]

By the late 1600s the Ojibwe were allied with the Dakota through trade and through intermarriage, an alliance encouraged by the French, though it likely began much earlier. Warren notes that much intermarriage took place in the area of the St. Croix River and Mille Lacs Lake. Intermarriage had a particular effect on clan structure among the Ojibwe, since odoodem or clan identity was inherited through the father. Warren notes that the children of Dakota men who married Ojibwe women were considered members of the Ma'iingan or Wolf clan; he also states that Ojibwe men who married Dakota women were members of the Nibiinaabe (Ne-baun-a-bey), Merman or Water-spirit, clan and "begat by them sons, who, residing among the Dakotas, introduced in this tribe the badge of their father's totem," and that ever since then all persons of the Wolf and Merman "recognized one another as blood relations." Few sources acknowledge the existence of clans among the Dakota, but Warren's statement may simply mean that Ojibwe members of a Merman clan living along the St. Croix were among those who married Dakota women. As it happens, Warren stated that the Merman or Water-spirit clan was a branch of the Wawaazisii (Bullhead; Awause), who, according to Warren, also claim some connection to the Me-she-num-aig-way or "immense fish," analogous to the Leviathan of the Bible. Both the Ma'iingan and Wawaazisii clans were particularly prevalent along the St. Croix River and at Mille Lacs in the 1800s. It should also be noted that according to Warren, the Dakota leader known to the French as the first Wabasha I was the son of a Dakota man and an Ojibwe woman who later remarried and was also the mother of a famous Ojibwe leader, Ma-mong-e-se-da of the Reindeer clan.[5]

The story of intermarriage and peaceful relations between Dakota and Ojibwe is not as well documented in histories of the two tribes as is war. Warren himself spends much of his history telling of the battles whereby the Ojibwe were said to have driven the Dakota out of the northern region of present-day Minnesota. In the case of Mille Lacs, Warren describes a great battle that took place around 1750, at two Dakota village sites, one at the Cormorant Point—probably later Indian Point—and the other at the outlet of the lake. Warren stated that misunderstandings had arisen between the two tribes involving an Ojibwe family from Fond du Lac. During the battle, Warren says the Ojibwe destroyed the two villages and the survivors took refuge at a new village site on the Rum River, only to leave the country for good by 1770.[6]

Similar traditions about the great battle of Mille Lacs were common in the nineteenth century, including among Mille Lacs Ojibwe. But among the Dakota of the same period the idea that they were driven away from Mille Lacs was not accepted. Their accounts and those of French sources suggest the Dakota were drawn to the south by the presence of the French there in the early 1700s. Further, given the history of intermarriage be-tween the two groups and the presence of the Ma'iingan people at Mille Lacs, it is likely the story of what happened needs to be much more nu-anced, as does the unrelenting history of warfare in the 1800s. Regarding the story of Dakota being pushed out of Mille Lacs and to the west, there is disagreement between Dakota and Ojibwe. At an Indian Reorganization Act conference in Hayward, Wisconsin, in April 1934, Paul Abraham, a Dakota representative from Pipestone, Minnesota, stated that Dakota had merely "heard the call of Horace Greeley, 'Go West, boys, and be a man.'"[7]

By the nineteenth century many Ojibwe communities in the area of Mille Lacs and along the Rum, St. Croix, and Snake Rivers contained mem-bers of the Ma'iingan clan. The leaders of these communities are shown in Table 1. (See the Appendix for additional biographical information about these and other Mille Lacs Ojibwe leaders from the 1820s to the 1880s.) Perhaps because of the presence of Ma'iingan clan members, the people of Mille Lacs and the Snake and St. Croix Rivers were instrumental in the 1820s and 1830s at a series of seasonal peace treaties with nearby Mdewakanton bands made at Fort Snelling and other locations, through which Ojibwe and Dakota agreed to share resources where they overlapped. This region stretched diagonally across the present state of Minnesota from southeast to northwest beginning north of the Twin Cities and following the bound-ary agreed upon between the two nations in the Treaty of Prairie du Chien in 1825. Indian agent Lawrence Taliaferro referred to this region as "the middle grounds." For anthropologist Harold Hickerson it was a "contested zone," a region where Dakota and Ojibwe fought in summer but which they shared in winter, a season when they rarely engaged in conflict. Taliaferro had reported that Bezhig (Lone Man), the Mille Lacs/Snake River chief, was the first Indian leader who came to him to request help in negotiating peace between Ojibwe and Dakota people. Bezhig was also a spokesperson for the Ojibwe at the 1825 treaty at Prairie du Chien, bringing with him a birch bark map to show the region claimed by the Ojibwe.[8]

In the so-called contested zone, winter deer hunting took place in back-water regions, up small streams and valleys away from the Mississippi and St. Croix Rivers. The Dakota from Kaposia, near present-day St. Paul, hunted on the lower St. Croix River. Dakota from Black Dog's Village and other sites of the lower Minnesota River hunted along the Rum and Sauk Rivers, both of which flow into the Mississippi north of the present-day Twin Cities. In these regions they often encountered the Mille Lacs and St. Croix River bands and reached agreements to hunt unmolested.

TABLE 1	
Clan Membership of Band Leaders at Mille Lacs and Vicinity in the Nineteenth Century	
NAME	CLAN
Ayaabens (Little Buck)	Ma'iingan (Wolf)
Bezhig / Biazhig (Lone Man)	Ma'iingan (Wolf)
Bizhiki (Buffalo)	Noka / Makwa (Bear)
Gegwedaash / Kay gwa dosh	Noka / Makwa (Bear)
Manoominikeshiinh (Rice Maker; after a kind of bird seen in wild rice areas)	Ma'iingan (Wolf)
Monzomonay (Plenty of Moose)	Ma'iingan (Wolf)
Negwanebi (Feather's End)	Ma'iingan (Wolf)
Noodin (The Wind)	Awause (Catfish/Bullhead)
Shaboshkung	Awause (Catfish/Bullhead)
Shagobay (Little Six)	not known
Wazhashkokon (Rat's Liver)	not known
Bizhiki (Buffalo)	Bear

Source: Warren, *History of the Ojibway People,* 17–25, 238–39; Brower, *Kathio,* 102–3; see also Appendix, page 267.

Although there were earlier accounts of seasonal treaties between Dakota and Ojibwe during winter hunting season, the presence of Indian agent Lawrence Taliaferro at Fort Snelling facilitated the sealing of such agreements. At Coldwater Spring, where the Ojibwe usually camped when they went to Fort Snelling, and at hunting sites along the St. Croix and Rum Rivers, Ojibwe and Dakota met, traded, and danced together to cement their relationships. They also participated in religious ceremonies that both shared, such as the medicine ceremony, called the Wakan Wacipi by the Dakota and Midewiwin by the Ojibwe.[9]

In December 1835 government interpreter Scott Campbell returned to Fort Snelling from the St. Croix River, reporting to the agent that "The Sioux & Chippeways were below the falls of St. Croix—on the Chip Land by invitation—Dancing—playing Ball & feasting together." Sometimes Dakota traded blankets, guns, and traps with visiting Ojibwe for maple sugar and birch bark canoes, which they used for ricing. Trading such items—which might otherwise have been provided by the Indian agent—may have been especially important for the visiting Ojibwe during the period after 1827, when Taliaferro was instructed by superiors that he was not to deal with the Ojibwe, who were supposed to go to visit their agent Henry Schoolcraft at Sault Ste. Marie or the subagent George Johnston at La Pointe. Taliaferro's location, close to Ojibwe villages on the Upper Mississippi and St. Croix Rivers, led Ojibwe from that region to continue coming to Fort Snelling.[10]

Indeed, Fort Snelling was where Ojibwe signed the tribe's first land cession treaty with the US government, the Treaty of 1837, on July 29 of that year. In Minnesota the area ceded under that treaty included land north of the 1825 Dakota–Ojibwe treaty line west of the St. Croix River, east of the Mississippi, and south of a line that crossed the north end of Mille Lacs Lake. During the treaty meeting hundreds of Ojibwe camped at Coldwater Spring. The treaty was negotiated near the Indian agency, south of the spring on the Minnesota River bluffs, west of the fort. Among those present were six leaders from Mille Lacs.[11]

Like several subsequent treaties involving the Minnesota Ojibwe, negotiation of the Treaty of 1837 was motivated by the desire of government officials to obtain a specific resource—in this case, pine. While Ojibwe people were reluctant to sell their land, government officials communicated their belief that the lands to be ceded would not be useful for white settlement very soon if ever. Since it was clear the Ojibwe would not remove from the region, federal negotiators put in the treaty a provision allowing for the Ojibwe's right to continue using all the resources available to them on the ceded land "during the pleasure of the President." Throughout the negotiations Ojibwe leaders from various locations made plain their understanding of the treaty. For example, Eshkibagikoonzhe of Leech Lake, known as Flat Mouth, stated:

> My Father. Your children are willing to let you have their lands, but
> they wish to reserve the privilege of making sugar from the trees,
> and getting their living from the Lakes and Rivers, . . . as they have
> done heretofore, and of remaining in this Country. It is hard to give
> up these lands. They will remain, and can not be destroyed—but
> you may cut down the Trees, and others will grow up. You know
> we can not live, deprived of our Lakes and Rivers; There is some
> game on the lands yet; & for that reason also, we wish to remain

upon them, to get a living. Sometimes we scrape the Trees and eat of the bark. The Great Spirit above, made the Earth, and causes it to produce, which enables us to live.

Later on Flat Mouth stated, "You know that without the lands, and the Rivers & the Lakes, we could not live. We hunt and make Sugar, & dig roots upon the former, while we fish, and obtain Rice, and drink from the latter."[12]

The leaders of the Mille Lacs and St. Croix area bands—among those most clearly affected by the treaty cession—said little about the terms of the negotiation. They were content to let other, better-known leaders speak for them. As a result of these negotiations, Article 5 of the Treaty of 1837 contained the statement: "The privilege of hunting, fishing, and gathering the wild rice, upon the lands, the rivers and the lakes included in the territory ceded, is guaranteed to the Indians, during the pleasure of the President."[13]

The words did not do justice to the richness of thought and language spoken by the Ojibwe leaders present, nor did they encompass an understanding of the specific places in this ceded territory important to various bands that signed the treaty. But the people of the Mille Lacs and St. Croix region would long remember their specific meaning and recall the words of the negotiators, when band members' own rights to remain in these lands and live on their resources were threatened in the years ahead.[14]

Shortly after the signing of the treaty at St. Peters in 1837, Indian agent Taliaferro accompanied a delegation of Dakota leaders to Washington, DC, to sign a treaty for Dakota lands east of the Mississippi River. Both treaties were ratified in 1838, bringing an influx of loggers and potential settlers into Dakota and Ojibwe lands east of the Mississippi. The increase in white population may have contributed to worsening relations between the two tribes.[15]

The first annuity payments under the Treaty of 1837 were made in the fall of 1838 at the head of Lake St. Croix. Though their late arrival had caused troubles for many communities, word that payments would thereafter take place at La Pointe on Lake Superior appeared even less desirable. In June 1839 a large number of Ojibwe from the Upper Mississippi River came to Fort Snelling to consult with Taliaferro about the payments. Among those complaining were Hole-in-the-Day, Rat's Liver, and Shagobay (Little Six). The Mille Lacs chief Negwanebi stated, "We are all of one opinion. We will never go there." The objections had to do with the sustenance necessary to support 2,800 Ojibwe on a trip to La Pointe.[16]

By June 21, 1839, Taliaferro wrote that there were 750 Ojibwe along with 870 Dakota present at the agency. Relations among those at Fort Snelling appeared cordial at first, with Taliaferro noting, "The Sioux danced at the Chippewa encampment [at Coldwater Spring] & in the evening ran foot races." More Ojibwe and more Dakota arrived. Among them were Mille Lacs Ojibwe who had come by way of the Snake and St. Croix Rivers and then, after a brief portage, had traveled through Rice Creek (which flowed from the area of Forest Lake in present-day Washington County, into the Mississippi in Fridley, just north of Minneapolis), as well as others. By June 24 there were 900 Ojibwe men, women, and children and 856 Dakota. As many as a thousand were there for at least a few days. After making their views known to Taliaferro the Oijbwe set off to return to their homes to the north.[17]

By the beginning of July 1839 Taliaferro heard a rumor that a party of people from the Dakota chief Šakpe's village, located near present-day Shakopee along the Minnesota River, was headed to attack a group of Ojibwe at the falls of St. Anthony. On July 2 Ojibwe from Leech Lake went to Lake Harriet, where they shot and scalped a respected Dakota named Neka (Badger). In retaliation, according to Taliaferro, 150 Dakota warriors set off in pursuit of the Mississippi Ojibwe who were returning to their homes. At the same time others from Little Crow's village headed for Lake St. Croix. Some Mille Lacs people, including Negwanebi, who had gone with one of his sons to Fort Snelling by way of Pokegama to persuade the Snake River leader Shagobay to accompany him, set off to return home by way of the St. Croix River.[18]

Within a few days Taliaferro received word of battles on the Rum River and around the present site of Stillwater on the St. Croix, in which many Ojibwe men, women, and children were killed. An army lieutenant who investigated the battle, which took place in a hollow along the river, stated that thirty-five to forty Ojibwe were killed there and another fifteen in canoes, while only three Dakota warriors were killed. Another officer, Captain Martin Scott, estimated many more killed on the Rum River. On July 21 missionary Frederick Ayer, whose mission was on the Snake River at Pokegama, stated, "The Chippewas lost 21 Killed 26 wounded on the St Croix-& 70 on the Rum River."[19]

While Leech Lake people had killed the Dakota Badger, other Mississippi bands and the St. Croix, Rum River, and Mille Lacs bands received the brunt of the retaliation. The Stillwater attack in particular was remembered by Mille Lacs people for generations. In testimony in court cases involving timber frauds in 1914, designed mainly to gather genealogical information, elders from the Mille Lacs and Mississippi bands often mentioned the deaths of relatives and the effects these deaths had on their communities. In some cases witnesses stated they simply did not know certain ancestors because they died at "the great killing at Stillwater."[20]

Gotigwaakojiins (Kodequahkojeence, also known as Negwanebi No. 2) in his 1914 testimony stated that he was a young boy at the time of the Stillwater attack. He was present when it happened: "If it wasn't for my being a fast runner I would have been killed too." Contemporary accounts also describe a heavy blow to the Mille Lacs Ojibwe. Edmund Ely stated, "not a Pokegama Indian was among the slain," at least at the Stillwater battle. But one man named Wattap lost his wife and four children; the elder chief Negwanebi was wounded in the shoulder, and his son was killed. Many of the survivors arrived at Pokegama. Makode or Bear's Heart, who with his wife was among those attacked on the Rum River, reached Pokegama on July 19. The Dakota who attacked their party had come on horseback. It was reported that Makode's wife, possibly Odahnun, who was Negwanebi's sister, ran "with a boy & girl in each hand, running beside her, & by her astonishing speed & strength outstripped her pursuers & saved the children." They reported that thirty out of the 105 among the party on the Rum River survived.[21]

Gotigwaakojiins stated that the battle in Stillwater, and presumably the one on the Rum River, had a direct effect on the population at Mille Lacs, because afterward there were only five lodges left there, on either side of the Rum River below the outlet from the lake, and "from these five lodges the Mille Lacs of today have come." This count may not have included those band members who spent part of every year on the Snake and St. Croix Rivers. At the time of the attacks, Gotigwaakojiins recalled that his grandfather Ozaawindib (Ozawandib) and his family were among the Mille Lacs people who survived the battles in 1839. In this sense, Gotigwaakojiins viewed his grandfather as a Mille Lacs pioneer who led the way for others to move there.[22]

They were soon joined by other St. Croix and Snake River Ojibwe. The attacks in 1839 led to an increase in aggression between Dakota and Ojibwe, despite the many earlier peace treaties. The Ojibwe themselves were often aggressors, but the Mille Lacs people were not the only object of retaliation. Ely noted that the Dakota seemed to make no distinction among those against whom they retaliated. Another Dakota attack occurred in the summer of 1841 at the community surrounding the mission on Lake

Pokegama on the Snake River. According to the missionary William Boutwell, a group of 111 Dakota attacked the community.[23]

Many more people from the Snake and St. Croix Rivers moved to Mille Lacs for year-round residence. In 1841 Boutwell said that three hundred more would winter at Mille Lacs the coming year. Mille Lacs leaders encouraged the mission to establish a school on the lake. By 1843 Boutwell noted that two families from Pokegama were not only wintering at the lake but also spending spring and summer there. Ely stated that few Indians had lived at Pokegama the previous winter. One band lived in a fortified village ten miles away; the others were at Mille Lacs. Boutwell described fish and rice as "the two great and never failing resources" found at Mille Lacs, making it an attractive place to live. Several families were already cultivating gardens there, and he suggested a mission be established at the site. In the years ahead many families continued to move to Mille Lacs, but others remained on the Snake and St. Croix Rivers. Descendants of these families established a thriving community in eastern Pine County that still exists today.[24]

CHAPTER 3

Seasons at the Lake

In testimony in 1914, Makode, the wife of Gotigwaakojiins, recalled that she was born in the late 1830s near the mouth of the Rum River, while her parents were "traveling, killing deer." Other months they lived near the outlet of the Rum River at Mille Lacs. Hunting at various times of year in the region of the 1837 treaty provided important resources, but Mille Lacs was a base of operations, a place for survival when all else failed.[1]

After the Treaty of 1837 was signed, loggers entered the territory ceded by the Ojibwe, often beginning to log without bothering to purchase land. The influx of whites into the region caused problems among Ojibwe communities. Far from loggers and other whites being in danger from the presence of Ojibwe in the ceded territory, it was the reverse: the Ojibwe were endangered by the presence of whites. While Ojibwe continued to make use of the many resources throughout the ceded territory, competition from whites encouraged the movement toward Mille Lacs already begun prior to the attacks of the Dakota. Mille Lacs was still more isolated and protected than other communities.

But news was spreading about the qualities of the large lake. A February 7, 1852, article in the *St. Paul Weekly Minnesotian* described Mille Lacs Lake on a winter evening. On the lake huge piles of ice lifted their heads "like the snow capped hills of Vermont." Along the shore "the smoke of a hundred wigwams go up towards the sky," while Indian children frolicked on the ice, "engaged in all manner of plays and capers." Hunters returned "overloaded with the game of the day." White blankets were planted on the surface of the lake, "denoting fishing grounds—the rising moon causing the frozen fish that lie scattered around to glisten like lead ore in the galena mines." The shores of the lake were covered with dense groves of maple trees, and at its mouth were three small rice lakes. Over five hundred Indians lived around the lake; they had a "pleasing appearance" and were welcoming to visitors. In the summer the water was as clear as crystal.

The soil was rich: someday it would "groan beneath the heavy crops of the white man."[2]

While the St. Paul newspaper account of the many resources available at Mille Lacs was idealized, accounts of Ojibwe people themselves describe how the area's bounty could feed a family for an entire year. One document used by many to typify the Ojibwe seasonal round is a narrative found in anthropologist Frances Densmore's *Chippewa Customs*. Densmore describes the memories of an elderly woman named Noodinens (Little Wind), a former resident of Mille Lacs who moved to White Earth, where Densmore met her several times starting in 1917. Recent research shows that Noodinens was Annie Noodinens Jackson, the daughter of Ayaabe or Buck, the leader of a small band at Mille Lacs in the 1850s and 1860s, one of the first Mille Lacs Bands to move to White Earth. Densmore reported that Noodinens was seventy-four when Densmore took down her story. This detail places her birth date in the late 1840s, meaning the information she gives can serve as a form of local history, describing the 1840s and 1850s in the Mille Lacs region, a time when it was possible for families to survive as they had done for hundreds of years before.[3]

Noodinens began her narrative with the following words: "When I was young everything was very systematic. We worked day and night and made the best use of the material we had." Because Densmore presented Noodinens's account in generic cultural terms, it is often used as a generally applicable description of the Ojibwe seasonal round throughout the Great Lakes region. But the Ojibwe seasonal round varied from place to place depending on available resources. Noodinens's account details the systematic way in which Ojibwe families made use of all the resources in the area surrounding Mille Lacs, living at different times of the year in various locations on or away from the lake. Noodinens described the physical setting of each kind of subsistence activity as well as the characteristic houses and other structures people used when engaging in it.[4]

The summer villages that were the base of operations for Mille Lacs Ojibwe were located near the shore on the southern portion of the lake. In the winter families went away from the lakeshore to hunt and trap either within the forested or wetland portions of the reservation or outside the boundaries of the reservation. Noodinens began her account in late fall: "My home was at Mille Lac," she said, "and when the ice froze on the lake we started for the game field," a region away from the lake where they lived in bark wigwams (wiigiwaaman).

Noodinens mentioned that when leaving the lake, her family carried bulrush mats, though they must also have had bark mats for covering their wigwams. "There were six families in our party, and when we found a nice place in the deep woods we made our winter camp. The men shoveled away the snow in a big space, and the six wigwams were put in a circle and banked with evergreen boughs and snow." Outside the door was a little shed made of cedar bark in which firewood was kept. There was a large central fire in the middle of the camp, where families did their cooking when it was not cold. The fire inside the circle of the wigwam had a rack for drying meat. The floor of the wigwam was covered with cedar boughs and "with blankets for our beds, the bright yarn bags being set along the wall for use as pillows. In the center was a place for a fire, and between it and the floor mats there was a strip of hard, dry ground that was kept clean by sweeping it with a broom made of cedar boughs."

In late winter Noodinens's family left the winter camp, traveling on snowshoes to the sugar bush. Records show the presence of sugaring places throughout the reservation, often very close to the summer village sites. "When we got to the sugar bush we took the birch-bark dishes out of the storage and women began tapping the trees. . . . Our sugar camp was always near Mille Lac, and the men cut holes in the ice, put something over their heads, and fished through the ice" using spears. As described elsewhere in Densmore's work, the equipment for sugaring was stored in permanent bark structures at the sugar bush. In addition, according to Noodinens, a food cache near the sugar camp contained wild rice and dried cranberries, potatoes and apples. "As soon as the little creeks opened, the boys caught lots of small fish, and my sister and I carried them to the camp and dried them on a frame." A number of small creeks and rivers flowed into the lake near village sites.

Once sugaring was over the people went to their summer homes: "The six families went together, and the distance was not long. Each family had a large bark house with a platform along each side, like the lodge in which the maple sap was boiled. We renewed the bark if necessary, and this was our summer home. The camps extended along the lake shore, and each family had its own garden. We added to our garden every year, my father and brothers breaking the ground with old axes, bones, or anything that would cut and break up the ground."

In keeping with Noodinens's account of gardening, Daniel Stanchfield, a lumberman who explored the region in 1847, recalled visiting the chief of the village on the south shore of the lake and enjoying a meal including game, corn, and potatoes.[5]

It is unclear whether the word *camps* was used by Noodinens herself or whether Densmore or her interpreter loosely translated an Ojibwe word in this way. Despite its tenuous connotation, Ojibwe families were based during spring, summer, and early fall at the same locations from year to year. Whites tended to describe these areas as temporary—rejecting the word *village* to designate them—even though these sites were used consistently from year to year for months at a time.

While continuing to live along the lake in the summer, the people gathered wild potatoes, blueberries, gooseberries, and Juneberries, which ripened along the lakeshore. Basswood bark and birch bark were gathered, "using our canoes along the lake and the streams." Toward the end of summer ricing began: "The rice fields were quite a distance away and we went there and camped while we gathered rice. Then we returned to our summer camp and harvested our potatoes, corn, pumpkins, and squash, putting them in caches which were not far from the gardens."

Many Mille Lacs ricing sites were located within the boundaries of the reservation, particularly on the three lakes below the outlet of the Rum River. They were within easy access of summer village sites, but families often moved close to the shores of these lakes for the ricing season. Later the women began their fall fishing, continuing often until after the first snows. "When the men returned from the fall trapping we started for the winter camp." Wetlands within the reservation provided many trapping opportunities.

As suggested above, Noodinens's narrative is helpful in countering one common attitude found in accounts by some nineteenth-century white observers of Ojibwe life that these people had a "nomadic" or unsystematic and random relationship with the environment and that their settlements could not be dignified by the term *village*.

The locations in which Mille Lacs Ojibwe people spent perhaps the greatest amount of time, and in which they socialized with the greatest number of other band members, were along the shores of Mille Lacs, where they lived for much of the season after leaving the sugar bush in early spring until they went to hunting camps in early winter. Throughout the year these locations were the places from which it was possible to travel to berry patches, ricing camps, and other less frequently used spots in the area around Mille Lacs. Such bases of operation were clearly villages by any normal definition.

In enumerating the regular and systematic nature of Ojibwe seasonal patterns, Densmore did show clearly that there were variations in the way of doing things. A failure of game or wild rice or garden crops might force an intensification of other activities, particularly fishing. At the same time, it is clear that changes in the systematic way of doing things occurred as a result of outside influences. At the time described by Noodinens, the Treaty of 1837 had already opened the region of the St. Croix, Snake, and Rum Rivers to lumbermen. Ojibwe people traded and sold their produce to loggers, and later to storekeepers in the developing settler towns of Little Falls, Isle, and Onamia, essentially incorporating these exchanges into an evolving seasonal round. Ojibwe men began working in logging camps and did wage labor for local farmers. In the twentieth century, work on highway projects and in local resorts would provide additional labor opportunities that could be incorporated into a seasonal structure of subsistence activities. The location of summer villages may have changed. Log houses became more common among the Ojibwe after the 1850s; many families built them side by side with bark wigwams at permanent villages. The log houses were used in cold weather, while the ventilated bark houses were used in warm weather. Bark houses were used all year round for travel, though tents came into use in the twentieth century.[6]

Perhaps the biggest changes would come after the 1850s when the Mille Lacs people faced continuing attempts to force them to leave Mille Lacs Lake. In that period the seasonal round became politicized and criminalized in ways few can imagine from Noodinens's idyllic account.

CHAPTER 4

The Reservation and Its Leaders

Each treaty signed by Minnesota Ojibwe leaders in the 1840s, 1850s, and 1860s seemed designed, in part, to correct a mistake in the previous treaty. For example, because of friction between peoples in the area ceded by the Treaty of 1837, which was exacerbated by lack of governmental authority to protect Indian people from the actions of settlers and lumbermen, the Treaty of 1842, for the land along the south shore of Lake Superior, included a provision to allow federal regulation of relations with Indians in the ceded territory, including a prohibition on the sale of liquor by so-called whiskey traders.[1]

In 1850 Minnesota Territorial Governor Alexander Ramsey led an effort to remove Ojibwe people from the 1837 and 1842 areas in Wisconsin into unceded land in Minnesota. One purpose was to use annuity payments for the Ojibwe as a means of encouraging economic development in the new territory, since such payments were usually spent quickly by recipients. At the request of Minnesota politicians, President Zachary Taylor issued an order on February 6, 1850, to remove these bands. The government effort was badly managed by Indian agent John Watrous and Ramsey. It was unsuccessful because Ojibwe band members refused all inducements to move, including tardy or suspended payments. As a result of government delays in payments in the early winter of 1850–51, many Native people died at or going to and from Sandy Lake. These events influenced Ojibwe people throughout Minnesota and Wisconsin to resist removal from their homelands in the years to come.[2]

During this removal period, federal officials thought of making Mille Lacs one of the destinations; however, except for encouraging St. Croix band members to move there, most efforts pointed Ojibwe people toward Crow Wing and Sandy Lake. No efforts were made at this time to remove the bands residing at Mille Lacs, although some St. Croix and Snake River Ojibwe were encouraged to move to the area near Crow Wing, twenty-five miles directly west of Mille Lacs. A muster roll dated September 1851 lists 288 St. Croix and Snake River Ojibwe who received annuity goods at Crow Wing. The Indian agent John Watrous trumpeted this payment as evidence that they had been removed, but it is not entirely clear where these people moved to or whether their movement had not been more gradual starting in the 1830s and 1840s. Among them was the leader Manoominikeshiinh (often called Rice Maker), a member of the Ma'iingan clan whom William Warren described in his 1852 history of the Ojibwe people as having "lately removed from St. Croix to Mille Lacs with his band." However, in 1914 Gotigwaakojiins stated that Rice Maker's move to Mille Lacs occurred earlier, right after the Stillwater fight. Rice Maker had three wives, two of whom were sisters, and his many children would lead the band in the coming decades. Warren stated that the leader was "a man of considerable importance amongst his fellows."[3]

One sign that Mille Lacs at this date was viewed as a desirable destination for the removal of Ojibwe people came when Indian agent Watrous hired a farmer named Levi Clark in 1851 to plow land on the west side of Mille Lacs Lake. While the Mille Lacs Ojibwe already had gardens, government officials there as in other places sought to encourage greater dependence on agriculture.[4]

The failure of this removal attempt led in part to further treaties, one in 1854 relating to lands in the arrowhead region of Minnesota and another in 1855 for lands in the Upper Mississippi region. Both treaties sought to correct the problem of competition between Native people and settlers for resources by creating reservations where band members could live without harassment from whites.

Negotiations for the Treaty of 1855 took place in Washington, DC, at the instigation of Minnesota politician Henry M. Rice, who was instrumental in many treaties and agreements in Minnesota in the last half of the nineteenth century. There seems to have been little consultation between Rice and Territorial Governor Willis A. Gorman, one of Rice's political rivals who had tried to reform the corrupt way in which federal Indian policies were carried on in Minnesota. Rice likely sought to hold the treaty negotiations in Washington to prevent Gorman's influence. At first only chiefs of the Mississippi bands were summoned with the Indian agent D. B. Herriman to Washington; the Mille Lacs chiefs were left out. A few weeks later Governor Gorman rectified this oversight when he ordered the trader Clement H. Beaulieu to accompany a delegation of four

Mille Lacs chiefs to Washington. These chiefs included a new generation of leadership.

Negwanebi—described later with honorific terms Gichi or Che Negwanebi—who had the leading role among the Mille Lacs chiefs, died in January, just before the 1855 treaty. The chief's son Wadena led the band until his death around 1861, including signing the Treaty of 1855. Accompanying Wadena to Washington was his brother-in-law Shaboshkung or Zhaaboshkaang, whose name has been translated as "He that Passeth Under Everything," a younger man of the Awause or Bullhead clan who was married to Negwanebi's daughter. Another leader at the 1837 treaty negotiation, Rat's Liver or Rat's Heart, had died in the 1840s, to be replaced by his son who was also known by the English name Rat's Liver. The fourth and final Mille Lacs signer of the 1855 treaty was Rice Maker. (More about these chiefs can be found in the Appendix.)[5]

Treaty negotiations began with several of the Mississippi delegations on February 12 and continued until February 22, when the treaty was signed. The chief negotiator for the government was Commissioner of Indian Affairs George W. Manypenny, who served during President Franklin Pierce's full term, from 1853 to 1857. Manypenny was initiating a new approach to remedy the wrongs caused by the previous removal policies. Many treaties negotiated by Manypenny or during his tenure involved the creation of reservations, where band members could live on their own without interference from whites, whether logging companies or settlers. Manypenny viewed these reservations as providing "a fixed, settled, and permanent home" for Indian people, where they could be "domesticated, improved, and elevated; that [they] may be completely and thoroughly civilized." Manypenny regarded the "policy of fixed habitations . . . as settled by the government" and believed it would "soon be confirmed by an inevitable necessity." According to Manypenny,

> it should be understood at once that those Indians who have had
> reservations set apart and assigned them, as well as those who may
> hereafter by treaty have, are not to be interfered with in the peace-
> able possession and undisturbed enjoyment of their land; that no
> trespasses will be permitted upon their territory or their rights;
> that the assurances and guarantees of their treaty grants are as
> sacred and binding as the covenants in the settler's patent; and that
> the government will not only discountenance all attempts to tres-
> pass on their lands and oust them from their homes, but in all cases

where necessary will exert its strong arm to vindicate its faith with, and sustain them in, their rights.[6]

In addition to Manypenny, Henry Rice, who had other ideas about Indian treaties, was present and would even, at some treaties, serve as a representative of some of the bands, which allowed him to participate in their otherwise private meetings and influence the results of negotiations.

Manypenny encouraged the delegates—in statements to six Mississippi chiefs before the Mille Lacs leaders arrived—to embrace agriculture. The dynamic Mississippi River chief Bagone-giizhig (Hole-in-the-Day the Younger, also known as Kwiwisens), as he often did, said to government officials what he thought they wanted to hear. It was recorded that he would "seek to notice what the white people do and to get his people, or near as possible to follow in their footsteps."[7]

In reply Commissioner Manypenny spoke of the importance of personal effort and labor, particularly in relation to making farms and producing crops. He stated that though the American government and country as a whole were prosperous, white men who went to Minnesota Territory were generally poor. However, he explained, when they settled on the "public domain" before the land was surveyed and offered for sale they were able to earn enough from their efforts to buy the land when it was actually put on the market. If the Ojibwe had only farmed instead of hunting they would now be in the same position: they would have pockets full of money.[8]

Manypenny stated that his goal was to purchase some of the bands' land along the Mississippi, which they would not need once they became "cultivators of the soil." Hole-in-the-Day responded to Manypenny's push for change in the Ojibwe way of life by stating that he was convinced that if "each generation adhered to the customs and superstitions of their ancestors, red men will always live in poverty." Still, he forestalled questions about the sale of land.[9]

That evening Manypenny held a meeting with a larger group of Ojibwe, including those from the first meeting, with the addition of the Pillagers from Leech Lake and Lake Winnibigoshish. Hole-in-the-Day, Flat Mouth, and Buffalo did most of the talking on this occasion. Once again the Mille Lacs leaders were not present. Exactly when that delegation arrived is not known.[10]

Another meeting with the Pillager bands occurred a few days later, on February 17. That afternoon the Mississippi bands, led by Hole-in-the-Day, returned. Discussion began in earnest on the issue of selling land and the price that would be paid. No Mille Lacs leaders spoke on this occasion; it does not appear that any were present. That evening the Pillager and Lake Winnibigoshish leaders joined the group.[11]

The Mississippi bands returned the following Monday, February 19. Hole-in-the-Day argued that the price offered for the land was too low and stated, "We want to change our habits and customs and live like the whites. How can we do this without the means to start upon and carry out your views?"[12]

Hole-in-the-Day and the Mississippi band leaders gathered that evening and then on the afternoon of February 20, 1855, when they requested that Henry Rice speak for them. Rice stated that those he represented wished "to be placed on the same footing as a white man, and leave the balance with the Legislature of the Territory of Minnesota, as to the proper time to make them citizens and enable them to enjoy its benefits." The extent to which these words represented the wishes of the Indian people he claimed to represent cannot be demonstrated from the treaty record.

Not until midway through this evening's interchange did the first evidence emerge as to the possible presence of the Mille Lacs leaders. At one point it was noted that Clement Beaulieu, who had left Minnesota with the Mille Lacs leaders, was said to have acted for his brother Paul, who had been there from the beginning, as interpreter. Nonetheless, no Mille Lacs leader appears to have spoken that evening. In fact, there was no record of any Mille Lacs leader speaking through the rest of the negotiations, which ended on February 22, when terms for the treaty were agreed upon.[13]

A few weeks later, after Congress ratified the treaty, the chiefs, who were still in Washington, again met with Manypenny, this time to discuss claims made against the bands for unpaid debts to traders. He presented to them a "paper," a document said to be a contract obligating the Mississippi Band of Chippewa to pay a total of $35,000 to a number of different traders, including $3,822 to Clement H. Beaulieu and $11,300 to Henry Rice, ostensibly in trust for other traders and their children. During discussion of that document the words of a Mille Lacs leader were finally recorded. According to the transcript, Manoominikeshiinh (Rice Maker) stated: "I do not know any thing about the paper. I have not seen it." Discussions continued for several more days, with no further evidence that the Mille Lacs leaders participated. Once negotiations on claims were concluded all the Ojibwe leaders returned to their homes in Minnesota.[14]

The major results of the treaty were the sale of land in north-central Minnesota by the Ojibwe to the US government and the creation of lands for their "permanent homes." Whether or not Mille Lacs leaders were present for much of the negotiation, the Mille Lacs bands did receive a reservation, embracing four townships along the south shore of the lake in land already ceded in 1837 and still undergoing government survey (42 North of Range 25 West; 42 North of Range 26 West; and 42 and 43 North of Range 27 West), as well as three islands in the southern part of Mille Lacs Lake. The townships are now known as Isle Harbor (42–25), South Harbor (42–26), and Kathio (42–27 and 43–27). To simplify, the townships will be identified as 42–25, 42–26, 42–27, and 43–27.[15]

Interestingly, a map marked by federal officials in the late 1850s shows another version of the Mille Lacs Reservation boundaries. This source, located in the collections of the National Archives in College Park, Maryland, consists of an 1859 printed map of public surveys in Wisconsin and Minnesota with Indian reservations drawn on it by hand. The shaded area for the "Mille Lacs Reserve" of the "Chippewas" includes townships 42–25, 42–26, 42–27, and 43–27, as listed in the treaty and shown on later maps, with the addition of 43–25 on the east side of the lake. The islands along the south shore of the lake are also shaded to indicate their inclusion in the reservation. An explanation for the map has not been found in Indian Office records, though similar ones using printed survey maps as a base were often used by federal officials prior to and after treaty negotiations to indicate lands set aside for reservations and other purposes.

Many years later, on Henry Rice's return to Mille Lacs to obtain an agreement under the Nelson Act, along with the same interpreter, Paul H. Beaulieu, Mille Lacs leaders discussed the reservation boundaries, asserting that those shown on a map Rice presented were not what they had understood from discussions at the time the treaty was made. Ma'iingaans (Maheengaunce), the son-in-law of Shaboshkung, stated that the boundary of the reservation on the west side of the lake should have extended three miles farther north than shown on Rice's map, to the mouth of the creek that flowed from Borden Lake into Mille Lacs, north of present-day Garrison. The Mille Lacs leaders noted that the land in section 13 of Garrison Township, which was the only area ever plowed for farming on the reservation, was excluded by Rice's map. It had been plowed during the tenure of Indian agent D. B. Herriman, probably before 1857, when Herriman left office. Shaboshkung noted that in general his understanding was that

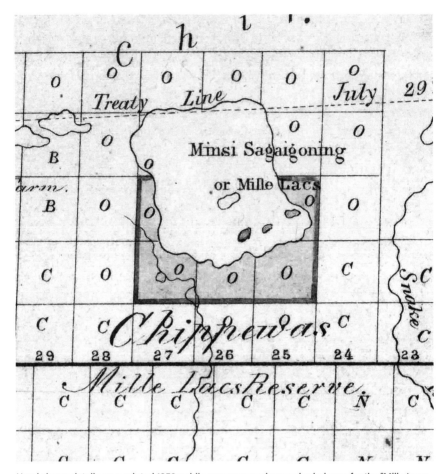

Hand-drawn details on a printed 1859 public-survey map show a shaded area for the "Mille Lacs Reserve" of the "Chippewas," including townships 42-25, 42-26, 42-27, and 43-27, as on later maps, with the addition of 43-25 on the east side of the lake. The map is from the collection Record Group (RG) 75 of the National Archives in College Park, Maryland.

when the survey of the reservation was done it would include six miles back from the lakeshore, which it did only at certain places along the south shore.[16]

This debate suggests that the Mille Lacs chiefs were present to discuss the boundaries of their reservation during the 1855 treaty negotiations and still recalled that conversation in 1889. However, the treaty journal also indicates that the Mille Lacs chiefs were not at the negotiations for the entire time, making it difficult to credit their acquiescence in the statements by Hole-in-the-Day and other Mississippi leaders about a desire to abandon old ways and become full-time farmers. As demonstrated in a 1902 "Schedule of Improvements," Mille Lacs Ojibwe did practice agriculture, and the reservation they received in the 1855 treaty provided them the opportunity to continue farming within the boundaries of the reservation. It also allowed them to continue hunting, fishing, and gathering on Mille Lacs and in the unsettled areas throughout the region.[17]

Evidence about these seasonal activities and a taste of what Mille Lacs band members might find in trying to carry them out in the years ahead is found in events that took place back in Minnesota during the treaty negotiations. It involved conflict between Mille Lacs band members and some of the lumbermen operating on the Upper Rum River. The lumbermen had built a dam at the outlet of Lake Onamia, designed to provide them with enough water to run their logs down the Rum River every spring. Unfortunately, the dam flooded rice plants in the three lakes above it. As Mille Lacs leader Negwanebi stated in a letter to Territorial Governor Alexander Ramsey, as taken down by Crow Wing fur trader Allan Morrison in 1852, the dam "floods the rice lake, in such a manner that we shall have no rice crops."[18]

Nothing was done by government officials to alleviate this problem until 1854, when Ojibwe people threatened to pull down the dam. Territorial Governor Willis A. Gorman attempted to mediate the problem, but the following year there was further conflict, resulting in the death of two lumbermen. Gorman, who as territorial governor had power over federal troops, ordered West Point graduate Lieutenant John Hamilton of the Third Artillery stationed at Fort Snelling to investigate the event.[19]

At the very time treaty negotiations were wrapping up in Washington, late in February 1855, Hamilton, commanding a detachment of twenty-five soldiers, reached a logging camp belonging to Joseph Day on the Upper Rum River. From there, accompanied by an interpreter, Hamilton went on foot for "Nicuanaby's [Negwanebi's] camp," although he did not mention that the chief had died the month before. Here "the Indians were informed that I wished to meet them in Council the next day at Mr. Day's camp." A few band members came, but none of their leaders. Then a messenger arrived "from the Indians on the North side of the Lake saying that if we wished to talk with them we would have to go there." Hamilton ordered his men to cut a road to Mille Lacs. Early the next morning, Hamilton wrote, "we started doubling our teams, and by noon had crossed the lake and were in the village." Through mediation, Hamilton was able to obtain the two young men said to be guilty of killing the lumbermen, to take them back to Fort Snelling for trial. Hamilton also heard the Mille Lacs Ojibwe's complaints about "the question of their sluice dam just below their Wild Rice Lake," although he did not resolve the matter.

Hamilton's letter contains many details documenting the hunting, fishing, and gathering rights of Mille Lacs band members under several treaties, including the fact that he referred to their possession of hunting and fishing rights in the area. Important to note are various references to locations used by Mille Lacs band members. Clearly "Wild Rice Lake" referred to in Hamilton's letter was present-day Lake Onamia. Later evidence suggests the dam was located at the south end or just south of the reservation, at the outlet of the lake. The lake provided two thousand pounds of rice a year, a large proportion of band members' annual subsistence.[20]

Hamilton's letter suggests that both the logging camp and Negwanebi's camp were located somewhere near Lake Onamia. Hamilton's use of the term "camp" to describe this location suggests it may have been a hunting camp or a sugar camp, rather than a summer village. Less clear is the location of the village Hamilton visited. It is difficult to imagine Hamilton was referring to Mille Lacs Lake when he said he received a message from the village on "the north side of the lake." Most likely he meant the north side of Lake Onamia. It is also possible the village was at present-day Mozomonie Point or Vineland; either location could have been reached by traveling across the ice on one of the small lakes on the Upper Rum River or on Mille Lacs itself. These locations and others were significant in the ongoing lives of the Mille Lacs Ojibwe on their new reservation, which band members, no matter their previous residence, now sought to make their permanent home.

By 1861 annuity rolls show six bands residing at Mille Lacs. These bands were under the leadership of chiefs Biidadens (Pe tud ance), Manoominikeshiinh (Mun o min e ca shin), Gegwedaash (Kay gwa dosh), Zhooniyaa (Sho ne yaw), Ayaabe (I aub ay), and Wadena (Wah de naw), totaling 653 people (see Table 2; for more on these chiefs see the Appendix). The exact locations of individual band members on the reservation is not known, but that total figure is close to the population given by Mille Lacs leaders in 1861. The bands listed included relatives living along the Snake River who had not removed to Mille Lacs, though full inclusion of scattered Ojibwe bands in the counts appears not to have happened until the 1870s. In addition to these bands the 1861 annuity rolls listed three bands of Episcopal converts of Mille Lacs origin—including ninety-five people—under the leadership of Menogishig (Me no ke shig), Saycosegay (Saw ca se gaw), and Kaykaykash (Kay kay ke), some of whom may have lived closer to the Episcopal mission at Gull Lake.[21]

TABLE 2 Individual Bands at Mille Lacs in 1861					
BAND LEADERS	MEN	WOMEN	BOYS	GIRLS	TOTAL
Biidadens / Pe tud ance	23	32	31	38	124
Manoominikeshiinh / Mun o min e ca shin	25	33	29	23	110
Gegwedaash / Kay gwa dosh	22	31	24	30	107
Zhooniyaa / Sho ne yaw	20	22	16	23	81
Ayaabe / I aub ay	16	10	11	6	43
Wadena / Wah de naw	38	47	50	53	188
Totals at Mille Lacs	**144**	**175**	**161**	**173**	**653**
Mino-giizhig / Me no ke shig	5	9	6	5	25
Saycosegay / Saw ca se gaw	8	9	12	10	39
Kaykaykash / Kay kay ke	4	8	9	10	31
Totals at uncertain locations	**17**	**26**	**27**	**25**	**95**

Sources: Appendix, page 267; 1861 Mille Lacs annuity roll, US Office of Indian Affairs, Chippewa Annuity Rolls, 1841–1907, MNHS M390, R.3.

CHAPTER 5

Permanent Home

The Mille Lacs Reservation from 1855 to 1861

Until almost the end of his life, Henry Rice would be seen by many Ojibwe, including some Mille Lacs band members, as their friend. However, in February 1856, only one year after the 1855 treaty created a permanent home for the band on Mille Lacs Lake, Rice wrote disparagingly about their continuing presence on their reservation to George W. Manypenny. In his letter Rice took the lumbermen's side in their dispute with the band over the dam the lumbermen had built at the outlet of Lake Onamia and stated that he believed the "alleged damage" to the rice crop "has little or no foundation in fact."[1]

Rice noted that logging was an important local industry but did not acknowledge that the Mille Lacs Band had been at Mille Lacs before logging had begun in the region. Instead he asserted that the lumbermen had purchased their lands (which were south of the reservation) prior to the creation of the reservation, so they "enjoyed this right [to dam the river] which custom had long conceded to them" and, given their great investment of money in purchasing land and erecting mills, they should expect to continue to enjoy that right. "Rum River is the great highway for the lumber men to take their produce to market," Rice stated. It was a public thoroughfare and the lumbermen should "be left to use it in the manner most advantageous to themselves," through the "interposition of Government." Rice wrote that if he had known about the problem before the treaty was negotiated, he would have taken action. Now it was necessary to enter into negotiations with the Mille Lacs Band "for an exchange of lands, so that they may be removed from all vexatious connection with the whites." If that could not be done, negotiations should take place by the government to obtain for the lumbermen the right to maintain the dam.

In apparent response to Rice's recommendation, Commissioner Manypenny wrote to Francis Huebschmann, superintendent of Indian Affairs of the Northern Superintendency, which included Minnesota, for the purpose of resolving the issue of the dam. Manypenny began by citing the Treaty of 1855:

> By the second article of the treaty with the Mississippi bands of
> the Chippewa Indians concluded February 22, 1855, it is provided
> that one tract of land amongst others, shall be set apart for the use
> of said Indians, to embrace the following fractional townships,
> viz, forty two north of Range twenty five West, forty two north of
> Range twenty six west, and forty two and forty three north of Range
> twenty seven west, it being understood by the parties that said
> reservation would include all the rice islands in the vicinity of Mille
> Lac, from which it is alleged the Indians have been accustomed to
> gather annually about two thousand bushels of rice, which formed
> a large proportion of their subsistence during a portion of the year,
> when they were usually most in want.

Meanwhile, he noted that the lumbermen had built, as an aid to running their logs, "a dam across the outlet of Mille Lac, called Rum River, within the reserve or very near to its southern boundary," the effect of which was to overflow and destroy "one half or more of the above mentioned rice fields."[2]

Manypenny believed the lumbermen had not "taken the proper view of the case—without denying the right of the Indians to indemnity, they have endeavored to throw the burden of compensation upon the government instead of assuming it themselves." He noted that, contrary to Rice's suggestion that the Mille Lacs Ojibwe be removed, he declined to negotiate this change, since "such a course would be unjust to the Indians and the Government."

Manypenny asked that Superintendent Huebschmann consult with the band and ask it to settle on a sum "to accept as an indemnity for the loss of their rice crops." He would inform "the Hon. H. M. Rice," who represented the lumbermen "in this business," about these instructions.

Huebschmann told the Ojibwe agent D. B. Herriman to investigate the matter. In doing so, Herriman learned of the agreement reached the year before between the loggers and the band, with the loggers agreeing to pay an annual fee for the continuance of the dam. He determined that no further negotiation was necessary. Later that summer, Huebschmann commented, sarcastically, that the request to transfer the payment to the federal government merely showed the "enterprising spirit" of some citizens of Minnesota.[3]

At this point Rice's suggestion about removal of the Mille Lacs Band was not taken seriously. However, his letter alluded to the precarious nature of the permanent homes secured for the Mille Lacs Ojibwe and the other bands who received reservations in the 1855 treaty, not to mention the untrustworthiness of Henry Rice. As for embracing agriculture as a way of life, the folly of exclusively depending on farming was demonstrated when Agent Herriman noted, speaking of the various Mississippi bands in the summer of 1856, that grasshoppers appeared at the end of July and "literally swept the whole country," affecting in particular corn and potatoes. Herriman stated that the infestation was especially difficult for those who cultivated the soil for the first time: "This is to be regretted this year more than any previous one, for it may discourage the new beginners and drive them back again to the chase."[4]

Some members of the Mille Lacs Band may have been among those who grew crops for the first time. Agent Herriman wrote that since the "clearing and breaking land" fund was low at the agency, he confined expenditures to the Rabbit Lake and Mille Lacs Reservations. He noted that much of the grubbing and clearing was done by band members themselves. As noted earlier, band members later stated that the land cleared was in the area on the west shore of the lake near present-day Garrison, within what Mille Lacs band members considered to be their reservation but which was not in the treaty boundaries as portrayed on Rice's map.[5]

Also making things difficult for the Mille Lacs Band were problems with wild rice crops. While the crop was flooded in 1855 because of the logging dam, in 1856 wild rice crops were only one-third of normal for all the Mississippi bands. The initial annuity payment of $1,000 from the treaty was helpful, but it had been paid out in winter, at Crow Wing, which required that band members pause during an important hunting season and travel all the way there and back.[6]

In August 1856 a road funded with $5,000 from Article 3 of the Treaty of 1855 was completed from the mouth of the Rum River to Mille Lacs Lake. Another road was built to connect Mille Lacs to Crow Wing. While the purpose of these roads was to provide access to the Mille Lacs Reservation, they may also have served the growth of settlement along the Rum River south of the reservation. A writer in the *St. Paul Advertiser* in March 1857 noted the potential for settlement, describing oak openings, prairies, marsh meadows with excellent hay, and tamarack groves for fencing. The pineries began about thirty miles from the mouth of the river, and ran all the way to the river's source at Mille Lac Lake. Hundreds of men were employed in the forest for half the year and required vast stores of provisions. Farmers had the best possible market and at the same time had access to cheap and abundant lumber.[7]

The next month the *Weekly Minnesotian* also trumpeted the potential of the Rum River country, claiming (without mentioning the reservation) that nearly every section of unoccupied land from the source of the Rum River to its mouth was open for preemption. The following year the *Minnesota Republican* wrote of a new town named Stirling, located on the southeast corner of Mille Lacs Lake, on a small, unnamed lake that was the "reservoir of two fine streams." This article also failed to mention the Indian reservation. It described nearby Mille Lacs Lake, noting its "beautiful bays and headlands and numerous fairy-like islands where wild fowls resorted in great numbers to 'incubate'" and that "There are excellent pickerels and herrings in countless numbers to be caught in vast quantities in almost all seasons." According to the newspaper the town was made accessible by the construction of a road from the Rum River Road and by other roads leading north to Lake Superior.[8]

The spread of settlement up the Rum River, difficulties with lumbermen, and the problems involved with establishing full-time agriculture on the new reservations all appeared to provide reasons why, from the point of view of whites, the "permanent homes" established under the Treaty of 1855 should be abolished. Around this time, abolishing the scattered reservations and creating a single reservation for all Ojibwe was often proposed as something for the benefit of the Ojibwe themselves. Agent Herriman wrote in 1855 that confining Indians "to small reservations, leaving the land all around them subject to claims," and forcing them to depend on agriculture before they had broken land to do so led to depredations by Indians, or at least, he acknowledged, false claims of depredations. In any case, he argued, gambling, drinking, and sexual relations were encouraged. Two years later another Indian agent, J. W. Lynde, used much the same reasoning to support concentrating all Ojibwe onto one reservation, preferably the Leech Lake Reservation, which could be enlarged to include lands that "will not be required for settlement for a long period of time."[9]

Mille Lacs band leaders and leaders of other Mississippi bands did not view the problems in the same way; they felt the challenges arose from the slow pace of changes promised by federal officials. In September 1860 Mississippi leaders including Shaboshkung and Manoominikeshiinh of Mille

Lacs asked for expenditures to help build houses. The petition included a reference to Article 9 of the 1854 Lake Superior Ojibwe treaty regarding the use of "arrearages" due under previous treaties. But the 1855 treaty included its own Article 9 provision stating that the Mississippi bands could "appropriate their means to the erection of houses" and other activities connected with "the cultivation of the soil." Superintendent of Indian Affairs in Minnesota William J. Cullen wrote a letter in October 1860 supporting the petition, stating that houses should be built at Gull Lake, at the Chippewa Agency at Crow Wing, and at Mille Lacs. He wrote: "I am well satisfied no more beneficial expenditure of their money can be made and the permanent agriculture progress of these Indians will thereby be materially advanced. They require cattle to improve their lands and I find that it has been attended with the most favorable results where stock has been given them and they made thereby to realize the advantage that accrues to them by protecting and enjoying the use of it."[10]

Around the same time Mille Lacs leaders also had concerns about the location of their annuity payments. In December 1861 missionary E. Steele Peake sent officials in Washington a petition for Mille Lacs band leaders Shaboshkung, Biidadens, Ayaabe, Manoominikeshiinh, Zhooniyaa, and Gegwedaash, representing the 664 Mille Lacs band members. They asked that their annuities be paid at Mille Lacs, recalling the promise that they would be paid there once the road from Crow Wing was completed. The road had been open for a number of years, and they wondered why they continued to be paid at Crow Wing. When annuities were paid in the winter, they were required to travel forty miles by foot, carrying annuity goods, and they lost time during their best hunting season. They also pointed out that they had received little benefit from the money set aside for agriculture and schools.[11]

In the fall of 1861 Clark Thompson, superintendent of the Northern Superintendency, gave his own reasons for suggesting that the Mille Lacs and other bands be paid on their reservations, to avoid the hardship of having to travel during cold weather. He wrote, "it would be better for the Indians and but little more trouble for the agent and superintendent." Lucius Walker, the new agent at the Crow Wing Chippewa Agency, also had suggestions for changes. He felt "compelled to state" that the Mississippi bands had "no farms under cultivation," despite the small expenditures of his predecessors, which was "entirely inadequate" to carry out the treaty provisions. With regard to the Mille Lacs Band he noted a dispute between band members and adjacent settlers regarding the

1855 reservation boundaries. He suggested a survey would resolve the difficulty. Though some of the townships around Mille Lacs had been surveyed in the late 1850s, survey of the reservation townships was not completed until around 1870.[12]

Even though the difficulties cited by Thompson and Walker related primarily to carrying out the 1855 treaty, they continued to be cited as reasons for scrapping the reservations and placing all the Ojibwe on one single reservation. Walker wrote that the single greatest challenge in making improvements on the reservations arose from the fact that they were disconnected. He raised also the specter of the "liquor traffic" and the difficulty of the agent being able to control it on these disconnected reservations. He wrote, "I would therefore suggest the propriety of removing these bands to one reservation."[13]

The 1862 Dakota Conflict

Further impetus for the creation of one large reservation for the Mississippi Ojibwe came the following year. As before, the agent of change was Hole-in-the-Day. The chief, who had done much of the talking at the 1855 treaty negotiation, was viewed by some government officials and many whites as exemplary of the changes they sought to make among the Ojibwe. Perhaps as a result of his speeches in Washington, he had personally received an entire section of land in fee simple, to include his house and farm, though he hired a white farmer to cultivate the land for him. In 1857, without mentioning the land granted to him, agent D. B. Herriman wrote that Hole-in-the-Day was "an exception to all Indians" and had "done more, unaided, to practically civilize his tribe than has ever been done by white men, backed up, though they have been, by the influence and money of the government."[14]

However, Hole-in-the-Day began to question corrupt practices by officials in the Indian agency. He went to Washington in the spring of 1862 to investigate fraudulent payments, but apparently achieved little change in the agency. Meanwhile, in August 1862 young Dakota men who would later be led by Little Crow attacked whites adjacent to their reservation in southwestern Minnesota. In mid-August, in what was believed by many whites at the time—and a few historians since then—to have been a coordinated attempt to join Little Crow's resistance, it was rumored that Hole-in-the-Day had sent messengers to the Mississippi bands to invite them to participate in a general attack against Americans. On August 18, the same day as the attack on white settlers by Dakota, several cattle were killed at the Crow Wing agency. Soon after this incident agent Lucius Walker dispatched soldiers from Fort Ripley on the Mississippi to arrest the chief, though without success. Hole-in-the-Day soon sent additional messages to various bands asking that they join him in making war against the whites.[15]

Mille Lacs leaders resisted Hole-in-the-Day's invitation. They sent a message to Commissioner of Indian Affairs William Dole, who was in Minnesota to make a treaty with the Pembina and Red Lake bands in northwestern Minnesota, informing him that they would not participate in Hole-in-the-Day's plans. According to Episcopal minister Ezekiel G. Gear, the Mille Lacs people were peaceable: "They condemned the movements of Hole-in-the-Day in council and told their young men that if any of them joined, they would never be permitted to return to the band again." In a letter dated September 3, Gegwedaash and Shaboshkung stated that they had no "animosity against any person and are happy to have the privilege to come and see our Great Fathers." They planned to arrive at Fort Ripley on September 6.[16]

That day, the missionary John Johnson (Enmegahbowh), who had been driven from Gull Lake, reported from Fort Ripley that Hole-in-the-Day had repeatedly sent his "braves" to Mille Lacs to persuade band members to support him, but they "invariably refused." Johnson spoke with Commissioner Dole and Superintendent Clark Thompson at Fort Ripley, suggesting that those "well disposed" Ojibwe ought to be separated from the "wild ones." The superintendent told him he intended to make "a general proposal" that all the Ojibwe now receiving annuities remove to a single reservation. He expected "to open farms, build houses and give cattle and all the comforts of civilized life to the good & civilized Indians." He asked Johnson to suggest a place.[17]

A meeting between Commissioner Dole and about fifty members of the Mille Lacs Band, including its leadership, took place at Fort Ripley on September 9. Dole in his annual report that year stated that as a result of the council meeting with the Mille Lacs Band "their friendship and good will [was] secured." However, it had been obvious from the beginning that the Mille Lacs people were opposed to Hole-in-the-Day.[18]

Missionary Peake also gave an account of the September 9 meeting, stating that the Mille Lacs leaders had come from their rice fields near Granite City (now St. Cloud) and Little Falls to go to Fort Ripley. Mille Lacs leaders made clear they opposed the actions of Hole-in-the-Day and the

Pillagers and did not wish to see any of the members of those bands in council. According to Peake, the commissioner promised the Mille Lacs people his protection and said their annual payment in the fall would be made on their own reservation.

Peake also reported that the chief Bad Boy (Gwiiwizhenshish) of Leech Lake and several of his band intended to move to Mille Lacs. Leaders at Mille Lacs wanted John Johnson to relocate to Mille Lacs to be their missionary. Shaboshkung talked with Johnson and Peake for a long time. Peake had learned that Dole told the Mille Lacs people they "must make arrangements to receive the friendly Indians" who might be removed to Mille Lacs. Peake also reported that Hole-in-the-Day and three hundred warriors showed up at Crow Wing on September 10 for a preliminary meeting with the commissioner.[19]

Another version of the meeting between Dole and the Mille Lacs leaders was recorded by missionary Gear, who wrote that the Mille Lacs delegation had "effectively and satisfactorily cleared themselves from all suspicion of complicity with Hole-in-the-Day." They explained how they resisted Hole-in-the-Day's invitations. Commissioner Dole praised their actions and assured them that all their wrongs would be righted and their fidelity rewarded. One of the Mille Lacs speakers alluded to annuities that had been withheld from them the previous year. They had received $12,000 less than usual, and the band members were sure it was just a mistake.[20]

A few existing records of this meeting with Dole refer to the band members who were there. Years later, on October 8, 1896, the *Princeton Union* newspaper reported on the death of Monzomonay "at the Mille Lacs reservation on September 3, at the advanced age of 85 years." The article, which was from the *Duluth News*, stated:

> The deceased was well and favorably known in the vicinity of Mille Lacs as a friend of the whites. In 1862, when almost all the tribes on the western frontier were hostile to the government, the Mille Lacs Chippewas remained loyal, mainly through the efforts of Mo-zo-mo-ny. He, with his father, the late Chief Ricemaker, arrived at Fort Ripley on September 9, 1862, and offered the services of the Mille Lacs Indians, who at that time numbered about 400 warriors, to suppress the Indian outbreak then existing in this State. This prevented the Leech Lake and other Chippewas, who were under the leadership of Hole-in-the-Day, and who had already commenced to pillage the settlers in the northwestern part of this

State, from doing further damage, and peace was restored, among the Chippewas, at least[;], as a reward for their services, the government granted to the Mille Lacs Chippewas the right to occupy the Mille Lacs reservation.[21]

A printed document submitted by band members to the Department of the Interior on July 21, 1897, recorded that on September 9, 1862, two band members, Shaboshkung and his nephew Mozomonay (Monzomonay), son of Manoominikeshiinh, received letters of introduction from Commissioner Dole and Superintendent Thompson describing their support and friendship "to the whites" and recommending them to everyone they met.[22]

Many years later, in 1914, a monument approved by the Minnesota legislature was erected at Fort Ridgely marking the contribution of Monzomonay and other Ojibwe in the opposition to Hole-in-the-Day. The monument referred to the "loyal and efficient services of Chief Mou-zoo-maunee (Monzomonay) and the Chippewa Indians during the Sioux outbreak and the Civil War." Writing of this monument, historian William Watts Folwell questioned Monzomonay's contribution and denied that he was a person of any importance at the time. In fact, Monzomonay, born around 1832, was coming into prominence as a Mille Lacs band leader. The next year he accompanied the Mille Lacs delegation to Washington, where, contrary to Folwell's assertion, he was one of the signers of the Treaty of 1863.[23]

The printed document from 1897 also recorded that the head warrior of the Mille Lacs Band who first refused to consider the proposition from Hole-in-the-Day was named Shagobay. There were various band members of that name at Mille Lacs at this time, but this may have been Zhowonaunahquodwabe, also known as Shagobay. He was the younger half-brother of Gotigwaakojiins and was also a nephew of the first Negwanebi. Born in the 1830s, he had achieved some prominence in 1857, when he and other band members were arrested in an altercation with a local militia in Chisago County. He was put on trial but was later placed in the hands of local officials in Taylors Falls, after which, according to Mille Lacs oral tradition, he made his escape.[24]

While separate negotiations between Hole-in-the-Day and Commissioner Dole stalled in early September 1862, Minnesota state officials became involved in negotiating with the Ojibwe bands. In mid-September the Minnesota legislature passed a resolution appointing the ubiquitous Henry Rice, retired missionary Frederick Ayer, and two others to act as commissioners to work with the commissioner of Indian Affairs to "preserve the peace and prevent an outbreak of the Indians on the northern frontier." Accompanied by Governor Alexander Ramsey, they set out for Fort Ripley. On the way they met Commissioner Dole, who suggested that "no amicable adjustment could be effected with those Indians" but encouraged them to make the attempt. They continued on to Crow Wing, where they met on September 15 with "the bands that had exhibited symptoms of dissatisfaction." Together they negotiated a treaty pledging peace and friendship, stating that all money due the Ojibwe would be paid and calling for an investigation of complaints by and against the Indians. No Mille Lacs leaders appear to have been involved in this treaty. Later in September the legislature urged the president to carry out the agreement, though Commissioner Dole stated it could have no binding effect on the US government because it had been negotiated without federal authorization. Nonetheless, the state treaty increased the pressure for a new federal treaty.[25]

In early October a meeting involving state officials and representatives of all the Mississippi bands, including Mille Lacs, occurred in St. Paul. At that time a number of Ojibwe from Mille Lacs and the Mississippi River offered their services to help American forces fight in the US–Dakota War. Historian Folwell reported that the offer was "respectfully declined," but there is some evidence that individual Ojibwe may have served in the fight against the Dakota.[26]

Kegwedosay, who was married to Noodin, a daughter of Manoominikeshiinh, was said to have served in the US war against the Dakota in 1862 and later. John W. Goulding, an early Princeton, Minnesota, resident, recalled that Kegwedosay had come to town in the fall of 1862 to inform the frightened settlers that his father-in-law and other leaders had refused to join Hole-in-the-Day in fighting against whites. Goulding also said that "old Kaig" had served in the US–Dakota War on the side of US forces, along with a Rum River lumberman, Captain Jonathan Chase. No official record has been found of Kegwedosay's participation, though Chase was mentioned as leading a "company of pioneers" on Henry H. Sibley's expedition against the Dakota in the summer of 1863.[27]

Goulding also stated that Kegwedosay had a particular animosity toward the Dakota because his brother, known as Same Day, was killed by Dakota warriors in 1857 along the Rum River. A similar account was given by Kegwedosay's granddaughter, Mille Lacs band elder Eqwaya (Jennie Mitchell), in a 1983 interview, according to Don Wedll and Tadd Johnson in their study of the events of 1862. They quote Eqwaya as stating that Kegwedosay's brother and wife were attacked along the Rum River, near Princeton, on their way back to Mille Lacs. The brother was killed, and his wife, with a baby in a cradleboard, ran away and swam across the river to escape.[28]

Later sources also refer to Kegwedosay's involvement in the war against the Dakota. An 1889 newspaper article stated that he had, in a meeting with some soldiers that year, "often referred to a letter which he carries written by Gov. Marshall, in which the scout's services in the [Alfred] Sully expedition against the Sioux are gratefully acknowledged." The reference to Sully may have been an error, since William R. Marshall himself was on the 1863 Sibley expedition. Furthermore, an 1897 newspaper carried a photograph of Kegwedosay with the label "Keg-way-do-say, one of Sibley's scouts," stating that he "was a scout with the Sibley expedition to the Missouri river during the Sioux uprising of 1862. He is eighty years old and has earned the right to wear the skunk skin the Victoria cross of the Chippewas, which can be worn only after a warrior has gained distinction on the battle field."[29]

Around this time the St. Paul photographer Joel E. Whitney did a series of carte de visite portraits of various Mississippi Ojibwe leaders. Many of these photographs were marketed with printed captions stating that the individuals had opposed Hole-in-the-Day "in his designs against the whites" or that they had offered their services to fight against the Dakota. Among them was Kishkanakut (Stump). A photograph of Shaboshkung was taken around the same time.[30]

After the October 1862 meeting in St. Paul, John Johnson (Enmegahbowh) wrote that Sandy Lake, Pokegama, and Mille Lacs Ojibwe would receive their payment at Mille Lacs, and Bad Boy's band, as well as Johnson, would go there to receive their payment. He stated that only the "rebels" would be paid at the agency.[31]

Pressure for a New Treaty

All of these developments increased pressure for a new treaty with the Mississippi Ojibwe, to arrange for their removal to a place more distant from white settlement. Commissioner William Dole, prior to encountering Governor Alexander Ramsey on his way to St. Paul, had written, "If it could be arranged to remove these Indians farther North towards Red Lake and Red River, I have no doubt that both the Indians and the white man would be benefited, and that it would be approved by the Government."[32]

The purported opinions of unnamed Ojibwe chiefs were sometimes cited in recommending that a new treaty be made. A. C. Morrill, who had been appointed as a temporary replacement for the previous agent, Lucius Walker, stated that in mid-September he held a council with some of the chiefs: "They said that they had no hostile intentions against the whites; they desired but one thing to wit: that a treaty should be made purchasing their lands and their removal on to one reservation more distant from white settlements." Subsequently, even John Johnson (Enmegahbowh) added his voice in favor of removal, although he did not specify that Mille Lacs should be one of the bands to move. On October 15, 1862, he wrote to Commissioner Dole, "I do sincerely believe the best thing that the government can do with the Indians is—to Remove them farther north and that immediately— better for the Indians, the whites & far better for the government."[33]

In October Superintendent Clark Thompson ordered the newly appointed agent, A. Lawrence Foster, to pay annuities to the Mille Lacs Band as well as the Sandy Lake and Pokegama bands at Mille Lacs, at a meeting that took place on October 27. The other bands were paid at Crow Wing later in November. In December, a new effort to invite the leaders of all the bands to come to St. Paul for a new treaty began. It appears that J. P. Usher, who was the assistant secretary of the Interior but would soon be appointed secretary, came to Minnesota to try to negotiate a treaty with the Mississippi Ojibwe at the annuity payment. Since that meeting included only some of the relevant bands, he returned to Washington, leaving a copy of the treaty language with the agent. Traveling through St. Paul on his way back east, Usher wrote a letter to Superintendent Thompson with instructions to assemble the bands "at some suitable and convenient place" to "make with them the Treaty proposed by me for their concentration at or about Leech Lake." He added that the removal of the bands was "deemed of the first importance to the Indians and the peace of the State." Thompson wrote to Agent Foster passing on these instructions and to Commissioner Dole asking for money to carry out the orders, since there were no funds in the agency for that purpose. Later in the month, at Thompson's suggestion, Commissioner Dole authorized having the negotiation take place at Crow Wing, because it was closer to Mille Lacs and would be less expensive to arrange.[34]

Shortly after that Assistant Secretary Usher wrote to Thompson with specific instructions about the content of the treaty. One goal, likely because of the hostility between the Mille Lacs Band and Hole-in-the-Day, was to put the Mille Lacs and the Gull Lake bands as far as possible from each other. Other terms were very similar to those in the Treaty of 1855, intended to give the Ojibwe "permanent homes where they could build themselves houses, and from which they would not be called upon to remove again." Usher stated that the treaty was much more for the benefit of the Indians than for the government. He threatened that if the bands did not sign the treaty, Congress might pass a law that would provide for their removal. Usher informed Thompson that he should "firmly insist upon their signing it," though there would be no payments as a result of the treaty.[35]

Usher also wrote a letter to be given to the chiefs and headmen in which he elaborated on his idea for the new reservation and made the same threats about their removal if they did not sign a treaty. He insisted the new reservation would be to their benefit because many whites were asking for their removal. Their annuities would be the same and, in the case of the Mille Lacs Band, he promised they would be paid at Mille Lacs, stating, "Your Great Father has kept his promise, but at great expense and inconvenience; but it is only promised this time, and he cannot be expected to do so again."[36]

Unmentioned in the Usher letter, surprisingly, was the bigger promise: that the Mille Lacs Ojibwe would be rewarded for their support of the Americans against Hole-in-the-Day. This promise was also not mentioned in the subsequent treaty negotiations at Crow Wing in January 1863, when government officials came determined to remove all Ojibwe, including the Mille Lacs Band.

A group of twenty-three Mille Lacs band members, including their leaders Gegwedaash, Negwanebi, Manoominikeshiinh, and Zhooniyaa, went to St. Paul in December, just before Christmas, to meet with Superintendent Thompson. According to a report in the *St. Paul Daily Union*, they were the Indians that, "during Hole-in-the-Day's tantrum, came in and offered their services to fight the Sioux, or even Hole-in-the-Day, if necessary." Unfortunately, the prejudice against all Indians was so strong in the city at the time that Thompson was unable to find the delegation any lodgings in a local hotel. In addition, it was reported that a group of German immigrants threw stones at them. Thompson offered a camping place in the garden of his house, on St. Anthony Hill, in the present area of the St. Paul Cathedral. In reporting these incidents, the newspaper scolded the city's residents for being unable to make distinctions among Indian tribes: "Really, we see no reason for maltreating the heathen. They will in all probability soon be removed in a peaceable manner."[37]

Negotiations at Crow Wing

What occurred during the consultation in St. Paul is not known, but it appears that the Mille Lacs delegation returned to Crow Wing for another negotiation. Agent Foster, who headed the discussions at Crow Wing, reported to Secretary Usher in late January that despite difficulties, including the fact that it was hunting season, the bands assembled between January 10 and 12. Since Superintendent Thompson did not appear, Foster began to council with them, continuing until January 21. Foster believed that if Shaboshkung had not exerted his influence the treaty would have been signed. The Mille Lacs chief had appeared with a delegation of ten and "had evidently selected to defeat the treaty." Foster wrote that at the first council Shaboshkung "declared that his arm would be wrenched from his body before he would touch the pen." Foster stated:

> The urgency of the treaty were so great that he soon relapsed in silence. He finally argued the absence of influential chiefs, that he was the guardian of a boy who was to be a principal chief by inheritance [a reference to the young man Wahweyaycumig, the son of the chief Wadena, who appears to have died prior to the treaty]. He said that he was aware of the perils that surrounded them, that if the government were determined on their removal, they did not want to locate around Leech Lake, but wanted time to look up a new home around Red Lake. He wanted the show to go off and finally withdrew from the council followed by the Sandy Lake and Pokegama delegations.[38]

Foster stated that Hole-in-the-Day, who had kept away, appeared at the last council but under the circumstances "could do nothing": "All seemed satisfied that the proposition came from their friends who urged it for their good to save them from consequences to be feared on account of the violent public sentiment prevailing among the people of Minnesota, that if the government insisted on their removal, they must submit."

Bishop Henry Whipple was also present at the negotiation and wrote to Commissioner Dole about the discussions with Mille Lacs leaders and their understanding of the promises Dole had made them in the fall. Whipple said the Mille Lacs leaders and Bad Boy stated that they had counseled with Dole in September: "They say that Dole promised that they would be protected and rewarded, and that Hole-in-the-Day and his followers should be punished." Other officials had promised the same thing. But now "the Mille Lac Indians say that they have lost their lands along with the bad Indians." Whipple noted that the Mille Lacs Indians said "that for months Hole-in-the-Day has been planning this outbreak and that he had made arrangements with Little Crow to have the outbreak begin with the Sioux at the same time." If Hole-in-the-Day were rewarded, it would "teach the young men to adhere to the fortunes of bad men, and this will lead to a more terrible outbreak." They asked for an investigation into what had occurred and protection for themselves from "the Great Father." Finally, they asked for Senator Rice to come to see them: "They say he is their friend and never speaks with a double tongue and that they will settle everything as he says." It was clear they had not heard of Rice's earlier call for their reservation to be abolished.[39]

Whipple appears to have been greatly impressed with the stand Sha-boshkung took, recalling it many years later in his autobiography. He noted that Foster, the government negotiator, seemed to have little knowledge of Indian character or the understanding that the land proposed for the new reservation was "the poorest strip of land in Minnesota, and is unfit for cultivation." He told Foster, "You propose to take their arable land, their best hunting-ground, their rice fields, and their fisheries, and give them a country where they cannot live without the support of the Government." But Foster persisted with the negotiation, advising the collected leaders to sign the agreement. Whipple wrote of Shaboshkung's reactions:

> As quickly as a flash of lightning, old Sha-boshkung, the head chief of the Mille Lacs band, sprang to his feet, and said:—
>
> "My father, look at me! The winds of fifty-five winters have blown over my head and have silvered it with gray. But—*they haven't blown my brains away!*"
>
> He sat down, and all the Indians shouted, "Ho! Ho! Ho!" That ended the council.[40]

John Johnson (Enmegahbowh) also gave an account of the contentious nature of the negotiations, including meetings between the various chiefs, in a letter written in February 1863. He reported that "there were some pretty hot times in the counsels among the chiefs themselves." Hole-in-the-Day and a Sandy Lake chief, unnamed and described only as an "old man," had quarreled. The Sandy Lake chief had spoken in public about how Hole-in-the-Day had sent tobacco, urging them "to rob & kill all the whites." Hole-in-the-Day taunted him and called him a liar, but the old man called on other chiefs and band members to verify that Hole-in-the-Day had sent braves and tobacco to Sandy Lake asking for their help. The Sandy Lake chief said Hole-in-the-Day was a child and talked like a child.[41]

Negotiations in Washington

According to John Johnson (Enmegahbowh), the chiefs were now planning a trip to Washington to see if they could stop the attempt to remove them. Pierre or Peter Roy of Little Falls, a person of mixed heritage with kin or marriage connections at Mille Lacs, was collecting the chiefs to leave in the morning, against the agent's wishes.

A few days later Bishop Whipple wrote to Henry Rice informing him of the delegations going to Washington and suggesting terms for the treaty. Rice received the letter by February 7 and replied, promising to do all in his power to make a treaty in accordance with Whipple's views, but he was not optimistic given the current political climate in Washington.[42]

By early February the delegation of Mississippi River chiefs left St. Paul on their way east, with John Johnson accompanying them. On February 16 Johnson wrote from La Crosse, Wisconsin, stating that they had gone with the encouragement of Superintendent Thompson. The delegation members were going to propose that the government "buy their present reservations and . . . give them the privileges of rights of selecting the country for themselves." The superintendent thought the government would be willing to do so. According to Johnson the leaders intended to ask for the Mille Lacs country. In particular, the Pokegama, Sandy Lake, Rabbit Lake, and Gull Lake bands, aside from Hole-in-the-Day, had agreed among themselves "to move & settle down permanently with the Mille Lackers and begin living after the manner of whites." Johnson wondered if the government would be willing "to give them that country or not."[43]

Because of what had occurred the previous summer and fall, Hole-in-the-Day did not go to Washington. Instead the chiefs represented many of the other Mississippi bands and Mille Lacs, including Shaboshkung, Manoominikeshiinh, Biidadens, Mino-giizhig, plus three others whose names had not appeared before in dealings with the US government.[44]

Although the collected journal for the 1863 treaty includes transcripts of government dealings with Hole-in-the-Day in June 1862 and the Lake Superior Ojibwe, who were present in Washington, DC, in February 1863, the first recorded meeting with the Mississippi Ojibwe occurred on

February 25, when Shaboshkung, Manoominikeshiinh, Biidadens, and Mino-giizhig met with Secretary Usher and Commissioner Dole. The journal records a series of meetings involving these and other chiefs over the next two weeks, ending abruptly on March 6, prior to completing the negotiation.[45]

Perhaps because Hole-in-the-Day was not present during these meetings, much of the recorded conversation involved Mille Lacs leaders, particularly Shaboshkung, who made clear the feelings of the Mille Lacs Band that it would not remove from the Mille Lacs Reservation. At the first meeting Shaboshkung reiterated the unhappiness they felt with the draft treaty that had been presented to them in the fall and winter, and the difficulty they had had in dealing with the agent and with the negotiator Foster, who had appeared in January. While the treaty had been thoroughly explained, the negotiator, when he first presented it at the agency, had seemed "a little severe," as though he intended to intimidate them into signing. For these reasons, Shaboshkung explained, they had set out from Minnesota to meet with the secretary and the commissioner. Manoominikeshiinh added that they were threatened with the loss of their annuities "if we did not touch the pen and put our names to the paper."[46]

Shaboshkung noted that the officials had been misinformed about the country to which it was proposed to move all the Ojibwes. It was, he said, "a country of starvation," nothing but sand barrens and swamps, and "you cannot cultivate corn enough to feed a squirrel during the winter, let alone feed several bands of Indians." This assessment was seconded by Nebawash, a Leech Lake Pillager, who said he knew the section of country well. He pointed out that the Leech Lake Band had already picked the best land for its own reservation.[47]

Shaboshkung made his offer that the Mississippi bands be concentrated at Mille Lacs, stating, "There would be sufficient land for all the Mississippi . . . provided the reservations extended around the lake." An unnamed Sandy Lake chief, whose band included ten wigwams, spoke of his willingness to remove to Mille Lacs. Many of them had gone there during the troubles of the previous summer and spoke then of their willingness to move. He said, "The idea is not changed now. We are all willing to remove to that place and make it our home."[48]

Dole and Usher's responses were tempered by acknowledgment of the services rendered by the Mille Lacs Band in 1862. Dole stated, "They came and promised to keep the peace, they aided us, and I am determined to be their friend in all their troubles." But Dole expressed the belief that

removal was in the best interest of the Indians themselves. It was important, he said, to remove them from proximity to white settlements for
their own safety. Wherever they were located would have to "satisfy the
people of Minnesota," because otherwise those people might "take the law
into their own hands and make war" on them. In other words, the Ojibwe
might need distance to protect them from the bad behavior of whites.[49]

Dole said it might be true, "and probably is true," that there was sufficient land around Mille Lacs for both whites and Indians, but it was unfortunately the case that adjacent land had already been surveyed and put on
the market, which would make it difficult to reclaim it for reservations. He
had not forgotten his promises to the Mille Lacs people, but their removal
had not been a subject for discussion earlier. Now that they were discuss-
ing removal, he could not promise that he would help them avoid it. However, "They [Minnesotans] may consent in the future for them [Mille Lacs
band members] to remain there forever if they will become good citizens.
But I am sure that we will not give satisfaction to the people of Minnesota,
however much it may be desired by the Indians, if we removed them all
to Millac."[50]

Dole's view was that at least the Gull Lake Ojibwe would have to remove farther north. Perhaps because of this apparent openness to the
ideas argued by Mille Lacs and other band leaders, John Johnson, writing
to Bishop Whipple on February 28, stated his belief that Dole and Usher
would approve the plan to concentrate some of the other bands at Mille
Lacs. He also noted that there was suggestion on the part of some in the
government to propose moving Lake Superior Ojibwe to Mille Lacs.[51]

Several days later, on March 3, negotiations began again, with a speech
from Commissioner Dole, in which he noted that it was difficult to separate things involving one set of Ojibwe from all the others. While the bands
closest to Crow Wing had caused the trouble, whites demanded the removal of all Mississippi Ojibwe in Minnesota. It would not be possible to
make a treaty that separated the Mille Lacs, Pokegama, and Sandy Lake
bands from the other Mississippi bands. However, given the Mille Lacs
band members' helpfulness they might remain where they were "at least
for the present," for a year or two, until "they themselves shall seek out a
new home to their satisfaction." But it would be better for them to make
haste because of "the bitter feeling that exists in Minnesota between the
white man and the Indian."[52]

In response Shaboshkung reminded Dole of the conversations they
had had at Fort Ripley in September. The Ojibwe had heard the pleasant

words spoken to them and treasured them "in our hearts and also in our minds." They were very sorry to hear "that there is one [Hole-in-the-Day] who has been the instigation of all the transactions of which we have to bear the brunt. He would be the proper one to listen to all the complaints made by the government." But they held to the stipulations of their treaties "and what has been promised to us," a reference to the Treaty of 1855. Shaboshkung ended the speech with these words: "When we wake up in the morning we have nothing to think of but those stipulations. How can it be possible to abandon our reservations when we were told to seize [cede] every inch of the land with the exception of the land for the Reserves. If it is not enough for an Indian to live upon—how can it be good enough for a white man to live on, where we are living now. We demand that we should be allowed to live on our Reserves."

Dole answered by acknowledging the service of the Mille Lacs people at Fort Ripley and the promises he had made, but asked Shaboshkung to also acknowledge that "the removal of the Indians from their present Reserve was not a subject of conversation or of council." He had kept his promise to them "that they should be paid at their reservation and that he would keep faith with them." The removal was "for their own good." The proposed removal was not to punish them but to prevent trouble from whites.

It was clear that the assembled chiefs were unwilling to accept the terms offered by the government. A telegraphic dispatch sent from Washington to St. Paul on March 6 reported: "The Indians have had another meeting with Commissioner Dole. They still seem averse to removal further North." If things had continued in this manner, no treaty would have been signed, at least not with the Mille Lacs Band. But then Henry Rice, opportunistic as ever, appeared on the scene. On the day he arrived, March 6, 1863, his term as senator from Minnesota had just ended. As a Democrat in a time when his party was not in favor in Washington, he had chosen not to run for reelection. His replacement was Governor Ramsey, who had resigned as governor and was now elected the new senator.[53]

Secretary Dole began the session introducing Rice, who was well acquainted with Mille Lacs band members and had now "consented to act as your friend." Dole stated, "he has known you for a long time, and he knows what is for your interest." Dole advised them to listen to Rice, who "knows more than you do and will give you any advice that is for your good." They should tell Rice everything they wanted, and Rice would tell the government officials, and "then we will see if we can agree." One way or another, though, it was necessary to act quickly. Rice responded that it was not necessary to say anything more: he had talked so frequently with the Ojibwe that they understood each other well. He was ready to meet with them at any time. Shaboshkung responded likewise: "We are willing to meet with the Senator at any time."[54]

The treaty journal noted that "the Indians then held a private consultation with Senator Rice at the office of the Secretary of the Interior." No record exists of this conversation or of any negotiations involving the treaty after March 6. The treaty was signed on March 11 and ratified by Congress only two days later, after some amendments. The president proclaimed the treaty on March 19.[55]

Explanations for both the private negotiations between Rice and the Ojibwe chiefs as well as the form of the treaty must be inferred from other evidence. On March 10 Rice wrote to Bishop Whipple suggesting that he was taking an active role in writing the treaty. He reported that he had not been well but that the previous afternoon he had "drawn up my first impressions in regard to a treaty." Then he had sat up until midnight "putting them into shape." He planned to send Whipple "the pencillings" and would forward the treaty once it was done, or at least, if his version were not adopted, he would send "the form I desired it."[56]

The very next day, on March 11, a treaty was signed. On March 18 Rice wrote to Whipple stating that he would soon send a copy of the treaty and that "Every word in it (save amendments made by the Senate) emanated from my pen. I consulted no one—Whites or Indians—and would not allow any changes." About the new reservation created under the treaty he wrote, "I did not like the location—but it was the best that could be done." He had marked out the boundaries to include all of the large lakes "in order to keep worthless whites from settling upon them." He thought he had done good "to the red men. Now if the Govt. & the whites will only do what is right—the poor savages will be enabled to see the light of Heaven."[57]

After writing the treaty on his own and getting it adopted by all concerned, Rice presented a document to the Indian department on March 17 which purported to be signed by twenty-four chiefs and John Johnson, making Rice the "true and lawful" attorney to act in the name of the Ojibwe "to ratify treaties, change the terms of existing treaties and to receive monies[,] purchase goods, and transact all and any businesses appertaining to the affairs of said tribes." Although the document was not notarized, it appears to have been signed by Johnson, along with Peter

Roy and two other men of mixed heritage, D. George Morrison and John George Morrison. In fact, Henry Rice had already been a signer of the treaty as a representative of the Ojibwe.[58]

The 1863 Treaty

At the time Rice did not explain how he handled the insistence on the part of the Mille Lacs Ojibwe that they would not leave their permanent home, their reservation. Given the wording in Rice's letter to Whipple it is an open question as to whether the Mille Lacs chiefs or the others there actually were made aware of the document's content before they signed it. On the other hand, the wording of the treaty as finally proclaimed does reflect the Mille Lacs leaders' demand that they not be removed from their reservation at Mille Lacs. While the treaty stated that the reservations of the Mississippi bands were ceded to the United States and that a tract of land east and south of Leech Lake was "set apart for the future homes of the Chippewas of the Mississippi," the treaty contained an important proviso regarding the Mille Lacs Ojibwe. Article 12 stated that:

> It shall not be obligatory upon the Indians, parties to this treaty, to remove from their present reservations until the United States shall have first complied with the stipulations of Articles 4 and 6 of this treaty, when the United States shall furnish them with all necessary transportation and subsistence to their new homes, and subsistence for six months thereafter: *Provided*, That owing to the heretofore good conduct of the Mille Lac Indians, they shall not be compelled to remove so long as they shall not in any way interfere with or in any manner molest the persons or property of the whites.[59]

The existing treaty negotiation record makes clear that the Mille Lacs leaders would not sign a document in which they would acquiesce in their own removal from the Mille Lacs Reservation to any new reservation. The Article 12 proviso stated that they would not be required to remove as long as they remained at peace with the whites, something they had pledged to do. As the Mille Lacs leaders explained on many occasions in the years to come, they understood the Article 12 proviso to be a clear promise. And statements like Dole's at the treaty negotiation, on February 27, in which he referred to the possibility that the Mille Lacs Bands could "remain there forever" if they became good citizens would certainly have contributed to this understanding.

The Meeting with President Lincoln

On February 25 Secretary of the Interior J. P. Usher told the assembled leaders that he wanted them to meet with the president. In a discussion transcribed in the treaty record, Usher greeted them warmly and said he wished them to stay in Washington, "until you have seen your Great Father, the President, until you have seen the capitol, our large public buildings, and the power and wealth that your Great Father controls." Subsequently, a variety of sources record a meeting with President Abraham Lincoln.[60]

According to several newspaper accounts in 1863, a delegation of Ojibwe from a treaty negotiation in Washington met with Lincoln on February 20. They may have been from Lake Superior, since the *New York Times* reported, in a garbled article, on Tuesday, February 24, that Thompson's delegation comprising the Mille Lacs and other Mississippi band chiefs did not reach the city until Sunday, February 22. However, corroboration for a later meeting of the Mille Lacs leaders and other members of the delegation with the president is found in an account published after the delegation left the city in late March.[61]

One of the earliest newspapers to report the visit with the president was the New Orleans *Daily Picayune*, on March 8: "Diplomatic Reception. The Chippewa chiefs, now on a visit here, had an interview on Friday, with the President. Commissioner Dole accompanied the Indians to the White House. They were much pleased at being introduced to their 'Great Father.'"[62]

No details were given about the treaty, though the article stated that the visit was on a Friday, possibly March 6. This date, however, is contradicted by a later article in the *Pittsburgh Gazette*, on March 18. It reported that the "Chippewa Chiefs" had concluded their business in Washington when their treaty was ratified "on Friday night," possibly on Friday, March 13, though in fact the treaty was ratified on March 12: "They called upon the President next day, accompanied by Senator Ramsey and others to pay their respects before leaving for their homes. They were well satisfied and had a 'big talk.' The President assured them of the good will and protection of the government as long as they deserved it, they promised good behavior in future."[63]

The last sentence and its reference to the "protection of the government" in return for "good behavior" was as close as the article got to the Mille Lacs band leaders' understanding of Article 12 of the treaty. The newspaper did mention that the agreement "contained some curious stipulations," among them the board of visitors—or ministers—which would be appointed to oversee Indian policy under the treaty. Article 12 may have been viewed in the same way, though it was not mentioned.

Another account of the treaty and the visit with the president was published in the *Chicago Tribune* of March 20, which contains a March 17 report from the newspaper's Washington correspondent. The article also stated that the visit with the president occurred the day after the Senate ratified the treaty, which would mean the meeting took place on Friday, March 13. This article included a description virtually identical to that in the Pittsburgh newspaper. The report described the treaty, stating that the Indians covered by it were then located around Gull Lake and would be moved to an area near Red Lake, and included the sentence: "The President assured them of the good will and protection of the Government as long as they deserved it, and they promised good behavior in the future."[64]

A later article in the Winona, Minnesota, *Daily Republican*, on March 23, gave an equally full report, possibly based on the same source as the reports published in the Pittsburgh and Chicago newspapers, and likewise stated: "The President assured them of the good will and protection of the Government as long as they deserved it, and they promised good behavior in the future."[65]

These articles were all somewhat confused about the destination of the removal of the Ojibwe under the treaty, suggesting they were to be sent to the region of Red Lake. While the *St. Paul Pioneer* of March 27 repeated many of the details in the other stories, it suggested that these reports were inaccurate about the location. However, the St. Paul newspaper ended with a similar account of the meeting with the president, including the refrain about "good behavior": "Before leaving Washington for their homes, the chiefs comprising the mission called upon the President accompanied by Senator Ramsey and other Minnesotians, to express their diplomatic efforts. They were well received and had a 'big talk.' The President assured them of his good will and protection of the Government as long as they deserved it, and they promised good behavior in the future."[66]

Surprisingly, Ramsey himself did not mention the visit with the president in the brief diary he kept at the time, perhaps because the treaty was not one in which he was involved. Earlier, before going to Washington to take office as Minnesota's new senator, Ramsey had met with Superintendent Thompson in St. Paul one evening in February. Thompson wanted to talk about the treaty with the Ojibwe which he hoped to help negotiate. Ramsey was informed that the treaty was intended to remove the Ojibwe people to a reservation between Leech and Cass Lakes, and he described his impression that "much of the motive for the (removal of the Ind) [and] bringing the Inds. to Washington is to give the Ind. officers an opportunity of going on to that city to their own business."

Ramsey did not otherwise express an opinion on the prospective treaty. While Thompson went to Washington with the chiefs, Ramsey was not there for the negotiation and did not arrive in the city until March 12, the date of the treaty's ratification. The next day he did, in fact, see the president, but his diary made no mention of the Ojibwe leaders being there, or of the recently ratified treaty. Several weeks later he again saw the president, but his interest at that time was "about the execution of the Sioux Indians yet unhung," that is, the Dakota men who had not been executed at Mankato in December and who would be imprisoned in Davenport, Iowa. The president told Ramsey it was "a disagreeable subject but he would take it up & dispose of it." Again the Ojibwe were not discussed, and it is unlikely they were there at that meeting.[67]

In the context of the newspaper accounts, which made no specific reference to the provision about the Mille Lacs Band, the statements attributed to Lincoln and to the chiefs might be interpreted as merely the usual assurances of good intentions made in such encounters. But in this case, given the context of what had occurred in 1862 and the insistence by Mille Lacs leaders that they were unwilling to leave their reservation, the newspaper accounts provide ample support for the understanding of the Mille Lacs leaders about the treaty and the assurance they received from the "Great Father," whether President Lincoln or Commissioner Dole or both.

The Mille Lacs Ojibwe's Understanding of the Treaty

In the years after the treaty in Washington, Mille Lacs leaders often recalled the assurances they had received on that occasion. Their recollections are discussed throughout these pages; only a few are provided here as examples. At the annuity payments in the fall of 1863, Bishop Whipple recorded in his notes of speeches made by Mille Lacs leaders: "Two chiefs

heard what promise [was] made by [the] Pres[iden]t. & would like the agent
to keep it. The Prest. [is a] great chief & we expect he will keep his word.
Good promis us, he said they would never take us."[68]

In an 1867 petition Mille Lacs leaders stated, in language very similar
to that recorded in the 1863 negotiation journal, "we have remembered
the words of our great father that he said to us six [sic] years ago when we
went down to Washington, if we would behave ourselves as we have done
before that we should be let alone on the land we had before occupied [sic]
for a hundred years or a thousand years or as long as we do not commit any
depredations."[69]

Nine years later, during another visit to Washington, Shaboshkung
recalled that a decade before, Mille Lacs leaders had met with President
Lincoln:

> The President took hold of our hands and promised us faithfully
> and encouraged us, and he said we could live on our reservation for
> ten years, and if you are faithful to the whites and behave yourselves
> friendly to the whites you shall increase the number of years to 100;
> and you may increase it to a thousand years if you are good Indians,
> and through our good behaviour [sic] at the time of the war, (we
> were good and never raised hands against the whites), the Secretary
> of the Interior and the President said we should be considered good
> Indians and remain at Mille Lac so long as we want to.[70]

There was no doubt the Mille Lacs Ojibwe understood that a clear
promise had been made to them by the president of the United States that
the provisions of the 1863 treaty meant they would be allowed to stay on
their reservation at Mille Lacs.

Henry Rice's Understanding of the Treaty

Less clear, at least in 1863, was how Henry Rice understood the treaty he
claimed to have written. Aside from his letter to Bishop Whipple, he did
not elaborate on his understanding of the treaty until twenty-six years
later. Right after the signing Rice had little need to explain since the provision was not mentioned, in 1863 or in following years, in public discussions about the treaty. The missionary John Johnson (Enmegahbowh),
who wrote a letter about his conversations with Henry Rice in Washington
during the treaty negotiations, made no mention of any requirement that

the Mille Lacs Ojibwe move from their reservation or even that they had sold it. Writing on March 13, he noted that some of the bands present, including Sandy Lake, Rabbit Lake, Gull Lake, Rice Lake, and Pokegama, had sold theirs. He did not say anything about the Mille Lacs Ojibwe.[71]

Rice also said nothing in response when several Mille Lacs chiefs sent a letter to "My Friend Mr. Rice" in 1877 stating, "I hope you remember me when I saw you in Washington sixteen year[s] ago. At that time I was prommis I should allwas keep our home at Millack."[72]

No answer from Rice has been found. However, in 1889 Rice came to Mille Lacs to carry out the provisions of the Nelson Act, designed to allot Minnesota Ojibwe reservation farmland to Ojibwe people, to sell pinelands, and to sell any surplus lands on the open market. On that occasion Rice explained to the gathered leaders of the Mille Lacs Band that their memories of what had occurred in 1863 had been correct and they had not forfeited their right to occupy their reservation.[73]

It appears, then, that in 1863 Rice understood correctly that unless he put in the treaty the promise to the Mille Lacs people that they could remain on their reservation at Mille Lacs, they would not sign the treaty. But he may have also thought they would be persuaded at some point to remove from Mille Lacs on their own. It is evident that Rice throughout his career had boundless faith in his ability to persuade, so he may have meant he had done his best to craft a treaty that would satisfy both the aims of federal officials and those of the Mille Lacs Band.

Commissioner Dole, who had said in the negotiation that it might be possible for the Mille Lacs people to remain at Mille Lacs, may have understood that the Article 12 provision was a temporary one, designed to allow them time to decide on where they wanted to go once they left Mille Lacs. Dole may have understood the provision allowing them to remain as temporary in the sense that he had conveyed in the treaty negotiation: that abrasive encounters were inevitable given conditions in Minnesota. But there was no language in the provision that made it temporary, and what neither Dole nor Rice may have counted on was the consistent good behavior of the Mille Lacs people and the stubbornness of their attachment to Mille Lacs Lake and their reservation.

CHAPTER 6

"They Shall Not Be Compelled to Remove"

Opposition to Removal

When the various delegations returned to Minnesota, there was some dissatisfaction about the treaty among many Mississippi bands. To a large extent this regret was encouraged by Hole-in-the-Day, who had not attended. Following a visit to Mille Lacs John Johnson (Enmegahbowh) reported on this topic in a letter to Bishop Henry Whipple on May 6, writing, "the life of the chiefs (Mille Lac) are very dangerous one[s]." Traders had told some at Mille Lacs that the band was "also included with the Removal Indians." However, many people appeared to believe that the Ojibwe as a whole would never be removed to the new reservation near Leech Lake created in the 1863 treaty and that the government would find a better place, possibly in the region of Red Lake, echoing some early newspaper reports.

Although Johnson had been at the negotiations in Washington, he did not appear to understand the treaty any better than anyone else. But he did not believe the government would enforce removal of the bands, either at Mille Lacs or from the other Ojibwe communities. He asked Whipple: "Have you seen the treaty & about Mille Lac? And what is expected of them from the government?" He said he would "like very much to go to Mille Lac" and discussed further plans for a mission there.[1]

In the fall of 1863 the Mille Lacs Band again refused to go to Crow Wing for payment. Superintendent Clark Thompson wrote that a delegation of Mille Lacs leaders had gone to Fort Ripley and while there had informed the commandant of their refusal to go again to Crow Wing for payment: "They claimed that they had understood while in Washington making their Treaty that they were to be paid again at Mille Lacs, that they would rather loose [sic] their annuities than go to the Crow Wing Agency for them."[2]

This refusal further demonstrated the understanding of the Mille Lacs leaders who had signed the treaty that they had not given up their reser-

vation. The place of payment had now come to symbolize the entire removal effort. In late November Shaboshkung and six other chiefs, most
of whom were reported to have been in Washington, touched the pen of
John Johnson (Enmegahbowh) in writing a petition, stating: "We the un-
dersigned chiefs of the Mille Lacs Band wish to express hereby our mind
that we don't agree in any way with the plans of Kwiwisens [Gwiiwisens,
nickname of Hole-in-the-Day] in regard to removing the Indians but wish
to stick to the treaty of last winter and further we will be friendly to the
whites as long as we live." Johnson added that they hoped the treaty would
be "carried out to the letter—and they think if one chief should spoil and
go against it[s] provisions [they] will have no confidence in the government. This is their own words."[3]

The petition made clear the degree to which the Mille Lacs leaders
viewed the treaty and the conversations with Commissioner William Dole
in September 1862 as a solemn promise to allow them to remain on their
reservation at Mille Lacs, and their concurrent obligation to be friendly to
whites as long as they lived. These were not temporary promises but ones
that could guide them in living in their permanent home.

At the same time, some whites apparently understood that claims of
misbehavior could be used to support the removal of the band from the
reservation. Perhaps in response to Article 12 of the 1863 treaty, white settlers in the counties of Isanti, Anoka, and Chisago, located between Mille
Lacs Lake and the Twin Cities area, sent a petition claiming that Ojibwe Indians near Fish Lake in Isanti County were camped there and were "fright-
ening women and children" as well as "pilfering and stealing in every
direction." However, as would often be the case in the coming years when
such claims were advanced, the Indian Office was unable to substantiate
them. In responding to the settlers' claims, Agent A. C. Morrill wrote that
he had learned there were Mille Lacs Indians hunting in the vicinity of
Fish Lake, but he had "failed to learn that they have committed any depredations." Morrill wrote that local whites were "timorous" because of
the events among the Dakota in 1862 and feared to leave their women and
children home alone while Indians were in the area. Apparently knowing
nothing of the guaranteed hunting and fishing rights under the Treaty of
1837, he had tried to keep the Ojibwe on their reservations but found it
difficult because they "derive nearly as much income from the furs they
collect as from their annuities." He believed this problem would remain
until they were removed and placed on the new reservation created in the
1863 treaty.[4]

In a letter to Commissioner of Indian Affairs Dole, Superintendent Thompson stated the removal of the Indians to the new reservation under the 1863 treaty could not be carried out because appropriations for the agency were inadequate. Thompson explained that Article 12 of the 1863 treaty stated that the Ojibwe were not obliged to remove from their present reservations until the government complied with Articles 4 and 6 of the treaty and supplied them with transportation to and subsistence for six months in their new homes. Of course, even if those provisions were fulfilled, it was still not compulsory for the Mille Lacs Band to remove from the Mille Lacs Reservation.[5]

The 1864 Treaty

In early 1864 Hole-in-the-Day and Misquadace of Rice and Sandy Lakes, supposedly representing all the other Mississippi band chiefs, went to Washington, DC, to negotiate a revision of the 1863 treaty, this time without the benefit of Henry Rice's aid. The new agreement was very similar to the one from the year before. Like the previous treaty, it contained language ceding the 1855 reservations, though a new provision set aside a whole section of land at Gull Lake, Sandy Lake, and Mille Lacs for the chiefs Hole-in-the-Day, Misquadace, and Shaboshkung, respectively. The new reservation for the Mississippi bands was to be in the same general area as the reservation created in the 1863 treaty but included more land. The treaty also preserved the right of the Mille Lacs people to remain, if they maintained their good behavior, and added a related provision for the Sandy Lake band, which was not required to remove "until the President shall so direct."[6]

At the end of December 1865 John Johnson (Enmegahbowh) wrote to Major Henry Bartling about a continuing belief on the part of the Mille Lacs leaders that government officials appeared to have misunderstood both the 1863 and 1864 treaties. They had heard that a general removal of all the Mississippi bands was contemplated. Johnson wrote that "the Chiefs thought that a general treaty ought to be given them by their great father the Secretary of the Interior that a general understanding between them and the government ought to be plainly understood on both sides—these are the main subjects that they wish & desire to see their great father the Secretary of the Interior for with other matters for their general welfare."[7]

To another official Johnson communicated that the Mille Lacs leaders would arrange to move to Canada rather than the place designated by federal officials.[8]

In February 1866 agent Edwin Clark reported that the principal chiefs including Shaboshkung wanted to make a trip to Washington to sort out the problems with the earlier treaties and recommended that permission be granted. Clark was in favor of taking immediate action to remove the Mississippi Ojibwe. In the last session of Congress an appropriation had been made to bring about the removal, but it did not include money to move the Mille Lacs people, "who because of their good conduct were not compelled to remove so long as they did not interfere with or molest the persons or property of whites."[9]

The next month Bishop Whipple wrote to the commissioner of Indian Affairs to criticize the continuing plans for removal. According to Whipple, each treaty seemed intended to pave the way for the next removal, which seemed designed merely for the payment of trade debts. In regard to the Mille Lacs Band, Whipple stated: "The Mille Lacs Indians were pledged peaceable possession of their present reservation. I am not prepared to say that the time may not come when it may not be best for all the parties that the Indians be removed. But I do say that unless the government desires to destroy its influence with the entire body of Chippewas they are bound to recognise [sic] to the fullest extent all its pledges to the Indians."[10]

While Whipple seemed to favor the ultimate removal of the Ojibwe to a reservation where they could take up farming and other features of what he viewed as a civilized way of life, he clearly recognized that a promise had been made to the Mille Lacs Band about their continued residence on their reservation—a promise that the government must keep if it wished to maintain its credibility among all the Ojibwe people.

For their part, the Mille Lacs leaders continued to emphasize their own pledge in Article 12 of the treaties and the commitment to agriculture that both the agent and their missionary John Johnson were urging on them. Johnson's influence was clearly being felt, as described below, though his hoped-for baptism of band leaders had been postponed.

In April 1866 Shaboshkung came to the agency, where he received a yoke of oxen and some seeds from the clerk James Bean. While there he had an extended conversation in which both the influence of Christianity and the emphasis on good behavior were evident. The chief recounted for Bean the tradition that seven hundred years before, in the woods between Lake Superior and Mille Lacs, Indians had found "a paper" recording knowledge about the history of the world. The paper recorded that when the Great Spirit made the earth he also made "monstrous animals or creatures." When these creatures met they "would fight and kill each other," which prompted spirits to appear to frighten them away. The spirits seldom appeared anymore, though they might "to Indians when anything is going to happen to them for their wickedness."[11]

Because of the wickedness of the people who had replaced the monstrous animals, a great flood came on the earth seven centuries before. And perhaps another flood could come again, or a plague would be brought by "a mysterious man, nobody knows who," who would appear in a village and cause everyone to die, either from disease or from fear. The paper also recorded that, someday, white people would come from another part of the earth, which would cause a great change in the earth, on the order of the earlier flood. That change was happening now. Shaboshkung spoke also of the "Spirit Land" but was reticent about going into detail about his people's beliefs. He said he pondered these subjects a great deal and sometimes would not sleep for several nights in a row thinking about them. He told Bean that when he was troubled he could not sleep, and that he could not sleep when he did not "do right," adding that "he always feels bad when he does wrong, but good when he does right." He told Bean that he wanted "to always do right": "He believes the Great Spirit made all men. That they ought to do right and live peaceably together. If they did, they would love each other and everything would go smoothly. There is only one in a great many that feels so. They are a great ways apart and between them a great many who are not careful and that makes commotion."[12]

Bean recorded the information for Bishop Whipple, perhaps thinking that the parallels between Christian beliefs and Ojibwe spiritual beliefs might interest him. Bean did not try to draw the connection to the situation of the Mille Lacs Ojibwe, a people held to a standard of good behavior in their treaty. Shaboshkung himself explained what motivated him to "behave well"—the pledges made in treaties on which his people's continued occupancy on their reservation now depended. The chief may also have intended to show that Christian beliefs were not alien to the Ojibwe, that their own spiritual beliefs had much in common with the white man's religion. But few whites in Minnesota at the time seemed to recognize the desire of Mille Lacs band leaders and band members to adhere to their pledge in the treaties.

Meanwhile, pressure increased for a general removal of the Mississippi Ojibwe to the new reservation created under the 1864 treaty. Petitions and individual letters were sent to Governor William R. Marshall of Minnesota, claiming that groups of Ojibwe were harassing settlers, although the identity of the groups was never clear. Eric Norelius, a Swedish emigrant in Isanti County, wrote in October 1866 that Indians had gotten drunk, broken into houses, and set fires that endangered the settlers' hay and their lands. Indians "tried to rob a girl of a few things she had in a handkerchief"; when she resisted "they drew up their [knives] and threatened to kill her." Norelius wanted these Indians "kept away from here."[13]

Governor Marshall sent the letter on to the secretary of the Interior, stating that there were frequent complaints about Indians leaving their reservations, "going among the white settlers [and] giving great annoyance and alarm to the latter." Marshall did not claim that the Indians had actually committed any depredations, but he wrote that since the Ojibwe could not be "readily distinguished from Sioux they are liable to be *Shot at Sight*." Therefore, he later wrote, in another letter to officials in Washington, it would be desirable for "the safety of both Indians and whites" that a general removal "should be speedily effected."[14]

Early in 1867 the Minnesota legislature sent a memorial to Congress urging efforts for the removal of the Ojibwe, who were said to "roam at pleasure throughout the frontier settlements of Minnesota and Wisconsin, and whose hostility is often manifest in stealthily murdering the whites, and pilfering, whenever opportunity occurs, and otherwise demoralizing to civilization." Like the earlier petition from settlers, the memorial did not identify the Indians and made no specific mention of Mille Lacs. Rather than requesting that the Ojibwe be removed from their reservations, it asked that "these Indians be kept on their own lands or reservations," which in the case of the Mille Lacs Band would have meant that they would continue to reside on their reservation at Mille Lacs.[15]

In January 1867 Joel B. Bassett replaced Edwin Clark as agent for the Mississippi Ojibwe. He quickly took on the task of removal, starting with accompanying Hole-in-the-Day and nine other Mississippi Ojibwe leaders to Washington to negotiate a new treaty.[16]

The 1867 Treaty

At the end of 1866 new requests had been made for a delegation of Mississippi band chiefs to go to Washington. Though complete details have not been found, a delegation went to Washington in February 1867 and a new treaty was signed on March 19. This agreement was designed to find a substitute for the reservation laid out in the Treaty of 1864. It ceded a portion of that reservation (retaining the remainder) and established a new reservation consisting of thirty-six sections of land to be laid out by the agent and representatives of the bands and to include White Earth Lake and Wild Rice Lake in northwestern Minnesota. Some early references to the location called it the Rice Lake Reservation, though it must not be confused with the Rice Lake Reservation located north of Mille Lacs Lake. Although the Mille Lacs leaders Shaboshkung, Gegwedaash, and Mino-giizhig were among the eleven chiefs who signed the document, the treaty did not include any provision requiring the removal of the Ojibwe from their existing reservations or rescinding the right of the Mille Lacs bands to continue to reside on their reservation at Mille Lacs under Article 12 of the 1864 treaty.[17]

Little has been written about the negotiation process for the 1867 treaty. No treaty journal has been found, though subsequent letters and other accounts provide some insight into the way various Ojibwe leaders and federal officials understood its meaning. Nothing suggested a change in the way Mille Lacs leaders viewed their tie to the reservation at Mille Lacs.

Removal Efforts under the 1864 and 1867 Treaties

While in Washington, DC, at the end of March 1867, Indian agent J. B. Bassett wrote a letter to the commissioner of Indian Affairs in which he discussed carrying out the stipulations in the 1864 and 1867 treaties. Without citing any new legal argument based on the Treaty of 1867, he urged "the propriety of immediate action in the removal of the Mill [sic] Lac Indians" because of "constant danger of difficulty growing out of their depredations on the settlements and their difficulties with the lumbermen on Rum River." He also referred to the recent memorial from the State of Minnesota: "so much complaint has been made that the Legislature of Minnesota have memorialized the President for their immediate removal." However, as noted above, this document did not mention the Mille Lacs Band specifically and did not call for the removal of the Ojibwe from their current reservations. Further, Bassett did not state he had conducted his own investigation to confirm whether the band had committed any depredations.[18]

In May Bassett again wrote to the commissioner of Indian Affairs to provide new reasons for the removal of the Ojibwe. He stated that their current locations were scattered and remote from each other, hampering his efforts to help them with farming. Further, they were "constantly coming into collision with the settlers on the frontier." Complaints regularly reached him "of their dogs killing the sheep of the frontier settlers and other complaints on both sides are being made." Their removal was "a matter of pressing necessity."[19]

Bassett acknowledged that "the Indians seem to be very reluctant to move from their old homes and the graves of their fathers and their children." However, this fact did not sway him from his conclusions: "In view of the forgoing, I submit the following recommendations: First that immediate steps be taken for their removal"—including selecting the place where improvements would be made and hiring the Indians themselves to do the work, thus assuring that the removal would take place peaceably and saving the government great expense.[20]

Throughout 1867 Bassett continued to press for the removals, joined at various times by other influential voices. In June Henry Rice wrote to Washington stating that "the longer the Indians are permitted to remain upon lands they have sold the more troublesome it will be to get them to leave." He added that "the Indians are roaming about thru the settlements—of course idle," but did not claim they had committed any depredations.[21]

In late July a group of leaders who had not been in Washington for the treaty sent a petition recording their opposition "to the Treaty made last winter with some of our people who had no authority from us to make such Treaty." They considered "that the recent Treaties made are not binding upon our people and we will never consent to remove to the new proposed reservation. We will die first in our old homes before we will ever consent to such removal." They asked to come to Washington to discuss the matter. The petition was witnessed by Peter Roy of Little Falls. Signers from Mille Lacs included nine chiefs, as well as two others from the area of Rice Lake north of Mille Lacs in the direction of Sandy Lake, Maynwaywayaush and Nishkegun. Kegwedosay and Mino-giizhig, who were listed as signers of the treaty of that year, signed the petition, while Shaboshkung did not. Next to their names someone in the Indian department put in a mark to indicate they had signed the treaty. Regardless, the treaty contained no provision revoking Article 12 of the 1863 and 1864 treaties, and the Mille Lacs leaders remained adamantly opposed to removal.[22]

In mid-July the secretary of the Interior, after consulting with Alexander Ramsey, ordered Agent Bassett to begin the work of contracting for supplies for the removal of the Mississippi bands. Two months later, in mid-September, according to Rev. John Johnson (Enmegahbowh), the

Mille Lacs and other bands were informed that they must remove either to Rice Lake (White Earth) or to White Oak Point on the Mississippi, the latter located north of Leech Lake.[23]

Major E. A. C. Hatch, a businessman and former Indian agent, appears to have been hired to assist in the removal of the Mille Lacs and other bands. He enlisted Rev. Johnson to assist in persuading the Mille Lacs Band to move. Johnson wrote to Hatch from Crow Wing stating that he would go to Mille Lacs to inform "the Indians of the importance of their immediate removal to their new homes, or near to that." He said, "in behalf of the included removal Indians," they were willing to remove at any time once the improvements had been made ready for them, as promised in the treaty.[24]

Johnson sent a copy of the letter to Bishop Whipple, along with his own to the bishop, in which he transmitted the doubts he had heard the Ojibwe express about whether it was really the wish of the Indian department, rather than merely that of their agent in Minnesota, to have them remove. Johnson repeated what he had written to Hatch, that Mille Lacs band leaders had expressed their willingness to remove but only once the promises in the treaty had been fulfilled.[25]

Whipple sent copies of both letters on to Secretary of the Interior Orville H. Browning, urging him to give orders that the removal should be postponed until the treaty provisions had been met. Whipple now began a relentless push on the issue of removal with officials in Washington. On September 21 he wrote again to Secretary Browning, reporting a meeting with Ezekiel Gear, a former missionary in Minnesota, now chaplain of the US Congress. Whipple stated that Gear had been present "with the Comr. (Dole) and the Mille Lacs Indians in 1862 and they were promised by Mr. Dole that as a reward for their fidelity during the outbreak they should never be removed." Whipple continued, "This promise was received by Sec. Usher and afterward incorporated in a treaty," referring to the 1863 and 1864 treaties. Regarding the 1867 treaty, he wrote, "The Indians were induced to make a new treaty under the positive pledge good men should be selected to go & choose a home with them & that they should have improvements made & then & not till then be removed."[26]

Meanwhile, John Johnson wrote to Whipple on September 23, giving more details about the sentiment of the Mille Lacs Band regarding removal. Major Hatch had sent him to urge their immediate removal "to their new reservation." They were to be told that once removed they would receive their annual payment—as soon as they got to the new reservation at White

Earth or White Oak Point. The Mille Lacs leaders responded that they were willing to go to the new reservation as soon as all the treaty stipulations were carried out to the letter and not before. They had no intention of going to White Oak Point to get a few trifles during their hunting season.[27]

Whipple wrote again to the commissioner of Indian Affairs on September 25, protesting the "premature removal of the Indians," without reference to a specific nation or band, although it was clear he was referring to the Mille Lacs Band of Ojibwe. It was, he said, a "wicked outrage." He wrote: "These Indians are our friends. Twice they were solemnly pledged that they should never be removed as a reward for their fidelity. When they were induced to sign a new treaty they were pledged that no move should be made until their houses were built and farms opened, and now at the beginning of the winter they are to be sent into the depth of the wilderness where there is no game, no means of support."[28]

The context of Whipple's letter was shown by its enclosure, a letter from Episcopal minister George DuBois, who wrote that he had seen Rev. Johnson, who told him that a delegation from Mille Lacs had gone to inspect the new reservation and saw that "no preparations have been made nor are making for their reception notwithstanding that they were officially promised that they should not be removed until houses had been built and ground broken on the new reservation," in addition to which an "officially formalized treaty promised that they should never be removed."[29]

According to Johnson, via DuBois, there were "four whitemen" at Mille Lacs trying to persuade bands to remove to Leech Lake to get their annuities. Echoing the earlier words of Johnson's letter to Whipple, DuBois stated that Mille Lacs leaders considered it an injustice for them to have to go that far to get "a mere trifle." DuBois also informed Whipple that Rev. Johnson had told him that the Mille Lac Indians had "a large crop of potatoes which with the fish which are very abundant are sufficient for their subsistence this winter." The Mille Lacs chiefs said they were living peacefully with their white neighbors, and so their removal would be "in direct violation of treaty stipulations." They would go on their own but only once the agreement regarding preparation of the new reservation had been fulfilled.[30]

Rev. DuBois wrote to Whipple again on September 29, recording an interview that morning with Indian agent Bassett on the subject of removal to the new reservation. DuBois was convinced that the agent was a "friend to the Indians" who would not do anything to prejudice their "welfare & happiness." Bassett assured DuBois that the removal "this fall will not be enforced in opposition to their wishes but only with their free consent to the measure." However, Bassett claimed that the Mille Lacs Indians "could not subsist themselves where they are for one month, if *restricted* to their reservation. That to live, they *must* trespass upon lands owned by bona fide settlers, who are constantly complaining to him of depredations committed upon their property, and who threaten to shoot the trespassers." This claim was another example of a constant refrain: that the Mille Lacs Ojibwe were not fulfilling the promise about "good behavior," and therefore would have to leave their reservation at Mille Lacs. Again there was no mention of any attempt to corroborate those complaints.[31]

According to Bassett, as reported by DuBois, the annuities due to Mille Lacs band members would give them only one dollar's worth of flour "a head." They would consequently be "utterly destitute this winter, and the temptation to pillage, with the consequent danger of trouble, stronger than ever." Bassett told DuBois that the rice crop had "entirely failed." Thus, stated DuBois, "Their only dependence will be fish and game and to obtain game, which is this year unusually scarce, they must send hunting parties far into the settlements," which could lead to violence. DuBois came away convinced that the Mille Lacs people, by the provisions of their treaties, would be required to remove once preparations were made on the new reservation, but he did not mention the Article 12 proviso allowing the Mille Lacs Band to remain on its reservation during good behavior.[32]

Bishop Whipple sent the letter from DuBois on to William T. Otto, assistant (and at that time, acting) secretary of the Interior. In the accompanying letter Whipple showed that, despite his sympathy for the Mille Lacs Band, he did, ultimately, support their removal: "The real trouble has grown out of pledges made by Comr. Dole & Secy. Usher that they should not be removed and now that they are asked to go before the improvements are made they fear the white man's promises." It appeared Whipple was willing to sacrifice the agreements made in 1862, 1863, and 1864, believing the Mille Lacs people would be better off at White Earth than they were at Mille Lacs.[33]

Meanwhile, Agent Bassett himself wrote to Whipple on September 30, expanding upon the views he had expressed to Rev. DuBois. He understood Whipple's feelings in the matter, but he was simply carrying out orders he had received for removal in the fall. Bassett claimed he had protested the order for immediate removal but learned that Henry Rice was pushing for it. According to Bassett, Rice believed it was important for the Ojibwe to be moved from the vicinity of settlement to avert a conflict, and if it became necessary the government would subsist them for a year or longer, espe-cially if they were making progress in farming. But Bassett agreed that the Ojibwe could not be compelled to remove until the government fulfilled all its obligations to them under the Treaty of 1864 (which he dated 1865, referencing the proclamation date). If the Ojibwe bands went before then, it would be of their own choice, and the offer Bassett made them, if they accepted, would avert suffering in the winter, especially since the rice crop had been a failure that year.[34]

In October 1867 officials in Washington, after mulling over Whipple's multiple protests, decided to leave the removal to the discretion of Agent Bassett. Soon after, on October 29, Bassett, despite the concerns he ex-pressed to Whipple, announced the decision to proceed with the removal. Bassett again emphasized that complaints by white settlers required the removal of the Ojibwe. And as usual the complaints were not specifically tied to individual cases or independently confirmed. Unnamed farmers in the region where the Ojibwe hunted complained that Indian dogs killed sheep and fowl. Unnamed Indians broke into houses of people who were away and rifled through their contents. Unnamed women and children who were not accustomed to seeing Indians were frightened by them. Removal was necessary to prevent the outbreak of "open hostility" on the part of unnamed settlers.[35]

Bassett stated that the Mille Lac Ojibwe "have been particular subjects of complaint," and he submitted "letters and petitions from citizens in relation to those depredations." One statement was from the sheriff of Todd County, sent from Long Prairie, more than sixty miles west of Mille Lacs Lake. According to him, "several bands of Chippewa Indians are now roving through this county to the great annoyance of the inhabitants." Without naming the bands involved the complaint described the Indi-ans "passing through fields and leaving fences down whereby cattle get in and destroy crops." The Indians were said to enter houses when the inhabitants were away and steal their provisions. The sheriff asked Agent Bassett to "adopt some measure by which all Indians under your control may be immediately and permanently removed from within the limits of this county."

A petition from Hartford, also in Todd County and equally distant from Mille Lacs, asked that steps be taken "to prevent the Chippewa Indians from coming into this county." Although there was no reservation in Todd County, the fact that Indians "infested" the county had a "baneful influence" on prospective settlers who came into the region and, seeing

Indians, abandoned their intention to settle there. The petition also complained that Indians hunting out of season destroyed the population of game, making hunting less productive for non-Indians who depended on the practice for meat and fur. It was "an unjust discrimination" against "those who are struggling with all the hardship incident to a frontier life and who are clearing the way for the future greatness of our common country."[36]

Another petition from the citizens of Melrose, west of St. Cloud in Stearns County, also more than sixty miles away, stated that most of the petitioners were settlers in the timberlands along the Sauk River. The continued presence of Indians, unidentified except in being "Chippawa Indians," interfered with their attempts to gain a livelihood. The Indians competed with the settlers for game. Beyond that, the presence of Ojibwe people in the region evoked the US–Dakota War of 1862, though Ojibwe people in general and the Mille Lacs Ojibwe in particular had not fought against white settlers. Women and children "having fresh in their memories the Indian outrages and murders of sixty two" were "timid and afraid of these roving savages."[37]

A fourth complaint came from one citizen of Big Lake in Sherburne County, more than sixty miles due south of Mille Lacs Lake, who stated that the people of the county were "pested with Indians they are killing sheep dayly." Like the other complaints, this one made no reference to the Mille Lacs Ojibwe.[38]

Interestingly, Bassett also included the cover letter from the private secretary for the state governor, who had sent him the complaint from Stearns County. He did not suggest the removal of the Ojibwe to any particular location but, in language similar to the legislative memorial from earlier in the year, stated only that "The Governor directs me to request most urgently that you will cause the Indians complained of to return to and remain upon their reservation."

Since none of the complaints identified the Indians any further than to say that they were Chippewas, it was unclear how the petitions demonstrated the need to remove any Ojibwe from their current reservations to another one, let alone that the Mille Lacs people "have been particular subjects of complaint."

However, based on these petitions, Bassett reported about preparations he was making to implement removal that fall, involving the Sandy Lake, Pokegama, and Rice Lake bands who had expressed a preference for the Mississippi bands' reservation near Leech Lake, which had been created in the 1864 treaty and partially retained in the 1867 treaty, and which was nearer to their old homes. Bassett began construction of houses for their chiefs on that reservation, known as White Oak Point. Because the Mille Lacs Indians were connected "by marriage and other ties of relationship" with the Sandy Lake bands, Bassett believed they would be induced to join their relatives at White Oak Point. Apparently some Mille Lacs band members had indicated a willingness to be removed to the Rice Lake [later White Earth] Reservation, once improvements were made there. Bassett wrote: "The Mille Lac Indians have always been the most reluctant to leave their homes and the graves of their friends but with these I should have had no trouble if they had not been influenced by unprincipaled [sic] persons who have always made their living by whiskey and stealing from Indians of whom Parrish [Peter] Roy and a few half breeds are principal." Bassett boasted of his efforts "to keep peace and quiet between the frontier settlement and Indians and effect their removal with as little disturbance as possible." He was optimistic that the removal could be completed early enough in the spring so that those removed could plant their crops.[39]

There were continuing complaints about Bassett's tenure in office, including that he was pushing the removal for financial interest. Bassett wrote to Whipple in mid-November to defend himself. At the same time he sought support from other prominent Minnesotans. In late November Governor Marshall informed Whipple that it was Henry Rice—not Bassett—who stood to be the "principal beneficiary" from the $40,000 profit in the removal contract, a charge previously made about Rice's self-interestedness in Indian removals. At the beginning of December Marshall wrote to Secretary of the Interior O. H. Browning to request that a special agent be appointed to investigate whether or not the Indians were being removed prematurely and who would benefit by their removal.[40]

That fall, Mille Lacs band members were paid their annuities at Crow Wing and Granite City (present-day St. Cloud). According to Peter Roy, Mille Lacs band members received less money at their payment than did members of the other bands—only $6.75 per person as opposed to $10 per person. They suspected it had to do with the strong effort being made to remove them. Twelve Mille Lacs leaders wrote to the commissioner of Indian Affairs in early December protesting this treatment. The payment, they said, was actually made by traders sent by the agent; the agent had not come to their reservation. They reminded the commissioner of the promises made in 1862, 1863, and 1864; they "remembered the words of our great father that he said to us six [sic] years ago when we went down to Washington, that we should be let alone on the land we had before

occupyed [sic] for a hundred years or a thousand years or as long as we do
not commit any depredations."[41]

The Mille Lacs leaders stated that they had behaved well and wondered
why 750 band members at Mille Lacs were paid an amount equivalent to
400 of the other Mississippi Ojibwe. Members of the other bands, which
had committed depredations on whites, were getting the best treatment.
The petition concluded:

> If it is the case it is no use for us to behave and ever remember the
> words of our great father at Washington we have not been used right
> by our Agent we demand that our payment be made at Mille Lac
> as we have been promised, and be paid equal to all other Bands, as
> regards so much money being taken away from us our children must
> suffer the present winter we therefore beg that our petition may be
> heard and further more ask that our interest pray be looked to and
> everything that is wrong made right and then we will be satisfied.[42]

Bishop Whipple wrote again to the secretary of the Interior on the issues involving Mille Lacs, stating that the continuing efforts of the agent
to remove the Mille Lacs Band were in violation of the word given to them,
as well as of the treaty itself: "One thing is certain that the Mille Lac Indians have our plighted faith as a nation that they shall be protected it is a
slight return for such fidelity. The treaty solemnly pledges that they shall
not be removed until Article 4 & 6 of treaty is fully carried out. Second, it
is almost certain that either the Government or the Indians are to be de-
frauded by the contract."[43]

Whipple did not mention the voluntary nature of the removal under
the promise made in the earlier treaties, nor band members' continuing residence at Mille Lacs under good behavior. However, he was at a
loss to determine who was at the bottom of the "iniquity." He called for
an unbiased investigation and went on to suggest more general changes
in federal Indian policy, "now that peace has been secured on our western
frontier," including that Indian lands be "inalienable."[44]

As complaints about Agent Bassett piled up, he continued to defend
himself to the Indian department in Washington. In mid-December he
responded to allegations about underpayment, complaining that he suspected the Mille Lacs rolls were padded. He had inherited no records or
rolls at the agency when he became agent, and some Mille Lacs band

members had come to the agency to be paid. He had expected there to be only 430 remaining at Mille Lacs, instead of 663.[45]

As for not paying the Mille Lacs Band at their reservation, Bassett's defense suggested he really was using the annuity payment as leverage to get the band members to leave the reservation, as they had suspected. He wrote that if he had "yielded to the point it would very much have weakened [his] influence over them & [his] ability to lead & direct them." Writing a similar letter to Bishop Whipple, Bassett ignored promises made by earlier officials, stating that it was important the Mille Lacs people understand "that the agent is not bound to run wherever their fancy might suggest."[46]

Despite Bassett's attempts to defend himself, dissatisfaction continued. John Johnson (Enmegahbowh) wrote to Whipple in January 1868 that he believed Bassett would removed from office soon: a special agent was to be appointed to investigate. Johnson noted that the Mille Lacs leader Mino-giizhig told him the agent had "a very wicked face." He asked Johnson why Indian agents all had been "represented being bad men." Johnson noted that Indians used to be given provisions when they visited the agent; now it was different. It was midwinter after a poor wild rice harvest and there were no rabbits, but Shaboshkung told Johnson he would "starve before he would call on the agent." Johnson expected that in the summer all the Indians, including those at Mille Lacs, were expected to remove, something he found desirable.[47]

It turned out to be an eventful spring for the Mississippi Ojibwe. Agent Bassett wrote that around the middle of May all the Gull Lake and 150 Mille Lacs Ojibwe "came to me and said they wanted to move to their new homes, as soon as I had some land plowed." Bassett "told them that treaty provided that all their land was to be plowed and Homes built before they was [sic] required to move. That it would take at least three months to do it, told them what was done and what I was doing, I also told them to go back and think the matter over for one week, and then if they decided to go I would take them along." He noted: "At the end of the week, about one hundred and fifty of the Gull Lake Indians and about the same number of the Mille Lac Indians decided to go. On the first day of June I started them and they, (on the first party they went in two parties) arrived the 12th. They expressed great satisfaction with their new homes. Most of them cut off their hair[,] threw off the blanket and went to work."[48]

Later on in the month, more groups of Mississippi Ojibwe set off for

White Earth. Among them were three small bands from Mille Lacs, including those under the leadership of Mino-giizhig, Ayaabe, and Saycosegay, each of which included Episcopal converts associated with the Gull Lake mission. As noted, Mino-giizhig had been a signer of the 1867 treaty. Now he wrote to Bishop Whipple that the reason they had gone to White Earth was directly related to advice the bishop had given him "about our future." Mino-giizhig stated that "they are now ready to embrace our religion. They are anxious that you should cause a church to be erected, and they are ready to follow your holy councils and advice."[49]

Agent Bassett repeated the claim that 150 Mille Lacs band members had moved to White Earth in July 1868, but annuity records show only Mino-giizhig and Ayaabe's bands, totaling sixty-one members, were paid at White Earth as late as 1870, while Saycosegay was still listed as a Mille Lacs chief, with thirteen band members. It should be noted that the total of seventy-four band members listed is less than the ninety-five members in these bands in 1861 (see Table 2, page 29). It may be that not all the band members were as eager to go to White Earth as the three leaders.[50]

Another possible explanation for the 1870 annuity roll is that some band members who went to White Earth found life difficult there and returned to Mille Lacs. Peter Roy wrote in January 1869 that he received a letter from "an upright Christian Indian—a man of High Character and has a position in the church," who wrote, "I have never heard my children crying for bread or food and at this time and on this Royal reservation they cried for bread and ate acorns with me." Food supplies were scarce for the new White Earth residents. Roy also described the letter as being from an "Indian missionary," which suggests it may have come from either Mino-giizhig or John Johnson (Enmegahbowh).[51]

In any case, the vast majority of Mille Lacs band members were opposed to going to White Earth and did not remove. They received some support from Peter Roy, who had been an interpreter at the treaty negotiation in 1863, when they were promised that they could remain on the Mille Lacs Reservation. In June 1868 Roy had written to Bishop Whipple that "the Mille Lac Band are not under the head as removal Indians and the Government has no Right to asked [sic] them to remove away from Mille Lacs at the present time." Roy added that he had told them not to go because the government had not appropriated any money for their removal. All the money in support of removal was for the Gull Lake, Sandy Lake, Rabbit Lake, and Pokegama bands, totaling 1,100 people.[52]

According to Roy the 1863 treaty gave the Mille Lacs Band the right to remain at Mille Lacs "as long as they are not injuring the interest of the whites." They had done nothing to require their removal. They had not killed any white person or destroyed any property belonging to whites. At Mille Lacs they were more out of the way of whites than they would be at White Earth. If the government spent one quarter of the money it would take to remove them to instead build houses for them at Mille Lacs, band members would not need to leave the reservation to hunt. He concluded: "Bishop, the Mille Lac Bands are naturally industrious and intelligent and good behaving Indians. You know the course they have taken in 1862. They prove[d] themselves to be the white men friends in time of need and they ought to not be forgotten."[53]

As groups of Mississippi Ojibwe set off to White Earth, Hole-in-the-Day, who now opposed removal to the reservation he had helped bring into being, was murdered in late June 1868 by warriors from Leech Lake. Perhaps as a result of this event, the general dissatisfaction with the agent, and the refusal of many to move to White Earth, rumors of hostilities at Gull Lake and Mille Lacs circulated. In August 1868 Brevet Major General Alfred H. Terry investigated. He wrote to Major General William A. Nichols describing the situation and noting that all but the Mille Lacs Band, because of its fidelity in 1862, were required to remove. Terry wrote that the Mississippi Ojibwe disliked their agent and had no confidence in him, while the agent blamed the dissatisfaction on "mixed bloods" and traders. He suggested that public interest demanded an investigation into Bassett to quiet the Ojibwe's complaints.[54]

In September 1868 Commissioner of Indian Affairs Nathaniel G. Taylor visited Minnesota to meet the bands opposing removal to White Earth, along with Agent Bassett and General John B. Sanborn, at the Chippewa Agency. Among those in attendance during a five- or six-hour session appears to have been Shaboshkung (erroneously spelled "Wa-bash-kunk"), whom Taylor called "an intelligent and influential chief." Taylor stated that the Mille Lacs leaders said they were "living faithfully up to their treaty engagements—not interfering with the whites nor intending to do so—and are anxious to remain where they are." They also asked that their annuity payments continue to be made at Mille Lacs.[55]

Taylor wrote that he was "satisfied that there is no ground for apprehending difficulty with these Indians, that kind liberal treatment, and faithful performance of treaty stipulations on the part of the Govt. are alone necessary to the perpetuation of peace with these Chippewas and to their rapid civilization as well as their material prosperity."[56]

Later in the fall, various Mississippi chiefs sent petitions to the commissioner of Indian Affairs to resolve matters left up in the air. The petitions were witnessed by Clement H. Beaulieu and Peter Roy, who sought to accompany the chiefs to Washington. Shaboshkung, Manoominikeshiinh, seven other chiefs, and four additional men signed a petition from Mille Lacs that called for "making some arrangement for our permanent location." While some band members had already moved to White Earth, the government had not lived up to treaty stipulations. The petition announced the appointment of Shaboshkung, Petudance, and Monzomonay to transact business for them, along with Beaulieu and Roy.[57]

Whether or not Commissioner Taylor actually believed that some new treaty was required to deal with the question of the Mississippi Ojibwe who would not move to White Earth, he left office in April 1869 without making any new agreements.

In July 1869 Brevet Captain J. J. S. Hassler was appointed to take charge of the Chippewa Agency in Minnesota. In October he submitted a report on the various Ojibwe bands under his supervision. He noted that under the Treaty of 1867 all the Mississippi Ojibwe were "to remove to the reservations at White Earth and White Oak Point, except the Mille Lac bands, who were permitted to remain on the land ceded by them during good behavior."[58]

At the end of 1869 further efforts were made by interests in Minnesota to call for the removal of Mille Lacs and other Ojibwe. In late December George A. Wheeler wrote to Senator Alexander Ramsey complaining that certain "Chipaway [sic] Indians" were "allowed to roam among the settlers" and asking why a treaty could not be negotiated with the Indians "so as to keep them away from these settlements entirely." Ramsey forwarded the letter to the Indian department. Around the same time he also received a letter from James Adams, a resident of nearby Isanti County, asking for the removal of certain Indians from the county, which Ramsey likewise sent on to the Indian department. Officials there made notes on the outside of the cover sheet: "Land [department?] will see whether these Indians have reservation in the vicinity, If something can be done."[59]

On January 20, 1870, Commissioner Ely S. Parker wrote to Ramsey regarding the Adams complaint. He noted that the letter had not specified which Ojibwe band was "committing the alleged depredations" and stated that "the nearest reservation to said county, is Mille Lac, which is about 36 miles from the same." He reminded Ramsey that under the treaty proclaimed on March 20, 1865 (the 1864 treaty), "the Mille Lac Band were not compelled to remove so long as they shall not in any way interfere with, or in any manner molest the property of the whites." He said it was not believed "that these were the Indians complained against as they have been uniformly distinguished for their good behavior." Definite information was required before any action could be taken.[60]

Ramsey, who had been in Washington at the time of the 1863 treaty but did not take part in its negotiation, responded a few days later asserting that the Indians complained about were members of the Mille Lacs Band and that the band "does not I am sure deserve the favorable opinion that you seem to have formed of them." He concluded: "They are a set of wandering Indians of whom there is great complaint, and I would respectfully suggest that a special agent be instructed to inquire into their status and conduct with the view of action looking toward their removal, if it should appear that they have not complied with the conditions upon which they have been allowed to remain." He offered no independent confirmation of the complaints.[61]

Ramsey's response was an indication of things to come. Politicians, businessmen, settlers, and other whites in Minnesota and elsewhere intended to continue their campaign to remove the Mille Lacs people from the Mille Lacs Reservation. In doing so, they affirmed, in a roundabout way, the meaning of the provision of the Treaties of 1863 and 1864 by which the Mille Lacs Band retained the right to remain on their reservation during their good behavior. If the right did not exist there would have been no need for anyone to refer repeatedly to the alleged bad behavior of Mille Lacs band members toward whites.

CHAPTER 7

Communities at the Lake

Despite the removal efforts of the late 1860s and the voluntary removal of some Mille Lacs band members to White Earth under the influence of the Episcopal mission, the vast majority of Mille Lacs band members remained on or near the Mille Lacs Reservation—and repeatedly asserted their right to remain under Article 12 of the 1863 and 1864 treaties.

As shown in Tables 3 and 4 (pages 79 and 81), annuity rolls from the 1870s and early 1880s document between 622 and 648 band members on the reservation and between 142 and 319 Indians living on the Snake River. Locations within the reservation are illustrated in Map 1 (page 80). The locations of the band's villages and developed sites provide one indication of the Mille Lacs band members' ties to the reservation.

In late 1866 Indian agent Edwin Clark reported to Commissioner of Indian Affairs Lewis V. Bogy that Shaboshkung had made his selection of land for the 640 acres he was awarded in the Treaty of 1864. The land was all in the northern portion of Kathio Township (43–27) and included parts of sections 16, 21, 22, 27, and 28. Together, the selections embraced the area of two points of land along the west side of Mille Lacs Lake, Shaboshkung Point and Indian Point, and some of the land in between. The total area was 653 acres, and Shaboshkung agreed to pay $1.25 per acre for the extra thirteen acres beyond that awarded him in the treaty.[1]

That land is today the location of Mille Lacs Band tribal government, schools, homes, a health center, and other important structures. Shaboshkung's selections provided a land base for Mille Lacs band members within the boundaries of their reservation in the years between the Treaty of 1864 and the early 1900s, a period when band members were under repeated assaults intended to drive them from the land in their permanent home.

The record of Shaboshkung's selections is one of the first that ties individual band members and communities at Mille Lacs to particular parcels of land on the reservation. Earlier sources give only vague references to the location of particular leaders and bands. While the names of band

76 ◆

leaders and some band members are known, it is more difficult to document the locations of these bands.

Some information on the locations of Mille Lacs band members on the reservation is found in the first federal surveys of the section lines of reservation townships, beginning with the northern part of Kathio Township in October 1865. The surveyor, Oscar Garrison, described the township as including "several beautiful bays on the eastern portion with a sandy shelving shore." He indicated on his map and mentioned in his notes Ojibwe villages north of the mouth of the outlet of the lake in section 33 and on what later was called Indian Point in section 27. He noted that both villages had "cultivated ground where they raise corn, potatoes, squashes, &c." He added: "this same village was mentioned by Father Hennepin (a reference to a Dakota village in 1679–80) and is noted in [David Dale] Owen's geology [of Minnesota]."[2]

Garrison also surveyed South Harbor Township (42–26) in October 1870. In his notes he described meeting the Mille Lacs leader Kegwedosay in section 15, in present-day Cove. Kegwedosay had a large garden, "which he claims as a reservation of 20 acres to himself at the sale of the balance of the reservation by the Mille Lacs Indians," an apparent reference to the Treaty of 1863, which Kegwedosay attended.[3]

The bulk of Lake Onamia is located in the southwest corner of South Harbor Township, roughly three miles southwest of Kegwedosay's land. Garrison noted in describing the township that "the Chippeway Indians have long occupied the shore of the lakes, cultivating small spots for gardens where they raise potatoes, corn, pumpkins, squashes &c and occasionally make maple sugar from the fine groves of sugar maple found scattered through the town. The lakes abound in fish which are easily caught and the small lakes are bordered by wild rice, *zinzania aquatica*, which can be gathered quite easily and forms the staple of the Indians."[4]

Maps from the 1870s and later depict the Mille Lacs Reservation, with some showing the locations of certain villages used by Mille Lacs band members. But these maps do not show the full extent of the connection between the Mille Lacs Band and their reservation or the off-reservation hunting, fishing, and gathering that took place during the seasonal round. Exact descriptions of where people lived and the interrelationships between band members, families, and communities are rare.

Oral histories give some evidence of the locations of band members, though they are not always very specific. In the 1914 testimony for the timber fraud lawsuits, Mille Lacs band members would sometimes give locations on the lake where particular individuals lived during this period.

According to one band member, Wazhashkokon, the chief who was the father of Bedud, lived at the source of the Rum River, on the north shore of the river, likely referring to the area of Lake Ogechie. The leader Kaykaykash was said to have lived "right at Rum River, where it joins the lake." Bahdushkahunch lived sometimes at the source of the Rum River on the shores of Mille Lacs, and sometimes at Cove northeast of Onamia. Noodin, who was the daughter of Manoominikeshiinh, granddaughter of Mezegun, and wife of Kegwedosay, said she was born on an island "this way, in this lake," possibly a reference to the islands at Wahkon or Isle.[5]

Gotigwaakojiins in his 1914 testimony recalled that his grandfather Ozaawindib (Ozawandib) and grandmother Kahjeje, who had raised him as a boy, had lived "just where that river, Rum River, runs from the lake, and on this [east] side. There was an old garden there." This description appears to refer to the shores of Lake Ogechie, which would support the theory, suggested earlier, that Negwanebi's village, visited by Lieutenant John Hamilton in 1855, was between Lake Onamia and Mille Lacs Lake.[6]

Another source that provides very specific evidence about the locations of band members is the record assembled in 1902 to compensate band members for the depredations committed on their villages and sugaring sites by white settlers in the 1880s and 1890s, during the first real wave of settlement in the area. As will be described later, in 1902 under a federal appropriation band members were to be compensated for any structures, gardens, clearings in sugar bush, or other "improvements" to the reservation they had lost through burning and other forms of harassment by settlers and county officials, as well as for those structures that were still standing and in use but on lands acquired by non-Indians. With the aid of community leaders, several officials made a section-by-section "Schedule of Improvements," pertaining to particular named band members. This list of "white depredations" provides a means for locating bands and band members in the period between 1862 and 1902.[7]

The list is a remarkable document, providing a detailed description of settlement patterns on the reservation. The data shows a concentration of improvements along the reservation's lakeshore, involving a combination of permanent summer villages and sugar bush. Of course, the data recorded by the federal government does not take into account wild rice beds, hunting and trapping grounds, berry patches, and other resources that were not seen as improvements.

Using this 1902 document along with other sources it is possible to get a sense of the way in which the Mille Lacs Band inhabited and made use of the resources of the Mille Lacs Reservation.

As shown in Table 3, in 1870 there were eleven bands enumerated at Mille Lacs, totaling 648 people, the most populous being the bands of Shaboshkung, Manoominikeshiinh, Monzomonay, and Zhooniyaa. Sources from this period and later describe Shaboshkung's association with villages located on the west side of Mille Lacs Lake in the area of the land set

TABLE 3

1870 Mille Lacs Bands

BAND LEADER	MEN	WOMEN	CHILDREN	TOTALS
Bands at Mille Lacs				
Shaboshkung / Zhabaashkong	23	28	46	97
Manoominikeshiinh / Mun o min e kay shien	30	28	60	118
Monzomonay	23	25	49	97
Zhooniyaa / Zhooneyah	21	29	58	108
Wahweyaycumig	8	12	13	33
Negwanebi	15	18	30	63
Biidadens / Pidud	13	20	24	57
Shaboshkung No. 2 / Zhabaashkong No. 2	4	6	8	18
Saycosegay	4	4	5	13
Maynwaywayaush	3	6	5	14
Nodinance	3	9	18	30
Totals	**147**	**185**	**316**	**648**
Bands at Snake River				
Negebwan	20	38	84	142
Bands at White Earth				
Minogiizhig / Min a ke shig	7	6	15	28
Ayaabe / I ah bay	9	11	13	33
Totals	**16**	**17**	**28**	**61**

Sources: 1870 Mille Lacs Annuity Roll, 1872 Snake River Band of Mille Lacs Annuity Roll, US Office of Indian Affairs, Chippewa Annuity Rolls, 1841–1907, MNHS M390, R.4

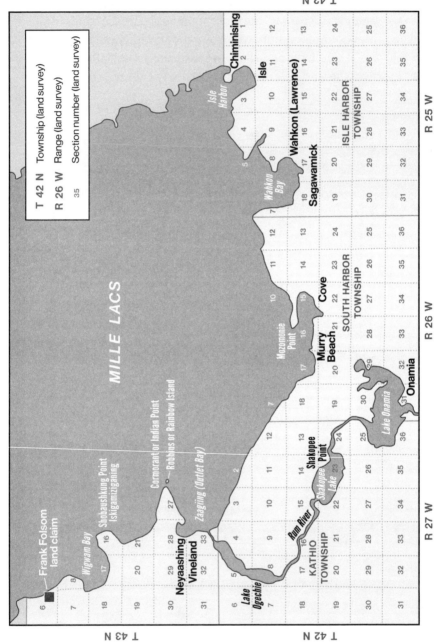

Map 1: Locations in the Mille Lacs Reservation

TABLE 4

Mille Lacs Leaders and Bands in 1881

BAND LEADER	AGE	BAND LOCATION	MALES	FEMALES	TOTAL
Shobaushkung / Shaboshkung	64	T43–R27, Vineland	48	65	113
Mahungaunce / Ma'iingaans	44	T43–R27	28	44	72
Pedud	77	At Mille Lacs	14	17	31
Monzomonay / Mozomonay	56	T42–R26, Mozomonie Point	48	49	97
Naygwunaybe / Negwanebi No. 1	56	T42–R25 Isle	64	55	119
Maynwaywayaush	49		21	15	36
Naygwunaybe / Negwanebi No. 2	54	T42–R26	42	44	86
Wahweyaycumig	28	T42–R25, Wahkon	28	40	68
Total Population Mille Lacs			**293**	**329**	**622**
Juyahn	49	Snake River	38	46	84
Mahjekewis	42	Snake River	18	16	34
Nubunayaush	29	Snake River	26	26	52
Mayyowub	52	Snake River	25	30	55
Ayndusokeshig / Endaso-giizhig	28	Snake River	26	22	48
Monzonce	69	Snake River	19	27	46
Total Population Snake River			**152**	**167**	**319**
Total Mille Lacs Population			**445**	**496**	**941**

Source: 1881 Mille Lacs and Snake River Bands of Chippewa Annuity Roll, NAM M390, R.5

aside for him by the Treaty of 1864. Shaboshkung's village, called Neyaa-shing, was located on what archaeologist Jacob Brower, in 1900, called Shaboshkung Point (now Indian Point), just north of Vineland or Outlet Bay. Brower located another village at the west end of Wigwam Bay. An earlier survey map of the township found in federal records from the 1880s shows a village site just north of the Rum River outlet.

Monzomonay was the son of Manoominikeshiinh, who had died in 1878. After meeting Monzomonay on a visit to Little Falls, Nathan Richardson wrote that he was a "quite large and muscular man" who "resides with his portion of the band on the south east side of the lake." Richardson obtained a biographical sketch of Monzomonay's life "from himself." Like many other Mille Lacs band members, Monzomonay had been born on the Snake River and came to live on the lake when he was a small boy: "It has always been a good place to live, the lake always yielding a great abundance of the finest quality fish, wild rice was generally abundant, and maple sugar as much as they desired could be made around the lake country. Wild geese and ducks were always plenty in their season, deer and other game were abundant until of late years, but game and fur are getting a little scarce. They cleared up land and planted potatoes and corn on some of the islands, where they frequently found the bones of dead men."[8]

Although Richardson wrote that Monzomonay's band was associated with the southeast shore of the lake, the naming of Mozomonie Point in South Harbor Township indicates a village location on the south-central shore.

As shown in Table 4 (page 81), the annuity roll for payments made in 1881 contains a listing for fourteen bands, each under a different leader, comprising the 941 people who were part of the Mille Lacs Band. Available information shows that 622 people, just less than two-thirds of the population, were part of the eight bands based at Mille Lacs. The other six bands, comprising 319 people, were based in the area of the Snake River. Together the leaders and the people who made up these bands would be the major participants in the coming decades of struggle over the lands of the Mille Lacs Reservation.

CHAPTER 8

The So-Called Settlers

The 1870s was a crucial period for the Mille Lacs Band. Logging was continuing in the upper Rum River valley. To get access to the pine forests located on the reservation, lumbermen made repeated attempts to open the reservation to land sales. Since it was understood that the only way to get access to these lands was to show that the Mille Lacs Band was not living up to the good behavior clause of the 1863 treaty, attempts to open the reservation were usually begun or punctuated by complaints about band members' behavior. This approach was recognition, of a sort, of the meaning of the 1863 and 1864 treaties.

Instructions, along with complaints about the band, were sent to Indian agent George Atcheson in January and February 1870. Atcheson wrote to Joseph Roberts (or Robert), a former Indian subagent who was now an adviser to the Mille Lacs Band. In reply, Roberts stated that the band leaders were "strictly opposed to leaving the reservation," just as they had been in 1866. He wrote: "They claim the right under the Treaty of 1863 or 4 that they should be allowed to remain at that reservation or the country they have occupied before, for four hundred years, providing they would commit no depredations, *which they claim they did not,* and they appeal to you to give them justice and that you should look to their interest, being that you are the only one that can do so at present."[1]

In the spring of 1870 Atcheson looked into some of the complaints against Mille Lacs band members. In one case, Charles Peltier, a settler eight miles from Little Falls, wrote that about twenty Chippewa Indians in the vicinity were "quite troublesome to my self and several of my neighbors" and that they caused "a good deal of fear for our lives & property."[2]

As would be the case in later years, many complaints came from white residents of Princeton, the seat of Mille Lacs County. Atcheson visited the town in early March and made inquiries. The problem, he alleged, was that band members came to the towns in the vicinity of their reservation and would "roam at will over the adjacent country, encamp in the vicinity of the farms, drink whiskey, carouse, gamble, and make hideous noises."[3]

The complaints resembled those of an earlier generation, involving charges of "inveterate begging," which occurred when Indians asked for food at "isolated farm houses, causing fear among women and children" who "through fear of imaginary results think they dare not refuse." Atcheson found that despite the fear, "aggravated cases of the kind . . . rarely occur." He advised the inhabitants of Princeton to furnish the Indian Office with proof of "interference or molestation . . . within a reasonable time" and noted that thus far "nothing positive touching the matter has been received by me."[4]

To learn more, Atcheson consulted with the leaders "Shaw-bah-skung [Shaboshkung], Be-dud-dunce [Biidadens, Pedud], and Shaw-ne-yaw [possibly Zhooniyaa]." Shaboshkung was "reticent in regard to the subject of removal," but, Atcheson claimed, he blamed the complaints on "Mo-zo-mo-nay [Monzomonay] and his band," numbering about a hundred people, who had "just gone down the country by way of Mille Lacs river to rove amongst the white settlements. This is what they always do." Atcheson reported that Shaboshkung had stated that Monzomonay was "the only chief who roves amongst the whites." The band as a whole was blamed for the actions of a few.

Atcheson wrote that he did not believe that "all the Indians have in a sufficient degree forfeited their right to remain at Mille Lacs under the protection of the treaty of 1865 [the treaty signed in 1864 but ratified in 1865]." A few, because of leaving the reservation, had "rendered themselves obnoxious" to the whites, "but of late years in no instance has it been shown that even these knowingly and willfully violated the provision of the treaty by interfering with or molesting the persons or property of the whites." He concluded: "the Mille Lacs appear to be very much attached to what they believe to be their country and doubtless could not be persuaded to remove voluntarily without heavy expense to the Government and possibly without resorting to compulsion in a few cases."

Around this time, questions appear to have been raised in other quarters about the rights of the Mille Lacs Band and the status of their reservation. On January 9, 1871, Indian agent J. P. Bardwell at Leech Lake wrote to the acting commissioner of Indian Affairs wishing to be informed as to "whether white men have a right to pre-empt land & cut timber on the old Reservation of the Mille Lac Indians ceded to the U.S. govt. in the treaty of March 19, 1867 [sic]."[5]

Settlers in Isanti County also complained about Mille Lacs band members. Their accusations came to the attention of Edward P. Smith, then agent at White Earth, in a letter from Governor Horace Austin. Smith spoke to Austin in person and also wrote him a letter on March 31, 1871, which was published in the *Minneapolis Tribune*. At the same time he reported on the topic to Commissioner of Indian Affairs Ely Parker.[6]

Writing to Parker, Smith noted that the Mille Lacs Band was "yet living according to treaty stipulations upon the Reservation," which had been "ceded to the Government on the condition that they should be permitted upon their old ground during their good behavior or the pleasure of the President." No provision had been made for their removal according to treaty stipulation. In the meantime "settlers have crowded upon them. Their lumber is being cut. The game is driven off." Smith believed there was little chance for them to survive unless they hunted beyond the lines of the reservation, which of course they had the right to do under the Treaty of 1837, a fact Smith did not mention.[7]

As for the complaints, Smith noted that a report of an investigation by soldiers from Fort Snelling showed that very little harm had been done through this so-called marauding. One cow was shot and a few vegetables had been taken. The "great harm which the citizens deprecate," said Smith, was simply "the alarm which prevails among the settler[s], who are mostly Swedes and entirely unacquainted with the habits of the Indians, and the fear of landowners lest these Indians by their proximity and frequent presence should hinder emigration to the country." The settlers appealed to Governor Austin, who authorized the organization of a county militia and issued arms with "instructions and authority to prevent the Indians from coming among the settlements." Smith feared there would be bloodshed and suggested to the governor that it would be better to use federal troops to keep order. Smith himself intended to go to Crow Wing to investigate.[8]

Later, on May 1, 1871, Smith wrote to Commissioner Parker with further thoughts on the troubles between the Mille Lacs Band and the settlers. He argued that the reservation, "though ceded by the Indians to the Government, should not yet be subject to entry, for the Indians not having been ordered or notified to leave, are, according to their treaty, yet entitled to all their rights upon it." He went on to say that the band members "clearly have possessory rights in the Reservation until they shall have received formal and sufficient notice to leave." In violation of those rights a lumberman named O. E. Garretson had sent men onto reservation lands and cut from two to three million feet of pine logs, which were on their way to market. The surveyor general had sent an agent to assess the stumpage on the lumber and collect it from Garretson. Smith believed the fee would amount to from $3,000 to $5,000, and he requested that whatever was collected be turned over to the White Earth Agency for the benefit of the Mille Lacs Band, to pay for their eventual homes there.[9]

But Smith raised a larger concern: he had learned from the register of the land office, presumably in Taylors Falls, that "the lands of the Mill Lac [sic] Reservation" had been "surveyed and the plats returned to the Register so that on the face of things there is no barrier to the taking up of all these lands by homestead or preemption." Smith stated that the Mille Lacs band members clearly had "possessory rights in the Reservation" and they asked that their lands not be "thrown open to entry, of any kind, so long as they remain, and that they be permitted to receive as compensation for the timber cut unlawfully upon their reservation, whatever stumpage may be awarded by the Surveyor."[10]

Smith later learned that not only was there no barrier to entry of land on the reservation but intrusions were already happening. On July 17, 1871, he wrote to the commissioner that the "whole Reservation has been covered since April 5th with scrip and presumptive claims filed in the Taylor's Falls Office." No order had actually been issued by the General Land Office to make the reservation subject to entry, but entries were nonetheless filed "under color of law." The surveyor general for Minnesota, who had discretionary power in his jurisdiction, had ordered the survey of the lands within the reservation: "When the Surveyor's bill for services was allowed at the Department it was considered to be an authorization of the survey." The plat of the land was then filed in the land office, and "that is considered authority to open these lands for public entry."[11]

Thus, wrote Smith, through these indirect means, "without permission of any sort from the Department, settlers and lumber men are taking possession of this Indian reserve." Smith declared this situation a double wrong: Indians were dispossessed without being removed, and members of the public did not have an equal opportunity to enter the lands, while "the very few men who in some way had knowledge of the time when entries would be received [were] ready to take the lands." A quarter of the lands were claimed with "half-breed scrip" from the Treaty of 1854, "which will be shown to be largely fraudulent." The scrip was intended to benefit only so-called half-breed people, but it was later transferred to timber companies. The other entries were preemption claims not made by settlers but "for lumbering purposes." Preparations were already underway to log the following winter. Smith asked that all these entries be canceled.

His request was fulfilled later in the summer. Smith received a reply from the commissioner of Indian Affairs on August 22, 1871, reporting the intention to cancel the entries. On September 1 Smith again wrote to the commissioner, stating that he had been informed that "three or more parties have engaged the services of men who are staying on the Reservation. These men will in a few days be ready to prove up their claims and receive duplicates, and then will be settlers in possession and it will be much more difficult to dislodge them." He suggested sending a telegram to the Taylors Falls Land Office to prevent further entries and that instruction be sent to the US attorney in St. Paul to prosecute "any parties trespassing on the Mille Lacs Reservation." He continued to fear bloodshed.[12]

Willis Drummond, commissioner of the General Land Office, notified the register and receiver of the land office in Taylors Falls on September 1, 1871: "You are now informed that these lands are still occupied by the Indians and are not subject to disposal." They were asked to advertise in a "newspaper of general circulation" that "all settlements & entries thereon are illegal and will not be recognized by this office." Whether or not advertisements appeared, a variety of newspapers around the country reported the facts of the order. In a front-page story the *Chicago Tribune* reported on September 5, 1871, that settlers were attempting to improve and cultivate lands on the "Mille Lac Indian Reservation in Minnesota" and that Commissioner Drummond had written to the land office in Taylors Falls stating that "these lands are still the property of the Indians, and are not open for either disposal to or settlement by emigrants."[13]

On September 11, 1871, the US attorney general informed the acting secretary of the Interior that, at the latter's request, the district attorney of Minnesota had been directed to "prosecute any persons who may be found trespassing upon the Mille Lac Reservation." Whether this actually happened is not known. Later in the month the acting commissioner of the General Land Office wrote to the governor of Minnesota asking that the state relinquish its claim to swamplands on the reservation.[14]

Meanwhile, on September 12, 1871, the officials in the Taylors Falls Land Office, John P. Owens, the register, and Oscar Roos, the receiver, wrote a detailed letter explaining their reasons for allowing entries on the Mille Lacs Reservation. They described how the reservation had come into being in the Treaty of 1855 and implied that the Mille Lacs Band had not fulfilled the requirement of good behavior. The land "was ceded by the Mille Lacs Band of Chippewas to the U.S. by the treaty of March 11, 1863 with certain conditions attached to be fulfilled on the part of the Indians. We have no official or other knowledge that they have ever fulfilled these conditions. The management of the land in question by the General Land Office as herein set forth would seem [to indicate] that the Indians had been derelict."[15]

The disingenuous statement implied that it was the Mille Lacs Band's obligation to prove a negative, that they *had not* violated the provisions of the treaty, rather than the federal government's obligation to demonstrate that there had been such a violation. But the behavior of the Mille Lacs people had not triggered the opening of the reservation; rather, as Indian agent Smith had described earlier, the actions of the General Land Office had provided indirect support for the conclusion reached in the Taylors Falls Land Office. The land on the reservation apparently had been opened for sale or entry regardless of any questions about whether the Mille Lacs Band had violated any terms of the 1863 and 1864 treaties.

Owens and Roos provided a long list of examples they asserted had provided the basis for opening the land to public sale. On October 16, 1869, for example, a plat from the surveyor general for one of the reservation's fractional townships, 43–27, was filed with his report for that month. On June 29, 1871, a list of swamplands covering the same township was certified by the General Land Office to the local office. The plats for all the other townships in the reservation were sent to the local office from the surveyor general on April 5, 1871. Owens and Roos noted that "there is a lapse of six days in the date of the Surveyor General's letter and the date of the Register's filing although the mail goes to St. Paul one day and returns the next. The Register took the intervening time to ascertain from the Surveyor General whether this was or was not Indian Land." The surveyor general, whom they described as "one of the best posted land lawyers in the State and who is an officer incapable of doing wrong to any living being[,] assured the Register that the plats should be accepted."

Owens and Roos listed many additional documents, a total of twenty-five, sent back and forth between Taylors Falls and Washington in the summer of 1871 that appeared to show the General Land Office had, indeed, opened the Mille Lacs Reservation to entry. Thus, if the commissioner of Indian Affairs had "any complaint to make in regard to this transfer to citizens he should lay the blame at the door of a [illegible word] Bureau of the

Department of Interior and not to the Register and Receiver of the Taylors Falls Land District."

After receiving notice that all entries allowed on reservation lands would be canceled, register Owens notified the commissioner of the General Land Office that "we have informal notice that all the cases will be appealed and I understand the papers are now being made out. The principal point of appeal is based upon the provisions of the first article of the treaty with the Chippewas of the Mississippi ratified March 11, 1863, wherein it is stipulated that among other reservations the Mille Lacs Reservation is ceded to the United States." Owens pointed out to the commissioner: "I see you make no note of the provisions of this treaty of 1863 at all; but decide these cases upon the provisions of the second article of the [illegible word] treaty of Feb 22d 1855 to which you alone in said letter refer."

The so-called settlers, who represented timber companies and whose land entries on the reservation were canceled, attempted in various ways to get their entries reinstated, none of which was successful. For example, according to agent Smith, attorney Ira H. Pierce made the argument that "a large number had gone upon the reservation in good faith for the purpose of making homes, and that by my notice of warning they had been compelled to leave their homes and crops and were waiting outside the lines of the Reserve (some of them in poverty and suffering)." Smith, accompanied by Pierce, went to investigate the allegation.[16]

The men held a council with the Mille Lacs Band—exactly where is not known, but it appears not to have been on the reservation—and told band members about the supposed condition of the settlers and the mistake under which these settlers had been allowed upon the lands. Smith asked if the band would relinquish the right of occupancy in one township for these individuals. The band members, doubtful there were actually any settlers on the reservation, called into question the facts that had been reported to Smith. The whites had come only to cut timber "and put up a few log shanties, which could not be intended for houses; . . . [band members] had not seen any families upon the reservation." If any settlers had come to the reservation by mistake the band members might "relinquish their right of occupancy to one township provided it did not in any way necessitate their removal from the Reservation."[17]

Finding it impossible to determine exactly the facts about any settlers on the reservation, Smith went there to investigate, along with Special Agent J. F. Stock, sent by Commissioner Drummond. They made "diligent inquiry" among traders and lumbermen, visited fifteen claims "on the reserve," and examined improvements. The men concluded that a large portion of the reservation had been entered using "half-breed scrip" or preemption claims. In all cases the claims were on pinelands "in preference to the hard wood lands which are better adapted to agriculture." Nearly all the "half-breed scrip" was "fraudulently obtained," while the entries by preemption were "largely made by parties who were employed and paid by the day and sent up in gangs of from 6 to 35 men to make improvements, prove up at the Land Office, and then transfer their titles to their Employers." Smith concluded that the entries made on the reserve were not for actual settlement but for "securing the pine timber," and he "respectfully request[ed] that no trespassing be permitted upon this reservation, and that the entries already allowed at the Taylors Falls Land Office be cancelled."[18]

None of the information publicly available at the time made clear who was behind the efforts to throw open the Mille Lacs Reservation to logging in 1870 and 1871. A year later, however, a name that will become more important in this account was first mentioned in connection with Mille Lacs. On November 8, 1872, Amherst H. Wilder, a St. Paul businessman involved in a number of railroad and transportation interests, and who was in Washington at the time, wrote a letter to Indian agent Smith, soon to be appointed commissioner of Indian Affairs, about the pine on the Mille Lacs Reservation. Wilder offered to buy the timber standing "upon their reservation" at the rate of two dollars per thousand feet.[19]

Smith, who was also in Washington, was clearly acquainted with Wilder and probably discussed the request with him. Smith immediately passed the letter on to the commissioner of Indian Affairs, lending his support for Wilder's plan and repeating the history of the reservation: that it was "ceded to the United States" in 1863, the Mille Lacs Band "reserving to themselves the right of continued occupancy during good behavior." Smith noted that since this right of occupancy was "the only original right of the Indians in this land," it was "evident that the government procured by this treaty nothing more than the right to compel the removal of the Indians in case of bad conduct." Smith believed the sale of the timber would assist the band in shifting to an agricultural way of life. He believed the proposed price was fair and that a contract should be signed with Wilder in acceptance of the businessman's offer.[20]

Interestingly, on this very same day, Wilder made a contract with agent Smith to buy all the timber on the Leech Lake Reservation. This offer was

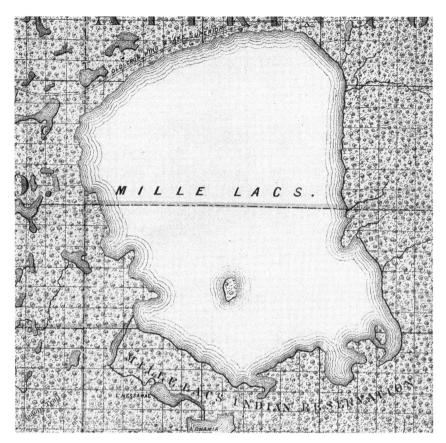

A map of the northern part of Mille Lacs County, from the 1874 A. T. Andreas *Illustrated Historical Atlas of the State of Minnesota,* shows the Mille Lacs Indian Reservation.

accepted, resulting in allegations of corruption against Smith. A federal commission appointed in 1873 cleared Smith of the charges, but a state commission then investigated the matter. In 1875 the US attorney revoked Wilder's contract.[21]

At the time nothing came of the plan for Wilder to buy the timber at Mille Lacs. Nonetheless, illegal cutting of timber continued on the reservation. J. H. Baker, surveyor general of Minnesota, wrote to the US surveyor general on July 3, 1876, reporting that large amounts of timber had been cut in townships 42–26 and 42–27. Upward of 300,000 feet was cut in section 36 of one of these townships. Baker asked the official in Washington if this would be considered school lands—as sections 16 and 36 of every township were normally dubbed—or still part of the reservation. He was unable to find any record in his office "that they are to be considered as other than ceded lands and subject to the same jurisdiction as other public lands." J. A. Williamson, commissioner of the General Land Office, replied that "the lands embraced in the reservation referred to are still under the jurisdiction of the Commissioner of Indian Affairs and your instructions from this office, as acting timber agent do not extend to lands reserved for Indian purposes, as are the lands in question."[22]

The continuing existence of the Mille Lacs Reservation was reflected in an important early atlas of the state of Minnesota, the A. T. Andreas *Illustrated Historical Atlas of Minnesota*, published in 1874. In both a full map of Minnesota and a detailed map of Mille Lacs County, the reservation was located with the words "Mille Lacs Indian Reservation" arcing across the four partial townships at the south end of the lake.

CHAPTER 9

The Sabin–Wilder Scheme

Despite federal instructions that the lands on the Mille Lacs Reservation were set aside for the use of the band and not open to entry or sale, further efforts were underway to reach a different outcome and throw open the reservation for legal cutting of timber. One individual formulating the plan was the same Amherst Wilder who had offered to buy the pine timber on the reservation in 1872. Wilder was associated in his new effort with Dwight M. Sabin, a Stillwater lumberman, window-sash and railway-car manufacturer, and politician. Sabin would later be known for his skill in using political connections to further his business interests. An 1883 article critical of Sabin stated that for him politics was "simply a branch of his business. . . . There is no sentimental Sunday-school nonsense or civil service reform humbug in his way of going at it." Much of what Sabin and others did in relation to the pinelands of the Mille Lacs Reservation appears to exemplify this statement.[1]

Wilder wrote to Sabin from New York City on March 17, 1876, with the outline of a plan formulated while he was in Washington, where apparently he had met with sympathetic government officials or perhaps with attorneys: "We conclude the best thing to be done is to have two men go on to the Farm Lands & make their preemptions—put up their Houses & act just as though they were there to stay for all time—let them make some improvements so that their papers will show well. I don't know just the legal steps to be taken by the preemptors but these you must have them follow to the letter.—When they have done certain things then they go to the Land Office to file their applications or whatever it is called."[2]

The men would not appear to be lumbermen at all, but settlers simply seeking to get lands for their homes. Of course, wrote Wilder, "the office will reject them," as it had been ordered to do in 1871. But an appeal would be filed and "taken to Washington & on this fight the whole question can be decided." Clearly Wilder expected his or Sabin's connections in Washington to overrule the decision of the local land office and the earlier ruling of the commissioner of the General Land Office. Perhaps he believed a new set of officials in Washington would take a revised approach to the Mille Lacs Reservation. Once the papers had made it through the Taylors Falls office and were on their way to Washington, Wilder stated, "I will then undertake to get the cases up & decided soon thereafter."[3]

Wilder wrote that it was important to have good men making the entries on the land, men who would follow the law so they would appear to be "what they represent themselves to be," that is, as Wilder made clear, actual settlers, though this status would be a masquerade. It was important that the preemptors did everything required of them, building a house or shanty, filing their papers in such a way that they could not be rejected in Washington on technical grounds: "The papers properly presented at the Taylors Falls Office & the appeal properly taken, I think will bring a favorable verdict for the preemptors at W[ashington]." This "favorable verdict" was assumed to be a probing wedge whereby the entire Mille Lacs Reservation would be opened to entry for logging.[4]

Wilder wrote to Sabin again the following day. He hoped Sabin would "Find the good men to make the preemptions named in my letter of yesterday—of course they will locate on the farming lands on the *so called* Reservation." The preemption must be done on farming lands, solving one of the problems that had occurred with the earlier attempts to open the Mille Lacs Reservation to lumbermen. In the earlier cases no genuine settlers had been involved. If a single settler's entry could be made and ultimately upheld on the reservation, the lands would be opened to entry, but without the taint of the preemption coming from lumber companies. In this case, Wilder's use of the phrase "*so called* Reservation" is revealing. The phrase and terms like "temporary" would be used in years to come by many who had an interest in the federal government opening the reservation for logging and, later, settlement. These words suggested something tenuous, even though the reservation's continuing existence was never challenged in a legal way.[5]

Both of Wilder's letters concluded by suggesting it might be possible to persuade the Ojibwe to move to White Earth, in part by enlisting Joseph Roberts to help. There is no information to suggest that Roberts assisted in the plan, but William H. C. Folsom, a veteran lumberman, newspaper editor, and politician in Taylors Falls, the location of the relevant land office, did. At the end of the March 17 letter Wilder stated, "Hope Folsom will get up his petition—it will do good at the Indian office & with the Committee." In his letter of March 18 Wilder wrote, "Push Folsome [*sic*] in his work." At this time Folsom, who was a state senator, had already introduced a joint resolution in the Minnesota legislature requesting that Minnesota's national representatives urge the government "for the necessity of the immediate removal of the Mille Lac band of Chippewa Indians to their permanent reservation," which, of course, was Mille Lacs. He added, "Their removal will release our settlements from the annoyance which their presence creates, and greatly improve their condition by the change."[6]

Around this time Folsom was involved in several petitions sent to Washington from people in the various counties south of Mille Lacs. Like many other complaints involving "good behavior," one of the petitions, from residents of Sherburne County, stated that the Mille Lacs Band, "located on their temporary reservation in Mille Lacs County," were a "great annoyance to the settlers" in those counties, for a variety of reasons. For one thing, the band did not "confine themselves to their reservation." The petitioners asked for the removal of the Mille Lacs Band "to their permanent reservation."[7]

These petitions were sent to Washington in April 1876. Folsom himself did not write to Washington until the following year. In the meantime, he had other services to provide for Sabin and Wilder. In particular, Folsom did his best to see that Wilder's scheme was carried out at Mille Lacs. He sent his son, Frank Folsom, as the chief preemptor in the Wilder and Sabin scheme to open the reservation.

Frank Folsom wrote to his father from Mille Lacs on April 28, 1876. He and a man named Gray had settled on two preemption claims, both in section 6 of 43–27, one on the shore, the other inland, both at the very north end of the reservation on the lake's western shore. They had built two houses and settled in the better one, where they intended to live, right on the shore of the lake; the other house was about a half mile away. Folsom was being paid five dollars a day and Gray two dollars a day. Folsom had hoped to make the lakeside claim his and give Gray the other one, but Gray "says he can not go on the other one & sleep occasionally and call it home & swear to it so I guess he will have to have this one."[8]

Folsom noted that he did not expect any difficulty from the Ojibwe "as they do not know how far their Reservation runs up & we are where there has been no claims here but in the southern towns. They are some what exercised about it & wanted to know what we was stopping at the trading post for but here they rather like the idea than not."

The trading post referred to was likely either at the mouth of Lake

Onamia or somewhere at the lower end of the Rum River near Mille Lacs Lake. Folsom gave his father instructions to file the claim in the Taylors Falls Land Office, stating, "So every thing is all straight so go ahead with the numbers. . . . Send me the number of acres that is in the Lot in Preemp No. 1 & also tell me which one I am to take."

A few days later, on May 1, 1876, William H. C. Folsom apparently prepared a "Declaratory Statement" of the kind required in the case of land preemptions for Frank Folsom to sign. It does not appear that the son could have signed it himself, but the document in Folsom's papers declares it was signed in the presence of Frank's brother, Wyman X. Folsom. The document stated that Frank Folsom had settled on several lakeshore lots in section 6 of 43–27, on land totaling almost 156 acres, "which land has not yet been offered at Public Sale, and thus rendered subject to private entry; and I do hereby declare my intention to claim the said tract of land as a preemption right under the provisions of said act of 4th September 1841."[9]

The statement was filed in the Taylors Falls Land Office shortly after and was refused on May 9 "on the grounds that by instructions from the Commissioner of the General Land Office said Lands is not at this time subject to pre-emption." The refusal was signed by the same register who had served in 1871, John P. Owens, and a newer office employee, receiver George B. Folsom—a brother of William H. C. Folsom and uncle of Frank and Wyman. McLuer and Marsh of Stillwater, acting as attorneys for Frank Folsom, filed an appeal of the decision of the Taylors Falls Land Office on May 12, 1876. The paperwork was sent on to Washington on May 17.[10]

Frank Folsom was staying at the Leland House in Brainerd on May 9 when he wrote to his father stating that he had just arrived there from Mille Lacs. He expected to return to the lake the next day. He reported on the problem of getting supplies, of the need for more money, and of his plans for planting on his claim. He noted that the traders on the lake had treated them well, but "what can you bet on them if this reservation is vacated what would become of their business. I would not insure my scalp there 24 hours at any time." He had returned to Mille Lacs on May 17 and had obtained more supplies. He expected to begin planting soon.[11]

On May 27 W. J. Baxter, acting commissioner of the General Land Office, wrote to the Taylors Falls Land Office to affirm the rejection of Folsom's claim: "The land is found to be within the Mil Lacs Reservation— See my letter to R&R Sept 1, 1871—and hereby is not subject to appropriation under the Pre-emption Law." Baxter stated that Folsom had sixty days to appeal his decision. An appeal was soon made.[12]

Frank Folsom continued to live on his preemption claim throughout the summer. While there, he and Gray and some other men who came to aid in the effort cruised for timber around the lake. He wrote to his father on June 16 that while he was living at his claim "some Indian hung a Dog[']s Heart up by a string, on some bushes, at the side of the lake where we get our water & launch our canoe. The Indians do not like our building where we did. This may mean business or there may have been only one connected with it, however I do not think the Indians will harm us. They may drive us off though."[13]

Folsom and the other men did some haying. Folsom wrote at the end of July that he was planning to dry blueberries. Around this time Folsom began to think about what might happen if the scheme was successful. He believed that once the policies were changed regarding the reservation and he was allowed to file a Declaratory Statement for his claim, the reservation would be opened to logging and to settlement. There would be no effective barrier against other claims. If that happened he believed he might be in danger from local residents. He wanted to make arrangements with his employers to get out while the getting was good:

> In case we are allowed to file our D.S. [Declaratory Statement]
> I suppose that will throw all the land into market & this would be
> declared not a Reservation, such being the case it would certainly
> not be safe for us to remain here & I suppose that would be all that
> the parties want of us. If this is right & it should take the turn I
> have described you had best notify us at once so that we can get
> out of this country as soon as possible, for it would certainly be
> *dangerous for us* to remain here, should the Reserve be set aside
> by this means.[14]

In mid-August Folsom was still on the claim. He had had no trouble from Mille Lacs band members, and his chief fear was about the coming winter. He did not think he or the men with him could stay in the claim shanty beyond November 1, though they could board with the local trader and "come down every 2 or 3 days & sleep in the shanty occasionally leaving our stuff in it." He asked for further instructions.[15]

It is not known when Frank Folsom left the lake. His assumptions about what would occur if his claim were upheld in Washington were not entirely borne out. As Wilder had predicted, officials in Washington handed down a favorable decision—but it did not disestablish the reservation or remove the Ojibwe on it. Rather, it simply provided a rationale for allow-ing the lands on the reservation to be sold to whites.

On March 1, 1877, Zachariah Chandler, secretary of the Interior and a former senator from Michigan, overturned the decision of the local land office in the case of Frank Folsom. Chandler reviewed the various treaties and, with respect to Article 12 of the Treaty of 1864, concluded: "It is true that, so long as said Indians do not interfere with the persons or property of the whites they cannot be *compelled* to remove, but it by no means gives them an exclusive right to the lands, nor does it in my judgement, exclude said lands from sale or disposal by the United States."[16]

Chandler did not question the existence of the Mille Lacs Indian Res-ervation, instead affirming that it would continue to exist even if the fed-eral government allowed non-Indians to buy land on the reservation. He only dealt with whether that land could be sold or claimed by individu-als other than Mille Lacs band members. Chandler stated that the lands on the reservation were open to preemption at the time Folsom made his claim and so his claim would be allowed. But since there were still Indi-ans on the lands and since there was no appropriation available for their removal, Chandler suspended execution of his decision "until the close of the next regular session of Congress, unless said Indians shall voluntarily remove therefrom prior to that date." Everything would be held in limbo and no further claims on the lands could be made. As for the earlier claims and entries on the reservation, their cancellation was said to be unaffected by this order since they had never been appealed to the secretary of the Interior.[17]

Chandler left office a few days after this, on March 11, but instructions carrying out his order were issued by the commissioner of the General Land Office on March 15, 1877. Folsom was allowed to file his Declaratory Statement in the Taylors Falls Land Office on March 23, 1877.[18]

Throughout 1877 various parties continued a concerted effort to re-move the Mille Lacs Band to White Earth. In late March 1877 William H. C. Folsom renewed his campaign to use his role as a Minnesota legislator to call for the removal of the Mille Lacs Band. It is unclear whether he was aware at the time that his son's preemption entry had been reinstated. On March 20, 1877, he drafted a letter to the secretary of the Interior, "by request of Citizens of my district" and referring to petitions "unani-mously signed from the people living in the district of the country." The letter stated that the "temporary reservation contains only about four townships of land which does not & can not sustain those one thousand

Indians in their uncivilized condition," confirming the substantial number of band members who remained on the reservation. It reported that the Indians roamed over ceded lands "annoying the inhabitants in divers [*sic*] ways," especially in those cases when Snake and St. Croix members of the Mille Lacs Band were paid at Brunswick, the seat of Kanabec County, on the Snake River. Not having been removed from Mille Lacs, the band was deprived of the schools, farms, mills, and utensils deemed necessary for "civilization" that they would receive at White Earth.[19]

The version of the letter in Folsom's papers also contains a statement— later crossed out—to the effect that: "These four townships of land, on which they temporarily reside, is wanted for settlement & use—a portion of these lands are covered with Pine timber and trespassers are annually destroying its value, by removing the timber & when the timber is gone, that portion of the lands becomes comparatively worthless."

This statement may have been too close to the truth to mention. Instead the final version of the letter emphasized the benefits to whites and Indians alike that would come from removal of the Mille Lacs Band. Folsom's letter was sent to Washington on March 26.

Around the same time, White Earth agent Lewis Stowe wrote to the commissioner of Indian Affairs suggesting "the propriety of immediately informing the Mille Lac Indians that no annuity payment will be made to them after the present year except in the case of their permanent removal to the White Earth reservation." Stowe may already have received a copy of Chandler's order, because he referred to "this proposed decision of the Department of using all legitimate means looking toward the settlement of the Mille Lac upon this reservation." It is unclear whether Stowe notified the Mille Lacs people about Chandler's order or received authorization to withhold annuities. However, in April Shaboshkung and other leaders wrote to the commissioner of Indian Affairs to say they had been informed by Stowe that they should be ready to remove to White Earth within one month. They asked that, instead, they be allowed to remain at Mille Lacs and take the lands of the reservation under the homestead law. The land there was good for farming, and they had "fish in the lakes, Wild Rice Game in abundance and we make plenty of sugar." Thus far they had lived "without the assistance of our Great Father." Included with and supporting the chiefs' petition was one from residents from Little Falls and Morrison County.[20]

Shaboshkung also decided to appeal to Henry Rice, who had been at the negotiations for the treaties in 1855 and 1863, for help in resisting this attempt at removal. On October 12, 1877, he and several other leaders went to Brainerd and had a woman named Caroline Morrison write a letter to Rice for them. Shaboshkung in his portion of the letter sought to remind Rice of the meaning of the 1863 treaty and its promise to allow the Mille Lacs Band to occupy the reservation. He said:

> I have this to tell you My Friend Mr. Rice. I have . . . called all
> my Boys together in Millack to tell them I was coming to Brain-
> erd to [drop] you a few lines. You know we are [quiet] Indians.
> We never [meddle] with others. I was quite sirprised when
> we heard this summer to be moved up to White Earth. I hope
> you will understan[d] what I mean. . . . My Friend Mr. Rice I
> hope you remember me when I saw you in Washington sixteen
> year[s] ago. At that time I was prommis I should allwas keep our
> home at Millack. I remember well what I was told from Gvoner
> [Governor?] and you know all that was sed to me at that time. At
> that time I was told we should all was keep Millack as well you do
> of Washington. I will never forget your White hand I last see you
> and shake hand with you. My Friend Mr. Rice I hope you will help
> answer this and tell me what to do.

In the same letter a chief named Fox [Waagosh] stated to Rice: "We depend on you Mr. Rice. You [are] the Best Friend I have to ask for advise [sic]." Clearly the band leaders believed Rice would corroborate their view of the meaning of the 1863 treaty and the promise that they would always have their reservation. There is no record of any response by Rice to this letter.[21]

During this period the Sabin–Wilder scheme was very much alive, thanks to Chandler's statement to the effect that his decision was held in limbo until the next session of Congress expired. The exact statutory expiration date for the session was June 20, 1878. Though Chandler had left office in March, his order lived on.

Chandler's successor was Carl Schurz, a former senator from Missouri known for his attempts to reform the civil service system. Just prior to the conclusion of the congressional session, on June 19, 1878, he sent a telegram to the Taylors Falls Land Office instructing it not to allow any entries under the Chandler decision until further orders. Those orders, sent on June 28, 1878, forbade any further entries on the reservation land until "the result of the action of Congress in relation to the right of the

Indians in question to occupy the tract of country known as the Mille Lac Reservation . . . shall have been determined."[22]

Evidence suggests that Schurz's order narrowly prevented further action in Taylors Falls. Chandler's decision had been read carefully and interpreted with a lawyer's eye for detail. On June 24, 1878, four days after the conclusion of that session of Congress, William H. C. Folsom wrote to the land office, noting that the first regular session of the 45th Congress had just ended, and in accordance with Chandler's decision he was now tendering the money necessary to enter his son's preemption claim.[23]

In a reply on the same day, John P. Owens and William H. C. Folsom's brother, George Folsom, stated that they had received a letter from the commissioner of the General Land Office directing them "not to allow any filing or entries of any kind on these lands until further orders. We are therefore compelled to decline complying with your demand."[24]

Schurz's order provided the officials in Taylors Falls and the lumbermen it held at bay with further cause for careful reading. The following year, on March 12, 1879, after another session of Congress had expired, the Taylors Falls Land Office allowed 285 entries for lands on the Mille Lacs Reservation. The entries were not preemption claims like Folsom's, but rather soldiers' additional homestead entries. People who had served in the military were allowed to obtain from the US government an additional 120 acres beyond the 160 acres to which ordinary citizens were entitled under the homestead laws. Soldiers' additional homesteads functioned like scrip, allowing the right to the extra homestead to be transferred prior to filing.[25]

In the case of Mille Lacs, the entries covered over 24,376.77 acres, almost half of some 61,028.14 acres of land on the reservation. Each of these entries was made in the name of a separate former soldier, almost all of them soldiers who had obtained homestead lands in states other than Minnesota. Forty-six percent of the entrants had obtained their homesteads in Springfield, Missouri. Another 15 percent had homesteaded on lands purchased in other Missouri land offices. Only four had entered their original homesteads at the Taylors Falls Land Office. Details about these entries are provided in Tables 5–8 (pages 106–11).[26]

It is highly unlikely that more than a handful of the individuals in whose names these 285 land entries were made ever saw the state of Minnesota. Instead, their rights to obtain the land were purchased from them in their home states. The process through which these rights were obtained was not known at first. A few years later it was reported that the entries had been made by a "Thomas H. Walker"—actually Thomas B. (also called T. B.) Walker, the well-known Minneapolis lumberman—using powers of attorney acquired from the former soldiers. In a version of events containing a few known errors, the *St. Paul Globe* stated that Walker "as attorney in fact" had filed

> about 350 [*sic*] solders' additional homestead claims on the Mille Lacs lands—taking about two-thirds of the reservation, including all of the pine lands, most of the lands fit for cultivation and the best water privileges. Although Mr. Walker appeared as attorney in fact, it is only an open secret that the real parties to the transaction are speculating capitalists (two) of St. Paul and Stillwater, who may or may not have Mr. Walker and others for partners. While the operation would naturally alarm the Indians, who are greatly attached to the locality and who have before been not a little damaged in their property by lumbermen and pine grabbers, it is also in the line of taking advantage of the white residents of the State.[27]

Later evidence concerning one of the 1879 entries provides useful information about the process through which the papers from the soldiers may have been procured. According to the *Princeton Union* of November 16, 1893, George A. Morris, a member of Company G, First Arkansas Cavalry, from 1862 to 1865, obtained a homestead of forty acres in Lawrence County, Missouri, on September 26, 1865. Ten years later, on April 2, 1875, Morris and his wife apparently signed a power of attorney transferring to T. B. Walker his right to an additional entry of 120 acres. Subsequently, in 1875 Walker attempted to enter in the name of Morris lots 5 and 6 of section 18, township 42, range 26 on the Mille Lacs Reservation—located south of current Highway 169 as it leaves the west side of South Harbor Township.

The application was rejected by the land office in Taylors Falls. Later, in August 1877, Morris, who was still living in Missouri and had never lived in Minnesota, signed an affidavit stating that "he had never knowingly assigned his right to Mr. Walker . . . that he had signed some kind of paper in blank, but that he had never received any consideration, and further that he had not constituted Walker as his attorney-in-fact." He asked for the right to obtain an additional homestead of 120 acres in Humboldt County, California, and his application was approved. Subsequently, on March 12,

1879, an entry was made for land on the Mille Lacs Reservation in Morris's name. The entry was canceled and reinstated several times, even more often than many of the other homesteads. In 1893 it was canceled by the secretary of the Interior on the basis that the right of a soldier's additional homestead was a personal one and nonassignable; it could be exercised only by the soldier himself. This ruling would have invalidated all the similar 284 entries on the reservation, but it was apparently later overturned. In June 1900 the patent for the Morris entry was issued.[28]

While it is likely that all 285 entries from March 1879 were made through powers of attorney executed by T. B. Walker, he did not become the owner of the lands in question. At some point the claims to the land became the property of Wilder and Sabin. Exactly what their arrangement was with Walker is not known, but it is likely Sabin and Wilder had in mind using soldiers' additional homesteads early on in their scheme. In fact, one of the surviving letters from Wilder to Sabin, on March 18, 1876, thanked Sabin for his "list of additional homesteads." Wilder stated that he would "at once send them to Curtis [their attorney] who will see that the matter is properly attended to."[29]

The involvement of Sabin and Wilder in the whole matter must have been well known in 1879. It was certainly known to officials in the land office, especially the receiver, George Folsom, brother of William H. C. Folsom and uncle to Frank Folsom. However, no published reports of the time stated the actual owner of the claims, beyond the vague references to anonymous businessmen in St. Paul and Stillwater. One account that named those behind the claims came many years later in the US Court of Claims case involving the Mille Lacs Reservation. David H. Robbins stated on August 6, 1909, that Dwight Sabin by using "Soldiers' Additional Scrip" was able to "scrip" the reservation and that Amherst Wilder financed the effort to buy the scrip with an investment of $42,000. Robbins's testimony also alleged that this scheme had been possible through an arrangement between Sabin and the officials of the land office at Taylors Falls. Robbins said the arrangement "was talked about openly. . . . The talk was that Sabin telegraphed to the man here the word 'Go,' and seven men worked all night and entered the whole of the reservation. He had seven agents there and they worked all night and entered the whole thing." According to Robbins, the official in Taylors Falls who made it possible was George Folsom. John P. Owens, the register, "told Folsom that he ought not to do it, but he went ahead and did it." Later on, said Robbins, the congressman and senator from Minnesota

William D. Washburn, who was Sabin's rival and had wanted to get title to the land himself, had Folsom removed from office.[30]

Existing records do not reveal the names of all the men who made the entries in the Taylors Falls Land Office on the night of March 12, 1879, but they do demonstrate that Folsom and the other men who "worked all night" did so methodically. The 285 entries, numbered 2551 to 2835, were entered starting with section 1 of 42–25, working through each section more or less in turn from section 1 to section 36, and proceeding to 42–26, then to 43–27, and ending with 42–27. At the end of the night a few soldiers' additional homesteads were entered on lands throughout the reservation, out of order.[31]

Early corroboration for the ownership of the land covered by the 285 entries from 1879 also comes from a more direct primary source: Mille Lacs County records. Tax records show that much of the land entered through this means was listed as being owned by Sabin and Wilder.[32]

The actions of the Taylors Falls Land Office in allowing the entries on the reservation under Chandler's order was a surprise to Secretary Carl Schurz. Federal officials seem not to have been aware of it until the returns from the office for the month of March 1879 were reported to Washington. At that point, in May 1879, Secretary Schurz wrote to the land office to cancel all 285 entries.[33]

Register John P. Owens responded in defense of the office's decision— and showing that officials in the Taylors Falls Land Office sought every opportunity afforded by implied loopholes in bureaucratic language, following the same practice of imaginative reading Owens demonstrated in 1871.[34]

Owens wrote that Schurz's instructions in 1878 had implied the continuing validity of Chandler's 1877 order. He said that Schurz did not actually revoke the order, but simply stayed its execution until certain measures were acted upon by Congress. Such measures were alive only until the end of the session in which they had been introduced. Owens reasoned that when Congress adjourned without issuing a report on the subject, the secretary's order had expired, and at that point Chandler's order of 1877 took effect. The end of that particular session of Congress occurred on March 3, 1879. Owens waited until March 12 for further orders, and "not having received any they felt they could not legally and in the discharge of their duty deprive the applicants, whose applications had been pending for nearly four years for the lands, of their rights any longer."[35]

It should be noted that the entry of 285 soldiers' additional homesteads by Wilder and Sabin did not decrease the importance of Frank Folsom's claim. On March 25, 1879, William H. C. Folsom paid his brother George Folsom $395.56 to perfect Frank Folsom's title in the property. He sent a copy of the receipt for the payment to Dwight Sabin and another to Sabin's lawyer in Washington, F. W. Curtis, of the law firm of Curtis, Earl and Burdett. William H. C. Folsom wrote that in consultation with "the officers," perhaps meaning Owens and George Folsom, "we agree in view this Preemption of much importance that the whole matter might hinge on it. And therefore thought best to make this a cash entry."[36]

On July 19, 1879, Curtis, Earl and Burdett filed a notice of appeal from Schurz's decision canceling the 285 soldiers' additional homestead entries. It took time for news about the entries and their subsequent cancellation to be widely known. However, in the summer of 1879, as if on cue, there was a renewal of complaints about the presence of the Mille Lacs Ojibwe in the region. To investigate the matter, Lieutenant Constant Williams was sent to the Mille Lacs area from the Department of Dakota at Fort Snelling, under orders dated August 8, 1879. He gave his report on August 21, stating that after speaking with everyone he could at Mille Lacs he found "that the white settlers of that region have no more to fear of these Indians than they have from each other."[37]

Williams found the reported evidence flimsy and based on the word of unreliable sources. He noted that the trader at the lake had reported theft during his own absence: "some maple sugar made by the Indians and put up in birch bark packages was stolen. They said that the thief or thieves opened many of these packages, evidently to find the best sugar." The trader was convinced that no Indian could have done it because "each Indian knows the quality and trade mark so to speak of every other in the land and so an Indian could at once without breaking a package have picked out the best sugar."

Whites were suspected of the theft. Furthermore, few settlers reported break-ins and few seemed afraid to leave their homes unattended. Williams was convinced that the reasons for the reports were simply that the Rum River passed through a reservation with fine timber: "Many white men are desirous of cutting timber there but owing to the fact that the Indians hold the country they cannot do so until the Indians molest the whites." He concluded, "I think that no further attention should be given the matter, unless it may be, in the future, to protect the Indians."

TABLE 5

Sabin–Wilder Land Patents (by location of original homestead)

LOCATION OF SOLDIERS' HOMESTEAD	TOTALS	PERCENT	42-25	42-26	42-27	43-27
AR, Harrison	6	2.11%	5	1		
IA, Council Bluffs	1	0.35%			1	
IA, Des Moines	4	1.40%	1	1	2	
IA, Fort Dodge	1	0.35%			1	
IA, Sioux City	2	0.70%		1	1	
KS, Concordia	4	1.40%		2	1	1
KS, Humboldt	11	3.86%	2		7	2
KS, Independence	34	11.93%	6	8	16	4
KS, Junction City	1	0.35%			1	
KS, Salina	2	0.70%		2		
KS, Topeka	7	2.46%	1	1	4	1
MI, Ionia	30	10.53%	10	8	10	2
MI, Traverse City	5	1.75%	4		1	
MN, Taylors Falls	4	1.40%	2	1		1
MO, Boonville	32	11.23%	8	2	16	6
MO, Ironton	7	2.46%	2		5	
MO, Springfield	132	46.32%	41	16	69	6
WI, Minarta	1	0.35%	1			
WI, St. Croix Falls	1	0.35%			1	
Totals	**285**	**100%**	**83**	**43**	**136**	**23**

Source: See tract books for reservation townships in General Land Office records, Tract Books of the United States, Mille Lacs County, Bureau of Land Management, https://www.familysearch.org/search/collection/2074276

TABLE 6

Sabin-Wilder Acreage (by location of original homestead)

LOCATION OF SOLDIERS' HOMESTEAD	TOTAL ACRES	PERCENT	42-25	42-26	42-27	43-27
AR, Harrison	646.44	2.65%	526.44	120		
IA, Council Bluffs	80	0.33%			80	
IA, Des Moines	320	1.31%	80	80	160	
IA, Fort Dodge	80	0.33%			80	
IA, Sioux City	170.2	0.70%		80	90.2	
KS, Concordia	454.9	1.87%		200	134.9	120
KS, Humboldt	968.85	3.97%	160		640	168.85
KS, Independence	2681.98	11.00%	480	644.01	1260.65	297.32
KS, Junction City	80	0.33%			80	
KS, Salina	166.15	0.68%		166.15		
KS, Topeka	622.8	2.55%	80	80	382.8	80
MI, Ionia	2588.39	10.62%	888.97	640	899.42	160
MI, Traverse City	397.25	1.63%	320		77.25	
MN, Taylors Falls	251.34	1.03%	131.34	40		80
MO, Boonville	2836.7	11.64%	780.52	160	1366.5	529.68
MO, Ironton	658.05	2.70%	200		458.05	
MO, Springfield	11213.72	46.00%	3197.03	1545.41	5951.23	519.55
WI, Minarta	80	0.33%	80			
WI, St. Croix Falls	80	0.33%			80	
Totals	**24376.77**	**100.00%**	**6924.3**	**3755.57**	**11741**	**1955.4**

Source: See tract books for reservation townships in General Land Office records, Tract Books of the United States, Mille Lacs County, Bureau of Land Management, https://www.familysearch.org/search/collection/2074276

TABLE 7

Sabin-Wilder Acreage (by date of patent)

PATENTED	ACRES ON THE MILLE LACS RESERVATION	PERCENTAGE OF ALL SABIN-WILDER ACREAGE	42-25	42-26	42-27	43-27
Unpatented	200	0.82%			80	120
4/5/1883	5513.45		1400	677.25	2040.35	1395.85
4/20/1883	584.89		86.28	292.16	206.45	
5/21/1883	80				80	
8/1/1883	80		80			
Total 1883	**6258.34**	**25.67%**				
5/15/1884	80				80	
Total 1884	**80**	**0.33%**				
1/23/1889	119.55					119.55
Total 1889	**119.55**	**0.49%**				
1/16/1891	2579.97		928.97	200	1291	160
1/23/1891	160				160	
2/28/1891	80				80	
4/20/1891	80				80	
6/17/1891	80		80			
6/20/1891	142.4				142.4	
9/23/1891	1537.32		840	240	457.32	
10/3/1891	5204.01		1431.86	1058.2	2713.95	
10/15/1891	414.75		200		214.75	
10/24/1891	597.8		80	197.8	320	
10/28/1891	2675.34		600	400	1675.34	

Source: See tract books for reservation townships in General Land Office records, Tract Books of the United States, Mille Lacs County, Bureau of Land Management, https://www.familysearch.org/search/collection/2074276

TABLE 7

Sabin-Wilder Acreage (by date of patent) *(cont.)*

PATENTED	ACRES ON THE MILLE LACS RESERVATION	PERCENTAGE OF ALL SABIN-WILDER ACREAGE	42-25	42-26	42-27	43-27
11/2/1891	80		80			
11/4/1891	1115.17		230.75	204.77	639.65	40
11/5/1891	80				80	
11/9/1891	1326.44		566.44	240	400	120
11/20/1891	754.5		240		514.5	
Total 1891	**16907.7**	**69.36%**				
1/22/1892	80		80			
3/1/1892	40			40		
Total 1892	**120**	**0.49%**				
1/21/1893	80			80		
Total 1893	**80**	**0.33%**				
8/30/1895	80				80	
10/15/1895	80				80	
Total 1895	**160**	**0.66%**				
1/22/1896	80				80	
11/21/1896	123.8				123.8	
Total 1896	**203.8**	**0.84%**				
6/7/1900	125.39			125.39		
Total 1900	**125.39**	**0.51%**				
8/5/1905	121.49				121.49	
Total 1905	**121.49**	**0.50%**				
Total	**24376.27**	**100%**	**6924.3**	**3755.57**	**11741**	**1955.4**

TABLE 8

Owners in 1910 of Sabin-Wilder Soldiers' Additional Homestead Lands on the Mille Lacs Reservation

OWNER	TOTAL ACRES	42–25	42–26	42–27	43–27
Boynton, A. J.	80	80			
Burns, Ralph H.	181.96	181.96			
Burroughs, F. A.	480	480			
Erickson & Westburg	46.28	46.28			
Everoth, Andrew P.	80	80			
Foley Bean Lumber Co.	16844.42		3506.27	11702.75	1635.4
Gold, Catharine W.	40	40			
Haggberg, O. A.	40	40			
Holland, Cora A.	160	160			
Holland, Cora M.	40	40			
Jenson, Andrew M.	120	120			
Johnson, Moses	160	160			
Kipp, Orrin	40				40
Langer, Charles D.	160				160
Lemden, Chas. F.	120	120			
Lewis, H. Peter	200	200			
McClare, Martha M.	38.25			38.25	
Olson, Carl	40	40			
Patterson, G. W.	4255.41	4255.41			
Rolson, J. R.	80	80			
St. Croix Lumber Co.	80	80			
Sammon, Joseph	89.9	89.9			
Samuelson, Frank	40	40			
Sharp, Gerald	160	160			

Source: 1910 Mille Lacs County Tax Assessment Rolls, Isle Harbor, South Harbor, and Kathio Townships, Minnesota State Archives, MNHS

TABLE 8

Owners in 1910 of Sabin–Wilder Soldiers' Additional Homestead Lands on the Mille Lacs Reservation *(cont.)*

OWNER	TOTAL ACRES	42-25	42-26	42-27	43-27
Smith, Frank M.	40	40			
Smith, H. C.	40	40			
Spaulding, George B.	40	40			
Sperry, Leonard B.	240	240			
Swanson, Frank	40	40			
Wallblom, Matilda	120				120
Unknown	280.05	30.75	249.3		
	24376.27	6924.3	3755.57	11741	1955.4

CHAPTER 10

A Deep-Laid Plot

During the fall of 1879, Mille Lacs band members first learned about the attempts by Dwight M. Sabin and Amherst H. Wilder to open their reservation. Mille Lacs leaders contacted their friend Joseph Roberts, who wrote a letter on their behalf in January 1880. He stated that the Mille Lacs leaders "claim that efforts have been made and are being made to defraud them of their lands; that they have been and are being robbed of their pine timber; that they are misrepresented—that their reservation rights are disregarded &c &c. And they wish me to ask you to oblige them by calling some of their head chiefs to Washington that they may personally lay before you their grievances." Roberts added that he expected good results for the government and for the Indians if the request were granted.[1]

Reports about the scheme to obtain title to the reservation pinelands began to appear in newspapers. In 1878 the *St. Paul Daily Globe* reported on the investigations of US attorney for Minnesota W. W. Billson into the various attempts to plunder the pinelands in the state, including the timber on the Mille Lacs Reservation. As early as December 1878 the newspaper hinted that T. B. Walker was implicated in these actions, making reference to the filing of "fraudulent additional soldier homestead scrip and other scrip." The newspaper questioned "by what legal right parties claim to own and control the entire tract of pine on the 'Mille Lacs Indian Reservation' in this state."[2]

The next day T. B. Walker (mistakenly called P. B. Walker) himself appeared in the office of the St. Paul newspaper to express his displeasure with the report on his activities. He admitted that he had been involved with securing soldiers' additional homestead scrip;

> That four years ago he did travel the country over to some extent, and purchased with good American dollars, enough soldiers' additional homestead claims to cover much portion of the Mille Lacs Indian reservation as had pine timber growing thereon. That he did

it with the malicious purpose of securing the land and making some money out of the operation, if it was possible. As attorney of record for various parties interested in the purchase, he has also been prosecuting the claim before the interior department for three or four years, and now says that he believes that the parties he represents are the honest, legal owners of the land.[3]

Walker's point was that his activities were not fraudulent, reasoning that

the Indian title to the lands of the reservation was extinguished in 1868 [sic], and the Mille Lacs band of Indians paid in full to relinquish their claim thereto. He further states that Mr. Zacharia [sic] Chandler, former secretary of the interior, rendered a decision just before retiring from that position in which he conceded the justice of the claim of the parties for whom Mr. Walker acts as attorney, and granting the legality of their title to the land covered by the soldiers' additional homestead scrip. The colonel further deposes and says that since that—of a—[son of a b---?] Carl Schurz was raised to the exalted position of secretary of the interior he has reversed the decision of the former secretary, and now holds the matter in his department without rendering any decision either for or against the claimants. "Now," remarked the colonel, "there was no secret about this matter, and all the facts are matters of record, and could be obtained at any time, and by anybody who would take the trouble to seek for them."[4]

The unadorned directness of Walker's account of his attempts to obtain title to the timberlands of the Mille Lacs Indian Reservation provided the *Globe* with evidence it reported in a number of articles in the following months. In January 1880 the *Globe* published an editorial on the matter, which was reprinted a short time later in the *Princeton Union*: "For many years the Mille Lac Indian reservation has been a choice morsel which has been looked upon with covetous eyes by the white men. All kinds of devices have been resorted to secure it. An effort to remove the Indians was made a few years ago, and drunken rows were fomented among them to make them appear lawless. Trespass was committed and a large amount of stumpage was secured."[5]

Now, said the *St. Paul Globe* newspaper, "the last game is to secure the valuable portion of the reservation by soldier's additions to the extent of eighteen thousand acres, embracing the very best portion of the reservation." The article referred to the entries made in March 1879 and their later cancellation and noted that since then "the ring has been wildly seeking some plan to allow their soldiers' additionals to 'stick.'" It was "aggravating and exasperating" to have the land slip from their grasp, "[h]ence the stir in the crowd that have this neat plum in tow and the strenuous efforts which are being made in Washington to receive the revocation of the cancellation order."

The article noted that Mille Lacs band members were seeking to travel to Washington to protect themselves from these efforts but could not get permission to go: "Evidently the Washington authorities do not desire to hear the 'other side.'"

The *Princeton Union* added its own commentary, asking a question which made clear some of the difficulty the Mille Lacs people were laboring against when they tried to defend against the lumbermen's actions. Even those arranged against the lumbermen might also prefer other uses for the reservation than allowing the Mille Lacs people to remain there: "Of what earthly use is the Mille Lac reservation to the Chippewas? They do not reside on their reservation. There is not an acre of it under cultivation. Why not throw it open to settlers? It contains valuable pine lands and we are informed that there are many excellent farming sections."[6]

Shortly after this publicity, band leaders enlisted the help of the nearby community of Little Falls in Morrison County, members of which had assisted them in getting a hearing in Washington in 1877. A report in the *Little Falls Transcript* of March 26, 1880, stated that during the previous week several Mille Lacs chiefs had come to Little Falls and asked for the help of white people in fighting any attempts by "pine speculators to enter the lands in their reservation and drive them from their homes." A public meeting was held at Vasaly's Hall in Little Falls, where the Mille Lacs representatives were given an opportunity to state their case: "They had an abstract from the records in the Taylors Falls Land Office; showing that over three hundred entries of lands located in their reservation were made March 12, 1879. These entries were afterwards canceled by order of the Commissioner of the General Land Office, but the interested parties, two well known capitalists of St. Paul and Minneapolis have carried the matter to the Supreme court, and expect a decision favorable to their interests."[7]

The newspaper repeated the well-known facts about how the Mille Lacs people had always been friendly and had offered to fight to protect white settlements. The Mille Lacs leaders asked the townspeople of Little

Falls to help them make their case to Congress. Several prominent community members "were elected a committee to take action in behalf of the Indians," including state senator and businessman Jonathan Simmons, former state representative Leon Houde, and former state representative Nathan Richardson. The newspaper concluded, "this scheme to rob these Indians is an infamous one."

It may have been with the aid of these men that the Mille Lacs leaders sent a letter from Little Falls on March 22, 1880, addressed to President Rutherford B. Hayes, stating some of the same facts and pleading their case. Evidence suggests Nathan Richardson may have transcribed the letter. The document was later printed in the Little Falls newspaper, with misspellings corrected:

> We, your Children, the Mille Lacs Band of Chippewa Indians desire to make known to you our grievance, and ask you to assist us, so that we shall not be driven from our home without having done any [w]rong to our white brothers and neighbors. In the summer of 1862, when other Indians made war on the whites, we stood by them and offered to fight with them against our own people. For our kindness our Great Father in Washington, and the great and good men with him, who ruled this great nation, made us a promise that we should inherit our home on the beautiful and to us, lovely Mille Lacs forever; or so long as we behaved ourselves well towards our white neighbors. We hear that many false accusations have been made against us and sent to our Great Father. If such is the case we hope he will not be deceived by them, and drive us from our home without giving us a chance to be heard. If we are charged with bad conduct, we demand a full investigation; and if proven to be guilty we will cheerfully submit to whatever punishment our Great Father may see proper, or may think best in his wisdom to inflict upon us. On the other hand, if we prove ourselves to be innocent, we shall ask for a new treaty or that the one we now have be made definite and perfect, so that pine land thieves will not dare to come upon our reservation, as they have done in the past and take our timber from us without our consent.

The petition explained the information the Mille Lacs Band had heard of the attempts to obtain title to land on the reservation:

We are informed that on the 12th day of March 1879 some person or persons to us unknown was permitted to enter all of our pine lands at the U.S. Land office at Taylors Falls, and that the Secretary of the Interior a Great and good man promptly canceled the entries; by which act he incurred the great displeasure of the pine land thieves; who are making a strong effort to secure his removal from office to make room for some one [sic] whose sense of honor and justice may yield somewhat to the persuasive influence of money.

As matters now stand and in view of what has been done and the efforts that are now being made to drive us from our home and rob us of the little valuable timber we have; we are continually laboring under great fear and are much distressed, for fear that bad men may prevail against us and succeed in robbing us of our most valuable lands. We therefore humbly ask and urge upon you to listen to our appeal to you for justice, and ask that you and our kind friend Carl Schurz, Secretary of the Interior; may without delay take such action as shall make us forever secure in our rights and home.[8]

The Mille Lacs leaders asked for a chance to visit Washington to make their case, since they had heard that their agent was on the side of those who were seeking to take away their pinelands. The leaders signing included some of those listed on band annuity rolls in the 1880s: Shaboshkung, Monzomonay, Maynwaywayaush, Wahweyaycumig, Negwanebi, Ma'iingaans (Maheengaunce), Biidadens (Pedud), and Kegwedosay, the last described as a "Brave."

The April 9 and April 16 issues of the *Little Falls Transcript* contained a complete account of the meeting with Mille Lacs leaders in Little Falls. It was reported that knowledge about the scheme by Sabin and Wilder to obtain title to the pinelands at Mille Lacs had come to band leaders the previous fall. Kegwedosay had gone to St. Paul to meet with the governor of Minnesota, John S. Pillsbury: "I went, and he asked me if I know what was going on, and stated that we were about to be robbed of what little we had." From the governor Mille Lacs leaders learned about the attempts to obtain title to reservation lands.[9]

Senator Simmons seemed skeptical of what the band leaders alleged. He asked how they knew that "any one is trying to get your lands away from you." In answer Monzomonay stated that no pine was currently being cut on the reservation, but he presented a certified copy of the entries made in the land office in Taylors Falls in March 1879, showing that they had been canceled. He said, "That paper is what we are afraid of . . . I am afraid of that paper; it appears to me like a match to burn up our country. My friends, I may not be able to speak eloquently, but I am afraid of that paper and I appeal to you, my friends, to give us a helping hand. My father [Manoominikeshiinh] helped make the treaty; and before he died he called me and asked me to preserve and keep the reservation."

Like other Mille Lacs people at the time, Monzomonay repeated his belief that the treaties had not taken away the reservation:

I have no knowledge that the reservation was ever ceded to the United States. Three chiefs once went down to Washington, and only one of them is now living. My father [Rice Maker] was there, and Hole-in-the-Day was the great man. I do not know what might have been done, but do not think the reservation was ever ceded to the government. We still believe it to be ours. Our purpose in coming here was to see our friends. We were told that our lands had been sold. We desire to be heard by our Great Father in Washington, and also by his right hand man, the Hon. Carl Schurz, Secretary of the Interior.

In response to these statements, the leaders of the Little Falls community expressed their sympathy. Richardson, in particular, noted that "it does really appear that the pine land grabbers and ringsters will not be content as long as there is a pine tree in the State that they do not own." These conspirators were behind charges made against the Mille Lacs Band but could offer no "proof whatever, beyond their bare assertions." He saw "no reason why we should not intercede for these Indians, and ask that justice be done them." A committee of those present was appointed to draft a petition, to be circulated for signatures among the community.[10]

By the time this report appeared in the *Little Falls Transcript*, details of the meeting had already been published in the *St. Paul Globe* of March 24, 1880. Headlined "Pine Grabbers," the article also repeated details the newspaper had first recorded two years before, about the scheme to obtain the pinelands on the reservation. The article stated that the "uneasiness of the Indians arose from rumors concerning the following transactions," one of which was Zachariah Chandler's order, described in the article as "clandestine," which may certainly be the case since there is no record of it having been communicated to the Mille Lacs people.[11]

The *Globe* stated that while those seeking to obtain reservation timber

were informed of the ruling, it was "concealed from the public and the Indians, although a certified copy of it was early pigeon-holed at the White
Earth agency office." Then, in March 1879, the land office in Taylors Falls,
"acting under this clandestine order allowed Thomas H. [T. B.] Walker, as
attorney in fact, to file about 350 soldiers' additional homestead claims
on Mille Lacs lands—taking about two-thirds of the reservation, including
all the pine lands, most of the lands fit for cultivation and the best water
privileges." It was an open secret that Walker only represented "speculat-
ing capitalists (two) of St. Paul and Stillwater, who may or may not have
Mr. Walker and others for partners." Secretary Carl Schurz had canceled
the entries, but "the St. Paul and Stillwater speculators have, however, appealed to the supreme court of the United States and mean, it is thought,
to hold the matter in abeyance until some one more complaisant than the
'd—d Dutchman,' as they term him, becomes secretary of the interior."

The Little Falls petition circulated in the area for some time. Then,
on May 15, 1880, it was sent with a cover letter to Secretary Schurz from
Richardson, Houde, and Simmons. The men stated that if time permitted
it would have been possible to obtain signatures from "every man in the
county," adding, "We are really satisfied that not only justice but good policy demands that these Indians of Mille Lacs be honorably dealt with."[12]

The petition itself repeated mention of the aid given by the Mille Lacs
Band in 1862. It noted their "uniform good behavior since that time" and
asserted that a "deep laid plot has been formed, including men in high
authority for the purpose of taking from them the pine that is on their
Reservation at Mille Lac." It noted that the principal success of such a
scheme depended on "belying said Indians and making the authorities
at Washington to believe that said Indians make a practice of committing
great depredations upon the white settlers adjoining their Reservation." It
stated that the Mille Lacs people were "orderly and inoffensive" and that
reports to the contrary "were concocted and promulgated by an association of pine land thieves solely for mercenary motives who have no regard
for and no interest in the Governments maintaining and carrying out in
good faith their pledges to these people."[13]

The petition further stated that the government should "take steps to
secure to said Indians their Reservation and home at Mille Lac and give
them such assurance as to dispel their present apparently well founded
fears and apprehensions of foul play and dishonorable dealing with them
by the Government."

Several months later, on July 9, 1880, the Little Falls people were sent a letter from L. J. Brooks, acting commissioner of the Indian Office, in answer to these expressions of fear about the reservation:

> In reply, I have to say that there is no law authorizing the sale or entry of any of the lands embraced within the Mille Lacs reservation, and in the absence of such law no such sale or entry can be made.
>
> It will be seen, therefore, that the apprehensions of the Indians, and of the people as well, regarding the disposition of the lands referred to, are not well grounded.[14]

On receiving the letter Nathan Richardson included it in a series of articles he was writing for the *Little Falls Transcript* about the history of Morrison County. On July 23, 1880, he commented that from the letter it would appear the current administration at least was willing to "protect the Mille Lacs Indians from the pine land sharpers." He sounded a note of alarm, however: "it is evident that a deep laid plot has been made and that they may yet succeed in robbing the Indians of their most valuable pine lands unless the parties engaged in it are sharply watched."

Wilder and Sabin had not abandoned their scheme despite the cancellation of their entries. Frank Folsom's property continued to be an important foothold on the reservation. On September 10, 1880, the property was finally patented to Folsom, although it is not evident how this step was compatible with Acting Commissioner Brooks's statement in July. In December the patent was in the hands of Dwight Sabin in Stillwater. On December 1, he sent it to William H. C. Folsom in Taylors Falls, requesting that Folsom's son, Frank, deed the land to his father, and that the sale be recorded at the county seat in Princeton. The purpose of this transfer was to make it more difficult for the patent to be canceled. The ownership of the land by William H. C. Folsom rather than Sabin or others who were part of the scheme was intended to divert attention. Sabin explained: "This transfer from Frank is absolutely necessary to go into some third party's hands as innocent holder, to prevent the possibility of having patent cancelled by the Department. The mere matter of record of patent in Frank's name will not prevent Department cancelling same, but when the land is sold and passes into other hands it is beyond recall, and I would think it best to have land deeded to you rather than to any of our folks that are interested in the matter."[15]

Sabin instructed William H. C. Folsom to go to Princeton to have the sale executed and recorded, and to have the patent and the deed returned to him. If Frank Folsom was working in the woods, "you must manage to reach him in some way. You perhaps could have deed made out and take his signature and acknowledgment up at the mill, provided there is a Notary Public there who also has a Notary stamp." Sabin added, "Under any circumstances, do not make any mistake on this." Sabin intended to go to Washington soon and hoped "to have this matter on record at least a couple of weeks before I go there."

Sabin scrawled another letter to William H. C. Folsom on December 5, 1880: "I think you had better hire someone to go into woods & find Frank— as soon as possible & get deed signed to you. $1 consideration is just as good as more—only *pay him the Dollar*." Sabin wanted to start for Washington "& want the patent & *deed* on *record* before I go—& would like to be so advised as it will make a great difference with my action there."[16]

Two days later Sabin asked Folsom to come to see him as he was "so hurried especially as my *expected* trip—is so *unexpected* that I have many things to see too [sic]." That same day the county auditor in Princeton wrote out a receipt to Frank W. Folsom for $4.94 in payment of the property taxes on his land—paid by William H. C. Folsom.[17]

After this transfer the Folsom family had no further role to play in the Sabin–Wilder scheme. Frank Folsom died in May 1881. William H. C. Folsom, in reminiscences written sometime in the 1880s, appears to have had second thoughts about his role in undermining the Mille Lacs Reservation:

> The Mille Lacs reservation covers about four fractional towns, bordering the southern shore of the lake. Since the treaty these lands have been covered by pre-emptions, soldiers' warrants and half-breed scrip, but are held by a doubtful tenure owing to the uncertain and various rulings of the land department. Under the provisions of the treaty, the Indians, a band of Chippewas, were allowed to retain possession until ordered to remove. In anticipation of this order settlements have been made at various periods, and patents have been issued to the preemptors in a few cases, but in many cases refused. Half-breed scrip has been laid upon thousands of acres under one administration at Washington, the permission to be countermanded by another. Meanwhile the Indians, not having received the order for removal, claim to be the owners of the land, and with some show of justice.

Although he did not accurately record the meaning of the 1863 and 1864 treaty provisions, Folsom acknowledged the continuing existence of the Mille Lacs Reservation and the band's justifiable claim to continuing residence on it.[18]

Dwight Sabin never gave up his desire to possess the Mille Lacs Reservation pine timber. He headed to Washington in December 1880 intending to further that aim in the context of a changing government bureaucracy. Carl Schurz continued as secretary of the Interior until March 4, 1881. He was replaced by Samuel J. Kirkwood, former senator from Iowa, who served until April 5, 1882. Under Kirkwood there were no further changes in the land situation at Mille Lacs. Nonetheless, it appears to have been widely expected that the plan was merely in abeyance. The *Princeton Union* stated on December 16, 1880: "If the Mille Lacs reservation is brought into market the pine land ringsters propose to gobble it up without paying one-fifth part of what it is worth. Secretary Schurz has blocked the game of the ringsters so far but then he will not be at the head of the Interior department much longer. He is very obnoxious to the ringsters."[19]

In December 1881 Commissioner of Indian Affairs Hiram Price wrote to Noah C. McFarland, Commissioner of the General Land Office, asking for a statement of what entries on the lands of the Mille Lacs Indian Reservation appeared on the records of his office. In reply, on December 30, 1881, McFarland sent a short list that included the allotment Shaboshkung had been given under the Treaty of 1864, as well as a homestead entry for the Ojibwe leader. A number of additional acres were still registered as swamplands patented to the state of Minnesota, never surrendered to the federal government in 1871. Folsom's cash payment was the only other entry. McFarland added that additional homestead and preemption entries "have been made from time to time for other portions of the land embraced in the reservation named, but all have been canceled save the entries, locations, and selections named above."[20]

On April 5, 1882, Samuel Kirkwood wrote to Commissioner of Indian Affairs Hiram Price asking for a history of the Mille Lacs Indian Reservation and for other details about the reservation and the Indians living there. Price replied on April 26, writing to Kirkwood's successor Henry M. Teller, a former senator from Colorado, appointed by Chester A. Arthur. In a lengthy letter Price reviewed the various treaties, their provisions, and the ways in which they had been interpreted over the years by assorted government officials. He examined the question of whether the Mille Lacs band members had done anything that would have forfeited their right to remain on the reservation under the provisions of the Treaty of 1864, concluding that "these people have never violated the conditions upon which their continued occupancy of the lands in question solely depends."[21]

Price went on to note that the position of the band on the reservation since 1864 was "an anomalous one." It could not be claimed that the Indians had "title or fee in the lands," nor was Price willing to say that "the lands are, by the terms of the treaty, excluded from sale and disposal by the United States," but he insisted "it is clear in my mind that the Government is bound to protect the Indians in the continued occupancy thereof, so long as they shall refuse to remove therefrom, unless they shall work a forfeiture of their right by future misconduct." The only answer, Price believed, was to ask Congress for authority to negotiate with the Mille Lacs Ojibwe "for relinquishment of their right to occupancy to the lands in question and for their removal to White Earth, for a specified sum of money."[22]

The new secretary of the Interior, Henry Teller, responded to Price's letter on May 10, 1882, focusing on Price's point that the Mille Lacs people did not have "title or fee in the lands" and that the lands were not necessarily "excluded from sale and disposal by the United States." Teller stated that he adhered to the decision made by his predecessor Zachariah Chandler five years before, believing there was nothing in the Treaty of 1864 that gave the Mille Lacs people an exclusive right to the reservation. He granted that they had not forfeited their right to remain on the reservation; they could not be asked to move voluntarily. However, the question was whether "they may occupy the whole reservation or only the part that is necessary to make good the promise of the provision of section 12."[23]

Teller said it was not claimed "that they originally occupied the entire reservation, or that it is now necessary to exclude white settlers therefrom to keep in good faith the treaty with them." He therefore concluded that "whatever the Mille Lacs people occupied in 1863, they are now entitled to occupy; if they have increased the area of their occupation, they are entitled to that, if such occupation was prior to the occupancy by white people."

Teller said nothing about the status of the reservation, only the status of the lands on the reservation. His reasoning departed from that of many of those who preceded Chandler. It also did not accord with the understanding consistently expressed by the Mille Lacs people themselves about the meaning of their treaty. Teller's novel interpretation suggested the need to determine the answers to the questions he raised, so that before any parcels were opened to settlement on the reservation those lands necessary for the use of the Mille Lacs Band were determined and held off the market. In keeping with the logic of his statement, Teller gave Price some instructions:

> I understand the number of Indians on that reservation is about five hundred [sic], while the reservation contains seven townships [sic] and three small islands. You will therefore ascertain as soon as practicable the quantity of land heretofore occupied by the Indians, as well as the quantity necessary for their support (if the quantity now occupied is insufficient) and report the same to this office, in order that such land may be reserved from the operation of the homestead and pre-emption laws, so that the remainder of the reservation may be occupied by the settlers who have in good faith attempted settlement thereon.
>
> If you think it desirable I will send an inspector there to examine and report on the area now occupied by the Indians, or you may ascertain the fact through your own agencies.

Teller's statement had a fair and cautious tone, concealing a number of important factual errors. He understated the Mille Lacs population, overstated the number of townships, and, of course, erred in suggesting that any Euro-American individuals had attempted to settle on the reservation in good faith. Errors of this kind also appear to have affected the examination that was subsequently made as a result of these letters. Nonetheless, Teller's reasoning made clear that regardless of the ownership or occupation of individual parcels of land, the Mille Lacs Reservation continued to exist and the Mille Lacs Band had a right to continue to reside within it. Further, that right had to be protected by the federal government.

CHAPTER 11

The Mille Lacs Reservation in 1882 and 1883

The first observer sent from Washington to examine the situation at Mille Lacs was US Indian Inspector George W. Chapman, apparently dispatched by Secretary Henry Teller with instructions on May 29, 1882. Chapman's first report to the secretary of Interior was on July 21, 1882, which he later described as "brief." This document has not been found. On August 25, 1882, Chapman sent a more detailed report.[1]

Chapman began with a description of the reservation's physical features: "The land is mostly low, flat and thickly interspersed with tamarack swamps, marshes, and sloughs, rising but little above the flow of the lake." He claimed that much of the soil was barren and unproductive, except for a band varying from a quarter to a half mile from the lake, which was "black sand loam, and productive of all grains and vegetables indigenous to the climate." Chapman wrote that the arable land was covered with sugar maple, basswood, butternut, and hardwoods. He mentioned several points of dry land extending into the lake, which when the region was accessible by railroad "will be desirable locations."

Chapman's opinion of the nature of Ojibwe occupation of the reservation was that it was "scattered and changeable." He wrote that "nearly all of these Indians have no fixed habitation, they go from place to place and pitch their tepes [sic] in the forest near some stream, or lake convenient for fishing, hunting, and gathering wild rice[,] in the summer and fall of the year the women and children gather ginsen[g], snake root, berries, and whatever else they can exchange for gun ammunition and trinkets." Chapman also described the three small lakes on the reservation (Ogechie, Shakopee, and Onamia) in which wild rice grew plentifully and referred to the importance of fish resources for band members, writing, "Fish are very abundant in Mille Lac and the other lakes and are easily caught at most seasons of the year, the wife of an Indian handily secures what the family require and for weeks at a time they subsist entirely upon fish." Of the 944 band members he described as existing on the annuity payroll, he noted that four hundred of the band were on the Snake River. There were thirty families on the reservation, living around tracts of land occupied by the leaders Shaboshkung and Monzomonay.

In addition to providing these clues to the lands occupied by these chiefs, Chapman recorded in some detail the section and lot numbers inhabited by band members on the reservation, as well as the acres of land they cultivated and fenced and the locations of their log cabins and bark houses. The data from Chapman's report, which is shown in the left-hand portion of Table 9 (page 126) and on Map 2 (page 129), provides some interesting information on band members' settlement patterns. The figures show use by band members of land around present-day Isle, Wahkon, Cove, Murry Beach, Onamia, Vineland, and Wigwam Bay.

The remaining band members were "scattered about the country, within a radius of thirty or forty miles" from the reservation. The "tepes [sic] are not permanently located, they are moved about the reservation as the season changes the conveniences for obtaining food. For this reason they prefer a wigwam to a house. Their head chief Shi a bus kunk [Shaboshkung] lives in a wigwam while a hewn log house, built for him, near his cabin, stands vacant, going to decay." Chapman was likely unaware that log cabins were used in the winter while bark houses, which were cooler, were used in the summer. He flatly stated that there were "no villages on the reservation," writing: "The wigwams are scattered along near the shore of the lakes on some bay or inlet when fish and game are plenty and located without any regard to garden or field with a few exceptions these Indians make no particular spot in the reservation their home the work they have to do fixes their habitation. 'Sufficient unto the day' is what the Indian deliberates to have a particular spot his home. To plant seed and prepare for coming want is a consideration he cares nothing about."

In Chapman's assessment Ojibwe people gave no attention to agriculture, since they did not have oxen or farm implements familiar to whites and did not cultivate the soil in ways he believed were most productive: "No field is fenced in a way that can be called a fence. There may be a few poles staked around some nook or corner to keep the ponies off. The ground planted this season on the reservation amounted to mere nothing, a few patches planted here and there by the women to corn and potatoes with the weeds as high as the crop is the extent of their husbandry. Nine acres will include all planted. There is much more ground formerly cultivated now grown up to seeds and brush than is planted this season."

Despite the prejudiced nature of some of these remarks, it is clear that

TABLE 9

Mille Lacs Reservation Use by Band Members 1882, 1883

	JUNE 1882						AUGUST 1883	
TOWNSHIP	SECTION	LOT NO.	ACRES CULTIVATED	[ACRES] FENCED	LOG HOUSES	TEEPEES OR WIGWAMS	LANDS OCCUPIED	LANDS RECOMMENDED TO BE WITHHELD
T 42 N, R 25 W								
	sec. 2	4	1/2			1	SE 1/4 of sec. 2	S. E. 1/4 of sec. 2
	sec. 3	1				1	sec. 3	sec. 3
	sec. 4	3 & 4						
	sec. 7	2			1			
	sec. 17	Island	1/2					
							NE 1/4 of sect 18	NE. 1/4 of sec. 18
T 42 N, R 26 W								
								sec. 11
								sec. 12
								sec. 13
								sec. 14
	sec. 15	1	1/4			1	sec. 15	sec. 15

Sources: Chapman to Secretary of Interior, August 25, 1882, and Wright to H. Price, June 27, 1883—both Special Case 109, NARG 75

TABLE 9

Mille Lacs Reservation Use by Band Members 1882, 1883 (cont.)

T 42 N, R 26 W (cont.)

	JUNE 1882					AUGUST 1883	
	2	1/4	1/2		2		sec. 18
	3	1/2	1/2		1		sec. 19
	4	1/4	1/4	1		N 1/2 of sect. 20	sec. 20
	6 & 7			1			sec. 21
sec. 16	5	1/4			1		sec. 22
sec. 17	1	1/2			2		sec. 29
	2	3/4	1	1	1		sec. 30
	5		1	1		sec. 18	sec. 31
sec. 31	2 & 3						sec. 32
sec. 32	1 & 2						
	3 & 4					sec. 31	

TABLE 9

Mille Lacs Reservation Use by Band Members 1882, 1883 *(cont.)*

	JUNE 1882					AUGUST 1883	
T 42 N, R 27 W							
sec. 3	3 & 4	1/4		1		SE. 1/4 of sec. 3	SE. 1/4 of sec. 3
sec. 4	2 & 3	1	1	1		NE. 1/4 of sec. 4	NE. 1/4 of sec. 4
sec. 23	1 & 2			1			
sec. 25			1		1	NE 1/4 of sec. 25	NE 1/4 of sec. 25
T43 N, R 27 W							
sec. 18	1	1/8		1		NE 1/4 of sec. 18	NE 1/4 of sec. 18
sec. 21							sec. 21
sec. 27	4	1/8		1		sec. 27	sec. 27
sec. 28	1 & 2			1		S 1/2 sec. 28	all of sec. 28
	3						
sec. 30						sec. 30	sec. 30
sec. 33	3 & 4	1 1/2	1 1/2	1		sec. 33	sec. 33
T 44 N, R 27 W							
sec. 31	2	1/4		1			

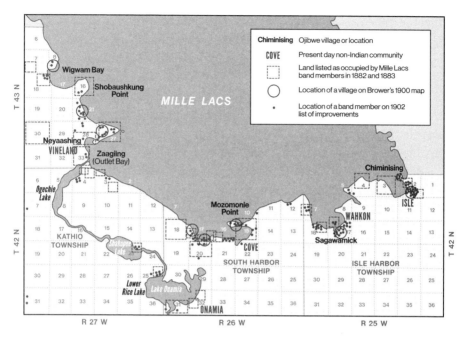

Map 2: Indian Occupancy of the Mille Lacs Reservation as Recorded by Non-Indian Observers, 1882–1902

Chapman essentially described the same seasonal patterns of activity Noodinens would tell in her narrative (see Chapter 3). His report shows that much if not all of the seasonal activities she described could be undertaken close to Mille Lacs Lake, within the reservation, although he gave few specific locations except for those of permanent summer villages.

Based on what Chapman believed to be the widely scattered and unsystematic nature of band members' use of the reservation, he suggested that, lacking an ability to remove them to White Earth, a plan should be formed to "contract the limits of their occupancy" by withholding from sale only a limited portion of their original reservation. The protected parcels would consist of two tracts, one currently occupied by Shaboshkung and the other by Monzomonay, along the west side of the lake and in the region including present-day Cove and Wahkon.

Chapman's statement was an implicit admission that the Mille Lacs Ojibwe made use of a large portion of the reservation. But Chapman believed this use was not warranted and should be "contracted," not particularly for their benefit but rather so that portions of the reservation could be turned over to whites.

Given Teller's instructions to Hiram Price in May, one might assume that the information Chapman gathered would have been used by officials in Washington to determine which lands were needed by band members and which could be disposed of by the land office. But this information was now not entirely relevant. By early August 1882, in an order given prior to the writing of Chapman's report, Teller made a decision that led to the reinstatement of the soldiers' additional homestead entries made by Dwight Sabin and Amherst Wilder in 1879, including some lands recommended by Chapman for use by band members.

This shift in policy occurred through the intercession of attorneys representing Sabin and Wilder. What happened was recorded in a letter written by the commissioner of the General Land Office, N. C. McFarland, to Teller on August 7, 1882. McFarland said he had received, unofficially, a copy of Teller's May 10 letter and understood from it that the reservation would be "reduced to the reasonable quantity needed for their support, and that the remainder of the lands (not so needed for Indian occupation) are to be opened to entry under the homestead and pre-emption laws." Such entry, he believed, would await the report that Teller had asked for in his letter.[2]

However, McFarland stated that the lawyers Curtis and Burdett, "representing a large number of soldiers' additional entries," had applied for reinstatement of these entries, claiming that under Teller's instructions of May these entries "should be considered as having been legally made at the respective dates thereof, in order that the same may be protected against any subsequent claims upon the same lands that may hereafter be presented."

McFarland could not see how he could reinstate these claims pending the results of the inquiry ordered by Teller in May: "I do not understand your letter to the Commissioner of Indian Affairs as authorizing me to take the action desired by Messrs. Curtis & Burdett, nor as determinative of the several questions which their application presents; neither is it my understanding that the report upon the examination required by you to be made of these lands has yet been submitted for your action and instructions thereunder." McFarland did not feel he had the liberty to reinstate the claims; nonetheless, Curtis and Burdett—who, McFarland noted parenthetically, had mentioned "they have had a personal interview with you upon the subject"—had asked him to submit their application to Teller "for any consideration and instruction you may deem proper in the premises."

Teller's response came not in a detailed letter that explained his reasoning, but rather in an August 7, 1882, endorsement on the back of McFarland's letter on its return to the writer: "I want all the entries heretofore canceled in the so-called Mille Lac Reservation reinstated for an examination as to their *bona fide* character, for if made in good faith the canceling of such entries was without authority of law, and in derogation of the rights of the parties making such entries. It is necessary to save the rights of such persons and prevent a conflict with others, to reinstate such entries, and therefore, this ought to be done at once." There is little further explanation for Teller's order given on the back side of McFarland's letter. Exactly what was said in conversation between the attorneys representing Sabin and Wilder and Secretary Teller has not been recorded. Teller did not explain the contradictions between his August order and his May letter.[3]

McFarland found the new order confusing enough on one score that he wrote to Teller the following week asking whether he was also to reinstate the canceled entries from 1871. Teller did not respond at all until sending a letter on February 13, 1883, which stated: "My meaning can hardly be made more explicit and certain by words than by the endorsement I made taken in connection as it necessarily must be with your letter. No reference is made directly or remotely to the canceled entries of 1871 and 1872."[4]

Teller offered no explanation for his differing treatment of Sabin and Wilder's 1879 entries and the canceled entries from 1871, but his intent to protect the later entries, and no others, was clear.

Meanwhile, in the fall of 1882 the Mille Lacs band leaders renewed their attempt to obtain permission to go to Washington to discuss their grievances. It is not clear if they had heard of Secretary Teller's reinstatement of the 1879 land entries. They stated that "we hear there is a move to steal our land; that we hope is not to take place. This effort to take away this land will have a bad effect with us and we appeal to you for relief, as we consider it our land." They also mentioned that a logging dam was being built on one of the lakes. Because it flooded the hay they grew in the meadows and damaged the rice crop, "we have stopped the same." The letter also mentioned the arrival of George Chapman during the summer: "We have seen [him] but once and have had no talk with him whatever, and we understand that he has gone back and made his report that we were willing to leave our home at Mille Lac. We deny ever having any talk with him and we are not willing to leave our home. We want to stay where we are."[5]

Perhaps in line with the Mille Lacs people's concerns, government officials apparently doubted that Chapman had provided them with adequate information. Commissioner Price, on May 9, 1883, sent John A. Wright, a special agent in the Indian Office, to visit Mille Lacs to get more information to provide to the secretary of the Interior. Wright filed his account of the visit on June 27, 1883.[6]

Unlike Chapman, Wright had no problem using the term "village" to describe the band's residences. The agent stated that, with the aid of an "educated full blood" interpreter named William Hanks, he had visited "every Indian village on the Mille Lac reservation and nearly every house apart from these villages." He described band members as poor "with few comforts around them, with scarcely anything to eat, at present, except fish which are caught in the lake by means of traps."

On the other hand, Wright insisted that despite the practice of agriculture by band members, one could not use the term "farm" to describe the places where they grew crops. "They live," wrote Wright, "mostly in birch-bark tepees though there are a few old log houses in tolerably fair condition. They have no oxen and but few ponies or plows, consequently their garden patches are small and poorly cultivated, so much so indeed that in no single instance do I feel justifiable in using the word farm. The ground is almost exclusively broken by the use of the shovel and spade."

In another observation shaped by his own cultural perspective, Wright wrote: "As a rule the men were lying idly around the lodges, while even the labor of taking fish from the nets and bringing wood and water was imposed upon the women," a statement that ignored the seasonal variations in men's activities. Wright did note that at various times of the year band members gathered wild rice, cranberries, and blueberries and "hunted deer, rabbits, and other animals when they can be found."[7]

Wright discussed the problems caused by the lumbermen's desire to log the Mille Lacs Reservation: "As the land on this reserve is mostly pine and much of it good quality, the pressure on the part of whites to secure titles to it has been persistent for years past but probably at no time greater than at present." There were no fewer than fifty "pretended settlers" now living on the reservation. They were paid monthly wages by lumber companies to claim land as settlers that they would later transfer to their employers after title was "proved up." Holding a low opinion of the land's potential for cultivation, Wright stated, "The idea of people settling in these woods with the intention of making their homes by agriculture or by any other means is simply absurd." He added, "The Indians are well aware of the hollow pretense of these people and are greatly irritated by their presence."

Based on what he had learned, Wright recommended what lands were necessary for the support of the band and should be withdrawn from sale through homestead or preemption laws, until the band could be removed to White Earth. These lands, he said would "afford them sufficient room for their lodges, gardens and other domestic purposes; maple and birch trees for the sugar season; maple, tamarack and pine for their canoes; fuel for all required purposes; cranberries, rice and, in fact, everything that the Indian values, obtainable from the reservation, can be obtained on these lands in sufficient quantities to meet their wants except game." The statement appeared to assume that hunting would take place in other areas on and off the reservation.

However, Wright could not definitely "locate the portions of the reserve occupied by the Indians twenty years ago, when the treaty was made." He believed the lands they now occupied embraced two-thirds to three-quarters of the lands occupied in 1863. He did not explain his interpretation. Using an inaccurate figure, Wright noted that of five hundred Mille Lacs Ojibwe people, 270 lived on the reservation and the balance on the Snake River. Sixty-seven of these people, under their leader Shaboshkung, lived in the northern portion of present-day Kathio Township (43–27). One hundred and fifty people under chiefs Monzomonay and Negwanebi lived in present-day South Harbor Township.[8]

The data given in the reports Chapman and Wright filed, though informed by some locations, do not appear to have accurately recorded all Ojibwe residents. It is not known, for example, whether even Wright's undoubtedly low estimate of 270 people living at Mille Lacs—let alone the 622 people reflected in the 1881 annuity rolls—could have lived in only seven log houses and twenty-two bark houses. It is also unlikely that, given the time of year when Chapman and Wright appeared on the reservation, they adequately accounted for other lands the Mille Lacs people used on their reservation, including hunting, trapping, and sugaring areas.

CHAPTER 12

The First Sabin–Wilder Patents and the Beginnings of White Settlement

On July 7, 1883, Commissioner Hiram Price sent John Wright's report to the secretary of the Interior. He seconded Wright's suggestions about the removal of the Mille Lacs Band to White Earth and recommended asking Congress for an appropriation to build houses at White Earth for the band. Pending these actions he noted that "considering the hostility of the Indians to the existing encroachments and the false attitude of the settlers as ascertained by Agent Wright, I would not be willing to give my consent to the opening of any portion of the reservation to settlement and sale. It is evident that the pretended settlements are the merest sham, and I do not think that the parties have any claim to consideration whatever. Indeed I think they ought to be forcibly ejected from the reservation." There is no record that Secretary Henry Teller responded to this statement that was so contrary to his own order written on the back of land office commissioner Noah McFarland's letter the previous August.[1]

Despite the pressure from some in Minnesota to remove the Mille Lacs Ojibwe to White Earth, opinions in the state varied as to the advisability of actually doing so. An article in a St. Paul newspaper suggested that statements about the "deplorable condition of the Indians and the hopelessness of remedying it as long as they remain where they are" might be true in relation to Mille Lacs, but "the hunger of private capitalists for their pine lands is not to be omitted from a consideration of the case." Parties were planting themselves on the reservation not with a desire to actually occupy the land but rather for the purpose of claiming the timber. The article suggested putting the Mille Lacs Reservation out of reach of the Preemption Act.

A copy of the article was sent to Secretary Teller by Knute Nelson, a representative from Minnesota in Congress. Nelson objected to the impending removal of the Mille Lacs Band, which was said to be "on the ground that the *Mille Lac* reservation is wanted for settlement." He stated that the reservation was mainly "pine land, rice swamps, blue berry and cranberry marshes and is not adapted to agricultural purposes." The settlers there were not "bona fide" but were "merely men hired by the pine land operators to gobble the pine on the reservation." The land was good for the Indians who lived "mainly by hunting, berrying and fishing." If any area should be thrown open to settlers it was White Earth, which was full of good agricultural land. These reservations were both in Nelson's district, and he wrote expressing the wishes of his constituents.[2]

Apparently unknown to Nelson and Commissioner of Indian Affairs Price, as shown in Table 7 (page 108), not only had some of the entries made by Sabin and Wilder already been reinstated and examined for their legitimacy as per Teller's August 7, 1882, instructions to Commissioner McFarland, but patents were already being issued for reservation lands. It is not known under what specific authorization this step was taken. On April 5, 1883, patents were issued on just over 5,513 acres of the Sabin–Wilder lands. A few more patents were issued later in April, in May, and in August, bringing the total of Sabin–Wilder lands patented in 1883 to 25 percent of all the lands entered in March 1879. Another eighty-acre parcel received a patent in May 1884. After that—as a result of the Act of July 4, 1884, discussed below—no more patents were issued on the Sabin–Wilder lands until 1889, although some were granted for other lands on the reservation. Nonetheless the original Sabin–Wilder entries remained viable, pending other governmental action. By early March 1883 Dwight Sabin was in a good position to look after the credibility of his entries on the Mille Lacs Reservation. The state legislature of that year elected him the new US senator from Minnesota. He began serving his term on March 4, 1883, just a month before the land office began issuing the patents for his land.[3]

Following the slowdown in patenting the 1879 entries after May 1883, new complaints about the behavior of the Mille Lacs Band appeared once again. In December 1883 a man named E. C. Ingall (or Ingalls) wrote to J. P. Owens, the receiver in the Taylors Falls Land Office. Ingall wrote from North Branch, a town in Chisago County around fifty miles southwest of the reservation. He stated that at the request of Orin Markel and five other parties "who have claims on the Mille Lacs Reservation and are kept from going there by the Indians," he was writing to describe "the great hardship" these claimants were under. They had gone there to "make their future home on their claims" at "great expense" but were "deter[r]ed on account of the Indians." He hoped Owens would interest himself in their plight and make it known in Washington. Owens, who had attempted to open the reservation to claimants a number of times earlier, sent Ingall's letter on to Washington, stating that it was an example of letters he was "continually receiving from settlers on the Mille Lacs Reservation." However, records of such claimants do not include the names of Ingall or Markel.[4]

Around this time, reports began to appear that the Mille Lacs people were suffering from a "state of utter destitution." The topic was much debated. A report was presented to Governor Lucius F. Hubbard by Jonathan Simmons of Little Falls and Joseph Roberts of St. Paul. They reported that the rice crop had been a failure that year due to the logging dam on the Rum River. Because of a lack of snow, loggers were not going into the woods and were not providing a market for the hay produced by the band. Deer hunting was also curtailed by the lack of snow. Hubbard relayed these details to Indian agent C. P. Luse, asking for aid for the Mille Lacs people.[5]

In January 1884 Luse went with the missionary J. A. Gilfillan to Mille Lacs to investigate. Later in the month he stated that the reports were not true, but the Mille Lacs people were simply "not clothed quite so warmly as usual" because their annuities, which would have included cloth and clothing, had not been paid. The nonpayment was due to a dispute between the band and the agent, who had insisted on paying them half in money and half in goods, contrary to previous practice.[6]

Many local people disagreed with Luse's report. Several who had been on the reservation said that Luse and Gilfillan had spent very little time there and did not have their facts straight. These locals suggested that another reason for the problems at Mille Lacs was a change in the game laws that had initiated a fifteen-day deer hunting season, which the Ojibwe were expected to observe. There had been no snow during the season that year, which made it hard to track deer. In addition, the cranberry crop had failed and fish were scarce.[7]

As a result of this dispute, Luse wrote to Price in February 1884 suggesting that a special agent be appointed to investigate the matter. Governor Hubbard, in sending the various affidavits to Washington in February 1884, repeated the information about the rice crop and noted that in revenge for the flooding, band members tore out the dam. There was also more competition from whites on the reservation for the hay band members normally cut to sell to loggers. Altogether the failed rice and cranberry crops and the reduction in hay had limited band members' income. The lack of cash annuities combined with these factors had caused suffering on the reservation.[8]

Hubbard believed the band members were facing real distress. A US Indian inspector, Robert S. Gardner, who went on the reservation in late February, supported this assessment, stating that poor conditions, added to the lack of annuities, had caused suffering at Mille Lacs. He reported that "Agent Luse did not give this matter the proper and necessary investigation and attention that the gravity of the case required."[9]

Further help for the Mille Lacs people came in early March 1884, when Joseph Roberts went to Washington to lobby for them. He met with and submitted a letter to Congressman Olin Wellborn, chair of the House Committee on Indian Affairs. He also presented letters from Governor Hubbard about the suffering of the Mille Lacs Ojibwe and documentation about the cutting of timber and the sales of land through the Taylors Falls Land Office. Roberts summarized the treaty history of the Mille Lacs people and their actions in 1862. He explained that Mille Lacs leaders had asked him to go to Washington in 1863 but he had been unable to travel. On their return he learned that they had been asked to sell their homes but had refused. They said:

> We told the interpreter we did not come to sell our homes, we could not, we had no authority to trade or sell any part of our land. But he (the interpreter) said the great father did not want the lands of the good Indians, he did not want our land but if we would sign with all the Chippewas he (the great father) would give us back our land, at once which was done, and in the treaty read to us the great father said because we had always been his friends we were to keep our homes forever.[10]

To this Roberts added "and I will say now that the said Mille Lacs say and believe this to this day." They did not consider the document they signed in 1863 as a treaty. Since then, said Roberts, they were "constantly sending for me to explain to them why the white men are now trying and have tried three times previously to take the land that was given to them forever, and they are constantly after the Government of Minnesota for the same purpose."

The disagreement about the actual condition of the Mille Lacs Band and Roberts's lobbying influenced Congress to pursue an investigation of the Mille Lacs Indian Reservation. In April 1884 the House of Representatives began to look into the situation, first by passing a resolution asking the secretary of the Interior for a report on the status of the Mille Lacs Ojibwe and their lands and about any bona fide settlements there. The letter was referred to the commissioners of Indian Affairs and the General Land Office for their responses. Following up on a request from the secretary of the Interior, Commissioner of Indians Affairs Price sent Teller his own letter from 1882 and Teller's response to that letter.[11]

At the same time, Commissioner of the General Land Office McFarland wrote to Teller summarizing the actions of the Taylors Falls Land Office over the years, the reactions of officials in Washington, and his own interactions with Secretary Teller. He mentioned the reinstatement of the 1879 entries and the issuance of patents on seventy-eight entries, representing over six thousand acres. He noted that the remaining 207 entries "are in the course of adjustment, many of which are in conflict with claims of the Northern Pacific Railroad Company, under land-grant acts, to tracts embraced in said entries." The Northern Pacific Railroad had received a land grant in the 1860s allowing it to claim lands on odd-numbered sections within twenty miles of the railroad line, which was located along the Mississippi River to the west of the reservation. The railroad now claimed some of the lands on the reservation, arguing that at the time of the land grant the sections in question had been public land. McFarland stated dryly that he had "no information whether *bona fide* settlements have been made on the land entered so far or whether such settlements had been made upon said lands prior to the entry thereof. Soldiers' additional entries do not require settlement as a condition of entry." This policy made such entries especially useful to timber companies, assuming all other requirements were met by the claimant or overlooked by land officials.[12]

McFarland added that the Taylors Falls Land Office was now allowing new entries on the reservation lands. From November 1882 to March 31, 1884, forty Declaratory Statement filings for preemption entries were allowed. Eleven were canceled. Altogether entries for 4,034.35 acres had been allowed. In addition, in the same period, there were cash entries for over 603 acres and homestead entries covering over 4,860 acres. McFarland noted that, except for a letter of August 15, 1882, which reinstated the Sabin and Wilder entries, no orders or instructions had been issued from Washington to Taylors Falls allowing these entries. It appeared the Taylors Falls Land Office had been acting as before, taking the slightest sign from Washington as though it were a forthright instruction to open the reservation to entry. McFarland stated: "it would seem . . . that without waiting for instructions from this office in the premises and as previously ordered, said officers have been acting upon their own judgment." This approach was certainly in keeping with the policies pursued by the Taylors Falls Land Office over the years.[13]

After receiving the report from the secretary of the Interior and the commissioners, Congress passed a law on July 4, 1884 (actually a provision of the annual Indian Appropriation Act) stating that the lands acquired from the Mille Lacs and White Oak Point bands under the treaty proclaimed March 20, 1865 (the proclamation date of the Treaty of 1864) "shall not be patented or disposed of in any manner until further legislation by Congress." As a result of this law, no additional patents were issued for the Sabin and Wilder entries for several years. However, despite the law the Taylors Falls Land Office did not suspend the patenting and disposition of lands within the reservation.[14]

In all, just under 1,242 acres were patented between 1885 and 1888, mostly as a result of cash sales. It is not known under what authorization this action was taken. Although none of the Sabin–Wilder lands were included, Sabin, under his own name, claimed and received a patent for eighty acres in January 1885. The land was located just north of Shakopee Lake.

The beginnings of actual white settlement on the reservation can be traced to this period. A few individuals drawn to the region by lumbering interests sought to claim land. Among them was David H. Robbins, who selected land in section 28 of 43–27, near Neyaashing, the village of Shaboshkung's band. Robbins arrived because of his connection with logging. In testimony before the Court of Claims in 1909, Robbins stated that he came into the region in 1882, representing a Wisconsin bank and Senator William D. Washburn, to find land for lumbering purposes. Discovering that the best timberlands had all been taken, he apparently decided to remain as a settler. In a reminiscence published in 1907, Robbins claimed to have "taken out the first filing made by an actual settler." He explained that his entry was permitted because "although the local land office did not have any order to open, it reasonably concluded that if a senator [Sabin] could scrip half of it a common settler could have a hundred and sixty acre tract." Once Robbins's entry was filed, he said, by the next winter "a large majority of the lands were covered with homesteads and pre-emptions." As will be seen, this statement was an exaggeration.[15]

This shift in practice occurred in the 1882–83 period. Robbins toured the lake in 1882 and found only two actual settlers, located outside the reservation. He brought in supplies during the winter of 1882–83 and began erecting a house on the land he subsequently purchased. He may have made a filing in the land office during this winter, although the tract book for reservation lands in the north part of Kathio Township (43–27) shows his homestead entry in section 28 on May 25, 1883, around the same period when patents were being issued for the Sabin–Wilder lands.[16]

Robbins stated that his arrival was the first information received by band members "that the government had opened the land to settlement." Robbins said that members of Ma'iingaans's band claimed "this whole point embracing the old town of Kathio." Men of the band confronted Robbins and two others, James Lochren and Tim Davis, who were helping him build his log house. The Ojibwe men asked to see Robbins's filing papers, which Robbins showed them. In response the band members made him understand that they would not allow him or any other white man to erect a house. Robbins and the two men left, after which band members were said to have burned the lumber Robbins had brought with him.

Robbins recalled that he went to Taylors Falls to speak with the officials in the land office. They "could not, or would not, give me any information in relation to how the title of the lands lay, except to say that the Indians had sold the land, received their pay and that the lands belonged to the government and were opened to entry." Then, for some reason, Robbins went to St. Paul to meet with Amherst H. Wilder. Perhaps he was referred to Wilder by the land office.

According to Robbins Wilder explained that he had "furnished the scrip for Sabin to enter the lands but denied knowing anything of the status of the Indians' claim to those lands." From this conversation and from what Robbins learned later he believed—erroneously, of course—that Wilder was "entirely ignorant of the way Sabin had acquired the land, but he said he [Wilder] would communicate with Sabin, who was in Washington, and have him notify the authorities as to the state of affairs." Wilder then hired Robbins to look after the lands he and Sabin owned at Mille Lacs.

Having been "assured" and having satisfied himself that "the Indians were wrong and that the government expected me to take possession of my claim and conform to the land laws," Robbins returned to the lake. He decided to reach his claim by boat, traveling up a portion of the Rum River and through the lower lakes. On the shore of Lake Onamia he encountered Shaboshkung and members of his band. When he informed Shaboshkung that he intended to return to the land he was claiming, the leader explained that he could not go there and would be harmed if he did. Robbins asked if he could stay on what would later be called Robbins or Rainbow Island, just off what was later called Indian Point, until an agent he believed would be coming from Washington arrived.

Robbins stayed on the island for seven weeks—during which he was subjected to some harassment by young men of Neyaashing, who fired their rifles at his tent from shore—until the arrival of Special Agent John Wright, clearly at the time of Wright's report on the reservation, which suggests these events occurred in the spring of 1883. Wright was accompanied by "the Indian agent and a squad of Indian police with an order from the Indian department to remove any whites he found occupying the reservation." However, when Robbins showed the men his homestead papers, Wright supposedly said "that superseded his authority. He said that the government officers, having taken my money for this land, were in honor bound to protect me."

Robbins's reporting suggests that Wright held the view that decisions of the Land Office in allowing land entries on the reservation superseded any attempt by the Indian Office to prevent the alienation of reservation lands. Wright is said to have stated that the Indian Office in Washington was unaware that any filings had been allowed. He called the band members together. According to Robbins, a council involving 1,500 Indians was held at the outlet for seven days, undoubtedly an exaggeration: "[Wright] finally prevailed upon them to agree to let the matter rest where it was until he could return to Washington and correct an affair which he assured them was all a mistake; that all settlers would be removed by the government."

Ma'iingaans (Maheengaunce), who claimed the land on which Robbins had filed, refused to allow him to occupy it. Instead Robbins worked out an arrangement that allowed him to live on the island, which he did for the next two years. During that time he worked for Wilder, "running lines for the division of his lands from vacant lands throughout the four townships." According to Robbins's testimony in the Court of Claims case, another reason for his examination of Wilder's land had to do with a dispute between Wilder and the county over $30,000 due in taxes on his timberlands. This detail may explain why much of the Sabin–Wilder lands were consistently listed as tax delinquent in county tax books in the 1880s, though there is no evidence that any of them were actually sold for back taxes during this period. It is not known if or when Sabin or Wilder paid the taxes on these lands.[17]

Among other things, Robbins examined the lands and compiled estimates of the timber on them. He had no trouble with band members, perhaps because they did not understand "the actual damage I was doing to them." In fact, while examining Wilder's lands he was also "noting locations to file settlers upon wherever Wilder had no script laid and I did file afterwards a large number upon these lands when they were open to entry again."

Robbins stated that during this period, for two years—roughly 1883 to 1885—no other white man who had a land claim in what would become Kathio Township (42–27 and 43–27), except Byron Carlton, whose claim was located south of Shakopee Lake adjacent to Warren Lake, attempted to live on his land claim on the reservation. A number of claimants "would come up and fish for a day or two at a time" from their actual homes elsewhere. For weeks at a stretch Robbins saw no sign of a white man.

A document in federal records shows that in May 1884 Robbins wrote to the commissioner of Indian Affairs to complain that he had lost $500 in hay and other crops to theft and fire. He alleged that band members admitted "they had burnt my hay but claimed they have done so to keep me from selling it to lumbermen and that they considered it was on their own land." Robbins claimed he had cut the hay "on my homestead." He also stated that "four tepes [sic] of them come and squat down on my clearing with every indication of staying all summer." Robbins requested that the band members be told "they must keep off of the settlers lands [there is] plenty of lands for them to occupy outside." Robbins did not receive a patent for these lands until March 1892.[18]

At this time Robbins may have hoped that further action in Washington would provide a forthright opening of the reservation and removal of the Ojibwe. Instead, as discussed above, Congress passed a law on July 4, 1884, that prohibited the patenting or disposal of lands in the reservation until it enacted further legislation.

This legislation prevented any action on the Sabin–Wilder land claims—one of several problems that plagued the business relationship of the two men beginning in 1884. In January of that year a company Sabin had organized, Northwestern Car and Manufacturing of Stillwater, Minnesota, began to have financial problems. The company, in which Wilder had invested, built railway cars inside the walls of the Stillwater State Prison, using prison labor. In January 1884 the four-story, three-hundred-foot-long factory burned to the ground, putting six hundred men out of work. Throughout the year and for many years thereafter, the company was burdened with debt, attributed by some to Sabin's bad management. The company reorganized in 1887 as Minnesota Thresher Manufacturing, which continued in operation until 1901. During the 1880s and until Wilder's death in 1894, Sabin and Wilder appear to have been at odds over the company's fortunes. It would appear that the failure of this business may have led Sabin to try even harder to fulfill the plans for the 1879 land entries on the Mille Lacs Reservation.[19]

Meanwhile, on the reservation, David H. Robbins made his own peace with band members at the site of his claim. He brought more lumber during the winter of 1884–85 and was allowed to build on his claim, which he attributes to "feeding the old chief well." Robbins claimed to have erected "the first frame house ever built at the lake, building it out on the point of land running into the lake on section 28, lot 1 of my homestead"—in other words, in the southeast corner of section 28, at the base of the south side of Indian Point.

For the next few years, as Robbins put it, "all land matters lay dormant" regarding federal policy toward parcels on the Mille Lacs Reservation.

> The writer, with others, made application to prove up, but our applications were turned down to await the action of congress. But there were numerous commissioners and special agents coming and going constantly. The Indian agents would tell the Indians the settlers were stealing their lands, and to make it as uncomfortable as possible without using violence that the government would soon remove us. Then would come a special agent from the general land office and he would tell the settlers they were all right, to keep cool and the government would soon remove the Indians. In fact their instructions were so at variance with one another that the Indian department could not have known what the land department was doing and vice versa.[20]

Confusion about government policy extended to the treatment of timber on the reservation. In November 1884 Milton Peden, special timber agent with the General Land Office in St. Cloud, wrote to Commissioner of the General Land Office Noah McFarland to say that he had investigated around one to two million feet of white and Norway pine blown down by a storm in the summer of 1883. The storm passed through the Mille Lacs Reservation in sections 11, 13, and 14 of 42–26, just east of Mozomonie Point, and extending to sections 17 and 18 of 42–25, around the present site of Wahkon. In doing his work, Peden was accompanied by H. A. Pemberton, a trader in the area of the reservation who was apparently interested in cutting the timber but also acted as an interpreter.[21]

During their investigations they stayed at the cabin of a chief named "Neg wase Natee," possibly one of the chiefs named Negwanebi (No. 1).

The next morning a group of Ojibwe appeared and informed them that a council had been held the previous night and had determined that no one should be permitted to cut timber without "first guaranteeing to them that they should receive the value of the same, and that they would burn his camp and kill his teams if he undertook to cut the timber." Through Pemberton the people informed Peden that the timber belonged to them. In reply Peden told them that since they had sold their land they could have no claim upon the timber, "but they were inexorable and would listen to no argument in the case." Peden said it was a pity for the timber to "lay there and rot, but there is no one who would undertake to handle it while the Indians remain in their present frame of mind."

Given the apparent demand for timber on the reservation, band members now made attempts to sell the timber directly, themselves. Apparently they viewed this activity as a way to relieve pressure to remove them from their reservation. In March 1885 a group of band leaders wrote to the secretary of the Interior asserting their wish to cut the timber themselves. They wished the commissioner's opinion "as regards our right to do so in accordance with our treaty to let our young men do the manual labor and to have a good and trusty white man to conduct our business." They reminded the secretary that their reservation was surrounded by white settlers, that the lumbermen had built a dam flooding their rice beds, and that their annuities were running out. It is not known how the secretary responded to this proposition, though at this time tribes were prevented by federal law from selling their own timber.[22]

In August 1885 newspaper editor and lawyer Gus Beaulieu wrote of another scheme to cut the fallen timber at Mille Lacs, employing members of the reservation to be paid in goods, provisions, farming implements, cattle, and other stock. Clearly this arrangement would have involved paying the government rather than the band members for the timber.[23]

Another special agent, this time from the Department of Justice, John T. Wallace, visited with Mille Lacs leaders at Brainerd in October 1885 about prosecuting liquor dealers who sold spirits to band members. Band leaders discussed the effects alcohol had on them, but they also mentioned the lack of money and the potential contribution that harvesting the timber at Mille Lacs would make toward improving their condition. Paradoxically, Wallace drew the conclusion that the resources of the reservation and the surrounding areas were one of the reasons for the harmful effects of liquor on band members. In other words, he reasoned that the Mille Lacs Band was much too prosperous for its own good.[24]

Wallace noted: "these Indians obtained large amounts of money from what nature has placed within their reach, such as blueberries, cranberries, fish, game and venison, mink, muskrat and otter, [*sic*] pelts, maple sugar and ginseng roots, and many of the young men are experts in running logs to the saw-mills. The Indians have more money that the white settlers." But, claimed Wallace, they spent "the greater portion of all their income" on whiskey.

Although no changes had been made in the government's policy toward the Mille Lacs Reservation since 1884, individuals seeking to enter the reservation continued to harass band members. Joseph Roberts in 1886 wrote to W. S. Holman, a member of Congress in Washington, about the situation. Roberts, who had met Holman during an 1884 trip to Washington, told him that the Mille Lacs band members' troubles were the same as before: whites were entering the reservation, attempting to preempt land, and spreading rumors that the band was to be moved without its consent. Roberts said: "The parties going on the reservation are the agents and employees of a lot of land jobbers and speculators who tell the Indians they have no right on the reservation and tell them they must get off and if they don't go peacefully, that they, the Whites, will put them off by force. The result is that the poor Indians are nearly frightened to death, and I hardly know what to advise them."[25]

Roberts wrote that if the intention was to allow the band to be driven off the reservation and "robbed of their homes the government at least ought to deal fairly enough with them by sending for some of their chiefs and making some kind of satisfactory arrangements."

Later that month band leaders wrote to Minnesota governor Lucius F. Hubbard stating that fifteen or twenty white men had come onto the reservation and settled within the month and had built houses "and tell us that we have nothing more to do with our Reserve." They had heard that "parts of our land has been taken up and patents given for same." They now wished to "inform the President and the Indian Commissioner that we protest against all this and ask that all this be cancelled and leave us in peace." For the sake of quiet they saw the best solution would be to sell the pine. The money could be used to build houses and educate their children. They had always lived in harmony with whites and would like to continue to do so, but many of the whites seemed intent on making trouble for them. They asked that something be done as soon as possible.[26]

Hubbard wrote a letter in support of the Mille Lacs Band to the commissioner of Indian Affairs the next month, stating: "The repeated assurance that has been made these people that they will not be disturbed in the enjoyment of their rights as guaranteed by the treaty to which reference is made in their communication to me, and that they will not be removed from the reservation they have occupied so long without their consent, are being disregarded in their view, by the occupation of lands within their reserve and the appropriation of the timber growing thereon, by parties whom they name and many others who have recently located among them."[27]

Hubbard thought it would be good for the band to move to White Earth but not without the band's consent and not until some arrangement had been made by which "their property rights upon their reservation may be disposed of for their benefit." Until then "it seems to me clearly the duty of the government to protect these rights from despoliation." Hubbard gave the letter to Joseph Roberts, who again went to Washington to lobby for the Mille Lacs people.

Meanwhile, the leader Ma'iingaans reported that a white man named Robinson was putting up claim shanties "in close proximity to the Indian wigwams, with a view of preempting land in case of removal of these Indians to White Earth." This person may have been Robinson P. Briggs, who would later receive a patent for land near Isle, or more likely, David H. Robbins, who was already claiming land in 43–27. Reporting to Commissioner of Indian Affairs John D. C. Atkins, Indian agent Timothy J. Sheehan stated that "fears are entertained that excesses may be committed on account of the action taken in erecting these shanties."[28]

CHAPTER 13

The Government Breaks No Treaties

A new attempt was made to get the Mille Lacs Band to consent to remove from their reservation in 1886, when the Northwest Indian Commission— including John Wright, the same special agent who had visited there in 1883; Episcopal bishop Henry B. Whipple; and Charles F. Larrabee—came to Minnesota to negotiate with various Ojibwe bands to resolve claims and make any changes in their reservations "deemed desirable by said Indians and the Secretary of the Interior," subject to ratification by Congress. The commission came to the Mille Lacs Reservation on October 9, 1886, meeting with band leaders at the outlet of the Rum River. Whipple was unable to attend this first meeting.[1]

David Robbins later recalled that the meeting took place "on what was known then as Spirit point on the hill now occupied by the hotel near the outlet." He said, in his typically derogatory description of the event: "It was then almost covered with Indian graves from which I supposed it derived its name. There was a perfect mass of boxes or hen coops and eleven hundred indians assembled to hear the good words spoken that the good Father at Washington had delegated three commissioners to tell them. They presented a very gaudy appearance, as many of them wore red blankets. The boxes were all well occupied and all looked very solemn. It was certainly a graveyard confab. It lasted a week and as usual a lot of fine promises were made them—never to be kept."[2]

Records of the commission meetings show that two gatherings occurred on October 9 and October 11, 1886. Larrabee began the first meeting by stating that the band had ceded its reservation to the United States almost twenty-five years before, "with the understanding, however, that you were not to be compelled to remove so long as you did not molest or interfere with the persons or property of the whites." Larrabee explained that this was "all the rights you have in this land—a very feeble tenure." He denied that they had any "actual ownership in the soil," despite what some band members may have claimed. Nonetheless, the Indian Office

had "upheld you in the right of occupancy during good behavior, diffi-
cult as it has been." Larrabee did not mention that the many failures of the
Indian Office to protect this right of occupancy were the only reason the
Mille Lacs Band could be said to have "a very feeble tenure."[3]

He and Wright spoke about the benefits of removal to White Earth,
about what a fine piece of territory the reservation there was, with plenty
of good land, wild rice, and fish, how prosperous they would become if
they removed there, how desirable it would be for them to be reunited
with others of the Ojibwe nation. On the other hand, if they remained at
Mille Lacs, "nothing can be done for you." If "greater poverty or misfor-
tune" ever befell them at Mille Lacs, the Great Father would simply have
to remind them that they had been offered a good opportunity at White
Earth and had turned it down.

Wright acknowledged that the Mille Lacs people had not forfeited their
rights through any overt act, but he insisted that "you know that your
reservation has been sold and the title passed to the United States. It has
been opened to settlers and many patents have been issued to white men."
In fact, this statement may be the first official, documented notification
the Mille Lacs Band received that the reservation had been opened to
settlement, although it is unclear under what authority it was made and
whether it was actually the case at this time. As noted, Robbins, describing the earlier meeting with Wright, suggested that band members were
not told at that time that the reservation had been opened to settlement,
although Robbins suggested that Wright believed then that actions of the
Land Office might supersede those of the Indian Office. In the future,
Wright said, people would continue to "raise false reports and give you
much trouble. Already reports have been sent to Washington, charging
you with evil doing, although, in justice, I ought to say that investigation
has found that they were not strictly true. A lie will travel 5 miles while
truth is putting on its moccasins. Your situation will be very unpleasant, to
say the least. I can understand how the old men hate to leave this beautiful
lake, but if you can better your children, it is but a small sacrifice to make."

Shaboshkung rose to speak, asking for the next day, Sunday, as an opportunity to study the proposal and to meet again on Monday, October 11.
After the meeting Nathan Richardson of Little Falls asked to see the proposed agreement in preparation to advise band members. The *Little Falls
Transcript* reported on October 8, 1886, that Richardson had been asked,
with other Little Falls leaders, to attend the meetings and he went "to
try and prevent the Indians from getting the worst of the agreement." In

response to Richardson's request Larrabee replied that he could have no dealings with Richardson on an official basis since Richardson was not a recognized agent or attorney of the band members.

At the Monday meeting the Mille Lacs leaders strongly resisted offers for their removal to White Earth. Shaboshkung said that the Mille Lacs people wished to stay where they were: "They are satisfied to stay here where they have lived in poverty. We have pity for ourselves and for our dead, and wish not to leave them. I wish rather that my bones shall bleach out on the shores of this lake." They had been told that they would be allowed to stay a thousand years if they wished. They had kept "their part of the contract to live in peace with the whites," making "their living quietly on their lands." He wondered: "Is the one thousand years up that the Great Father sent you here?"

Endaso-giizhig (also Ayndusokeshig), the son of Monzomonay, reiterated, speaking for the young men: "We will not go anywhere. This is why we reserve this land to make a living on. We shall never go anywhere else. We reserve this for this purpose and we are carefully taking care of our land. We think a good deal of this indeed, and shall never leave it. We do not wish anybody to trouble us on our land."

Wright responded testily that he was surprised to hear them say that "God placed you here and that the land is yours. Then why did you sell it? The records show that you did and got your pay all but Shaw-bosh-kung's land. The records say so, and as you know the treaty said you might remain during good conduct, and you have been permitted to remain twenty-five years." He denied that they had been promised to be allowed to stay one thousand years—and he insisted that "the Government never breaks treaties."

Here followed a discussion about whether the reservation had been sold or ceded and what exactly that meant. The band leaders held to the position that they had a right to remain and did not believe that the land could be sold out from under them. They were incredulous at the possibility that the document signed in 1863 could be interpreted this way.

The government agents insisted that the land had been sold and that any provisions about the right to remain there under good conduct essentially meant very little, an admission either that the treaty had been a lie or that the government was simply breaking it. Yet, Larrabee asserted that the treaty was "plain and to the point." He said they were "well aware of the difficulties the Indian Office have had in protecting you against the encroachments of the whites on account of your feeble tenure." The Indian

Office had done its best to protect them, "to keep [them] in peaceable possession." Why had the office and its representatives been unsuccessful? He did not explain, stating only that it was now "too late to attempt anything for your advancement here." Their only hope was to remove to White Earth.

The band leaders continued to be puzzled by the commissioners' assertions. They could not believe that they could be asked to leave Mille Lacs if they had not violated the terms of the treaty. The commissioners insisted that this should not have been a surprise to them. Larrabee commented: "you know from correspondence with the Indian Office and from numerous inspectors, special agents, and other friends who have visited with you and talked about it, that the status of your land is just what I have stated it to be." Their only right to the reservation was to stay there during good behavior, nothing more. There was no reference to the proposals of George Chapman and Wright himself in 1882 and 1883 to set aside lands for the use of the band and the frequent discussions about removing illegal settlers from the reservation.

In response Shaboshkung made clear what the record shows, that the implications the commissioners drew from the treaties were not at all what band members had learned from their interactions with the Indian Office. Further, Special Agent Chapman in 1882 and Wright himself had not made this clear: "Inspector Chapman came here and played checkers with that man [pointing to one of the Indians] all the time he was here. Special Agent Wright sat over there on that point yonder and cooked and ate his meals."

Toward the end of the meeting, Wright, faced with continuing questions about the cession of the reservation, asked, "Why did the Government issue so many patents on your reservation, if it did not belong to the Government?" It was a good question with many answers that have been discussed in this narrative. And once again it raised the question of whether the decisions of the Land Office could supersede those of the Indian Office and the treaty itself, but Wright did not supply answers, any more than he had done, according to Robbins, in 1883. The meeting ended when Kegwedosay gave the final refusal to accept the offer and the band leaders and commissioners politely shook hands, "the Indians taking to their canoes."

A little less than a month later the commissioners, now with Bishop Whipple present, again called the band leaders together. The commissioners were unhappy with the way the previous meeting had gone. The report describing the actions of the commission asserted that the band leaders had stubbornly refused to accept the offer made to them. They denied they had ever ceded their reservation and said they would never move. The commissioners stated that the only possible explanation could be that they "had been tampered with before our arrival. . . . They had received their lessons from outside and had committed them to heart." The commissioners seemingly could not imagine that the band may have simply been repeating what they remembered of their rights under the treaties they had signed with the United States.[4]

Hearing of the band's refusal, the secretary of the Interior asked the commissioners to try again. This time the meeting took place at the farm of Hans Jebe, twenty-four miles east of Brainerd, just north of the reservation on the west side of the lake. Every possible argument was tried again and a further offer of $25,000 was made to the band to give up the same right of occupancy the commissioners had seemed to find so tenuous at their previous meetings. As before, the commissioners stated that band members "were determined not to yield their consent." Meetings took place on November 3, 4, and 5, 1886. On the last day Shaboshkung mentioned his own 640-acre tract, given under the Treaty of 1855, suggesting that if deprived of any of the rest of the reservation he would fall back on that land. No matter what else happened and what other band members did, he did not wish to sell his own land to the government.[5]

> Let me live in peace on my own land. I ask that of you in pity: just let me live here on my own land. I wish to look at myself on that land this winter and see how I will do. I am going to carry out this view till spring and see what I can do there this winter. If I had been alone I think I would have complied with your request; for a month or so, perhaps longer. I say so that the Great Father, the Commissioner of Indian Affairs, and the law-makers may know what I say. I want to stay here with my sons. I wish to ask you one thing. I have your promise of one ax, one spade, one plow, one rake, one scythe, &c. I do not think there would be room enough for every child in one family to put their hands on one ax. There are just three articles I have in my garden, and the children grab the articles from each other when they want to use them. I have been fifty years in gardening and digging the ground up with my hands and nails, and Still I am making enough to live upon. I am very old, as you can see, but I am not afraid that I shall die of starvation. The traders take

care of me. I purchase my flour, tea, sugar, and pork from the traders in the towns about here, and also what agricultural implements
I need. I do not depend upon anybody else, and for that reason I ask
you in mercy to allow me to sit here on my land.

The commission left to continue its work. In words that that were contradicted in part by Shaboshkung's speech, they condescendingly stated in
their report that they believed the people who resided at Mille Lacs were
"an idle, shiftless, vagabond set. They have no fixed habitations anywhere,
and but for the fish with which the lake abounds, their women and children would starve to death. With the exception of three or four log shanties there is not a house on the reservation. They live, summer and winter,
in small and poorly constructed bark wigwams." When furs were abundant they were comfortable wearing them, but as it was now they must
suffer "intensely for many months of the year." Women and children lived
in a state of "absolute barbarism, half starved, without shelter from the
cold" and without enough clothing to cover their nakedness. These were
bitter words flavored no doubt by the deep frustration of not reaching
the agreement the commissioners desired, to force the Mille Lacs people
to move to White Earth against their own will.[6]

CHAPTER 14

The White Trespassers

After the last meeting of the Northwest Indian Commission at Mille Lacs, the *St. Paul Pioneer Press* reported about the band's refusal of the commission's offer. Noting that band members lived by hunting, gathering, and selling cranberries, it stated that the people who purchased the berries and who sold the Ojibwe whiskey were "believed to be the persons who have influenced the Indians to resist the overtures of the commission."[1]

Although it is highly unlikely that band members were actually induced to take the position they did by those with whom they traded, some with whom they did business did encourage them to continue to assert their belief in their rights under the Treaty of 1863. Nathan Richardson's appearance was a prime example of the continuing role played by the people of Little Falls. Jonathan Simmons, who had also been invited to appear at the commission meetings but had been unable to, purchased 250 saddles of venison from band members in December 1886, as well as several hundred partridge and a large number of furs. Such trade was a prime demonstration of the continuing possibilities of hunting and gathering in the Mille Lacs region, belying the commissioners' words about the need for band members to remove to White Earth to improve their circumstances.[2]

Band members found other ways to raise money. While the Mille Lacs people were not permitted to sell the timber on reservation land for their own benefit, it was reported in late 1886 that Shaboshkung had made a contract with James Lochren—the same James Lochren who had helped David H. Robbins in his initial effort to build a cabin in 1883—to cut the pine timber on lands in sections 27 and 28 of 43–27. Despite the fact that this land had been set aside for the Mille Lacs leader, Reuben F. McClellan of Princeton wrote to the secretary of the Interior in December 1886 that "understanding that the disposal of these lands was restricted by the Act of July 4th 1884 have thought best that your department have knowledge of this matter." He stated that active preparations were underway to cut and dispose of the timber during the winter. The author of the letter was a cash purchaser, in March 1883, of 144.5 acres of land in section 10 of 42–25, just west of present-day Isle. Despite the Act of July 4, 1884, he received his patent for the land in March 1886. Other evidence suggests that Shaboshkung did sell some timber for $2,000 during the winter of 1886–87.[3]

The provision preventing disposal of lands on the reservation convinced no one that such restrictions would remain permanent, especially considering the tone the commissioners took in the fall of 1886. A few settlers came onto the reservation, locating themselves in close proximity to Indian communities. They seemed surprised at the hostile reaction they got. Earl Tucker, a logging company employee who eventually obtained a patent for lands in section 33 of 43–27, in the area north of the outlet of the Rum River on Mille Lacs Lake, wrote a letter full of misspellings, in March 1887, stating that he had

> a good substanshall house erected here on my claim at the Lake
> and the Chief Shaw Bosh King come and ordered me to [leave] and
> [declared] he would burn my buildings. I expect he will do so the
> first time I leive. I haft to leive my claim sometime for too or three
> weeks at a time to make a living. I was going cross the Lake to drive
> and will be obliged to be goin several weeks when I will no doubt
> he will burn it as it is the third or fourth one he has destroyed in the
> last three years.[4]

Other settlers, led by David H. Robbins, put together a petition to White Earth Indian agent Timothy Sheehan asking for a stop to "harrising & pilfering" by the Indians. They stated that "the Government gave us these preemptions & homesteads and expect us to comply with the laws and live here we have waited for the Government to settle this land title for four years p[ati]ently but our keeping quite seams to only incite those Indians to a more radical [illegible] system of pilferings and abuse." They stated that Shaboshkung and Ma'iingaans had been going around to the settlers to tell them to leave and stating that they intended to burn them out in the spring. The settlers organized for their own protection and told the chiefs that they would kill the first Indian who molested their property.[5]

Despite the statements by these individuals, it appears that none of them had actually obtained title to the land from the federal government. Seven of the twelve men who signed the petition are identifiable as subsequent recipients of patents for land on the reservation, but none of them had yet received patents for their land—and would not until 1891 or later.

At the time of the petition, their rights to the land they claimed depended directly on changes in government policy toward the reservation.[6]

After receiving the petition, Agent Sheehan sent it to the commissioner of Indian Affairs, saying that he intended to investigate. What results came of this investigation are uncertain. Meanwhile, John Wallace, special agent of the Justice Department, continued to investigate the liquor traffic. His report to the attorney general in Washington at the end of April noted that the Mille Lacs Band was located on the south shore of the lake on lands "that have been sought after by white people for many years, and notwithstanding the many attempts to open this Reservation to settlement by the white people the Government has allowed the Indians to retain their title."[7]

Wallace said that a number of white men had located claims on the reservation and were reported to keep whiskey "and often employ Indians to cut and save hay, and pay the Indians with whiskey." Wallace asked that Agent Sheehan be instructed to remove "these white trespassers" from the reservation, which would help suppress the whiskey traffic. Wallace was apparently unaware that the government had already permitted some "trespassers" to obtain title to reservation lands, or that his words contradicted those of the members of the Northwest Indian Commission that visited the Mille Lacs Reservation in 1886.

In January 1888 Henry Rice's brother, Edmund Rice, who was a congressman from Minnesota, wrote to the Indian Office enclosing a petition from the Mille Lacs leaders. It repeated the history of the Mille Lacs Band and their support of whites in 1862. It noted that in order to survive if removed to White Earth, they would have to make a great change in their lives and depend on charity. The abundance of Mille Lacs included plenty of fish, wild rice, maple sugar, game, and cranberries. Band members could easily get work with lumbermen and had a good market for their hay. White Earth had none of these benefits. The Mille Lacs people were firm in their determination to remain at Mille Lacs. They had been told that they had ceded their reservation and could occupy the reservation only during good behavior, but they never intentionally ceded the reservation, and they asked the president to give them a small piece of land so they could remain. They would take allotments from the land on the reservation. In the meantime, they mentioned the squatters, the problems caused by the dam, and that whites were cutting the best hay on the reservation. Whites were committing depredations and cutting timber. Band members asked the government for help.[8]

In a letter written at the same time, Jonathan Simmons of Little Falls supported these requests. He said the Mille Lacs leaders were again requesting the opportunity to go to Washington to settle their affairs. He repeated the story of the actions of the Mille Lacs Band in 1862. He noted that the band members continued to fear they would be moved to White Earth without their consent: "White men are cutting timber on the reservation and squatters are taking claims all around them and on the very lands they are living on, and the Indians report that in several instances the squatters (white men) are cutting their choicest maple trees, claiming that they are doing this for the purpose of opening farms, but this we know is not so and it looks to me as if it is being done for the purpose of annoying the Indians and to get their pine."[9]

CHAPTER 15

A Mouthful Here and a Mouthful There

In January 1888 Minnesota congressional representative Knute Nelson introduced a bill designed to effect changes in the boundaries of the Red Lake Indian Reservation. Over the course of the next two years the bill was broadened to cover all other bands of Ojibwe in Minnesota. As finally passed in December 1888, the act provided for the removal of Ojibwe throughout the state, except those at Red Lake, to White Earth, except that any Indians residing on any of the reservations could take allotments on the reservations where they lived, instead of going to White Earth.

Such a provision, if carried out completely and fairly, would have allowed Mille Lacs band members to obtain title to considerable portions of the Mille Lacs Reservation. The main difficulty for the Mille Lacs people lay in another provision of the bill, one credited to Senator Dwight Sabin, in Section 6, stating that "nothing in this act shall be held to authorize the sale or other disposal under its provisions of any tract upon which there is a subsisting, valid, preemption or homestead entry, but such entry shall be proceeded with under the regulations and decisions in force at the date of its allowance, and if found regular and valid, patents shall issue thereon." David Robbins suggested that the provision was not in initial versions of the bill as passed by the House of Representatives through Nelson's efforts. In the Senate, however, the bill "metamorphosed to suit Senator Sabin," Robbins wrote, and "That cooked the goose." All of Sabin's entries as well as those of some later settlers, including Robbins himself, were protected under the provision.[1]

Sabin's involvement in the passage of the Nelson Act was discussed by William W. Folwell in his history of the state. Folwell noted that the bill, originally passed by the House on March 8, 1888, was later altered by the Senate. A complete substitute was introduced by the Senate Committee on Indian Affairs on October 3, 1888. Folwell wrote that the bill was the result of consultations with lumbermen in the West who had no interest in the matter but who were invited to comment because of their expertise.

Part of the bill had been "mapped out" by them. Citing the *Congressional Record*, Folwell wrote that Senator Henry Dawes of Massachusetts said in debate that Dwight Sabin had "the bill in charge"; but Sabin insisted that Dawes was the author of the bill. One way or another, Section 6 had Sabin's fingerprints all over it. It clearly benefited him directly.[2]

The bill passed the Senate and went to a conference committee in October. By December 21 the conference committee report had been approved by both House and Senate. The bill was passed on January 14, 1889, and went to the president for his signature. Interestingly, at this time Dwight Sabin was up for reelection to the Senate. His opponent was William D. Washburn, one of his rivals in the lumbering business. Sabin and those supporting him were heavily lobbying state legislators to give him another term as senator. A later investigation took place into charges of bribery on both sides. One of those giving testimony, a legislator named J. W. Underwood, stated that a member of the House had come to him and told him that there was "a deal to get Mr. Sabin elected to the United States Senate." A "syndicate," said Underwood, or "several men associated together" seeking "to get the pine land on the Red Lake Indian Reservation," wanted to offer him $2,000 or a certain percent of the Red Lake pineland free after Sabin "got the bill through Congress and these parties had secured the land." The idea, apparently, was that a man named Buckman would be appointed to be surveyor general. He would manipulate the survey to affect the valuation placed on the timber so that it could be obtained "without costing too much." Underwood was offered the opportunity to go to a meeting at the home of T. B. Walker, the Minneapolis lumberman involved in obtaining powers of attorney used for the soldiers' additional homesteads at Mille Lacs in 1879, where Underwood would be able to get the money.[3]

The bill in question may have been the Nelson Act—which had just been signed by the president—although it is apparent that the important part of the scheme outlined was not in the passage of the act but in getting the appointment of the right person to a key position. Unfortunately for Sabin, he lost out to Washburn in the Minnesota legislature on January 17, 1889. Nonetheless, Section 6 of the Nelson Act would do its work for his benefit.

It is unclear at what point Mille Lacs band members became aware of the effect the Nelson Act could have on them. During 1889 band members faced continued pressure from lumbermen and settlers seeking to make use of the Mille Lacs Reservation. On March 15 a petition was sent by thirty individuals—including David H. Robbins—claiming to represent "the majority of those interested in the Mille Lacs Indian Reservation—so called—in said county, by having bone-fide entries in said reservation . . . living and residing upon the same." Predictably, they claimed many depredations had been committed by the Mille Lacs Indians, amounting to a value of over $25,000. Over twenty settlers' houses had been broken into. Overt acts of violence had taken place. Most of the complainants had "resided here for five years" and believed the Indian agent at White Earth would not investigate properly since, in the past, he had always "endorsed the denial of said Indians, accepting their denial for the truth." They asked for an investigation as soon as possible.[4]

Relations between the settlers and the Ojibwe on the reservation deteriorated badly in the spring of 1889. From newspaper accounts of the period it is impossible to say precisely what occurred in these incidents. The *St. Paul Pioneer Press* in a series of articles spread false rumors that Mille Lacs band members were planning to drive all whites from the region in a "general uprising" and that as many as eighteen settlers had been killed. In fact only one man was injured, a settler named Sven Magnuson. Kegwedosay's son Wadena was accused of having shot Magnuson, though a jury in September 1889 acquitted him of the charge. Magnuson survived the shooting.[5]

As was often the case in articles about Indian people, the newspapers told exaggerated stories of the role of liquor in the conflicts. In the original reporting, the *St. Paul Pioneer Press*, under the headlines "A Redskin Menace," "Indian Murderers," and "Drunken Red Men," blamed liquor for the violence said to have been committed; paradoxically, it later credited the use of liquor for the fact that these things had not actually occurred. In addition, the newspaper acknowledged the fact that band members were dissatisfied about the settlement of whites on their reservation. It also mentioned band members' fears that whites were planning to build a canal from the lake across the reservation, intended to bypass the ricing lakes on the Upper Rum River. Band members were also fearful when, as in the 1855 incidents, troops were called to go to Mille Lacs to bring about peace, this time 117 men in three companies of infantry from Fort Snelling.[6]

Aside from gathering information it is unclear what the troops accomplished on their visit to Mille Lacs. While there is no record of actions taken by the troops against band members, the settlers greeted their arrival "as occupants of a besieged fort might welcome reinforcements," so it may be that the soldiers' presence made clear to band members that the

US government was willing to back the rights of illegal squatters over the rights of band members to reservation lands.

Accounts of the 1889 incidents provide additional information on the locations of particular villages of Mille Lacs band members. A report in the *St. Paul Pioneer Press* on June 16, 1889, mentioned villages of about six hundred located on the Knife and Snake Rivers southeast of the lake, in addition noting that "the main body of the Indians at the village on Mosomeny bay [the bay at Cove enclosed by Mozomonie Point] number 300," a figure slightly higher than the total given in 1881 of members of the three bands associated with this area of the lakeshore. The newspaper mentioned Wadena and other band leaders from this region, including his father, Kegwedosay, and Monzomonay, who was said to have taken a conciliatory role in the events. It also reported that there were about sixty band members camped on an island about eighty rods from a "ranch" inhabited by two brothers named Briggs—signers of the petition submitted earlier in the year—in the southeast shore of the lake. Later records suggest this ranch was in the area of Wahkon. However, the newspaper report stated that "the real trouble" was on the southwest shore of the lake around present-day Cove. According to the report, the eighteen feared dead in early reports had been whites who had settled in that area and simply decided to leave after the talk of a general uprising had started.[7]

Special Agent Robert Gardner of the Indian Office—who had been at Mille Lacs in 1884 to assess the condition of the band—returned to investigate. He reported to Commissioner of Indian Affairs John Oberly that Wadena had not intended to shoot Magnuson, but rather Andrew Berg, a Swedish American who had settled on lands in section 15 of 42–26, at the site of the Mozomonie Point village. Gardner said this spot was where "these Indians for 50 or more years have made their summer homes and held their Religious or Medicine dance," explaining that "this encroachment upon their lands, by Mr. Andrew Berg has engendered strained relations, or hostile feelings," which culminated in the shooting.[8]

Gardner reported that there were ninety or so white settlers on the reservation; they had filed on the land, built houses, and made three- to eight-acre clearings for cultivation. These settlers reported that Indians sometimes ordered them to "quit cutting maple trees" and leave the reservation, but the settlers stated that they had no fear of a massacre. Gardner concluded that "if the same number of whites had been treated as these Indians have been in the past they would not sit tamely down and have complained of it, but would have revolted and possibly engaged in wholesale hostilities and murder." Gardner, having heard about the commission appointed to put the Nelson Act into effect, advised the band members to make an agreement and move to White Earth.

Negotiations with the Mille Lacs Ojibwe for the implementation of the Nelson Act began on October 2 "in the woods on the bank of the lake." The commissioners included Henry Rice, Bishop Martin Marty, and Joseph Whiting, but Rice and Indian agent B. P. Schuler, who accompanied them, did most of the talking. Already well known at Mille Lacs for involvement in the negotiations in 1855 and 1863, Rice began his speech with an acknowledgment about the Treaty of 1863: "It was a wise treaty, and if it had been properly carried out, you would have escaped all the trouble that has befallen you. Men who cared more for themselves than they did for you, thought they had found a hole in it, and that they would take advantage of that and deprive you of your rights." Rice said these men thought they would drive the Mille Lacs people from "this Reservation." But the band had had some friends who worked in their favor, including Joseph Roberts, who had recently died. With respect to Roberts and what he had fought for, Rice said he wanted to correct some mistakes and set the record straight: "The time has come when I am able to tell you that all he said, all I have said to you, all the chiefs told you who were there and made the treaty, is correct: that the understanding of the chiefs as to the treaty was right. Here is the acknowledgement of the government that you were right—that 'you have not forfeited your right to occupy the Reservation.'"[9]

During subsequent negotiations it became clear that Mille Lacs band leaders would continue to maintain their desire to remain on the Mille Lacs Reservation and to receive allotments there, although there were suggestions that the boundaries of the reservation as agreed to in 1855 and those incorporated into law were different. Monzomonay and Ma'iingaans insisted that the reservation's northern boundary should have included land three miles north of the reservation boundaries shown on Rice's map. They noted that the only government plowing for the benefit of the band had taken place there, in section 13 of 44–28 (the township containing Mille Lacs shoreline just north of the reservation), on land now belonging to a settler named Dinwiddie. Rice promised to look into it, and the commission's report confirmed that this description of the land that had been plowed was correct.[10]

Rice made clear that the Mille Lacs people could take allotments on agricultural lands, as well as hay lands, hardwood lots, and sugar bush. Their children could each select forty acres of land, something whites could not obtain under homestead laws. He said, "There is nothing now to prevent your taking allotments that are not claimed by others or occupied." When the agreement was ratified in Washington, surveyors would show them the lines of their allotments "so everything will be not only convenient for you but correct." As for the pinelands, it would take time to put them on the market.

Ma'iingaans wished to know if they would have a sawmill at Mille Lacs, a farmer to show them how to farm, a blacksmith, and a schoolmaster. Rice said he would recommend these things, and he hoped the people would improve and advance. Cultivating a folksy manner, he said it was not the intention of the government to "pull out your teeth and tell you to eat tough meat."

Another matter of concern were dams on the Rum River. Ma'iingaans said that settlers came on the reservation to take control of the meadows and steal hay from the Indians. What would become of the whites who came to take lands on the reservation? Would they go away soon? He asked, "And is this question forever settled so far as the Indian is concerned? Are we going to meet with any more difficulties relative to our land and our possessions here, and our rights?" Ma'iingaans noted: "When the whites come amongst us, the first thing they do is to take a mouthful here and a mouthful there. We look at them; they take what belongs to us; we don't say a word. What will be the final arrangement as to this matter?"[11]

Kegwedosay added that it was important to take pains to solve this problem, since "We have had trouble enough heretofore." In response, Rice said that as to the dams, this was a matter for the state to look into. In regard to the hay and timber trespassers, this was a matter to discuss with their agent. As to the settlers "upon your lands," this was a matter to be handled in Washington. Some of these people had "papers which they have received, and they know about the position they occupy." But Rice did not think any more settlers would "come upon your Reservation, and perhaps some who are merely visiting you will leave." While there were "some other cases that are different," Rice said these matters would be carefully looked into and "whatever is right will be done for the best, in the interest of justice and to your satisfaction." To this Agent Schuler added, "any white man who cuts hay upon your reservation without permission is liable to prosecution" and any hay or timber cut on "your reservation" could be seized and sold for the Mille Lacs people's benefit.

There was a significant difference between what Rice and the other commissioners said in this meeting and what the commissioners of 1886 had said about the Mille Lacs Reservation. Rice forthrightly stated that the Mille Lacs people were correct in their interpretations of the treaty, and he referred to lands on the reservation as theirs; Schuler made clear that those who cut their hay and their timber were trespassers and that when the hay and timber was sold the moneys would be used for their benefit.

The words were welcome. Ma'iingaans exhorted the other assembled band members to not look on the event as a mockery: "This is a settlement of all our past difficulties. We have suffered in the past; do not let us be children. Do not let us miss this chance. They tell us that we are going to stay here forever, and that they are going to make allotments here to us. Let us trust them."[12]

Nonetheless it should be noted that there was some ambiguity in what Rice told these band leaders about how the intruders on the reservation would be dealt with. Kegwedosay mentioned that when he had encountered two lumbermen who came to cut timber on the reservation he told them he did not think they could because "the land was occupied by Indians." But the men told him they had received a patent for the land. Kegwedosay wished to know who had opened the reservation so that patents were issued for pinelands. Rice did not give an answer but said he would send the leader's words to Washington.[13]

Later on Ma'iingaans brought up the matter again: "Those who are inside the Reservation,—the people wish to know positively that the whites will be removed immediately—that is what we wish." Rice's response reiterated some of the ambiguity of his first statement, telling them their words had been written down and it was a matter to be referred to Washington for the government to decide. In the meantime they should "keep quiet and disturb no one" and wait until they heard from the Great Father: "If there is anything wrong he will correct it; he will not permit you to do so. The law has come to stay, and when it is appealed to, its decisions will be made in the interest of justice, without regard to the preferences of the Indian, the white man, or the black man,—the rich or the poor. Any rash act might destroy all that has been accomplished."[14]

Negwanebi accepted this response, saying he knew the Great Father would fulfill all that was being said, to "fix all the difficulties that surround us." Shaboshkung too seemed pleased by the meeting. He noted that it had long seemed as though "this Reservation was shaking all the time, on account of the excitement and conflicting interests." They wished to quell the shaking and depended on Rice to do it. Everything was to be gained by being quiet, and they promised to do so. Shaboshkung concluded by summarizing what the assembled people wished out of the treaty: "They say they wish to have their allotments made here, and made solid under their seats, solider and solider every move of their bodies; that is what they want." Then the leaders signed the documents presented to them, with Wahweyaycumig saying, "Let us raise our hands as a token of sincere friendship."[15]

The agreement signed by the Mille Lacs leaders confirmed the existence of the reservation, stating that it was being signed by those Ojibwe "occupying and belonging to the Mille Lac Reservation under and by virtue of a clause in the twelfth article of the treaty of May 7, 1864." The agreement provided that the signers would ratify and accept the Nelson Act "and each and all of the provisions thereof," which would include the provision allowing them to take allotments on their own reservation. Finally, the agreement provided that the Indians did "forever relinquish to the United States the right of occupancy on the Mille Lacs Reservation, reserved to [them] by the twelfth article of the Treaty of May 7, 1864." This statement appeared to confirm that the government viewed occupancy as an important right and bargained for relinquishment of that right by offering to provide allotments to band members within the reservation.[16]

Throughout the meetings Henry Rice held out to the Mille Lacs leaders the prospect of allotments on their reservation and the removal of whites from their reservation. Perhaps more than anything he acknowledged that their reservation existed and that justice would now be done to them, despite the mistakes of the past. Unclear is the extent to which Rice believed what he was saying and whether he knew these promises would not be kept.

According to the reminiscences of David Robbins, Henry Rice pretended to be unaware of the Sabin–Wilder claims on reservation lands, as well as the claims made by subsequent settlers. Robbins said he told Rice at the time of the negotiations that "he ought not to be surprised as one of his near neighbors and townsmen, A. H. Wilder, was the owner of about one-half of the reservation and explained that almost all the rest had been filed on by pre-emptors and homesteaders." In fact Rice and Wilder lived less than a block apart from each other along Summit Avenue, St. Paul's wealthiest street. Yet Rice's response may have been strictly accurate; he merely asserted that officials in Washington were unaware of "any such state of affairs." Robbins said he presented to Rice a set of township plats, furnished to him by Wilder, showing that all but five thousand acres had been "segregated from the public domain."[17]

In fact Robbins exaggerated the degree to which the land on the reservation was already claimed. Even if there were an estimated ninety settlers at Mille Lacs and all of them were legitimate and all obtained homesteads of 160 acres, these claims would have taken up only 14,400 acres. Indeed, the majority of the lands remaining after the entry of the Sabin–Wilder claims in 1879, except for the land taken up by a handful of settlers such as Robbins, was not claimed until 1890 and 1891. There were in fact plenty of lands available for allotment. Robbins's memory of his conversations with Rice may have been colored by his knowledge of what happened soon afterward.

Nonetheless, Robbins recalled that Rice read to him from the instructions he had received as to what to tell the Ojibwe: that they would all be given agricultural land; some pine would be reserved to build houses, barns, blacksmith shops, schoolhouses, and sawmills; and they would be given teams, wagons, and cattle. The balance of the timber would be sold to finance purchases for the band members.

Robbins claimed he laughed at Rice and asked how he could tell the Indians "foolish stuff as that knowing you cannot carry it out." Robbins said he told Rice "it was strange that the government, knowing the facts in regard to this matter, should still insist in carrying out a system of deceit." Rice told Robbins that if what Robbins said were the case it was doubly important for the Mille Lacs leaders to sign the treaty because it would allow them to go to White Earth where they could share with other Indians. Robbins wrote, "He also claimed that in dealing with Indians it was extremely necessary to deceive them for their own good and that the present instance was one of them."

Despite Robbins's memory of this conversation, Rice's correspondence with Commissioner of Indian Affairs T. J. Morgan after the 1889 meetings reflects the content of his conversations with the Mille Lacs leaders in these negotiations. Rice noted that the band members had assented to the proposition presented to them and "signified their intention to remain where they are, and will take allotments upon that reservation." Rice recommended a portable sawmill be built at Mille Lacs to provide them with lumber and a farmer be appointed to aid them in agriculture. In addition, he noted that there were now probably a hundred squatters on the reservation; "Some of them took the gardens the Indians had made, and built thereon, appropriating to their own use the fields which the Indians had broken and cultivated with much labor." Rice stated that band members claimed no patent could have been issued legally for land in the reservation, "consequently no authority has or can be given to dispossess them of any part of it without their consent." Rice noted that since many of the settlers had only board shanties "they can leave at any time without serious loss." Rice believed "in the interest of justice this subject cannot too rigidly be examined, or at too early a period."[18]

As demonstrated here, Rice and Schuler, in carrying out the Nelson Act at Mille Lacs, explicitly recognized the existence of the Mille Lacs Reservation and the rights of the band to that reservation. In signing the Nelson Act agreement it is clear Mille Lacs band members anticipated that the effect on their reservation would mainly be in the sale of the timberlands that loggers had been trespassing on and lumber companies had been trying to get from them for twenty years or more. They questioned Rice about whether it would be possible for them to sell the timber without selling the land, but he had resisted the notion, and so they had signed the agreement. In return they believed they would receive allotments which would make their position at Mille Lacs less precarious in the eyes of government officials. The exact size of the allotments they would receive at Mille Lacs was not made clear to them. Rice boasted that white people under the Homestead Act received only 160 acres but Mille Lacs band members' children would receive forty acres apiece. It may have been that government officials anticipated giving adult signers of the agreement 160 acres, the amount called for in the Dawes Act, from which the Nelson Act was in part derived. Later, in 1891, the Dawes Act was amended to reduce the size of allotments to eighty acres.[19]

However, assuming the Nelson Act had been carried out as described by Rice, how much of the reservation would have been sold and how much kept for the allotments of band members? The commission's census counted 895 band members in 1889. Even assuming that band members received forty-acre allotments, the population of 895 people would have obtained allotments totaling 35,800 acres—more than half of the reservation, but it still would have granted Sabin and Wilder the full amount of their 285 soldiers' additional homesteads, the best pinelands on the reservation. Knowing the reservation and the portions of it that contained pine timber, Mille Lacs band members likely anticipated this probable outcome, one they could live with because other whites, those who came to settle on their reservation and displace them, would be asked to leave by the government.[20]

What they would not have expected, given everything Henry Rice said to them during the deliberations, was that during the next ten years not only would 99 percent of reservation land be patented to whites but the Mille Lacs people would be treated as trespassers on their own lands, their villages burned to the ground, their resources taken by others, with no defense of their interests by government officials. They had trusted Henry Rice. They did not expect betrayal.

CHAPTER 16

The Aftermath of the Nelson Act

The several years after the 1889 visit of Henry Rice and the other commissioners were confusing ones, not only for band members but also for federal Indian and land officials, lumbermen, settlers, and railroad companies. Band members, who thought they had a clear understanding with Rice about obtaining allotments on Mille Lacs Reservation lands, would soon discover that other government officials had no intention of following through. Shaboshkung, who died around February 9, 1890, did not live to see how the Nelson Act played out. Government Indian and land officials, lumbermen, settlers, and railroad companies all sought in various conflicting ways to make the government's Indian policies serve their particular needs, but they often found themselves working at cross-purposes.[1]

In late December 1889 the commissioners submitted their report about the agreements reached with the various Ojibwe bands. In it they referred to the government's history with the Mille Lacs Band and the treaties of 1863 and 1864, "which confirmed the belief [of band members] that they were not only permanently located, but had the sole occupancy of the Reservation." The commissioners noted that the Interior Department now held that "The Mille Lac Indians have never forfeited their right of occupancy, and still reside on the Reservation." But in spite of this understanding, the report said, "white men were permitted to rob them of their pine and for years to settle upon their agricultural lands, and there to remain in quiet possession to the great injury and fear of the Indians." Some had the "shameless audacity to take from the Indians land the latter had, with much labor and perseverance, put into cultivation." Squatters "are now settling this reservation and the interest of the Indian ignored."[2]

To be sure, many people went onto the Mille Lacs Reservation "believing they had a right so to do." They were thus persuaded by the actions of those "who not only sought the rich pine forests thereon, but actually secured as is believed patents to many acres thereof." It was possible matters could be arranged to give protection to the well-intentioned but misled whites who had homes on the tract, but "the question of right should be settled at the earliest possible moment," since waiting would only make it more difficult. The commissioners made clear that the "principal fault" of the Mille Lacs Ojibwe seemed "to lie in possession of lands that the white man wants."

Some of this information was repeated in the letter from Secretary of the Interior John Noble to the president transmitting the commission's report on January 30, 1890. Noble pointed out that white men had been permitted to rob Mille Lacs band members' pine and settle on their agricultural lands. He repeated that "the question of right should be settled at an early date." Noble did not make any distinction between Mille Lacs and any of the other reservations mentioned in the Nelson Act. Thus it was not just in relation to Mille Lacs but rather all the reservations that Noble suggested it might not be "prudent to urge individual allotments elsewhere than at White Earth." Nonetheless Noble made clear that before ceded lands on any of the reservations could be disposed of to whites, they had to be categorized as pinelands or agricultural lands. Only those agricultural lands not allotted to Indians could be disposed of to actual settlers under the homestead law.[3]

Although not mentioned in this January 30 letter, Noble had recently reached a decision involving a dispute about land on the Mille Lacs Reservation. David H. Robbins contested one portion of the land upon which Shaboshkung had already received a patent, arguing that Shaboshkung had not improved and resided on the land as required by law. But the merits of the Robbins claim were not really at issue in the secretary's decision. Rather, the question of whether the Nelson Act was the "further legislation" mentioned in the Act of July 4, 1884, and whether it confirmed land entries suspended in 1884, was posed. After recounting the long and complex history of laws and governmental decisions, Secretary Noble stated that, while it might be correct to assume that the Nelson Act confirmed these earlier entries on the reservation, this could not happen until the president actually approved the agreements made under the act. At the end of his decision Secretary Noble addressed the proposed construction by certain lumbermen of a canal through sections 17, 20, and 29 of 42–26, "which is a part of the 'Mille lac' reservation." He found "no pretense of authority for digging this canal" and directed "the proper Indian agent" to "take the necessary steps to protect the rights of the Indians and all parties concerned." It is not known how widely publicized this decision was nor whether the implications it might have on the desire of the Mille Lacs Band for allotments on their reservation were understood.[4]

Around this time, Nathan Richardson, who continued to advise and support the Mille Lacs Band, had worried about the number of new settlers coming onto the reservation since November 1889. Richardson wrote to Noble pointing out that the commission had promised band members the chance to remain at Mille Lacs and accept allotments. The Mille Lacs Band had demanded that the squatters be removed from their reservation, and the commissioners had told them the matter would be submitted to Washington. After the commissioners' departure, new squatters were coming onto the reservation and were "crowding in on them very much; in some instances where the Indians have garden spots cleared going upon them and putting up their shanties."[5]

These interlopers thought the Nelson Act would allow squatters' claims at Mille Lacs. Richardson saw nothing in the act that would permit this to happen, but if that were the case, he hoped the president would withhold his approval of the agreement. Some people claimed that Section 6 was put in the act to protect fraudulent land entries; if that were the case, it should be stricken before approval by the president. Richardson felt the Nelson Act was "vague and defective" and should be overhauled before the agreement was approved.

In another letter written the following month, Richardson elaborated upon some of these points. He identified Dwight Sabin as the individual who had claimed the best pinelands on the reservation and who, it was said, had had Section 6 inserted in the Nelson Act. Richardson believed that if the matter were brought to the attention of the president he would have it thoroughly investigated to find if any part of the law was designed to legalize fraud. Richardson believed that, under Secretary of the Interior Noble's recent decision, no entries "that have ever been made on the reservation has been legal." But Richardson learned that after the decision Sabin immediately went to Washington and was "still there looking after this matter and doing all in his power to get the President to ratify the law just as it is."[6]

Richardson further stated that a large number of whites had gone onto the reservation, so that now "nearly all the lands of the Reservation are claimed by squatters." Nearly every Indian's garden had a shanty put on it. Band members reported that "the whites are more insolent since the treaty than before," telling them that "they will be removed from the

Reservation." Band members followed the advice Rice gave them at the commission meetings to remain quiet, and now they "submit to the indignities heaped upon them very meekly believing that the Government will deal justly with them and fulfill all the promises made to them." Richardson sought help for the Mille Lacs Band to prevent what he believed to be a "great wrong and swindle."

However, everything proceeded as though the government intended to carry through on the promises Rice made to the Mille Lacs Band. By March 4, 1890, the president had approved the agreement made by the Rice commission and sent the report on to Congress. His approval meant the agreement took effect from that date. But under the Nelson Act land sales could not occur on reservation lands until parcels were classified as pinelands or farmlands. After that the Indians would have a right to allotments. Only then could the remaining agricultural lands be available to settlers. And none of the lands, pineland or agricultural, on the Minnesota Ojibwe reservations, including Mille Lacs, could be open to sale or settlement until advertisement of that fact. All persons found unlawfully on the lands would be dealt with as "trespassers and intruders." Mille Lacs was one of the places where a circular to this effect was distributed. A public notice sent out by the secretary of the Interior on March 5 made clear the desire of the Indians to obtain allotments where they lived and that this policy applied to the Mille Lacs Reservation.[7]

Around this time Agent B. P. Schuler was carrying through on his promise to look into the theft of pine from the reservation. While at Mille Lacs for the commission meetings, Schuler met with Benjamin R. Briggs, a settler in 42–25, and discussed some of the illegal timber harvest going on around Mille Lacs. He asked Briggs to keep him informed. In mid-December Briggs wrote to Schuler at White Earth to follow up. He had been in Milaca overnight and heard from a number of lumbermen "talking about lumbering on the Mille Lac Reservation as soon as there came snow enough to haul." He learned that Henry Webster and Page Brothers had the contract to "haul some Pine Lumber" for Sabin. Eli Buskey was also planning to cut timber, and Briggs had gotten inquiries about it from the deputy US marshal in St. Paul. Briggs noted that everything was quiet at Mille Lacs Lake among the band members, "for they have but little money." Briggs offered to help any official who came out to Mille Lacs to investigate the cutting. Agent Schuler sent the letter on to the commissioner of Indian Affairs, saying he had asked Briggs to keep him informed "concerning illegal cutting of timber by White men on the Mille Lac Reservation."[8]

Later, in March Agent Schuler investigated conditions at Mille Lacs and found band members ailing, but in other respects more concerned about "the encroachment of squatters on their land." Since the agreement, whites believed the reservation would soon be thrown open to settlement, what Schuler described as "legal plunder." Band members said that nearly every quarter section was now taken and much of it occupied by whites cutting timber on their claims and "even depriving [band members] of their gardens and meadows." Many of the band members' ponies were suffering from want of hay, which had been taken and cut by the squatters. The squatters drove the ponies from the haystacks and even killed one of them. Band members continued to follow Rice's advice, "submitting quietly, believing that the time will soon come when their rights will be protected by the Great Father at Washington." The Ojibwe were led to believe that "this should be their home of those who wished to remain and take their allotments and not leave their old home." They asked Schuler to protect them and their land against the squatters, but in the absence of any instructions and because of the number of squatters already there and the uncertainty of the situation, he said, "I have taken no action in the matter."[9]

Schuler's letter was sent to the commissioner of Indian Affairs and forwarded to the secretary of the Interior. On March 20, 1890, Secretary Noble, after reading Schuler's letter, wrote to the commissioner, mentioning that Schuler was taking no action because he had received no instructions. Noble called this important matter to the commissioner's attention and said that "the rights of the Indians must be protected and you will please report to me what steps are being taken to remedy the evils complained of. If you need additional force you will let it be known."[10]

On March 22, 1890, James Cooper, working for the Indian Office, also wrote to the commissioner of Indian Affairs, reporting on the distribution of the notice from the secretary of the Interior about the lands acquired under the Nelson Act. He reported no trouble on the reservation "at present," but stated that there were ninety white men located in the Mille Lacs Reservation, including a few men with homestead and preemption filings. What should he do in the case of men who had "straight filings from the U.S. Land Office"? The response to this letter has not been found.[11]

In April 1890 Endaso-giizhig, the son of Monzomonay, went to work on the spring log drive. He was gone from home for two months. When he returned he found "a new house built on his premises, and his own house being used as a blacksmith shop." He spoke to the man in English but then learned that he was a Scandinavian. Through an interpreter,

Endaso-giizhig asked the man why he had taken over this property and learned that the man had entered a claim at the land office. Endaso-giizhig found another place on the reservation on which to live. It became a common story for band members in this period.[12]

As the months passed it became clear that something was afoot that would prevent the allotment of lands at Mille Lacs. Henry Rice appeared to hold out hope that the Indians would be able to obtain allotments there, but he was less certain than he had been in 1889. He wrote to Commissioner of Indian Affairs T. J. Morgan on July 18, 1890, asking whether "that part or portion of what is called the Mille Lac Reservation—not claimed, occupied or otherwise disposed of, be subject to pre-emption by Chippewa Indians under the provisions of the foregoing Acts."[13]

Meanwhile, others were seeking to make sure that no lands would go to the Indians. Among these was a politician in Princeton and the editor–publisher of the *Princeton Union* newspaper, Robert C. Dunn. Through his newspaper and other means in the years to come, Dunn enthusiastically supported the settlers on the reservation and did everything he could to bring about the removal of the Mille Lacs Band. Nathan Richardson wrote to the secretary of the Interior on June 27, 1890, stating that, on a visit of Minnesota newspaper editors in Washington, DC, Dunn had been petitioning for the removal of the Mille Lacs Ojibwe "from their reservation at Mille Lac Lake." Richardson had not seen the petition but reported that Dunn was himself trying to make a 160-acre claim on reservation lands. He had also been "officious in getting other white men to go on to the reservation, knowing they had no legal rights there."[14]

No record has been found of a claim by Dunn on reservation lands. However, Dunn's newspaper provides many examples of his calls for the removal of Mille Lacs band members. A report in the July 17, 1890, issue of the *Princeton Union* stated that a decision was expected at any moment. The article said that "the white settlers believe that the rights of the Indians were extinguished by the act of 1884 [sic], and that they have remained at Mille Lacs only by sufferance. The opinion is also held by prominent attorneys."[15]

It appears the newspaper was referring to the Amanda Walters case, a petition to the secretary of the Interior that was working its way through the offices in Washington. It had been filed on behalf of Amanda Walters, the widow of James Walters, a former soldier who had never lived in Minnesota but obtained a homestead in Boonville, Missouri, and later transferred his right to an additional homestead to Sabin and Wilder (or indirectly to them through T. B. Walker). As it happened, when the Sabin–Wilder entries were made on March 12, 1879, the entry using Walters's documents was entered in section 1 of 42–25 and was given certificate number 2551 by the Taylors Falls Land Office, the first certificate issued that day. Though the entry was later canceled and reinstated, no patent was issued for it in 1882. Thus it was on the top of Sabin and Wilder's list of lands they now sought to have patented. Assuming Nathan Richardson had been correct in February 1890, that Sabin had gone to Washington in support of his land claims, it must have been the Amanda Walters case that concerned him.

The decision in the Robbins case clearly anticipated some of what subsequently occurred in relation to the Walters case. A petition "on behalf of Amanda Walters, *et al.*" was filed with the Department of the Interior on March 17, 1890, asking that the patents on these lands be issued "without further delay." On January 9, 1891, Secretary of the Interior Noble decided in favor of the petition, holding that the Nelson Act was the "further action" called for by Congress in 1884, since the Nelson Act referred to prior entries that would be allowed to proceed to patent under its provisions. However, despite his previous insistence on protecting the "rights of the Indians" with respect to the proposed canal on the reservation, he now believed that Mille Lacs was not a reservation within the meaning of the Nelson Act—because it had already "been declared open to entry by successive decisions from the Department"—and therefore band members could not take allotments there under the Nelson Act. In other words, the failure of federal officials to protect the rights of Mille Lacs band members to the land was now viewed as a precedent permitting further failures. It was another of many legal shell games.[16]

Of note is that Noble's decision contained the misleading and erroneous statement that, "pending the consideration of this question, by the Secretary, the Mille Lacs, as reported by the Chairman of the Chippewa Commission [Henry Rice] have prepared to move to the White Earth reservation, and would not now, in all probability, take any allotments on the lands in question, even if so entitled." If Rice actually made such a report, it was at odds with everything the Mille Lacs leaders said to him in 1889. It is not known how else Noble reached a conclusion so contrary to the people's consistently expressed wishes.

The reaction of settlers and those who fought on their behalf was joyful. The *Princeton Union* reported about Noble's decision in successive issues of the newspaper, starting January 15, 1891. "The settlers on the Mille Lacs reservation" were to be congratulated "that they will get their lands." The decision "as a matter of right and justice" was "probably without a flaw." It was a fortunate thing that the Mille Lacs Band had been removed "to a reservation where there are other Indians located." The only problem, the newspaper pointed out, was that those settlers who had made claims on the odd-numbered sections of the reservation—including the so-called settler Amanda Walters—would have to deal with the claims of the railroad companies to their land. This situation would take time to sort out. Otherwise, the settlers on even-numbered sections could secure title by making proof of "actual settlement and show a valid title to the lands."[17]

The newspaper's correspondent in Washington reported that the Indian Office was hard at work to bring about the removal of the Mille Lacs band members to White Earth. The longer they were in Mille Lacs County, "the more intense the feeling there will be against them and . . . having no rights there they were bound to cause trouble and annoyance not only to the white settlers but to the department." As for the railroad claims, the newspaper stated that "first class attorneys" in Washington believed the railroads had no title to the lands in question. In any case, the Department of the Interior was disposed "to treat people honestly and fairly, and no fine points or hair-splitting technicalities" would be allowed "to interfere with the just rights of the settlers on public lands."[18]

The decision at first only affected claims already filed in the land office. The register, Edward C. Gottry, announced in a letter published in the *Princeton Union* on February 5, 1891, that he had received instructions from Washington to proceed with entries and filings already received, but to allow no new entries or filings "within what is known as the Mille Lacs reservation" until he had further instructions from the Land Office in Washington. It was his understanding that the decision did not change the status of "squatters" who had made claims on the "Mille Lacs reservation" after the act of July 4, 1884, but applied only to claims of record at that time. He believed the department intended to adjust existing claims first and "when the exact status of the remaining land is ascertained, to open it." He anticipated the early opening to filings and entries and was "in hopes that it will not be long before the settlers who have gone on the reservation in good faith will get their rights." The "further instructions" referred to in the letter from Washington would no doubt resolve remaining issues about new claims.[19]

At the time of Gottry's letter, patents had already begun to be issued for the Sabin–Wilder lands. As shown in Table 7 (page 108), on January 17, 1891, patents were issued on another 2,579 acres of land filed under soldiers' additional homesteads in 1879. Patenting continued apace throughout 1891, so that over the year patents were issued on 16,907 acres, or almost 70 percent of the Sabin–Wilder lands. Thus, together with the lands patented before 1884, by the end of 1891 a total of 96 percent of the Sabin–Wilder lands had been patented. This figure was, of course, in addition to any other land parcels patented to actual settlers.

As a direct result of Secretary Noble's decision, settlers filled the Mille Lacs Reservation in 1891, despite the problem with the railroad claims to the odd-numbered sections. On February 5 the *Princeton Union* reported that David H. Robbins was "down from the lake" in Princeton the week before. He reported to the newspaper that "every 160 acres in the so-called reservation, outside of the Sabin & Wilder lands, is occupied. Scores of log and frame dwellings have been erected within the past two or three weeks." Settlers were anxiously awaiting Secretary Noble's decision on the odd sections claimed by the railroads.[20]

Settlers on the reservation had the support of their elected representatives in Washington who were busy trying to further their interests. On February 12, 1891, the *Princeton Union* published a letter from Senator Cushman K. Davis, who said that he would do everything in his power for "every settler in the Mille Lacs reservation, no matter whether he is located on an odd or an even numbered section." This statement reflected the kind of man Davis was, the newspaper said: there was no railroad corporation rich enough to "hire Cush Davis to work against the settlers."[21]

Meanwhile, there did not appear to be anyone representing the Indians in any way, least of all Henry Rice. Whatever Rice had communicated to officials in Washington prior to the Walters decision, he now tried to make clear that there would be no dire results from an outcome that so contradicted the understanding of the Mille Lacs band members. Even in this context, however, he continued to act, as many would subsequently, with the assumption that there was still a Mille Lacs Reservation. Writing from St. Paul in January 1891 he reported: "A delegation of Mille Lacs Indians called upon me last night. They are aware of the recent decision of the Hon. Secretary of the Interior in regard to the Reservation they occupy; although disappointed, they will yield to the inevitable, which will be for their good as I told them; not only for the present but in the future."[22]

Rice reported in February on his attempts to move the Mille Lacs Band in his role as chairman of the Chippewa Commission. He stated that when the secretary of the Interior's decision had become known, a new batch of settlers had gone onto the Mille Lacs Reservation "and took every available tract of good land, much to the annoyance of the Indians; and at one time, it was feared trouble would follow." But renewed efforts were made to remove them to White Earth or elsewhere, and with "gratifying results." Already eighteen people had been removed and nine others started that very morning to select allotments. Of course it was cold and the ground was covered with snow, but it was best for them to go now, to select homes, build houses, and prepare for planting season, "than remain in idleness about Mille Lac."[23]

Things were not all sweetness and light for Rice, however. As it became clear that Rice's call for quiet and trust among the band members was not justified, there was increasing tension. Settler Robert Briggs and others sent petitions to the commissioner of Indian Affairs and Henry Rice, asking for the removal of the Mille Lacs Band to White Earth. They stated that Indians were breaking into houses and threatening to kill settlers if they did not leave the country. It is not known if these incidents happened, but it would have been understandable had there been a few such cases, given the band members' frustration about the unfulfilled promises made to them in 1889.[24]

Rice communicated with the Indian Office after receiving this petition. Despite the complaints Rice did not anticipate trouble, though "a small cause may at any time bring on a collision between such opposing elements." He expected that within sixty days he would have enough band members removed "to quiet all fears." The eldest son of Shaboshkung and the five sons of Ma'iingaans would go and several others would follow in a few days. By March 1, 114 band members had removed to White Earth. Rice announced that the Mille Lacs band members were "now satisfied that their interest points to White Earth as their future Home." (The departure of Ma'iingaans himself was reported, perhaps prematurely, in the *Princeton Union* on April 9, 1891.)[25]

At the same time Rice wrote to Briggs and the other petitioners saying that the best efforts were being made to remove the Indians. He asked for the petitioners' understanding since the move was two hundred miles, the weather was severe, and the Ojibwe poorly clad. White Earth was mostly prairie and the "highest and coldest region in Minnesota." To remove the Mille Lacs Band before shelter could be provided would be "inhuman": "You know their attachment to the homes of their fathers is great, and also that objections to remove to a strange country and settling amidst a people whom they have looked upon for years as unfriendly, although of the same tribe, cannot be easily overcome. They honestly look upon you as the aggressors and it is natural they feel oppressed. If you are forbearing and patient, I am satisfied I can, without much further delay, secure a peaceful adjustment of existing annoyance."[26]

A few days later Rice wrote once more to the Indian Office, referring again to the conditions at Mille Lacs. Complaints came on every side, Indian and white. "The determination of the settlers to possess every foot of valuable land without ceremony, and the reluctance of the Indians to give up their long cherished homes, especially when they feel that injustice is being done them," along with the introduction of whiskey, to say nothing of the bad weather, made Mille Lacs "a danger point." But Rice was on top of things. His best efforts were directed "to Mille Lac settlement." He was "constantly and fully posted as to the situation."[27]

Meanwhile, the *Princeton Union* was pleased to report the latest information on the new settlers at Mille Lacs. Many came from or passed through Princeton on their way north. Mr. and Mrs. James F. Wray went to Mille Lacs in early March. Mr. Wray had a fine claim there for 160 acres in section 20 of 42–25, just south of present-day Wahkon, on which he had filed his Declaratory Statement a month before, on February 5. The Wrays intended to remain there several months. The claim was twenty-six miles north of Mora, the nearest railroad station, but there was a store a mile north on the lake. Just about two miles east of the Wrays, Henry Fillmore from Princeton had a homestead entry for 160 acres filed on February 11, on a site where someone unnamed—possibly band members—had picked three hundred bushels of cranberries the previous fall.[28]

In April 1891 the *Princeton Union* reported that the General Land Office had rejected the claim of the railroad companies to the odd sections of Mille Lacs land. No explanation was given for the decision, but it appeared the companies' claims outside the twenty-mile limit of the grant were denied. Since few settlers on the reservation had claims within twenty miles of the railroad line, there was general rejoicing. Still, the matter would certainly be appealed to the Interior Department and beyond that to the Supreme Court, if necessary. The companies would be "[loath] to surrender all claims to these valuable lands." Nonetheless, the decision was carefully drawn and seemed likely to hold. Among those who rejoiced at the decision of the General Land Office was Alvin Barrett, who had a preemption claim, "one of the richest claims on the so-called Indian reservation," consisting of 160 acres in section 29 of 43–27, just southwest of the present Mille Lacs casino. The paper reported that Barrett moved into his "cozy little house one day last week."[29]

It is unclear when Barrett first moved onto the reservation, but many of the settlers had been there "for years"—some perhaps as many as eight years—and had expended anywhere from $100 to $1,000. The Princeton newspaper stated, "if they lose their claims they will be irretrievably ruined." Still, the paper had every confidence that things would turn out all right. Business was brisk at the lake. Every man had more to do than time would allow. Claim shanties were going up in every direction. The only scarcity was lumber, since Garrison was the closest point to obtain it and supplies were limited there.[30]

The townships were now organizing. Robbins, present-day Kathio, was organized on March 24, 1891. David H. Robbins, after whom the township was first named, reported the new post office of Vineland. South Harbor and Isle Harbor Townships also organized that year.[31]

Late in April Henry Rice wrote to Francis Campbell, the agent at White Earth responsible for preparing for the removed Indians. Rice was disappointed that so little had been done in building homes for them prior to planting season. Around the same time Rice wrote to Commissioner T. J. Morgan that he could say with confidence that the work of turning the thoughts of Mille Lacs and other bands to White Earth as their future home had been accomplished and "that too, without engendering a disturbing element." At one time Rice had feared difficulty between Mille Lacs band members and whites who had taken over what the Ojibwe "believed were their rightful homes." The danger had now "probably" passed. Those removed seemed satisfied with what had been done for them, even though, Rice added, Campbell had not done a good job at White Earth.[32]

Settlers were going to the land office in Taylors Falls to "prove up" their claims. In some cases there were other claimants to the land, so that "some lively swearing" was involved. One requirement was to give testimony showing residence and cultivation of the land, often provided by other settlers. In such cases the *Princeton Union* published a notice from the claimant of his intent to make final proof before the register of the land office. Once the case was brought it might take seventy days before the land office made a decision. Land contests were "tedious and expensive."[33]

The Princeton newspaper alternated between reports complaining about the presence of the Mille Lacs Band and others suggesting the contribution band members made to the local economy. The May 7, 1891, issue stated that the "Indians on the so-called Mille Lacs Reservation are a continual annoyance to the settlers, and their presence retards the growth and development of one of the most picturesque regions in Minnesota."

The sentiment was that it would be better for all concerned if the Indians moved without further delay. The following week, on May 14, the newspaper reported that a number of Indians had been working on the logging drive on the West Branch of the Rum River.[34]

After reading the statements in the *Princeton Union*, Henry Rice wrote to the newspaper that he had been doing his best to secure the "desired end" of removing the Indians. The citizens should be patient, keeping in mind the strong attachment Mille Lacs band members had for the country, which had been their home for many generations. Readers should remember what had happened in 1862 when the Mille Lacs leaders had protected settlers. Rice announced that nearly two hundred Ojibwe had been removed to White Earth and emphasized that the Indian Office was doing its best to carry out the job so that the Indians would cease to be a "continual source of annoyance to the settlers." Soon after this letter, Henry Rice resigned as chair of the Chippewa Commission, to be replaced by Darwin S. Hall, who would hold the job at various times for many years.[35]

Around this time reports surfaced suggesting that Rice had not been as successful as he claimed. The *St. Paul Pioneer Press*, in an article reprinted in the *Princeton Union*, suggested that the estimates of the actual removals from Mille Lacs were inflated because they included mainly mixed-heritage people who were related to the band but "few of them ever saw Mille Lacs lake." They were enrolled purely for the purpose of getting land, while the "old-fashioned blanket Mille Lacs Indian" boldly "says he will not leave Mille Lacs for the government or anyone else." In the meantime three hundred white settlers on the "so-called reservation" claimed they were in continual fear of drunken Indians and Indians who were continually breaking into their houses and robbing them of their contents and committing "other depredations." But the settlers remained quiet, waiting for Commissioner Hall to give the removal of the Mille Lacs Indians his "early attention."[36]

The reason for Rice's resignation is not known. He may have reached the limits of his ability to carry out a policy that was contrary to his words to Mille Lacs people in 1889. In September 1891 a newspaper reported that the Mille Lacs Ojibwe felt "exceedingly bitter towards ex-Commissioners Rice and Bishop Marty, as they attribute the wrongs they are suffering to the treachery of the ex-commissioners, in whose promises they had unbounded confidence." With the appointment of Hall, however, came the announcement that allotments at White Earth would shrink from 160 acres to eighty acres, which did not help motivate any Mille Lacs band members to move there.[37]

Late in the summer Darwin Hall granted a St. Paul newspaper an interview, during which he was asked why it was necessary for the Mille Lacs Band to leave Mille Lacs. For the simple reason, he replied, that there was "no land for them around Mille Lacs." Some time ago the reservation was "thrown open, and actual settlers have crowded in and taken claims." It was better, Hall asserted, for them to move to White Earth. The land was more suited for farming there anyway.[38]

CHAPTER 17

The Seasonal Round in the 1890s

The Mille Lacs Band never wavered in its belief that it retained the sole occupancy of its reservation under the 1863 and 1864 treaties. Importantly, throughout the late nineteenth century it was clear from the interpretations of federal officials that the Mille Lacs Reservation continued to exist as laid out in the Treaty of 1855. These officials understood that though the Mille Lacs Band sold the reservation to the government in the treaties of 1863 and 1864, band members had the right to continue to reside on the reservation as long as they behaved well toward white settlers, that the federal government was obligated to protect that right, and that the band retained that right when Congress enacted the Nelson Act in 1889.

However, according to some of the conflicting federal interpretations in the early 1880s, even if it was an Indian reservation, the Mille Lacs Band did not have the exclusive right to reside on it. These interpretations allowed lumber companies and white settlers to obtain title to land within the reservation until Congress put a stop to the practice in 1884. Even those who opposed the continuing residence of Mille Lacs band members in the region of Mille Lacs Lake and sought means to remove them elsewhere affirmed, explicitly or implicitly, the reservation's continuing existence. As the Nelson Act was implemented, federal agencies and officials, starting with Henry Rice himself and including the Department of the Interior, acknowledged that they had accepted the existence of the Mille Lacs Reservation all along.

Nothing in the Nelson Act had any effect on the appearance of the Mille Lacs Reservation on federal, state, and commercial maps of Minnesota in the 1890s and early 1900s. Among maps from this era, two of Indian reservations in the United States, produced by the Bureau of Indian Affairs in 1892 and 1904, delineated the boundaries of the Mille Lacs Reservation, even though the location was spelled erroneously as "Mille Lac."

Many companies like Rand, McNally, & Co. of Chicago, the Matthews Northrup Engraving Co. of Buffalo, C. S. Hammond & Co. of New York, and others produced commercial maps of Minnesota showing the Mille Lacs Indian Reservation with some slight variations as to boundaries. Rand, McNally maps of Minnesota published in 1899, 1903, and 1904 were issued under the name "Railroad Commissioners' Map of Minnesota." The 1904 map stated that it was produced "under the direction of the Commission," that is, the Railroad and Warehouse Commission, an official body of the State of Minnesota's executive branch. All of the maps portrayed the continuing existence of the Mille Lacs Reservation.

◆ ◆ ◆

Throughout the 1890s Mille Lacs band members continued to survive in the region of the lake using the same seasonal pattern of resources described by Noodinens about the period fifty years earlier. But this cultural pattern had experienced some profound changes. The presence of white settlers hampered band members, making some activities more difficult, if not impossible. On the other hand, band members did have more opportunity for outside work, such as day labor for the timber companies that were finally beginning to log the reservation. All of these undertakings are described in the pages of Robert C. Dunn's *Princeton Union*, which is in many ways the most complete record of what was happening at Mille Lacs, including the activities of both band members and settlers. Of course, the news accounts were highly biased toward the settlers' point of view. Dunn made no apology for this slant: Indian people were considered an obstacle to be overcome, and Dunn wished to do his best to bring about the removal of the band. In 1891 the newspaper stated that the "vagabond Indians" were "the only stumbling block that retards the growth and development of this region." But they would soon be removed to White Earth, and "the hardy industrious white settlers will reap their reward for long years of toil and waiting and that country will bloom like a rose."[1]

Writers in the *Princeton Union* were gleeful in reporting the deaths of band members on the theory that the only good Indian was a dead one. Indeed, an article headlined "Another Good Indian" reported the death of one band member. The newspaper gave inflammatory accounts of drunkenness and blamed nearly every bad thing on the Indians. Band members were accused of almost all cases of theft and vandalism that took place on the reservation. The newspaper reported that there were many fires around the lake and blamed the Indians for them, although the weather was dry and rain was needed. In 1892 the newspaper compared Indians unfavorably to insects, noting that there were two pests the residents of

South Harbor Township wanted to get rid of: "mosquitoes and the Indians. We can get along with the former but d—n the latter."[2]

Despite the biased nature of the newspaper's reports, it is possible to learn from them a great deal about the band members' struggle for survival. These accounts also make clear how band members fought to maintain the seasonal round on a reservation that was being occupied by settlers a quarter section at a time. Many of the conflicts between settlers and band members had to do with the resources of the reservation upon which band members had long depended.

Haying

In the summer of 1891 Benjamin Carter, who had been on the reservation since the 1880s, prepared a petition from the settlers to Governor William R. Merriam. Their fears had to do with haying season. As described earlier, band members had long harvested hay from the meadows for their own use and to sell to lumber companies for cash. Carter explained that the Indians did not want the settlers to cut the hay on their claims, but settlers were determined to do it despite the fear of trespassing Indians. Something had to be done or there would be serious trouble. Merriam passed the petition on to Indian Agent B. P. Schuler and Commissioner T. J. Morgan, writing that the settlers were in fear of their lives as well as wanting to protect their hay.[3]

In one case the settlers complained that they had claimed a large meadow and planned to cut the hay on it, but band members "had the impudence to post up notices warning off the white men and threatening them if they dare even go on the land." A petition was sent to the governor. Despite the threats, haying went well. A crew working on an area called "the big meadow," possibly an unclaimed parcel near Lake Onamia, had put up seventy tons of fine hay. But they had to stop work when, as they claimed, the Indians burned the workers' camp and all their supplies. When the workers complained, the Indians were said to have threatened to burn the hay and to have given other threats.[4]

A settler named Lynch, possibly Martin Lynch, who had land between Cove and Lake Onamia, was ordered to stop cutting hay. A fight ensued with threats from both sides. A knife and gun fight was reported involving a settler named Jewell at the south end of Lake Ogechie, though no one appears to have been injured. A few weeks later it was reported that the information about the burning of the camp on the big meadow was incorrect:

"No supplies were burned to amount to anything, neither was the crew obliged to quit on account of the burning of the camp, they worked six days after the camp was burned." No further statements were made to suggest that the Indians had caused the fire.[5]

The settlers' complaints about haying season got the attention of Governor Merriam, who was considered a great supporter of the newcomers. He met with Benjamin Carter, who presented him with petitions. Merriam promised that if the federal authorities did not protect the settlers and their rights, state authorities would do it. Commissioner Morgan reported to Merriam that he had brought the matter to the attention of Darwin Hall, telling him to take measures to "remove the cause of the disturbance and restore amicable relations and good feeling between the whites and Indians upon the reservation named." Hall investigated the trouble and announced, predictably, that the cause of it was whiskey furnished in towns surrounding the reservation. The whiskey sellers had always opposed the removal of the Indians to White Earth.[6]

At the end of July 1891 Hall was at South Harbor Township to visit with "the head chief," apparently Monzomonay, whose band was located there. Few band members showed up "as they all [knew] he was coming and had gone off in every direction." Hall attempted to convince the assembled to go to White Earth: "He told them plainly that they must go; that they had no rights here now; that all the land was given to white men; that they had the papers to show for it, and that the government would sustain them in holding their lands; that the white men wanted the hay, and they must not in any way trouble them."[7]

Hall did not record a response. The following year the *Princeton Union* reported on August 18, 1892, that Hall had forbidden band members to cut hay on the reservation. Nathan Richardson was said to have advised, possibly as a joke, for them to turn their sixty-some ponies out and let them starve "and then make the government settle the bill." This story of course outraged the *Princeton Union*, which suggested that the Mille Lacs Band should "submit to the inevitable" and go to White Earth.[8]

Two years later a settler named Olof Johnson, who was attempting to assert the right to a claim next to Shaboshkung's land at Neyaashing, found that Indians removed the fence from his garden and turned their ponies into it to feed—perhaps a way of dealing with the lack of hay. Johnson "applied to the strong arm of the law" for help: the following week he complained before a judge in Princeton. Sheriff A. F. Howard went to the lake in June to arrest a man named Skinaway on Olof Johnson's complaint;

apparently Howard brought three or four men to Princeton, one of whom was Migizi, Shaboshkung's son. William Campbell, chair of the Chippewa Commission, was invited to "convince the Indians that they were trespassers and must not interfere with Johnson, but Mr. Campbell did not come." The Indians were said to have agreed not to molest Johnson "and to keep off his lands." The county surveyor would "run out the lines" to make the boundary clear to everybody. The newspaper stated that "perhaps this is the best disposition that could have been made of the case."[9]

Band members cut two stacks of hay on the island claimed by Charles Malone in 42–25, now known as Malone Island. They were engaged in "slaughtering game right and left without any regard to or fear of the State laws." They were "quiet but surly." The hay crop was damaged by fire in September 1894 at the time of the famed Hinckley Fire, which occurred at the end of a very dry summer. It was reported that 125 tons of hay burned in one of the lake townships. Rain in late September saved some of the crop.[10]

Summer Fruits and Rice

The variety of other resources that had traditionally been harvested by band members in late summer included berries and rice. Berry season came in July and August. Band members sometimes went long distances to find blueberries. Darwin Hall encountered band members picking to the north of Mille Lacs near Kimberly in August 1892. In 1893 the newspaper reported that some had gone to Aitkin and others to Willow River for blueberries. Local Euro-Americans picked also, but there were no conflicts over berries recorded in the *Princeton Union*. However, later testimony from band members suggests that they were driven from berry patches.[11]

A report by Chairman M. R. Baldwin of the Chippewa Commission in July 1895 stated that Indian men were still on the log drives—which went on into late summer that year—while women were making canoes and baskets and others were preparing to go to the blueberry fields.[12]

Both berries and rice were featured in an 1891 account of a boat trip through the lakes in the Upper Rum River. The report in the *Princeton Union* emphasized the beauty of the Mille Lacs area, a beauty it suggested was marred only by the presence of Indian people. The writer described going by boat from Lake View, apparently near the outlet, through Rice Lake. This name appears to have been applied sometimes to Lake Ogechie and sometimes to Lake Onamia. If a writer was specific, the former was

Upper Rice Lake and the latter was Lower Rice Lake. In this case, from the description it must be Ogechie. The newspaper account stated that the lake was "almost a solid bed of rice." As far as one could see on either side of the channel were "solid fields of green rice, just in blossom." How could the Indians be starving? If they would only work and harvest the rice they would have enough to last two years. What's more, in the fall the rice beds would be alive with ducks.[13]

From Rice Lake, the writer and friends went into Shakopee Lake to visit the pleasant home of the Thomas J. Warren family, which had 173 acres in the area between Shakopee and Onamia Lakes. A pleasing walk through pine woods—there was "no end of stately pines in this vicinity"—led to the home of a settler named Henderson south of Shakopee Lake for a "bountiful dinner," followed by a walk through some pines to a cutover area of about two hundred acres covered with raspberries. The party filled their pails and went on their way, returning to Shakopee Lake and the home of James Degan, who had "by far the best garden in this end of the Mille Lacs county." It was a "magnificent country," and when the Indians were removed it would be a "perfect paradise and as prosperous and contented a settlement as there is in Minnesota."

Despite the suggestion in the article, band members continued to harvest wild rice in the Mille Lacs area. As noted earlier, rice had its ups and downs. Earlier logging dams caused great damage to the rice crop, but there were fewer complaints in the 1890s. Ricing was still done extensively on the lakes of the Upper Rum River. It was reported at the end of August of the same year that the Indians were in South Harbor Township tying up their rice, as they usually did to protect it prior to harvest. This rice crop was the best it had been in ten years. Harvesting took place on Rice Lake at the end of August, and rice was sold for two dollars a bushel.[14]

Rice harvesting was reported in 1893 when it was stated that, following a familiar and normal pattern, "the Indians have entirely deserted Mo-zu-mi-na [Mozomonie] Point, all having moved to Rice Lake [Lake Onamia] to gather rice and berries." Rice was one of the few crops that whites did not attempt to harvest on their own, even though it was becoming a more salable commodity outside the area of the reservation. In February 1897 several thousand pounds of it were gathered by band members at Mille Lacs and sold to traders who shipped it to St. Paul wholesalers—the first year the commodity had been handled in such large quantities.[15]

Later on, in Court of Claims testimony, band members reported that they were sometimes prevented from harvesting rice. No record of this complaint was found in the *Princeton Union*. Disputes if they came would likely have arisen from settlers who claimed lands along the lakes that were traditional landing and rice processing sites, the areas where band members camped during ricing season.

According to newspaper accounts, there was more competition for cranberries than for rice. No mention was made of harvesting rice in 1892, but that year the settlers were "nearly all busy picking cranberries." They expected trouble because the Indians announced their intention to pick where they pleased. By request two Mille Lacs County deputies came to Robbins to protect the settlers from "marauding Indians." If necessary, the sheriff said he would send a posse of a hundred men. Governor Merriam also promised to send "one or a dozen" National Guard companies if county authorities could not handle the situation. Another sarcastic comment in the newspaper stated: "Should there be any blood spilled at Mille Lacs lake the vexed Indian problem will be speedily disposed of for all time to come without any assistance from the Federal authorities or Nate Richardson either."[16]

Fall and Winter Activities

For many years, going back to the Treaty of 1837, fall had been the time for annuity payments. But Darwin Hall had suspended those payments at Mille Lacs. In the fall of 1891, as Hall was attempting to get the band in full to agree to removal, he enlisted Jonathan Simmons of Little Falls to aid him. The idea was to persuade the band to move "in a body" and "by squads." Simmons, believing he could bring about their removal, went to Mille Lacs and held a conference at what the *Princeton Union* called Tucker's Point, that is, the area just north of the Rum River outlet. All willingness to reach an agreement with the government seemed to have disappeared. Band members would not even agree to meet with Chairman Hall. Simmons reported that their acquiescence to the Nelson Act was not "as it appears in the government record"; the wording of the agreement they signed did not reflect their understanding about what they were agreeing to. For this reason, "they fear that any agreement they make may appear in the records as entirely different from what was understood by them and they are therefore unwilling to make any further agreements with the representatives of the government." They were in an angry mood.[17]

In October Chairman Hall, along with Simmons and Richardson, met with Mille Lacs band members. Hall told them they had no rights at Mille Lacs and they must remove. Simmons agreed, but Richardson appeared to be supporting their resistance to removal, at least from Hall's perspective. Richardson spoke about the fact that the government was going back on its promises. Nonetheless, he said, they may have signed away their rights; it was something he would have to look into. Hall then stated that there was no alternative: they had to move. He asked if anyone would be acceptable to corroborate the fact that they must move. At this Monzomonay arose and pointed at Richardson, saying he would be governed by him. Monzomonay added: "We wish the promises of Mr. Rice your predecessor carried out. We want his promises . . . fulfilled. They are in print, you can see them. You don't have to take our words for those pledges. They were made with uplifted hands, by him, let them be redeemed."[18]

Afterward Hall was disgusted with Richardson, although Richardson told him it would be possible to remove the band, but not this fall. However, Hall was forced to concede that, in the council's proceedings with the band in 1889, promises were made "which it is impossible for us to fulfill," another admission that federal officials lacked the will to carry out the Nelson Act agreement. He was not discouraged, however, and would continue to do his best. The settlers were pleased with Hall and thought of him as their friend. Hall returned to Detroit Lakes, intending to stay away from Mille Lacs, to give the band the opportunity to consider the proposition he had made to them to remove to White Earth. Later that fall Hall or someone who had seen his report of the events sent a version of it to the *Princeton Union*. The statement blamed Richardson and Leon Houde for poisoning the minds of the band members and confusing them. The newspaper reported that the account was written by "a gentleman thoroughly conversant with the facts."[19]

As a result of this failure, Hall requested Commissioner Morgan to instruct the Indian agent at White Earth not to pay annuities to the Mille Lacs Band unless members came to White Earth. The order was sent by telegram in December. In response Agent Schuler stated that he would follow the instructions but wondered if the order was not quite severe "on the old and destitute and women and children." He also wondered if more could not be accomplished "by car[r]ying out all agreement[s,] thereby keeping faith with them and allaying their distrust and keeping them in good nature." Hall's policy was followed for several years in the 1890s, encouraged by Henry Rice. The *Princeton Union* of November 23, 1893, taunted the band members on this subject: "Unhappy Indians. No payment at lake. No one to buy venison for Milaca people to carry away in the night and tell how cheap it is out of season. Hungry with White Earth so near. What will the winter bring forth." The explanation for this sarcastic note appears in a letter written by Monzomonay at Cove to the president in February 1894, stating that the previous fall band members gathered during hunting season to await the agent for the payment, but the agent never came; because of the policy they had lost the opportunity to hunt during the season.[20]

In January 1892 the Princeton newspaper complained that band members were killing moose. Settlers wondered why game laws were not being enforced against band members, although the newspaper conceded that whites were also violating game laws. This reporting was despite newspaper publisher Robert C. Dunn's contention that game in the area of the reservation was almost extinct. In November 1892 it was reported that "The Indians are all moving away to their hunting grounds and getting ready to slay the deer." A Swedish settler in Opstead, north of the reservation on the east side of the lake, reported to a Swedish-language newspaper that he had seen Indians with a lot of ammunition in February 1893. He feared an uprising. It was not a likely scenario: a later report in the *Princeton Union* complained that band members were slaughtering deer and selling the meat; there were two or three loads of venison going out of Lawrence (present-day Wahkon) every week.[21]

In July 1894 the *Princeton Union* reported that Indians were netting fish and killing deer by the score, although this complaint may have been more general than actually referring to current actions. Enforcement of game laws and seasonal limits increased in the late 1890s when Executive Agent Samuel F. Fullerton of the State Game and Fish Commission concluded that Indians had no more rights outside of reservations than any other citizens, contrary to the usufructuary rights (that is, the right to hunt, fish, and gather) recorded in the Treaty of 1837. At the same time Mille Lacs became a popular attraction for sportsmen, though more for waterfowl drawn by the region's wild rice than for deer.[22]

If late winter hunting was unsuccessful, food shortages sometimes occurred. In 1897, as the federal government began to place more emphasis on helping the band at Mille Lacs than in forcing their removal, food supplies of pork and flour were delivered to band members in March.[23]

Dances took place in midwinter and were sometimes attended by the Euro-Americans. What were called "gift dances" were described in the February 23, 1892, issue of the *Princeton Union*. E. W. Case, a resident of Cove who was a frequent visitor at such dances, "thinks he has the step to perfection now. It takes a person with an ear for music to learn to dance after their band." A series of dances over three days took place at "Brigg's house" possibly in 42–25, near Isle: "The drum has been going for three days and nights. Feathers, paint, calico and ribbons are used in profusion."

Sugaring

Because of the many maple groves long described in the area south of the lake, sugar making was a popular activity for band members and later for settlers. It was also the occasion of many conflicts. Five Indian families moved onto Annie Warren's claim just west of Neyaashing in 1892: "They intend to be in time for sugar making. But the settlers will surprise them by making sugar themselves this spring" noted the report. Indians were moving into the township every day getting ready for sugar making.[24]

Among those troubled was William A. Wallace, who proved up his claim to 160 acres in section 19 of 42–26, in the area between Mille Lacs Lake and Lake Onamia. Band members were later recorded as having sugaring areas on adjacent sections of the township. Wallace reported to the newspaper that relations between the Indians and the settlers were strained and there was "liable to be serious trouble before the sugar making season is over." In the same issue the newspaper reported that "the settlers are expecting trouble with the Indians as they still persist in making sugar in spite of all the warnings. They are erecting their teepees wherever they have a mind to." Apparently not all settlers sought to prevent band members from making sugar: some had allowed them to do it, "but others have refused and the feeling is bitter."[25]

The *Princeton Union* accused Charles H. Beaulieu, a French-Ojibwe employee of the Indian office at White Earth, of having told the Indians "to go ahead and make sugar." Beaulieu replied in a letter to the editor the following week that he had given band members little support: "On the contrary I told them these settlers had papers from the government for these lands, and that it was trespass for any one to come on their lands when forbidden by the owners; that if they, the Indians, would come to White Earth they should have papers for better land than there was at Mille Lacs, and that no one should step on it or cut a timber without they said so. I can only say that every person should advise these Indians move."[26]

One conflict that occurred in the spring of 1891 may have been related to arguments over the ownership of sugaring places. In early April the *Princeton Union* reported that H. C. Head of Princeton, who had with the aid of three men put lumber on the ground to build a house on his claim in lot 1 of section 18 of 42–26—just northwest of present-day Murry Beach along the lakeshore—found that band members cut up the timbers and destroyed the foundation. It was reported four years later, after his house was finally built, that it was located in a "maple knoll" that Head christened "New England Point."[27]

In some cases grievances might be appealed to the Indian Agency or settlers might take matters into their own hands. Indeed, the Princeton newspaper said that "the settlers all hope that Mr. Head will give the redskins a lesson that will be remembered." The lesson given, however, was that county officials now did their best to support the settlers in driving away band members. How this case was handled, described below, might have had to do with the fact that Head was a person of influence in Princeton. He later represented Mille Lacs County in the legislature.[28]

In April 1892 Che no ten (Che Nodin or Giche Nodin, meaning Big Wind), also known as Big Pete, was arrested for destroying a set of four sill beams that Head was going to use to build a house on his property in South Harbor Township. A later source, the 1902 "Schedule of Improvements," shows that Head's claim was near a number of band members' houses and a sugar bush in adjacent section 17. Among these was "Kichenodin [Giche Nodin]," who had three cultivated acres, a log house and log barn, and sugar bush in lot 5. Workmen hired by Head stated in a criminal complaint that when they were constructing the house, Chenodin [Che Nodin] had threatened them with a Winchester rifle and then told them not to do any more work. They continued to work, but the next day they came back to find the eight-by-eight-inch sills chopped up in pieces. Chenodin [Che Nodin] was bound over to the next term of court, with the bail fixed at $200, which was paid by two whites. In the fall term of court the case was dismissed—though it would surface later on.[29]

Enos Jones, who had a claim of 160 acres in section 12 of 42–26, just east of present-day Izatys, did his own sugaring in April 1893. Gilbert O. Jahr, who had land nearby in section 11, including part of present-day Izatys, went to St. Paul around the same time to ask the new governor, Knute Nelson, what help he could give to prevent Indians from sugaring on settlers' claims.[30]

Several incidents occurred in 1894. On March 12, according to a settler's complaint, a group of band members "did commit unlawful trespass on the property of said Harvey M. Bennett by moving to his land and Building wigwams and Preparing to make maple sugar." Bennett's land was in section 8 of Isle Harbor Township, the northern portion of present-day Wahkon. Bennett stated that John Skinaway and some women "came on his land and commenced to build a wigwam, that he notified her to leave and she refused to go and said she was going to make maple sugar there on his land, that on the 14th day of March the lot of them moved on and commenced to cut trees and build wigwams." Among them were Chison, some women, and an "Indian named Pisonegesic and others to him unknown only one he could identify being John Skinaway."[31]

As it turned out, Skinaway was prosecuted for the offense of trespassing for the purposes of maple sugaring, a prime example of how state officials criminalized the seasonal round in this period. He was arrested, tried, and sentenced to thirty days in "the village lock-up." At the same time the *Princeton Union* reported from Lawrence (present-day Wahkon), describing further arrests of band members attempting to gather sugar: "The Indians are beginning to find out that they are not in it here any longer. They started in to make sugar upon Mr. Haggberg's place and he at once ordered them off. Mr. Bennett had two or three arrested upon his place, but could only make out a case against one of the Indians, and he was taken to Princeton. The Indians should, by this time, have discovered that there is no hope for them in this region."[32]

Later in March the newspaper reported that six band members, including James King, Sha-wa-ba-to (possibly Shaywoub or Kecheshaywahbekito), and Cheneton (probably Che Nodin, the man who had allegedly destroyed the sill beams two years before), were arrested for trespassing on land of E. E. Warren in South Harbor Township—perhaps at the base of Mozomonie Point in sections 10 and 15. "The Indians had established a sugar camp upon Mr. Warren's land and had cut down several trees." They were sentenced to thirty days in the county jail by a justice of the peace and were later released, according to the *Princeton Union*, because it was "beyond the jurisdiction of a justice of the peace." The paper's editor, Robert C. Dunn, then swore out a fresh complaint against the Indians, though it was later withdrawn. Nonetheless the newspaper stated that "the Indians have been taught a much-needed lesson and have learned that the settlers have rights which must be respected. No further trouble is apprehended at the lake."[33]

These events encouraged whites to take up their own sugaring. On April 12, 1894, the *Princeton Union* contained a report from Vineland stating that "nearly all the settlers are taking advantage of the nice weather and are busy making sugar." Elmer E. Dinwiddie, who had a claim of 112 acres in section 17 of 43–27, on the south shore of Wigwam Bay, had tapped five hundred trees.[34]

Sugaring was poor in 1894–95 for both band members and settlers. In 1897, however, further conflicts were reported. Wahweyaycumig stated that a band member named "Bechebe"—possibly Bizhiki—complained that he had been driven away from his sugar bush and had his kettles stolen by settlers who also cut his bark house into pieces and threatened him if he came back to plant potatoes in his clearing. The settlers were named "Jay Jwe Jaw" and Tupper. It is possible the first was Gilbert O. Jahr, the man in section 11 of South Harbor who had complained to Knute Nelson in St. Paul in 1893. The second may have been Clara Tupper, who lived near Jahr. A band member named Bizhiki would later be compensated for losing the improvements he had made near their claims, in section 12.[35]

After receiving Wahweyaycumig's complaint, Gus Beaulieu informed band members that under recent rulings of the secretary of the Interior they were entitled "to occupy the Mille Lacs Reservation and use the sugar bushes therein if they are not on patented lands." He referred to rulings, discussed below, recognizing that the lands in the reservation were, in fact, reservation lands subject to the Nelson Act.[36]

Spring Activities

There is no record in this period of disputes between band members and settlers over the vast fish resources of Mille Lacs Lake. As described by Noodinens, fishing in the creeks that ran into the lakes often took place around the time of sugaring season. Noting that sugar making was over and the sap had been very sweet, the *Princeton Union* of April 19, 1894, stated that "the heart of the red man is glad for fish are running up every small tributary of the lake." A week later the ice was out on the big lake—earlier than ever before—and everybody was feasting on fish. Ducks and geese were also seen in great numbers.[37]

After sugaring season, it was time for men to go on the log drives. On April 21, 1892, it was reported that the "Indians are removing rapidly—not to White Earth as we expected, but to the log drives." At the same time, some men and women planted gardens in plots near their summer villages. Gardens had always been a feature of Ojibwe life at Mille Lacs, although one frequently ignored or disparaged by observers. While the clearings used by band members for gardens made attractive sites for settler homes, settlers would also complain that the Indians damaged their gardens. Wadena, for example, supposedly took possession of the home and garden of Sven Magnuson, the man he was tried for shooting in 1889. It was said that "he refuses to surrender the same," and later, in the fall, that Wadena had ordered Magnuson to vacate his house and land at gunpoint. In October 1892 it was reported that Earl Tucker, the settler just north of the outlet in section 33 of 43–27, who "had one of the finest gardens at the lake," found his garden "totally destroyed." Tucker was reportedly driven from his claim with knives. On a tour of Mille Lacs Lake in 1893, Robert C. Dunn claimed that the only Indian gardens around the entire lake were to be found in a clearing at Neyaashing. Dunn criticized the technique and said he found the hundred potato vines in one garden there "spindling."[38]

Midewiwin ceremonies took place in June. In June 1891 Indians were gathering for the "grand dance" on Mozomonie Point: a "gentleman reported that six or seven hundred Indians were there and more coming." The newspaper asked, "Looks favorable for getting rid of the pests, eh?" Two weeks later it was reported that the dance was still going on; drums could be heard at night for miles. A break-in at the home of A. K. Trask was blamed on the Indians. An "annual medicine dance" lasting two weeks was reported in June 1892. As was typical, the accounts complained about "hideous" noises and suggested that all the money earned on the log drives would be spent on liquor. Other dances were described in the fall. An account from November 1891 described "pow-wows," first at Mozomonie Point, then Tucker's Point at the outlet. A group of Dakota people came in from Little Falls to participate and stayed. Once again there was an attack on Trask's house and the Indians were blamed.[39]

Celebrations on July 4 sometimes involved Indian dancing. E. W. Case, the man at Cove who was said to have appreciated Indian dancing, apparently had a more cordial relationship with band members than many settlers. In 1895 Case and Arthur Snow, the storekeeper at Cove, put on a July 4 celebration that included a reading of the Declaration of Independence and dancing by a hundred men and women of the band, led by Wahweyaycumig and Negwanebi. An uncharacteristically favorable report stated that "some of their costumes were beautiful and it was worth going a long distance to see."[40]

As indicated here, Mille Lacs band members attempted to continue their seasonal patterns of resource use in the face of frequent harassment and competition from settlers. These patterns included participating in logging and harvesting resources such as rice, sugar, berries, and game, which could be sold for cash. In addition, band members made improvements in their lives of the kind that federal agents frequently encouraged them to do but would not provide for them unless they moved to White Earth. For example, though there was no government school for children of band members, some children began to go to school. It was reported in 1895 that despite objection from some, several Indian children attended the Lake Shakopee school, where they showed "the greatest interest in the school and learned very fast."[41]

CHAPTER 18

Land Claims

The issue of title to land was a muddle at Mille Lacs for many years after 1889. Partly this confusion had to do with the continuing and contradictory decisions of the Land and Indian Offices in Washington. Despite the many complaints about Indians, a writer in the *Princeton Union* in 1891 suggested that the question before the secretary of the Interior about the claim of railroads to odd-numbered sections of the reservation—the main problem settlers found in the Amanda Walters decision—was "the only drawback that retards extensive improvements around here."[1]

A decision in September 1891 seemed to provide a solution, even if it involved another shell game on the part of federal officials. The *Princeton Union* noted that within the odd-numbered sections were about two hundred soldiers' additional homestead entries that were now the property of "well known capitalists and business men of St. Paul and other Minnesota cities." The Interior secretary reached the same conclusion as the commissioner of the General Land Office. According to the newspaper, John Noble had stated that the lands in question "while not an actual Indian reservation, were reserved for the use and occupancy of the Indians until the legislation of 1889, when all rights of the Indians were extinguished and provision was made for their removal to White Earth." In asserting that all these rights were extinguished in 1889, Noble did not mention the Nelson Act provision allowing the Mille Lacs band members to obtain allotments on the reservation or the promises made by Henry Rice that they could remain and receive allotments on the reservation. However, because Noble recognized that the lands had been reserved for the Indians' use and occupancy until 1889, they were "excepted from the withdrawals for the benefit of the [railroad] company, and their [the railroad company's] rights could not attach in this same legislation." As in the case of other lands under the Nelson Act, the Mille Lacs lands would now have to be divided into agricultural lands and pinelands and be surveyed and disposed of following the provisions of the act. Nonetheless, "valid pre-emption and homestead filings" would be respected, and since "all the lands were mostly covered by filings there was nothing left for sale and appraisement." The case would certainly be appealed to the Supreme Court.[2]

The decision brought rejoicing among the settlers: the "entire reservation" was buzzing with the news that Noble had "decided in favor of the settlers." Albert J. Porter, who had "the best ranch on the so-called reservation," 160 acres of land in sections 21 and 22 of 42–26, directly south of Cove, was overjoyed. He reported that "the boys" had had a reception at his house on Sunday night and "none of them thought of going to bed." Everyone praised Secretary Noble.[3]

One might wonder what to make of a decision that suggested that while the Mille Lacs Reservation was not actually a reservation after 1863, it was nonetheless "reserved" for the occupancy of the Mille Lacs Band until the approval of the Nelson Act agreement, which meant that it was, in that sense, a reservation for the use of Indians. What was the implication for land titles obtained prior to 1884, not to mention those in 1891? Such questions did not trouble the settlers at first. It was enough that the decision checked the claim of the railroads. The decision provided many settlers the opportunity to prove up their claims.[4]

Among those for whom the decision does not appear to have brought resolution was Annie M. Warren, who was seeking to obtain a patent for land in the northeast quarter of section 29 in 43–27, just west of the present-day Mille Lacs casino and within the twenty-mile limit of the Northern Pacific Railroad land grant. The land had originally been entered under a preemption claim by her father, George H. Warren, on February 7, 1891. George Warren died in August 1891, and Annie subsequently made a homestead claim on the same land. Despite the secretary of the Interior's decision in September 1891, her entry was later canceled because it was within the grant's twenty-mile limit. Warren fought for this land for a number of years, and her efforts were regarded by some as a test case of the rights of the railroad and of settlers in the odd sections.

Oscar Taylor, an attorney in St. Cloud, filed Warren's appeal in 1892. In the document he argued that, by the provisions of the Treaty of 1863, the Indians had ceded the Mille Lacs Reservation to the government conditionally. Taylor argued that the reservation remained a reservation after this agreement. The band had relinquished their absolute rights for a "conditional title." He argued that the provisions of the treaty amounted "to an estate in the Indians of which they could not be legally divested during their continued good behavior." It was "unreasonable to presume that the treaty contemplated the transfer of the land from the Government to other grantees while the land was in the occupation of the Indians thereby placing the Government in a position where it would be impossible for it to protect the conditional estate granted the Indians." The idea of such a transfer or other disposition of the land so long as the Indians lived up to the provisions of the treaty, Taylor concluded, "is repugnant to the provision and must therefore be rejected." The government possessed at the time of the railroad grant not a full title to the land but "merely a reversionary interest." The lands were therefore expressly excluded from the parcels available for the grant.[5]

Ed Gottry, the receiver in the Taylors Falls Land Office, who frequently gave Warren advice regarding her claim, wrote to her in 1894 explaining the significance of her appeal in relation to the many land claims on the reservation. He stated:

> The whole thing to one who has had much dealing with the department is perfectly plain. The questions raised in your appeal are vital to the interests of many of the Soldier's Additional entries on the reservation and in fact upsets the whole course of dealing with the question, but the principals [sic] laid down in your appeal are sound as the very foundation of all law and every principal [sic] is one of fundamental application and is elementary in its nature and it will when eventually recognized overrule the whole course that the Department has pursued in the matter. For that reason it is hard for us to get them to take hold of the questions and give a decision on the merits of the case.[6]

Apart from the legal questions raised, Annie Warren's case demonstrates the conflicting nature of the various claims made for land at Mille Lacs and the inability for anyone, including the governmental agencies who had the task of doing so, to apply a consistent legal or administrative policy that would make sense of the way the reservation had been dealt with since the 1870s. How could the claims of Dwight Sabin and Amherst Wilder, the railroad, and the settlers—not to mention those of the Mille Lacs Band to their reservation—be sorted out? To do so was to tie government policy in knots.

As time went on the settlers had less reason to be happy with federal decisions. In April 1892 Secretary Noble held that his ruling of the previous September meant that the Mille Lacs Reservation had been a reservation in 1889 and that its lands must be disposed of under the provisions of the Nelson Act. This approach had the advantage, according to the *Princeton Union*, that "all rights of the railroad companies are entirely rooted out," but it effectively threw out all land entries on the reservation since 1889, some two to three hundred entries. It would also give the Mille Lacs band members the right to select allotments on the reservation lands. It was, the newspaper wrote, a "tangled skein."[7]

Settlers at Mille Lacs were confused. A correspondent from the town of Robbins wrote: "What is Secretary Noble trying to do about this land? Why can't he just leave us in peace, just as we have towns organized and thinking we were somebody. Surely he will decide in some way in our favor and we will all retain our homes. This is too pretty a country to remain in possession of these horrid Indians." The editor responded that all was actually well: Noble in his decision was really fighting "the battle of the settlers against the great railroad corporations." One way or another, "the Indians will go and the settlers will remain in undisputed possession of their homes." This opinion was given on the authority of Senator Cushman Davis.[8]

Reactions were not nearly as sanguine to "a damnable decision" made by Acting Commissioner William M. Stone of the General Land Office in November 1892. According to the *Princeton Union* of November 17, 1892, Stone's decision carried through the April 1892 decision of the secretary of the Interior, stating that the "only valid land claims on the reservation are those initiated prior to July 4, 1884." The newspaper commented, with twisted logic: "The decision cannot stand. The so-called Mille Lacs reservation is not an Indian reservation, nor has it been since 1863." Appeals should be perfected and all pressure should be brought to bear on the state's elected representatives in Washington.[9]

The only path out of the confusion was a joint resolution of Congress to reinstate the land entries that had been made since 1889. In fact, Senator William Washburn had already put forward such a measure. In November Washburn succeeded in getting Commissioner Stone to revoke his decision to give time for the legislative discussion. It would take months, but a resolution legitimating land entries between the Amanda Walters decision in March 1890 and the decision in April 1892 was eventually passed by both houses of Congress, going through the Senate on December 11, 1893. The resolution's title referred to the "former Mille Lacs Indian Reservation," though the body of its text stated that it applied to "entries allowed within the Mille Lac Indian Reservation" between the dates of the two decisions. Bona fide preemption or homestead entries entered on the reservation between those dates were "hereby confirmed where regular in other respects." Clearly the resolution was a means for going around what the *Princeton Union* had called the contradictions between the two decisions, that "tangled skein."[10]

Senator Washburn earned praise for his role in the resolution. The newspaper reported that on the floor, at the time of passage, Washburn took part in debate about the precedent the bill set. Another senator wondered whether it was wise to introduce settlers with title to property upon an Indian reservation. In reply Washburn stated that the Mille Lacs Reservation was "really no longer an Indian reservation. The Indians are remaining there only through sufferance." The band members were to be removed to White Earth, so the joint resolution really had no effect on their rights, "or anybody else, so far as that is considered." Another senator asked whether there was "any contest on the part of the Indians against being removed from the reservation." In response Washburn gave a short but breathtakingly inaccurate answer: "None whatever. There is no contest that I know of anywhere."[11]

The resolution did not solve the problem of the Mille Lacs Reservation for settlers because of the competing claims that still existed as to reservation lands and because the Mille Lacs Band continued to contest its removal. As time went on, however, the railroad companies' claims fell by the wayside. The Northern Pacific Railroad eventually relinquished its claims to the lands on the reservation in return for land elsewhere. The Northern Pacific lost its contest for Annie Warren's land in 1896, and she received a patent on November 4, 1899.[12]

In contests with the railroad, settlers and their supporters were, thus, sometimes forced to take the position that the Mille Lacs Reservation had in fact existed after 1863. But in cases where the railroad claims were not involved, the same individuals might take the opposite stance. The problem was illustrated perfectly in the course taken by Oscar Taylor, the attorney who had crafted Annie Warren's appeal. In 1896 Taylor wrote a congressional resolution introduced by Senator Knute Nelson that simply declared that all the land "formerly within the Mille Lacs Indian Reservation" was subject to entry by "any bona fide qualified settler under the pre-emption laws of the United States." The resolution would also legitimate all previous homestead and preemption filings.[13]

Arguing in favor of the resolution, Taylor dealt with the question of whether or not the Mille Lacs Reservation had existed after 1863 in light of a recent finding by the acting secretary of the Interior that the intention of Congress in the 1884 Act was to "protect these Indians in their right of occupancy of the territory" as stipulated in the 1863 treaty. It had appeared to the acting secretary that since the Act of July 4, 1884, the lands of the reservation had not been open to settlement and that any persons who had gone there for that purpose were "trespassers." Taylor responded vehemently, contrary to the position he took in his appeal for Annie Warren, that for twenty-five of the thirty-three years since the Treaty of 1863, the Mille Lacs Reservation had been treated as part of the public domain. Taylor claimed that there were fewer than 150 Indians living at Mille Lacs, that "but one of these claim the right of possession adversely to any settler," and that the entire opposition to the rights of the settlers arose from a few interested "squaw men."[14]

As it happened this resolution was not enacted, though another one passed in May 1898 to declare public lands formerly within the Mille Lacs Reservation subject to entry. The later resolution also set aside 120 acres of land in section 33, 43–27 for a burial ground for the Mille Lacs Ojibwe. Thus, despite a series of decisions that went against the settlers on the reservation, few of them—either the real settlers or the so-called ones represented by the Sabin–Wilder claims—were expelled from their lands except in the case of contests involving other settlers.[15]

Further, apart from Shaboshkung's selection, there was only one case of a piece of land at Mille Lacs being allotted to a band member before 1925. Still, band members continued to press their claims for fulfillment of the promises made to them in 1889, including through attempts to get support from federal officials as well as ongoing assertions on the reservation itself that they had a right to be there. These declarations brought them in increasing conflict with the county of Mille Lacs, which at every turn supported the position of the settlers.

These conflicts did not involve the lumber companies. Logging did not begin in earnest on the Sabin–Wilder lands until the mid-1890s. By then Sabin and Wilder no longer owned the lands. One township—42–25 or Isle Harbor Township—had been given over to Weyerhaeuser interests, as a result of a defaulted loan of $50,000 from Frederick Weyerhaeuser to Sabin. The timberlands in the other townships were sold by the Sabin and Wilder interests to the Foley Brothers and became the property of the Foley Bean Company, which finally undertook the logging over the next ten years. As shown in Table 8 (page 110), Foley Bean in 1910 still owned almost the entirety of the Sabin–Wilder lands in the fractional townships that made up

South Harbor and Kathio. Paradoxically, now that there was no question about the ownership of the timber on the reservation, relations between the lumber companies and band members improved. Lumber companies had little reason to want to remove the Mille Lacs Band, especially since its members provided a valuable workforce.[16]

Most well-documented land disputes involved settlers—like Olof Johnson, who had claimed the land adjacent to Shaboshkung's parcel at Neyaashing. After the arrest of Migizi and others in 1893, mentioned earlier, there continued to be friction between Johnson and band members, though there is no record of any arrests or violence. In December 1897 Johnson sought to make final proof on this land before the clerk of district court in Princeton. On the same day Migizi filed an affidavit of contest stating that he had lived with his family on two of the three lots claimed by Johnson from 1882 to 1897, had erected a house and barn on the land, and had improved and cultivated it. A hearing was held the following year in the St. Cloud Land Office, which decided for Johnson. On appeal the commissioner of the General Land Office found that Migizi and his relatives had been in possession of the land for many years prior to Johnson's arrival, "that their people were buried on the place and that Johnson must have known the facts."[17]

The General Land Office had recognized the rights of Indians against the intrusion of settlers in several rulings in 1884 and 1887. Accordingly, the ruling in favor of Johnson was reversed. This decision was then appealed to the secretary of the Interior, who reviewed the testimony in the case. Secretary Ethan A. Hitchcock noted that it was not sufficient to say as Johnson did that Migizi had abandoned his claim and lost his rights to it, since the record showed that Migizi "was driven from the land by the threats of the defendant, accompanied by a display of fire arms, followed by his arrest in the summer of 1893 by the sheriff, who took him to Princeton." Migizi was released after promising not to return to the land except "to gather his growing crop." Johnson did not bother to deny making the threats "but admits that he caused the arrest for the purpose of driving the Indian from the land, which, it appears he was successful in doing."[18]

Hitchcock noted that homestead entries were permitted only on "unappropriated public lands." The rules of the General Land Office had prohibited entries by whites on lands "in the possession, occupation and use of Indian inhabitants." In this case the land was clearly in Migizi's possession and use at the time of Johnson's entry in 1891. Secretary Hitchcock also noted that the land in question was as of August 1899 subject to an Indian allotment application from Migizi. In October 1907 Migizi received a patent for this land, in a document indicating that it was an Indian allotment, which may mean that Migizi's allotment was the only one granted to band members prior to 1925 by the federal government for lands at Mille Lacs.[19]

If the decision in the land contest involving Migizi had been applied to Mille Lacs as a whole, it would have emptied the reservation of settlers. But the only other known attempt to follow this reasoning was less successful. This case involved Che Nodin or Big Pete and his conflicts with H. C. Head—later state representative for Mille Lacs County—in South Harbor Township. After Che Nodin's arrest in 1892, he and Head appeared to reach an understanding. Head agreed to pay Che Nodin five dollars a year either to "avoid being molested" or to look after the property when he was absent, or both. Che Nodin, it appears, sought to prevent Head from using only one of the lots Head claimed. Head subsequently relinquished his claim to lot 5 in section 17 to Che Nodin. On this land federal officials later recorded the presence of prior improvements by "Kichenodin," including three cultivated acres, a log house, a log barn, and a sugar bush. During the course of a separate contest involving the lands, Che Nodin had claimed to occupy lot 5 in section 17 for about fifteen years and cultivated a portion of it.[20]

However, the contest involving Head was not from Che Nodin but from another settler named Thomas D. Anderson, who contested Head's right to lot 1, section 18, stating that Head had abandoned the property and not lived on it the required amount of time to warrant his homestead entry. Testimony indicated that while Head had built a substantial house on the property, it was used largely as a vacation cabin. He came there for only a few weeks during the summer, "having a good time." The secretary of the Interior ruled in favor of Anderson, stating that such periodical visits "cannot be accepted as actual permanent residence on the land."

This decision did not end the story, however, nor Che Nodin's connection with the land. At some point in the process he himself applied for an Indian allotment on both of the parcels that H. C. Head had originally claimed. In both cases, at different times, the land was awarded to Thomas Anderson. Thus, despite Che Nodin's recorded occupation of the land prior to the arrival of Head or Anderson, the reasoning applied in the case of Migizi does not appear to have governed disputes anywhere else on the reservation.[21]

Another unsuccessful allotment application involved land just east of Che Nodin's claim. It came from Gogee, a band member in section 17 of

42–26, who stated in June 1901 that he had, prior to 1863, made improvements in lots 1, 2, and 3 of the section—which consists of present-day Murry Beach—including building a dwelling and other houses and clearing and cultivating the land. He had occupied the land continuously. In fact his frame house and barn were recorded in the 1902 list of improvements (under the name Kogee) in lot 2 and other portions of the same section, and he made application to the Chippewa Commission to receive an allotment on the land, though he never received a response. Despite this application and despite Gogee's continuous occupation of the land, William Wallace, who as noted earlier had made a preemption claim on land in nearby section 19, had made a homestead entry for Gogee's land in 1898 and had subsequently received a patent for it.[22]

Gogee objected. He had "relied wholly on the promises made by the commission which secured the assent of the Mille Lac Band of Chippewas to the act of 1889, that we would receive allotments on this reservation before it was opened to settlement, otherwise I might be able to secure the land in question by applying for it at the local land office in St. Cloud." Gogee asked that Wallace's patent be set aside. He ended by saying: "I have more than twice as much improvements on the land as he has. Besides this I do not care to remove from this place, for I wish to remain here the balance of my life." He asked for an investigation. It appears that none came.

CHAPTER 19

The Burning of Villages

While some band members were blocked in the 1890s from residing on lands they had occupied all their lives, some found that the Sabin–Wilder pinelands—unoccupied by settlers—were places where they could live unmolested. The *Princeton Union* reported in October 1891 that some Indians were building "houses and barns in a nice piece of pine belonging to Wilder. They cut anything they want. It does not look as if they expected to move this fall."[1]

Throughout the 1890s band members were also able to continue to make use of important village sites along the lakeshore. When Minnesota archaeologist Jacob Brower and anthropologist David I. Bushnell from the Peabody Museum at Harvard came to the Mille Lacs Reservation in 1900, they described the presence of village sites at Wigwam Bay, Neyaashing (Nay Ah Shing), Murry (or Murray) Beach or Portage Bay, Mozomonie Point, Sagawamick (present-day Wahkon), and Chiminising (present-day Isle). By then Shaboshkung's band was under the leadership of his son, Migizi. Monzomonay had just died. The leaders in the area of Cove were now Monzomonay's son Endaso-giizhiig (Ayndusokeshig) and Kegwedo-say's son Wadena. Wahweyaycumig continued at Sagawamick—as well as providing leadership for the many Mille Lacs bands. Negwanebi No. 1 led the bands near Isle. Brower named the prominent leaders but had little to say about other band members, except in relation to place names given in their honor. For example, Brower noted that Lake Shakopee was named after the band member who currently lived on the north side of that lake.[2]

Brower and Bushnell went around the lake once by boat and then along the south shore by wagon. Brower described how the Mille Lacs Ojibwe lived in areas that showed evidence of long habitation by their own people and their predecessors, the Dakota. Modern villages and modern graves were found throughout the reservation. Though Brower's visit was mainly designed to locate and map the ancient mounds around the lake, he developed an interest in and sympathy for the modern Ojibwe residents. He was shocked at the recent history of the band, at first commenting mildly, "Why all white people seem to desire the downfall of these poor people, I fail to appreciate." His comments became more heated as he traveled along.[3]

The Ojibwe, because of their long residence in the area, had given names to places throughout the reservation and around the lake. They did not need Brower and Bushnell to name these places. According to Brower, Neyaashing, where Migizi was located on the land inherited from his father, meant "shore view." Brower called the peninsula Shaboshkung Point, although that name is now applied to the next point up the lakeshore, just east and south of Wigwam Bay. Brower called that point Sagutchu Point, after a band member he met there. Because of the maple sugar groves located there, an Ojibwe name for that point is Iskigamiziganing (sugar boiling camp place). Another name is Zaagajiw-neyaashi (point where a hill protrudes out over a bay).[4]

On the peninsula Brower called Shaboshkung Point he found many mounds as well as "many evidences of modern Indian occupancy which includes several old Ojibwa graves." Brower went on a tour of the shoreline to the end of the point and then went west along the north shore to the west side of present-day Shaboshkung Bay, where there was a modern Ojibwe village. On this trip Brower found "many evidences of long continued Indian occupancy, pits, old graves, lodge sites, evidences of cultivated ground, hundreds of sugar maple trees." Throughout this area and the entire reservation many modern Ojibwe graves were found on top of prehistoric mounds.[5]

Exploring naming traditions, David I. Bushnell wrote:

> Sag-a-choo is a typical Ojibway Indian good natured and apparently accommodating if treated as a human being. We asked him the meaning of his name in English and he explained it thus: We were standing on a ridge of ground at the time, he told us to remain there and he went down about fifty feet and walked slowly up to the top all the time holding his hands out before him. When he reached the top he went through the motion of looking over it. That is what he did when he first walked unaided [as a child] about fifty years ago. Sa-ga-choo means to "look over."

Zaagiing (Sahging) was the Ojibwe name for Outlet Bay, referring to the outlet of the Rum River. The waters just below the outlet, just before

Ogechie Lake, were called the "place of dead pine," a reference to flooded forests there, perhaps due to the raised water levels brought about by the dam at Lake Onamia. Brower's map shows villages on the south and west sides of Portage or Onegaming (Onigaming) Bay.[6]

At Mozomonie Point, along Cove Bay, Brower saw additional mounds and the fresh grave of Monzomonay at a "small grain field." Brower stated that the Ojibwe name for the bay was Wequagamong, meaning "Bay of the Lake." Nearby Sagawamick—the name was a reference to the island just offshore—now Wahkon, Brower had extensive conversations with Wahweyaycumig and his wife and a number of other Ojibwe leaders, who were cordial and friendly to him. At his camp there Brower heard drums through the night. The next day at Wahweyaycumig's house he found a "circle of Mille Lac Indians pounding the drum and playing the moc[c]asin game." They continued throughout the day. Arrangements were also being made for a so-called medicine dance, and "couriers are being sent out to notify all Mille Lacs Indians to attend."[7]

The next day Brower moved on to Isle and commented that "the name will hardly hold for so interesting a region." A better name was Giminising, he thought, though, more accurately, it would have been Chiminising, as it is known among Ojibwe people now. The name came from *gichi*, meaning large or great, and *minis*, for island, which he said referred to "the Biggest Island," the largest island of the lake found at the mouth of Isle Harbor. The Ojibwe village associated with Negwanebi No. 1 was in section 2 of 42–25 on the banks of what is now called Malone Creek or Thains River. Brower stated that band members occupied the site of the ancient village that was located on both sides of the riverbank, where they had "bark houses, small cornfields and patches of ground fenced in." Brower speculated further on what was happening to the Mille Lacs people: "Why not propose to drown them in Mille Lac, or bury them alive? They have held this region since they drove out the Sioux, and they know no other home. Fathers, mothers, and ancestry are buried here, and men like Na-guan-a-be, who have lived here 100 years, know no other home, are acquainted with no other land. Why push them away?"[8]

It was clear that despite the increasing numbers of settlers all over the reservation, band members still had a strong presence there. But settlers, egged on by people like newspaper editor Robert C. Dunn, continued to maintain that Indians had no place at Mille Lacs. Intent at first on establishing their claim to small parcels of land spread throughout the reservation, settlers appear to have avoided confronting concentrations of band members at the village sites described by Brower. Beginning in 1900, however, the settlers, aided by Mille Lacs County officials, became bolder in their strategies toward the band.

In a deposition given in 1909 at Cove, the leader Negwanebi No. 1, from the Isle area, now around ninety years old, recalled how he had once lived on the reservation but had been "driven off" by "that man; that bad man that mistreated the Indians, Malone." Charles Malone had come bearing a land patent. Negwanebi had asked him, "How do you come to own this land?" Malone said, "The government, the Big Chief told me to come here and own the land." Negwanebi told him: "I don't think the government would tell you that. . . . I own this land because my old ancestors had owned this land and planted their gardens there." Malone would not accept this assertion, asking Negwanebi who gave him the land. Negwanebi told him, "The Great Spirit who own[s] us all gave me this land, that is why I am here." Malone had no more to say.[9]

The incident must have occurred in the 1890s. Charles Malone now owned Malone's Island in the mouth of Isle Harbor and had reported Indians making hay on the island in 1892. Negwanebi's memory suggests that at one point band members had had gardens on this island and were expelled by Malone after he laid his claim in November 1891. If so, band members appear to have joined others along the Chiminising River near the eastern shore of Isle Harbor. Soon they would be driven off again.[10]

In May 1901 the Mille Lacs county sheriff forced twenty-five families of Negwanebi's band from their land. Newspaper reports in the *Princeton Union* were at first reticent in details about how this removal took place, although—following the usual pattern—the account included gratuitous slurs intended to provide justification for the official's actions: "Sheriff Claggett went to Mille Lacs lake this week and removed a band of Indians from the property of Pete Kenedy, where they had settled and refused to move. The Indians were inclined to be ugly but finally gave in and moved their effects, with the assistance of the officers. They settled again a short distance away on the townsite recently platted by the Isle Harbor Land company. The Indians claim this place also and will probably refuse to vacate."[11]

Interestingly, in light of the earlier military expeditions to Mille Lacs, the incident took place at the same time it was announced that a regiment of state militia, on a practice march from Milaca to Aitkin, camped out along the south shore of Mille Lacs Lake. It was reported beforehand that "the conditions will be, as nearly as possible, those which would surround a regiment of infantry in a hostile country." Apparently for whites the Mille Lacs Band simulated a hostile army. It was reported in Milaca's *Mille Lacs County Times*, for example, that band members were "massing" near Onamia "to view" the regiment when it marched through the region. Once again there were reports of a planned uprising: "Vague rumors are in circulation that the Indians are calculating on checking the advance of the regiment, having an idea that it is an attempt to drive them from their old hunting grounds. As a necessary precaution against any hostile moves on the part of the natives the Princeton company will lead the advance in open skirmish order." Despite these reports no violence occurred between band members and the soldiers. During visits to Onamia and Vineland band members gave what the newspapers described as a "powow" to entertain the troops and, in return, the guard's military band gave a concert.[12]

Still, vague rumors of some planned violent resistance persisted. Seeking to tamp down these tales, the *Princeton Union* reprinted a story from a St. Cloud newspaper, describing it as a "pipe story." However, the newspaper insisted that the band members' imputed anger was the result of the recent eviction: "It is claimed that some weeks ago Sheriff Claggett of Mille Lacs county visited the Indian village of Isle and ordered the Indians off the land covered by the village on the theory that the land belonged to a white man. The Indians were given until May 11 to move, but they disregarded the order and May 26 the sheriff again appeared and after giving the Indians a day in which to move their effects, set fire to the buildings. It is said that some fifty bark houses and log shacks were burned by the sheriff."[13]

The article went on to say that some of the younger band members were bent on resistance and wanted to shoot down the sheriff and his deputies, but that elders counseled against taking action. The newspaper stated that "later the young men were brought home off the [log] drives and a council was held" during which "the Indian who killed the settler Magnussen"—an obvious reference to Wadena and the 1889 allegations about him—"counseled an outbreak." Instead band members decided to bring a civil action against the sheriff. They wrote to the commissioner of Indian Affairs asking him to take action in favor of the band. The newspaper referred to a provision in the 1894 Indian Appropriation Act that allowed Indians who were entitled to allotments of land under any law of Congress but who had not received their allotment to take the matter "to the proper circuit court of the United States." The newspaper stated, with its usual sarcasm, that the law allowed Indians to "obtain title to the land without taking the long way via the land office."[14]

A letter describing this or another incident was sent to the commissioner of Indian Affairs by David H. Robbins for Migizi in June 1901. Robbins stated that a delegation of band leaders had asked him to write to the secretary of the Interior to use his influence and authority to stop forcible ejections "done by different parties from their houses and lands under color of State laws—and their houses being burnt." Robbins stated: "For fifty years they have occupied several pieces of land cultivate[d] and live on the same as a home but parties went to the local land offices and by false statements that no one lived or occupied the same home, obtained filings." He noted that even the land that had been set aside as a burial ground by federal law in 1898 "was forcibly taken possession of."[15]

In July a special agent named Eugene MacComas wrote to the commissioner reporting further facts about the incident. He stated that the county sheriff and his assistants had forcibly removed twenty-five Mille Lacs families from the lands they occupied and burned their houses. MacComas learned that the Mille Lacs Indians whom the sheriff had removed had decided to go to court to "redress their wrongs" and bring suit in state court against the sheriff and posse and in US court against the settlers to have their patents set aside. MacComas saw these steps as a way to avoid federal action: "It occurs to me that if these Indians are going to work out their own salvation in this way there is no need for the Department to carry on this investigation in their behalf." In keeping with previous federal efforts regarding such actions, he recommended that no steps be taken. As a result, it appears that nothing happened.[16]

In November 1901 S. M. Brosious of the Indian Rights Association wrote to the commissioner of Indian Affairs that "the lands upon which said Indians were living up to the time of eviction have been their home for many years, their grandfathers lived there before them." The eviction, Brosious said, was the result of "the vacillating policy of the government," which had made two or three "varying decisions" on the right of settlers to the lands, the last one providing for the disposition of parcels under the Nelson Act, which would give the Indians the right to locate allotments on the land. The government was duty bound to protect the Indians, either by bringing action to dispossess the intruders or allowing the Indians to employ lawyers to bring suit themselves at government expense. In the course of the letter Brosious pointed to the precedent suggested by the Migizi case. It is not known what response was made, but a note on the letter indicates the commissioner believed there was no possibility of getting an attorney to handle the case.[17]

This same year Brosious authored a pamphlet for the Indian Rights Association on the topic of "the urgent case of the Mille Lacs Indians." In it he described the history of the Mille Lacs Reservation and a number of cases of band members who were driven off by settlers or by government officials. He noted that throughout the 1890s "the entire political machinery of the State seems to have set to work to force the Mille Lacs off their homes and to locate them on the White Earth Reservation."[18]

In August 1902 archaeologist Jacob Brower attended a council that would have a major effect on the band, during which Indian agents James McLaughlin and Simon Michelet arrived at an agreement with a number of Mille Lacs band members that the agents believed would get them to remove to White Earth. In the following years Wahweyaycumig and other band members who had been resisting going to White Earth finally agreed to go. For Brower, who believed the band had little choice but to leave Mille Lacs but who was outraged by the way in which he believed the band had been cheated out of their lands, the event was a sorrowful spectacle. After attending for a short time, he left in disgust.

For some band members who signed the agreement and removed following the council, a motivating factor was a federal appropriation of $40,000 designed to pay band members for any structures, gardens, clearings in sugar bush, or other "improvements" to the reservation they had lost through burning and other forms of harassment by settlers and county officials, as well as those structures still standing and still in use. They understood that these moneys would pay for "damages done to the Indians on the Mille Lac Reservation by the settlers in burning our houses and taking our gardens away from us and driving us away from our rice fields, from our homes and our rice fields." Band members hoped to make use of the money to buy land at Mille Lacs. With the aid of community leaders and David H. Robbins, agents McLaughlin and Michelet made a detailed list of all these improvements, who was responsible for them, and what was believed to be their value. In part it is a list of what might be called "white depredations."[19]

The 1902 "Schedule of Improvements" is a remarkable document, providing a detailed description of settlement patterns on the reservation. The data shows a concentration of improvements along the lakeshores of the reservation, involving a combination of permanent summer villages and sugar bushes. Of course the data recorded by the federal government does not take into account wild rice beds, hunting and trapping grounds, berry patches, and other resources that were not seen as improvements.

Beginning in the 1890s Robbins attempted to estimate the value of the reservation to the band members, including the number of tons of maple sugar taken, the amount of hay taken and sold to lumbermen—said to have been five hundred tons—and the amount of wild rice gathered each year—around 2,500 bushels. Robbins later stated that assessing the value of the improvements was difficult. This earlier estimate amounted to around $76,000—politically impossible to achieve. The bill to pay for improvements lost to the band limited the amount to $40,000, so when Robbins and the agents constructed their list in 1902 they were forced to "cut it down" to make it fit the available funds. Thus, this list is not complete in terms of the resources it covers or the values it specifies.[20]

Another record of Mille Lacs Band use and the depredations done by settlers after 1900 came in the depositions given by band members in a later Court of Claims case. Endaso-giizhig spoke about the promises Henry Rice made to remove the early settlers on the reservation. However,

> Instead of moving them off they came onto the reservation in big swarms, like mosquitoes and settled there after the treaty was signed. . . . When you got a mosquito bite on your finger it only sting[s] you a little while but these white people when they came there and took possession of all our property, our little gardens, even our blueberry patches; we could not pick our blueberries there, they drove us out of our rice fields, we could not get our rice, they would not let us pick our rice there. . . .
>
> For myself I know that I had a little house built there and a little garden. I was driven twice out of my little house, they did the same thing to all the Mille Lac Chippewas there. Even they went so far, in our little villages, they came around and drove us away but when we didn't go they would take our household stuff and set it on fire and drove us away and scattered us all over.

Endaso-giizhig complained that no allotments had been given after the 1889 Nelson Act: "We have been waiting for ex-Senator Rice to fulfill his promises. We are waiting for what ex-Senator Rice promised to be fulfilled, what he promised."[21]

Such statements, when combined with the list put together by Robbins and the commissioners in 1902, provide a rich record of places used by individual band members and their families and helps to make the experiences of the 1890s much more tangible. But of course the record is frozen in time. It does not tell what happened later, of the ways in which settlers and those seeking to develop the reservation for tourism would work to further hinder the actions of band members. The depredations against band members did not cease in 1902.

On another front, the increasing enforcement of game and fish laws designed to benefit sportsmen at the expense of Native residents provided further reason for whites to question the continuing residence of the Mille Lacs Band at Mille Lacs. Writing to warden J. P. Saunders in Brainerd in 1904, Commissioner Samuel F. Fullerton of the Game and Fish Commission praised him for making a trip to Mille Lacs. Fullerton said that a good warden was needed near there, though his committee did not have the money to pay one. The particular problem was the Mille Lacs Ojibwe: "I kind of wish those Indians were away from there; they are a source of constant worry and white men use them to violate the law. I am glad you have notified the store-keepers and others about buying the fish and game. If there was no one to buy, there would not be anyone to sell and hunt."[22]

CHAPTER 20

The Court of Claims Case

While some Mille Lacs band members accepted the offers of Darwin Hall and other members of the Chippewa Indian Commission to remove to White Earth, many did not. The 1902 act, to which some band members assented, reserved their rights regarding unsettled claims, stating that "nothing in this agreement shall be construed to deprive the said Mille Lac Indians of any of the benefits to which they may be entitled under existing treaties or agreements." Together, band members at Mille Lacs and those who had removed to White Earth persisted in their quest to seek justice.[1]

Pursuing tribal lawsuits against the federal government required Congress to pass a "jurisdictional act" that waived federal "sovereign immunity," permitting a tribe to file a lawsuit in the US Court of Claims. A number of Native tribes were able to get authorization for such lawsuits in the early 1900s. The first version of an act regarding the Mille Lacs Band was introduced by Minnesota congressman J. Adam Bede on March 30, 1906. The bill was not passed before the end of the 59th Congress in March 1907, though the House Committee on Indian Affairs issued a report on the topic in February 1907.[2]

At the beginning of the 60th Congress, in December 1907, Bede reintroduced the bill, which passed in February 1909, becoming "An Act for the relief of the Mille Lac band of Chippewa Indians" and authorizing the band to file suit in the US Court of Claims "on account of losses sustained by them . . . by reason of the opening of the Mille Lac Reservation in the State of Minnesota, embracing about sixty-one thousand acres of land, to public settlement under the general land laws of the United States."[3]

The act and the subsequent lawsuit did not presume that the Mille Lacs Band had ever given up its claim to the reservation. The lawsuit dealt with the question of land ownership within that reservation and the fact that the federal government had made portions of it available for public settlement without protecting the rights of the Mille Lacs Band. The lawsuit provided an opportunity for a full accounting of the process of dispossession,

allowing many band members who had lived through it to give depositions and record in eloquent words their memories of what had happened.

In May 1911 the Court of Claims found in favor of the Mille Lacs Band,
affirming the continuing existence of the Mille Lacs Reservation and the
right of the band to reside on it under the treaties of 1863 and 1864: "The
language of the [Article 12] proviso would be difficult to construe in any
other way than the granting of a right to occupancy to the Mille Lac Band.
That they shall not be compelled to remove was certainly equivalent to a
right to remain. Remain where? Why, on the Mille Lac Reservation, for
all other reservations had been by the treaty ceded to the Government."[4]

The court noted that the provision of Article 12 of the two treaties "confirmed rather than extinguished their rights under the treaty of 1855. The
language of article 12 is not ambiguous and if considered apart from the
context of the whole instrument could convey but one meaning." And
the court referred to the "dogged persistence with which they retained
their residence on the Mille Lac Reservation under the most discouraging
circumstances until subsequent to the cession of 1889." Further, the court
noted that despite the decisions by Secretaries of the Interior Zachariah
Chandler and Henry Teller allowing lands on the reservation to be entered
by or sold to whites, both decisions respected "the rights of the Mille Lac
Indians acquired under the treaties of 1863 and 1864."[5]

The basis for the court's award of damages was that the federal government, contrary to the provisions of the Nelson Act, had opened the land
on the Mille Lacs Reservation to "entry and settlement under the general
land laws," rather than through the processes for identifying pineland
and agricultural land and dealing with them separately. Yet, the court
noted, the federal government had, as late as July 1890, "treated the Mille
Lac Reservation as Indian lands" in an act approving a right-of-way for a
railway company through the reservation and awarding to the Mille Lacs
Band "damages incident thereto."

The court ruled that the Mille Lacs Band was entitled to damages for the
way in which lands were sold so as "to deny the claimants of the benefits"
of the Nelson Act. Among them, the court noted, was the refusal to grant
band members allotments—"It must not be overlooked that under the act
of January 14, 1889, the Mille Lacs were entitled to allotments on their reservation in common with other Indians"— although it is not clear that the
court's damage award took into account this fact.[6]

The federal government appealed the decision to the US Supreme
Court, which heard the appeal in April 1913 and rendered its decision in

June. The court sidestepped a ruling on the meaning of the Article 12 proviso, finding that the dispute was resolved by the Nelson Act, in which the government accepted the Indians' contention as to the status of the reservation, while the Indians accepted that the pre-1884 Sabin–Wilder entries could be patented. Although this is not how Henry Rice explained the Nelson Act to band members in 1889, it meant that damages could only be awarded for lands entered after 1884. The Supreme Court sent the case back to the Court of Claims to reassess the damages had the act of 1889 been rightly applied. The amount finally awarded was $711,828.47.[7]

The decision may have given some sense of justice to the Mille Lacs Band, but the damages awarded, under the terms of the Nelson Act, went to the fund created by the act for the benefit of the Chippewas of Minnesota, not directly to the band, a fact in much dispute for many years after the decision.[8]

CHAPTER 21

More Burned Villages

As the Court of Claims case proceeded, Mille Lacs band members, indi-
vidually and in their villages, were still fighting harassment and indignities, still asserting their right to remain on the Mille Lacs Reservation.
Frequently they faced more forced removals at the hands of the Mille Lacs
County sheriff. In August 1910, C. B. Miller, a Minnesota congressman
from Duluth, wrote that he had received a visit from several Mille Lacs
band members, who protested the actions of the sheriff in relation to Jack
Boyd, a band member who lived on lots 1, 2, and 3 of section 8 of 43–27.
These lots were on the north side of Wigwam Bay, at the village site described by Jacob Brower in 1900. Boyd told Miller that on August 3, 1910,
the sheriff went to his place, "took all his belongings, together with his
brother's, and put them out in the road, and destroyed the house [and] belongings of his brother," and then threatened to come back and burn his
house down. Boyd said he had resided on the land for over twenty years
and wanted to keep his home there.[1]

Darwin Hall, once again a member of the Chippewa Commission,
responded to Congressman Miller's account. Hall had investigated and
learned that Boyd had been served with notices asking him to vacate, noti-
fying him that the land was owned by "private parties who had paid taxes
on it for many years." Hall took the opportunity to explain that all the
land around the lake was owned by "private parties who paid taxes on the
same" and that band members could not get allotments there but could do
so at White Earth.[2]

It was an old story, one now taking place in the context of a new reality
in the Mille Lacs region. The area was becoming a vacation destination for
increasing numbers of urban and rural Minnesotans. Construction had
begun in 1907 on a Minneapolis, St. Paul and Sault Ste. Marie (Soo Line)
train track from Brooten to Duluth, along a diagonal line past the south
shore of Mille Lacs Lake. Intermittent service to the new town of Wahkon
started in August 1908, and regular service on the rail line began in the

spring of 1910. Its construction inspired promotion of the Mille Lacs region as a summer resort. A 1917 book on the town of Wahkon urged Minnesotans to "Spend . . . Vacations at Mille Lacs," where they could "enjoy the bathing beaches and delightful fishing and excursion trips upon the lake." The booklet described in vague terms "the sturdy redmen" who had lived along the lake, but a caption next to a photograph of an unnamed Native cemetery described "the shade of the sturdy oaks that cover the shores of Mille Lacs where for centuries occurred the spirit worships, councils of state and war, feasts, and dances of powerful tribes, most of whose history is locked with its many silent mounds."[3]

Such statements suggest that although Mille Lacs band members and other Native people may have been seen as an obstacle to tourist development in the region, they were beginning to be appreciated for the touch of exoticism they gave to popular perceptions of the landscape.

In 1911 the Mille Lacs Investment and Improvement Company put out a promotional booklet for a development on Mozomonie Point, a place that would be called Izatys, the Dakota word for the people who lived in the region (it does not correspond to the current resort of that name). The brochure emphasized both the region's present-day natural beauty and an Indian history described as being largely in the past:

> Fortunately the original and characteristic name [Izatys] is not to be lost, being preserved as the name of the park-like shore that lies at the base of the promontory long known as "Mozomonne [sic] Point" in the remembrance of Old Chief Mozomonne. So strong did his followers find the chain of ancient association that for thirty years after their claims to the lands about the lake had been, by their own consent, abandoned to the government, a remnant of the tribe under the leadership of Mozomonne's son and grandson, lingered in their old haunts, obstinately clinging to the home of their ancestors in the face of the encroachments of white settlers and promoters of civilization. I understand that only very recently did Ain-dhu-so-ge-shig, the last of Mozommone's race of chiefs, submit to the inevitable and depart from his native shores forever. In fact there is among the last handful of loiterers on the shore, the belief that one part of the lake is theirs forever by supernatural authority.[4]

Masked by the booklet's sentimental literary tone was the sketchy nature of Indian policies since the 1863 treaty and the sorry story of ensuing

deception. The booklet also concealed goings-on at the time of its publication, through which the Native residents of the area were forcibly removed from the very site of this new development and the remains of their
village burned. This process, like that pursued in relation to the village at
Isle in 1901, began with a civil suit, followed by a notice of eviction and the
eventual forced removal of band members by the county sheriff.

In 1910 a group of at least nine families was living around the base
of Mozomonie Point, led by Kegwedosay's son Wadena, now known as a
chief. Although Endaso-giizhig, Monzomonay's son, was listed in the census as a resident of South Harbor Township in 1910, there is evidence that
he and his family and other members of this community left for White
Earth sometime during the next year.

Another resident of the Mozomonie Point village was Pewaush (also
spelled Beewash), who gave a deposition at Cove in 1909, at the age of
fifty. When asked where he lived, he said "right over here, right beyond
this point, on this shore" on the lands of "old man Wadena." When an attorney for the government asked if Wadena owned the land, Beewash said,
"We always lived there." Were settlers claiming the land now? "Yes, I think
so." The Indians didn't cultivate any land, did they? "Yes, they have some
gardens." Just small gardens? "Yes." How did they live? By fishing, small
gardens and day labor? "Yes."[5]

On August 11, 1910, the development company filed suit against Wadena
and eight other Mille Lacs band members to remove them from its property in portions of sections 10, 11, and 15 of South Harbor Township, an
area which included the group's village at the base of Mozomonie Point.
After the band members were served with the plaintiff's complaint, the
case was continued until the April 1911 term of the court.[6]

By early spring the development company had obtained the proper
permits, and their plans were reported in the *Princeton Union* of March 23,
1911. The development was to consist of two hundred acres at the base of
Mozomonie Point: "The landscape work has been completed under the
direction of Theodore Wirth, superintendent of the Minneapolis city
parks, while Albert Graber of Hennepin county has superintended the
engineering work. Streets have been cleared and roadways are now being
built. Mozomonie Point is one of the beauty spots of Mille Lacs Lake. It is
finely wooded, has a magnificent beach and is certain to become a favorite
summer resort." Another article mentioned that the plat of the development had been approved on March 22 by the Mille Lacs County Board of

Commissioners, but no mention was made of the current inhabitants of the site in either article.[7]

The trial took place on April 5, and the results were reported in the *Princeton Union* of April 6, 1911: "Mille Lacs Investment & Improvement company vs. Chief Wadena and a number of other Indians. Action for ejectment. W. S. Foster for plaintiff, John A. Keyes and H. V. Gard for defendants. There was no appearance on behalf of defendants. Plaintiff waived jury trial and introduced evidence of title, and findings were ordered in its favor."[8]

It is not known why the lawyers for the band members failed to appear and presented no evidence. However, as described earlier, they had argued in a response to the original complaint that began this lawsuit that the band members had for more than thirty years been in "continuous, peaceable, exclusive and adverse possession of the premises described in the complaint and the whole thereof, claiming title thereto, and that these defendants" and their ancestors had "made improvements on said lands of the value of several hundred dollars," and that their possession and occupation of the land had been "by authority, grant, and acquiescence of the United States Government, and that none of said defendants have ever surrendered their rights to said lands or any portion thereof." At this date, however, no one representing the US government appears to have been interested in supporting these arguments. Sporadic attempts were still underway to remove any band members remaining at Mille Lacs to White Earth.[9]

As a result the judge issued an order "for the recovery of . . . real property" against the defendants, which was carried out by county sheriff Henry Schockley in early May. The sheriff's own account was written on the back of the judge's order, where Schockley certified that on the basis of the writ "I have on the 3rd & 4th days of May 1911 removed all of the within named Defendants from the within named real Property and delivered the said real Property to the Plaintiff." On a statement of expenses he noted that he had hired seventeen men and several teams to assist him in the work, most at two dollars per day for two days, though the actual "service of writ of restitution, removing each of said defendants and occupants and putting said plaintiff corporation into possession of the premises, thereby removing nine families," incurred a twelve-dollar charge.[10]

There were several other reports of what occurred that day. On May 11, in keeping with the tone of earlier accounts of interactions with Mille Lacs people, an article in the *Princeton Union* described the event as though it were a battle on the western frontier. It is possible the origin of the tale was the sheriff himself, or someone else who sought to aggrandize the sheriff's role in the events. The article reported that Sheriff Schockley with nineteen "stalwart men" arrived at the village on May 4. It was reported that forty men of the band "had taken up positions behind trees on an eminence and were resting their gun barrels awaiting the order of Chief Wadena to pour forth a volley of lead." The sheriff, said to have been "undaunted by the hostile reception," "ascended the eminence and gathered Wadena into his clutches" and dragged him down "into the valley." When Wadena refused to ask the men to drop their firearms, the sheriff put him in manacles. It was claimed that after an hour Wadena agreed to order his men to throw down their arms. The manacles were removed and "late in the day the old chief and his tribe with their personal effects, moved silently along in single file down the trail until they found another tract of land which suited their fancy. There they settled down and will remain until such time as the paleface owner again drives them forth."[11]

A slightly more sympathetic treatment of the band members' plight was given in a *St. Paul Pioneer Press* article many months later, on October 29, 1911. The author of the article saw the events as an arraignment of "the white race," from which there "will be no appeal forever." The article reported that the village from which the band members had been evicted to make way for a "summer colony" was "an ancient village" where there had been a burial ground: "Upon the wide and shadowed base of Monsomonnoe [Mozomonie] Point the village lay, the various teepees and dwellings scattered as fancy or convenience dictated through the copse, sheltered mostly from the keen sweep of the north wind by thick growths of timber or natural hummocks. There were half a dozen squat log cabins used for winter quarters; three frame structures tar papered outside, and a straggling collection of round-topped birchbark wigwams with their characteristic adjuncts of outdoor living rooms with a large porte cochere made of poles with a covering of green boughs, a most comfortable and picturesque arrangement."[12]

The unknown author of the article appears to have had knowledge of some of the familiar Ojibwe seasonal patterns as well as the role that such villages played as bases of operation for a variety of activities. Still, the author could not resist some culturally biased commentary: "Many of the village dwellings were always empty, the band being characteristically absent on various important business, berrying, fishing, harvesting wild rice, or hunting in season (which is all the time for the Indians) but mostly intent upon the serious work of doing nothing in particular."

According to the author, "Wadena's family, his son's families, and perhaps half a dozen others were all that remained." Wadena was "an individual of strong personality and quiet, if smoldering temper." Apparently efforts had been made to remove him earlier, by "various magnates and potentates [who] were aching to build stucco and cobblestone and concrete palaces." He lived "in the exact middle of the street," presumably as it was laid out in the plans designed by Theodore Wirth. As time went on, "the band of seven or eight families had increased to fourteen, numbering about sixty-five," with the apparent intent of helping Wadena and his community retain their village. "It was by this time late in the spring, and highly necessary to the white settlers to open the highway bisecting the point and clear the cross streets leading to the small private docks on either side"—and it was at this point that the sheriff and his men appeared to do their job.

The article suggested there was no initial attempt to resist the sheriff. In fact, the band members began to dismantle their own bark houses: "The Indians themselves quickly removed and deftly rolled up the strips of birchbark covering the poles of the wigwams." Meanwhile the sheriff's men "unroofed and tore down the frame structures, and piled the lumber at one side not caring to destroy property; they also unroofed the winter cabins and piled the logs in heaps." However, by afternoon "the sheriff set fire to the ruined village." Whether or not this included the lumber the sheriff had been so careful to save from destruction is not known.

At this time, the author said, Wadena, who had been observing all of this activity, "made a move toward his rifle." The sheriff "immediately seized Wadena and after a sharp struggle put him in irons, a man of rank and importance, but nevertheless a man with a breaking heart. In irons he watched his home burned[,] then he was deported a mile or two and liberated." He and his relatives set off in search of a place in which to live: "As twilight stole over the great lake the two wagons laden with household goods lumbered along the highway to dump their burdens in some other spot the Indians did not own and from which they would be compelled to move in time. Women and children plodded after them, patiently, silently, hopeless and hunted."

The article concluded with what appears to be a sarcastic comment rather than an expression of fact: "Wadena, though, will have the last laugh, a laugh of poetic justice. He has bought a lot in the summer colony and will build a stylish cottage."

Shortly after the events on Mozomonie Point, the Milaca *Mille Lacs County Times* reported on June 15, 1911, that another village on the lake had been burned: "The Indian village at Wigwam Bay on Mille Lacs lake between Garrison and Vineland was destroyed by fire the past week probably due to the work of incendiaries. The village consisted of a frame house, several log huts and wigwams. The people have been anxious to get rid of these trespassers who have refused to go to White Earth to take up their allotments, and it is reported that the chief's wigwam was burned while he was strapped to a tree a short distance away."[13]

Aside from expressing the climate of opinion among some whites in the region about the continuing presence of the Mille Lacs Band, the exact circumstance of this event are not made clear. It could have been the work of the county sheriff, considering the threats reportedly made against the residence of Jack Boyd and his brother at Wigwam Bay the year before.

The *Princeton Union* of the same week reported the complete destruction by fire of the Wigwam Bay village—said to consist of a number of wigwams and log cabins. But the article denied that the event was caused by "incendiaries." The newspaper first copied a report from a Brainerd newspaper "to the effect that an old chief of the Chippewas living on the west side of the lake was strapped to a tree and his wigwam and all his belongings burned to the ground in front of his very eyes. While the tears coursed down his cheeks and he begged for pity the fire ate up his home." From several sources the newspaper stated that though the village had in fact burned down, it was most certainly an accidental occurrence: "There were only a few Indian families at Wigwam bay and they never gave the white settlers any trouble." The newspaper insisted on what may appear to have been a surprising point, that "the settlers around Mille Lacs lake are not savages and they have never dealt harshly with the Indians." The explanation for events such as the one that clearly occurred at Mozomonie Point only a few weeks before was simply what the newspaper had been saying for many years: "There is no land left for the Indians at Mille Lacs and it would be far better for them if they were to join their brethren at White Earth where they would be comfortably cared for by the government and could in time become self-supporting and independent."[14]

CHAPTER 22

Setting the Stage for Allotments

Federal officials, following the lead of the Court of Claims and the Supreme Court, began, finally, to make efforts to provide allotments for Mille Lacs band members. Through the influence of Minnesota congressman C. B. Miller, the general appropriation act for the Bureau of Indian Affairs in 1914 provided: "That not to exceed $40,000 of this amount may be used in the purchase of lands for homeless non-removal Mille Lacs Indians, to whom allotments have not heretofore been made, to be immediately available and to remain available until expended, said lands to be held in trust and may be allotted to said Indians, in the discretion of the Secretary of the Interior subject to the provisions of the Act of February eighth, eighteen hundred and eighty-seven, as amended."[1]

The process took more than ten years to implement. James McLaughlin came back to Mille Lacs that year and later to negotiate for the purchase of land parcels. By September 1917 land had been purchased at Vineland, amounting to 709 acres, costing $19,578, and in Isle, 193 acres for $6,087.[2]

The process of obtaining land involved dealing with the neighbors of band members, many of whom had strong feelings about the continuing presence of the band at Mille Lacs. In notes taken around this time McLaughlin described some of the meetings he had. In September 1914 he called on Charles Wallblom of the Wallblom Furniture and Carpet Company in St. Paul about Wallblom's land at Vineland, which included portions of Shaboshkung's land tract. Wallblom stated he had purchased it twenty-two years before for $2,000, supposedly from Nathan Richardson acting under a power of attorney for Shaboshkung. The 1910 assessment rolls for Mille Lacs County show the land was owned by Matilda Wallblom. Further details on the process through which this land was allowed to be taken from band members have not been found. Wallblom had been paying taxes on the property. Later, Charles Wallblom sold all of it except sixty acres for $16 to $22 an acre. He would only sell the remaining land with lake frontage for $150 to $200 an acre. The rest of the land was now owned by E. A. Cooper of Minneapolis.[3]

Charles Wallblom, according to McLaughlin, was "bitterly against the Indians and also against the members of Congress who were instrumental in having legislation enacted providing for the purchase of lands for the depraved sots of Indians remaining at Mille Lacs." McLaughlin concluded that Wallblom was "an old crank."

In general, it was difficult to find land the government could afford to buy. While many settlers of the 1890s had obtained their homesteads for the filing fee (preemptors got their land for $1.25 an acre), in most cases land prices had now risen well above $20 an acre. David H. Robbins, who had 102 acres west of Migizi's allotment, valued his land at $100 an acre. Two years before he had sold two acres for $300. Cutover lands of the Foley Bean Lumber Company—inland from the lakeshore in the area of Neyaashing—were now either owned or handled by the D. S. B. Johnson Land Company. According to another land owner, what was left of this land was being sold for $25 an acre.

McLaughlin sought to buy parcels in areas where band members had land already. In addition to Migizi's allotment there were a few small pieces of land owned by band members in other places on the reservation. Of the 120 acres in 42–27 that had been set aside in the 1898 congressional act, eighty-six acres were still held for the band. McLaughlin wrote that it was "nearly all good meadow land, only about 2 acres in the extreme south end is suitable for burying ground." The land contained a number of burials from former times, but band members had not interred anyone there for twenty-five years. Instead burials took place in the Neyaashing area, where Shaboshkung had been laid to rest.

In addition, at Isle eleven band members had gone together and bought forty acres of "very rough land." It was about two miles northeast of Isle, upriver from the mouth of the Chiminising or Thains River, near the site of the old village destroyed in 1901. In a letter written in 1920 Mike Sam or Wahbegwon stated that the land had been purchased six years before, in other words, just at the time of McLaughlin's arrival. When McLaughlin visited the site in 1914 there were ten houses with board roofs, walls covered with tarpaper, located on this land.[4]

Because of these earlier land parcels, McLaughlin arranged to get land around Neyaashing and Chiminising. But band members continued to fight for the right to remain on land in other places.[5]

For example, Shagobay or Shakopee lived on the lake near Onamia that takes his name. Shakopee and his relatives, including Joe Shakopee, his nephew, were living on lot 1 of section 23 in 42–27, the area on the north side of the lake now called Shakopee Point. McLaughlin said they had received permission from a landowner to go onto the land about five years before, although, as noted by Brower, Shakopee was living on the lake, probably at the same location, in 1900. Shakopee continued to reside on the land and refused to vacate. Joe Shakopee intended to move from this spot to the new lands to be purchased for the band the following spring, but McLaughlin did not learn of the elder Shakopee's plans and made no effort to purchase lands for them.[6]

To a large extent, then, the purchase of lands for Mille Lacs band members was shaped by their previous ability to obtain title to land in particular places. To begin with, there was no real attempt on the part of the government to redress previous wrongs or to buy land where all band members preferred to live.

McLaughlin also looked into the Mille Lacs band members who lived along the Lower Tamarack River, in Pine County. They too had purchased land on their own, and in 1917 McLaughlin was negotiating for the purchase of nine hundred acres to supplement what they had already. McLaughlin reported thirty families living there consisting of 160 people.[7]

In 1917 McLaughlin heard further complaints about Shagobay but once again made no attempt to purchase lands for band members in this area. He wrote to the secretary of the Interior that "it is a matter for the County officials to enforce, which can doubtless be effected without much difficulty." It is unclear if McLaughlin was aware of the earlier village burnings accomplished by county officials.[8]

Once lands were bought, it took almost ten years before they were allotted. In 1916 David H. Robbins, who over the years appears to have had a considerable change of heart about the place of the Ojibwe people at Mille Lacs, wrote to Senator Thomas D. Schall asking for help in stirring up the Indian department. The land had been bought but it had not been allotted nor had any improvements been made. Robbins also asked for a division of the funds awarded by the Court of Claims for the loss of the Mille Lacs lands. It was a "great mistake of justice" to put the $700,000 received in the general Chippewa fund without any provision for the Mille Lacs Indians themselves.[9]

As noted, the land purchased by the Indian department had been located at Vineland and at Isle. But this territory did not represent the full extent of band residence in prior years, nor did it include all the lands on the reservation where band members were actually living. Chief Wadena, for one, continued to live on the land at Cove, in South Harbor Township. In a letter from Onamia in April 1917 Wadena stated that he wished the government to buy land for them between Lake Onamia and Mille Lacs and also by Shakopee Lake. He stated: "We want the land because we will make our living there. We just have to have this land so please help us to have the land purchased for us." They did not want the land at Vineland or Isle.[10]

Superintendent J. E. Hinton of the White Earth Agency, when asked to respond to the letter from Wadena, stated that he did not know if it made sense to buy more land at Mille Lacs or whether the land requested by Wadena could be obtained at a reasonable price. As soon as he could he would visit Mille Lacs and investigate. He noted that Wadena had been requested to move to the land already purchased but refused to do so. Hinton blamed this choice on a dispute between Wadena and Migizi, without recognizing the possibility that Wadena might have strong reasons for wanting to stay where he was. In September Hinton went to Mille Lacs, and he later expressed more sympathy, noting that one had to take into account "the fact that they have heretofore claimed through their ancestors, from time immemorial, all the land, or at least large tracts thereof, in the Mille Lac country." But nothing more appears to have been done in regard to Wadena's request for land to be allotted in South Harbor Township.[11]

CHAPTER 23

Lake Fishing

While federal officials were searching for land to buy for Mille Lacs band members on the reservation, the activities of band members themselves in making use of the traditional seasonal resources at Mille Lacs continued. In some cases there were new opportunities for such usufructuary—or treaty-guaranteed—activities. Band members incorporated novel ways to support themselves while facing familiar patterns of opposition and criticism from local whites.

Beginning in 1917 with the outbreak of World War I, the need for the country to supply food, particularly meat, for the troops sent to Europe created a nationwide shortage. The federal government encouraged the civilian population to conserve resources and seek alternative sources of protein—including wild-caught fish. The Ojibwe residents of the Mille Lacs Indian Reservation, living on a large lake with plentiful fish, had the skills and opportunity to aid this effort.

Leading the way in Minnesota was the Commission of Public Safety, also known as the Public Safety Commission, a new agency vested by the state legislature with extraordinary powers for the duration of the war to "do and perform all acts and things necessary or proper so that the military, civil and industrial resources of the state may be applied toward maintenance of the defense of the state and nation." Among other things, the Public Safety Commission had the power to override fishing regulations, including the prohibition on commercial fishing, a long-running feature of state law.[1]

For years state officials had tried to restrict Indian hunting and fishing while denying the existence of any reserved treaty rights, viewing Native hunters and fishers as poachers. The demand for Americans to eat more fish did not change the attitude of state officials toward treaty rights, but it allowed them to ignore existing laws when required for the current emergency.

State officials developed a plan to allow and encourage commercial fishing on some of Minnesota's larger lakes, including those within Indian reservations such as Red Lake and Mille Lacs. Under the authority of the Public Safety Commission, Carlos Avery, commissioner of the state's Game and Fish Department, instituted a plan to purchase fish directly from fishermen, ship the catch to population centers, and sell it at low prices, either to dealers or directly to the public. State fish dealers were permitted a profit margin of no more than three cents a pound. According to a December 1917 issue of the Game and Fish Department's magazine, *Fins, Feathers and Fur*, fish were distributed through game wardens, representatives of the Public Safety Committee, meat dealers, and other stores and individuals. Once fish began to be marketed, demand exceeded supply. Customers at the first fish sale in the St. Paul city market could not buy more than two or three fish apiece, "lest restaurants monopolize the supply."[2]

Fishing was not restricted to so-called rough fish, those species least desirable for sports fishermen, a limitation which had been one of the features of state law until then. Of the 1,547,306 pounds of fish produced by the state fisheries in 1917 and 1918, over 37 percent were walleye and northern. Most were produced at Red Lake, at Mille Lacs, and in the lakes around the town of Ely.

The commercial fishing program at Mille Lacs began in early 1918 with a state-run commercial fish-purchasing agency or market in the town of Wahkon. Charles E. Lucas, a former fish and game warden from Wisconsin and later mayor of Wahkon, was put in charge. By March the commission was actively purchasing fish out of Mille Lacs Lake, beginning with 160 pounds of burbot or eelpout.[3]

The state fisheries program at Mille Lacs produced both game and rough fish. Although Avery made a point of preventing walleye fishing during spawning season, he did allow it once spawning was over. Records show that over 15,000 fish were produced by the state fishery in Mille Lacs in April 1918, including pickerel or northern pike, suckers, and perch. Walleye fishing began in May, reaching a peak of almost 13,000 pounds of fish in June 1918. Over 20,000 pounds of tullibees were produced by the fishery in November. By the end of the year 71,049 pounds of all kinds of fish had been produced at Mille Lacs. State records indicate that $3,193.27 was paid out for purchasing fish from all fishermen at Mille Lacs, an average of just under five cents a pound.[4]

According to state records for 1918, twenty-four Mille Lacs band members received $509.24, or 15.9 percent of the total amount paid to fishermen. These figures suggest that band members produced around 11,300 pounds of fish during the course of the year. The leading fisherman, according to these records, was Jim Boyd, who received $143 or just over 28 percent of the total paid to band members. Another fisherman, Maqua (likely John Gahbow Sr.), received 12.33 percent of the total. Of the remaining twenty-two fishermen, none received over six percent. Unknown is to what extent any of these fishermen represented families or groups of fishermen working together. No women's names appear on the list even though later evidence shows that women participated in the fishery, particularly fishing with nets for tullibees and whitefish, a traditional activity for Ojibwe women.

The success of the state's fishing program led to its continuance after the war ended in November 1918. However, since the basis for the program had come from the extraordinary powers of the Public Safety Commission, the authority for which ceased three months after the Armistice, the only way it could continue was through legislative authorization.[5]

The possibility that commercial fishing would cease to be legal for Mille Lacs band members was of special concern to Harry D. Ayer, the federally licensed trader who had only recently taken over the former trading post of D. H. Robbins near the outlet of the Rum River, at Vineland. Early on Ayer had sought ways to broaden economic opportunities—and seasonal activities—for the Mille Lacs Band, trading for and buying Indian produce and crafts, building fishing boats, and hiring band members to serve as guides for visiting fishermen. Ayer's participation in carrying out oversight at Mille Lacs was of considerable value to federal officials. In late 1919 C. V. Peel, special agent in charge at White Earth, wrote to the commissioner of Indian Affairs noting, in relation to Ayer, "We have a very excellent man down there, who is the licensed trader, and he is taking a great deal of interest in the Indians, and doing everything possible to help them along."[6]

Ayer wrote to Carlos Avery on February 8, 1919, suggesting the importance of continuing the state fisheries. He asked specifically about whether it would be possible to market "meesi [mizay]," the Ojibwe name for eelpout, which were now running. Mille Lacs band members had asked Ayer to handle the sale of the fish for them. He reported that Charles Lucas at Wahkon had told him there was currently no authority to buy eelpout. In reply, on February 10 Avery affirmed that Ayer could not purchase or ship any fish caught with nets, though they could be speared at any time and sold without restrictions. By law net fishing was allowed for whitefish and tullibees in the fall but not for commercial purposes.[7]

Apparently Avery's reply worried Ayer. He wrote the next day, February 11, giving his opinions about the state fisheries program, including that discontinuing it would be a great mistake. He believed the shallowness of Mille Lacs Lake and the presence of stony reefs and sandbars likely limited the lake's popularity for "outings." But the waters of the lake teemed with fish: paying a fair and constant price to licensed fishermen would build an industry "that would permanently support a large number of families of both white men and Indians." Here was an opportunity to give several families of Indians a chance to follow a livelihood to their liking. During the six months ending July 15 about ten tons of fish, mostly pike, "which were without exception hook and line caught," were marketed from the village at Vineland.[8]

Ayer went on to say that the catch the year before would have been greater, but there had been no time to build boats or put up ice (in the winter, for the storage of fish in the summer). Ayer asserted that the supply of fish could be maintained through proper regulation, licensing, and controlling the numbers of fishermen. In supplying this information Ayer stated that the Mille Lacs band members were banking on being able to fish commercially in the spring. Avery responded to Ayer on March 8, saying that the fisheries program was in danger in the legislature: "A great deal of opposition has arisen coming chiefly from the interests engaged in handling fish, claiming the state should not be in competition with them."[9]

Authorization for continuing the state fisheries program came in part from a law passed that session allowing the Game and Fish Department commissioner to remove rough or nongame fish from state waters if he found they were interfering with the propagation of game fish, providing that such waters were not suitable for angling and that such removal would not deplete any species of fish, was "necessary and desirable to properly cultivate and preserve any species of fish therein," and was "in accordance with the generally accepted principles of scientific fish culture." Fishing would be carried on by contract or by day labor, using nets or other means, the proceeds going into a revolving fund that would allow the fishery to support itself. The provision concluded with the statement that "no fish shall be taken under the provisions of this act from any lake of less area than two hundred square miles."[10]

Although the law appeared to apply only to nongame fish, other provisions provided Avery with authorization to continue commercial walleye fishing. Wording in the main game and fish law that year specifically stated that bass, trout, and muskie could not be bought and sold, but the section of the law dealing with walleye and northern stated that "walleyed pike, except those taken from water which may be open for the sale thereof by the commissioner, may not be bought or sold at any time."[11]

Whether or not legislators intended it, the practical effect of these changes in the law was that the state fisheries continued for all fish at Red Lake and Mille Lacs but ceased everywhere else in the state. When Avery interpreted the law in writing to a man from Backus on April 30, he stated: "the sale of bass, pike and trout is entirely prohibited. Other fish may be sold when legally caught. The Game and Fish Department is not authorized to purchase fish and no state fishing will be carried on under the law except in Mille Lac and Red Lakes." Similarly, in his report for 1920, presented on June 30, Avery wrote that the legislature of 1919 had continued the state fisheries program but "also limited the operation of these fisheries to waters of a certain area thus confining it to two lakes, Red Lake and Mille Lacs."[12]

At Red Lake and Mille Lacs the state fisheries program started up again in May 1919. Sources suggest the renewal was a boon for band members at Mille Lacs. A. B. Hostetter, US Department of Agriculture district agricultural agent, who visited Vineland in May to survey current activities, noted in an interview published in the *Duluth News-Tribune*: "Just now the Indians are engaged in fishing. They catch from 1,500 to 2,500 pounds of fish a day and find a ready market for it with the government. Most of their fishing is done with lines, [with] only the women engaging in net fishing. The county agricultural agent [Hostetter]'s staff decided that perhaps they should be encouraged in following this vocation and that farming should be with them only a side line."[13]

State records indicate that commercial fishing took place on Mille Lacs in May, June, and October of 1919. A total of 45,614 pounds of fish was caught commercially in the lake, almost half of that walleye—over 12 percent of the fish produced by the state fishery that year. No figures have been found to indicate the proportion of that caught by Mille Lacs band members. Fish continued to be sold to the public at below-market prices. Avery wrote in his report for 1920: "The fisheries have been a benefit to the public and to the Indians and settlers on Red Lake particularly."[14]

CHAPTER 24

New and Continuing Opposition to the Mille Lacs Band

Despite the state fishing operation's overall success, opposition began to develop around Mille Lacs Lake, focused on the program itself, on the state officials involved, and ultimately on band members' participation. Petitions against the fishing operation circulated at the same time as a new round of complaints about the continuing presence of the Mille Lacs Band on their reservation. Local white residents made use of many of the same arguments used in previous decades. It was difficult to determine whether commercial fishing was the chief complaint or whether the mere reminder of the presence of the Mille Lacs Band had been enough to stir up the familiar grievances among whites.

While some petitions circulated at Mille Lacs in the fall of 1919 demanding a stop to commercial fishing, others requested the wholesale removal of the Mille Lacs Band. Some combined both issues and originated with the same petitioners. A. P. Jorgenson of Vineland, for example, circulated a petition complaining about Indians at Mille Lacs and asking that they be removed from the lake. According to White Earth special agent C. V. Peel the complaint declared that Mille Lacs band members refused "to obey the state game and fish laws, taking fish and killing game whenever they feel so inclined and think they can get away with it." It also stated that the Indians "scatter over the country in the hunting season, the sugar making season, the rice season, and for berry picking."[1]

Peel sent these comments to Harry Ayer, who answered the charges point by point. Regarding game and fish laws Ayer wrote that the Indians had broken such laws, illegally catching pike from Mille Lacs and selling them to whites, who illegally bought them. The same was true of ducks. But this practice was common among all residents at Mille Lacs: until 1918 "the law in this locality has been lax and practically no one, white or otherwise, observed it." In the spring of 1918 Mille Lacs was opened to commercial fishing by licensed fishermen "as a war measure." Band members obtained licenses and had been observing the laws.

On the charge that Mille Lacs band members refused to cultivate the soil, Ayer stated that gardening was part of the annual seasonal round, further noting the great similarity between the seasonal round practiced by Ojibwe at Mille Lacs and that of white settlers living in the cutover lands cleared of pine by the timber companies: "None of the white settlers have made complete livings from their farms but have supplemented their farm work with road work, lumbering, working in the Dakota harvest fields, etc. In fact, many signers of the petition gain their livelihood practically as do the Indians; they raise a garden, hunt, fish and work out by the day. It is absolutely necessary. Up to the year 1918, game was plentiful."[2]

Regarding agricultural practices, Ayer described a system of community gardening in keeping with Native traditions of sharing. He mentioned six acres of land purchased in 1919 from D. H. Robbins, one of the first whites to come to the reservation in the 1880s. According to Ayer part of the land "had been previously cleared by the Indians for a village before Robbins homesteaded it." The band divided the acreage into sixteen tracts, "distributing these among as many different families by drawing lots." Ayer stated that the Indians "fertilized their fields, worked them as well as they could with the tools available and kept them free from weeds. The yield proves it."

The Indians planted corn, beans, potatoes, rutabagas, squash, pumpkins, and an eighth of an acre each to cucumbers, which they sold for pickling at the Gedney Company's "salting station" at Wahkon. Ayer supplied P. R. Wadswoth, the agent at White Earth, with a receipt from Gedney's local manager reporting payment to seventeen band members for 21,637 pounds of cucumbers, worth $379.40.[3]

The growers additionally raised and sold twenty-two bushels of beans. They cultivated enough potatoes to feed their families through the winter. Ayer stated that band members had sent an exhibit of their products to the Minnesota State Fair. Some families had several pigs. Some had chickens. Three families had cows. In all they had fifty small horses. Together the community made 150 tons of hay, "working on a cooperative basis and dividing the labor and the hay according to the number of horses owned."

As for the claim that band members did not have permanent farms, Ayer mentioned a variety of Ojibwe cultural practices often critiqued by whites, though he emphasized that many in the community did have homes which whites would recognize as such. However, he also noted that every family had a barn "large enough for a team and very warm." For some families these barns served as a home: "These buildings are permanent as much so as any new settlers log house or shack is permanent. They live in them during the winter entirely, in the summer, many substitute the birch wigwam for the house. They have their reasons for it. They are cooler and when performing various kinds of permanent labor for whites, they often erect their birch wigwams near their work on account of having usually to board themselves."

Such birch structures were also useful for band members when they hunted, picked berries, and harvested sugar and rice. Why anyone would complain about their use of such "natural gifts" was not clear to Ayer, and he observed that no complaints were made about their trespassing when ricing. "On the contrary," he noted, "many [whites] desire them to camp on their land for the privilege of obtaining a supply of rice."

Similarly, Ayer provided information on the charge that band members refused employment from white farmers "at the regular going wages" and that they refused to help out in the fields and meadows in 1918 "at the top prices offered them when the whites were being called on for the World War." He found only two cases where complaints were made. One farmer hired four Indians to make hay, paying them $2.50 a day. While they were working, a lumberman from Brainerd arrived and offered them $3.00 a day, with room and board, to work on the log drive. The four men took this job but "arranged for the completion of the haying by sending young men from the village to take their places."

In the second case Vineland resident A. P. Jorgenson, an instigator of one of the petitions, complained about the cost of labor. He had needed help in haying, but had offered only $1.50 per day at a time when the going wage was $3.00 to $3.50 per day, with room and board. Jorgenson was, of course, unable to find any workers, which made sense because Indian labor was in demand throughout the region for haying and potato harvesting. Ayer also noted that a great deal of the land being cultivated by white farmers "has largely been cleared by Indian hired labor or was cleared for Indian village sites before being taken up by whites."

Ayer's various activities in supporting the Mille Lacs Band were described in a letter by N. J. Oredson, cashier at the Soo State Bank of Wahkon, who complimented Ayer on the success he was having in "assisting and interesting the Indians in your neighborhood in farming, gardening and other industries." He praised the band members' industriousness in clearing land, making hay, and other "heavy work," stating further that "if the

Indians should be removed to another location this Mille Lac Lake region would lose one of its interesting attractions."[4]

P. R. Wadsworth, the supervisor in charge and later superintendent at White Earth, relied extensively on Ayer's letter in writing his own report to the commissioner of Indian Affairs on May 12, 1920. In addition to rejecting each of the white residents' charges discussed in Ayer's letter, Wadsworth wrote that the "charge that the Indians did not do their part in the recent war is a stretched statement," noting that he had "met a young Mille Lac Indian soldier boy last week at Vineland who was wounded at the front in France." He reported his belief that Jorgenson was motivated to lead the petitioners in part because he had been unable to get the federal government to buy his land for the Indians, which explained his animus. Wadsworth concluded that "the charges in the petition against the Indians are naked and bare statements and not supported by evidence." The entire petition should be disregarded.[5]

Meanwhile, Carlos Avery and other officials of the Game and Fish Department sorted through complaints about commercial fishing written by some of the same local white residents. Three letters from residents of Vineland opposed to commercial fishing on Mille Lacs reached Carlos Avery in March 1920. W. M. Humason wrote on March 15 that as a taxpayer and resident of the shores of Mille Lacs Lake he protested further netting for commercial purposes. He stated that the practice was an injustice to the people in the area and to the sportsmen of Minnesota. The fish were scarcer year after year, and another season of commercial fishing would finish the lake as a resort for sportsmen. The only people advantaged by the netting and selling of fish were some Indians and a dealer or two, while the country was being robbed of an asset it would never be able to replace.[6]

Peter Evans wrote from Vineland on March 16 describing the "wholesale fishing" carried on at Mille Lacs the last few years with "seines, nets, hooks, and line." The lake was opened up during the war in order to provide cheap fish for the people of the state, but still the fishing continued. The state buyer Charles Lucas was there strictly for what he could make. He had been accused of selling to commission houses rather than entirely to the state, and Princeton people could verify this accusation. Evans also complained about Harry Ayer, who took the Indian-caught fish to Lucas. Ayer and Lucas worked together. "We settlers," said Evans, saw no reason the situation should continue. The wholesale fishing had made fish scarcer, so that there was danger of a person not getting enough for his personal use. Evans stated that those engaged in fish dealing did not live on the lake permanently and had not done anything to build up the country, but were out for what they could get in fish, game, and trade. Evans believed other white residents thought the same as he did and promised that his neighbor from Garrison would be writing to Avery on the same subject.[7]

E. E. Dinwiddie, a settler at Wigwam Bay who had many complaints about the state fishing program and Mille Lacs band members, wrote an outraged letter to Avery on March 15. He asked if there was any way commercial fishing in Mille Lacs could be stopped: "It is certainly a shame to allow the Indians and a few trashy whites to skin our lake in the way they have been doing of late and the way they intend to do this spring." Dinwiddie claimed that he and his neighbors went to considerable trouble to stock the lake and the Game and Fish Department promised there would be no commercial fishing allowed. Why was the practice continuing? In wartime it made sense, but now there was no excuse. Two weeks later, on March 30, Dinwiddie again wrote to Avery to inform him that petitions were circulating. He stated that he had lived on Mille Lacs Lake since 1882 and believed that fish were more scarce compared to a few years before. Only Ayer, Lucas, and the Indians were in favor of commercial fishing—and those who had reaped the benefit should restock the lake. He hoped the petitions would persuade Avery. And he noted that since the roads were almost impassable many people would be unable to sign the petitions.[8]

The petitions Dinwiddie mentioned did not arrive in St. Paul until after the first week in April 1920. Sent by W. M. Humason, they repeated some of the arguments already expressed in the earlier letters, protesting commercial fishing on the belief that all kinds of fish in the lake were rapidly diminishing "so that fishing for home consumption and for sport is seriously jeopardized."[9]

State officials' reactions to the complaints mirrored those of federal officials. Writing to Humason on March 18, Avery stated that the legislature provided for commercial fishing on the grounds that a limited number of fish could be taken from the lake without depleting it, and in this way the industry could be maintained, which was of benefit to quite a number of people. Legislative hearings had shown that the industry benefitted from this fishing. As to whether the lake was harmed by overfishing, Avery noted that the Game and Fish Department had the power to limit the quantities of fish taken. A considerable number of fish died in the lake every summer; he did not know whether there was an excess of fish in the lake, as some had claimed. He rejected the claims of the writers that they had been responsible for the health of the fishing population in the lake through their stocking: "Mille Lac Lake has never been stocked in any effective way and never required it, there always having been an abundant supply of fish in the lake." Avery made many of these same points in his letters to Evans and Dinwiddie. However, he tried to be diplomatic. In replying to each of the correspondents he stated that if it could be shown that commercial fishing was in fact harming the lake he would certainly order that it be stopped. He asked for more evidence from the local people.[10]

Further investigation by members of a committee of the Crow Wing Game, Fish, and Bird Protective Club in Brainerd, including its field secretary and county game warden A. P. Cardle, helped explain the connection between opposition by local whites to the fishing program and opposition by the same individuals to the continuing presence of the Mille Lacs Band. Writing on May 5, the committee's chair, J. F. Woodhead, explained that most of the commercial fishing at Mille Lacs was being done by Indians at Vineland. These Indians were harmless and their catch was such a small percentage of fish in the lake that it seemed ridiculous to stop commercial fishing. He noted that several of the chief opponents to commercial fishing had ulterior motives, in particular A. P. Jorgenson from the Vineland area, who had written a number of the letters opposing the fishing and the Mille Lacs Band.[11]

According to Woodhead, Jorgenson was resentful for several reasons. Harry D. Ayer, as a licensed trader, was getting all the Indian trade Jorgenson formerly enjoyed. Jorgenson also tried to sell his property at an exorbitant price, but the government decided not to buy the land. He was bitter and wanted to get the Indians out of the country. If he couldn't do it peacefully, Jorgenson was heard to say, he would tie a rope around their necks and drag them away. Cardle and the committee working with him were not impressed with Jorgenson. Any statements he made were propaganda. The committee interviewed several farmers who were against commercial fishing, but they did not believe the fishing was depleting the lake. Fish were so plentiful that in the spring great numbers of dead fish could be found along the lakeshore.

Summing up, Woodhead wrote that commercial fishing would not harm other fishing and Indians were in no way interfering with anyone else's rights. The committee talked to the band members through an interpreter and believed they were right in saying that their ancestors lived and fished at Mille Lacs without encroaching on white men's rights. He added, "We feel that if the farmers and resort keepers in that neighborhood would give this matter some thought they cannot help but see the advantage of keeping these people from an advertising standpoint as they are a most interesting tribe and people would go miles to see them." Woodhead concluded by saying that any attempt to do away with commercial fishing or the Indian was purely selfish and should not be considered by the State of Minnesota.

Woodhead's comments were seconded by state senator Hilding Swanson, also from Brainerd, who had been corresponding with Avery on the topic. Since hearing from Avery on April 26 he had given the matter more thought. He appreciated Avery's statements to the effect that the whole matter was a misunderstanding, but Swanson believed the opposition was not well grounded and was based on jealousy. Swanson was interested in the matter as a sportsman. The whole question was seen in a different light during the war "to reduce the high cost of living," and so Swanson had supported the passage of the 1919 law that provided for commercial fishing to continue. But there was another important reason for supporting the industry: it "gives a useful occupation to the Indians about the lake." Referring to Harry Ayer's encouragement of farming and fishing, Swanson noted: "They make a little money to properly provide for their families. They have spent money to get ready for the present season and are now informed that they cant fish, at an industry that they know how to do. Others too have spent money to get ready for this season." According to Swanson the Indians' interest in fishing meant no one would be accusing the band members of being lazy.[12]

On May 6 Avery received a sympathetic letter from Richard Hamer, a state senator from Milaca who had voted against continuing the state program because of the many arguments presented by the "lake people," that is the local whites from Mille Lacs. Among other things he mentioned the common fear that declining fish populations would harm the lake's value as a resort. He noted that Avery's experience demonstrated how hard it was to please everybody. In response Avery wrote that he did not feel he could open state fishing on Mille Lacs until he could check on the situation and he hoped people would come to some amicable understanding. Personally he did not believe that taking a limited amount of fish for food purposes would deplete the lake, but on the other hand there was no great need to carry on the fishing. Whatever action was taken should be in the best interests of the lake and the people in general. He had received a number of communications and petitions and had had someone check into the matter. He also expected to visit the area and interview people himself.[13]

On May 11 Avery received another letter from J. F. Woodhead of the Crow Wing Game, Fish, and Bird Protective Club, reporting the results of its investigation into commercial fishing at Mille Lacs. Woodhead stated that "a motion was made and carried that our club go on record to approve of commercial fishing in Mille Lacs Lake for this season and that the report of the investigation committee be accepted."[14]

A few days later Avery notified many of the opponents of the fishing program that he would be going to Wahkon on May 19 "to dispose of the matter relative to the commercial fishing." He asked them to inform others that he was interested in meeting with "anyone who is interested or concerned."[15]

The day before the meeting P. R. Wadsworth at the White Earth Agency wrote to Avery giving his opinion thus: "all things considered there were no good reasons for stopping the Indians doing such fishing and inasmuch as it is quite important to the Indians I sincerely hope that they will be allowed to fish this year as they did last."[16]

However, it appears that even before going to the meeting at Wahkon Avery was already inclined to alter the state fishing program. His rationale appears to have been his desire to come to an amicable understanding "in the best interest of the lake and the people in general." As a public official charged with enforcing unpopular laws he could make no decision that would alienate large numbers of the population. Throughout the early years of wildlife management in Minnesota, commercial use and Native use had always been presented as contrary to the best interests of game and fish. Thus, despite ample evidence to the contrary, any decision Avery reached was likely to be dictated by the consensus of "the population in general," that is to say the non-Indian side of the argument.

Even if Avery was not already inclined to alter the fishing program, the meeting in Wahkon provided additional impetus in that direction. In an account written the next day, Avery noted that there were 250 to 300 people from the towns along the lakeshore, nearly all of whom opposed "the continuation of the fishing for pike with nets." It seemed preordained: at the meeting Avery proposed that he would issue an order acquiescing in the consensus of those present. An article the next day in the *Wahkon Enterprise* reported that "At a hearing here Wednesday afternoon by Carlos Avery, executive agent of the state fish and game commission, Mr. Avery ruled that hereafter only hook-and-line fishing would be allowed in Mille Lacs lake, and that the fishermen could sell their catches on the open market."

Avery's order, entitled "Permitting the sale of Pike-Perch or Wall-eyed Pike when Taken from Mille Lac Lake," stated that "It is hereby ordered that pike-perch or wall-eyed pike, legally caught with hook and line within legal limits from Mille Lac Lake, Minnesota, may be sold as provided for in Section 73, Chapter 400, General Laws of 1919." The order would be in effect until January 1, 1921, pending further authorization or changes in the law. Avery used as a basis for his decision the statement that "wall-eyed-pike, except those taken from water which may be open for the sale thereof by the commissioner, may not be bought or sold at any time."[17]

As reported in the *Wahkon Enterprise* of May 20, henceforth only hook-and-line fishing would be allowed in Mille Lacs and fishers could offer their catch on the open market rather than being forced to sell to Charles Lucas. The article reported, with irony, that there had been petitions protesting commercial fishing, but "that is just what has now been made permissible. What was in operation in the past year was state fishing." The article stated, "Mr. Lucas, who has been in charge of the state market here, will now be in the fish business or [for?] himself." Avery declared the charges against Lucas to be unfounded.[18]

Exactly what this compromise meant and what Avery thought of it was explained in a series of letters to various individuals who had written to him about it. Avery replied to P. R. Wadsworth that he felt a personal interest in the Indians' welfare and sympathized with Ayer's efforts. However, he had found it necessary to change the management of the state fisheries at Mille Lacs "to some extent on account of the sentiment of the people around the lake." He had issued an order that would enable band members to sell walleye caught with hook and line. It was further agreed and understood that the state fisheries would continue to handle tullibees and whitefish caught with nets in the fall. He concluded: "Under these arrangements, the pike fishing will not be so profitable as it would be with fishing with nets, but it will allow some of the older Indians and women to fish if they wish to do so and sell their fish. I think that there is no particular hardship on the able bodied men who can do some other kind of work." He hoped this decision would be satisfactory to the Indians' interest. It was the "only settlement we could make to the controversy."[19]

Harry Ayer seems to have thought Avery's compromise a good one, although his letter to Avery has not been found. In a reply on May 22 Avery wrote that he appreciated Ayer's comments: "It is very gratifying to me indeed and I hope that it will all work out for the best. I could see no other way out of the dilemma." Avery admitted he was responding to public pressure, but in such situations, he said, "we are of necessity compelled to be responsive to a great extent to public sentiment particularly when the sentiment tends toward conservation rather than away from it." There may have been unworthy motives, but there was no question people were against pike fishing with nets. He regretted the arrangement would cause a loss to Ayer and Lucas. He did not think the revised policy was a victory for anyone, but a reasonable adjustment of a difficult situation. He noted that he had also received a letter from W. M. Humason of Vineland, a vocal opponent of commercial fishing, expressing satisfaction at the outcome.[20]

Although Harry Ayer was happy with Avery's settlement, it is not clear whether it was satisfactory for Mille Lacs band members. There were immediate suggestions that Indian people were disregarding the rule against using nets. On May 27 Avery wrote to A. P. Cardle, enclosing a letter from commercial fishing opponent A. P. Jorgenson, who stated that there were a dozen gill nets being used near Indian Point. Avery asked Cardle to investigate and confiscate any nets he found. He indicated faith in Harry Ayer and his ability to control the band members' fishing, but if Ayer could not do it, the sale of walleye would have to be discontinued. On May 31 D. E. Emmons, one of the earlier petitioners, wrote to Avery saying there were nets set in the lake. He had not seen the nets himself and did not know to whom they belonged, whether Lucas or someone else, but in any case that person was not afraid of Lucas in his role as game warden.[21]

Around the end of May A. P. Cardle apparently confiscated some nets and seized the catch from Indian fishers, although the details of what happened are not entirely clear from available documents. Writing to D. E. Emmons Avery reported that agents had found several nets in use by Indian women; the Indian agent had given them permission to use the nets to take fish for their families. However, Avery said that even if the nets were used in this way "it cannot be allowed under this agreement and I think they will be kept out of the lake."[22]

Writing to Cardle on June 1 Avery stated that he approved of what Cardle had done. Avery mentioned that he had received a letter from Harry Ayer and one Ayer had written to Cardle, advising the agent to instruct band members not to employ nets even for their own use while this regulation was in effect: "I will write Mr. Ayer it will be necessary to keep the nets out of the lake entirely while this arrangement is in effect because it would be impossible to know from our own knowledge whether fish were taken with nets for sale or not, and, even if the Indians were acting entirely in good faith and catching fish with nets for their own use only, this would not be sufficient explanation to those who would be inclined to criticize." There was no other way but to instruct everyone that all nets must be kept out of the lake.

Avery's decision not to allow nets in Mille Lacs Lake for any purpose appears to have caused some confusion, since it contradicted his earlier letter implying that older Indian women would be allowed to continue to use nets for fish other than walleye. Harry Ayer appears also to have concluded that Avery would allow the Ojibwe to use nets when they fished for personal use. Replying to a letter on this topic from May 31, Avery wrote on June 2 that the Indians should not use nets even for their own personal fishing because doing so would "give rise to accusations which cannot be disproved so I think that it would be best to instruct them accordingly." Avery appeared to be saying that because local whites might conclude— as state game officials consistently had in the past—that all net fishing done by Indian people was for commercial purposes it was advisable for the band members to do no net fishing. The advice was seconded by agent P. R. Wadsworth on June 25, who wrote that it would now be best for the Indians not to use nets in any way, "and then there will be no trouble."[23]

Despite the handicaps under which the Mille Lacs band fishers were now operating, Harry Ayer wrote to Hilding Swanson on June 6 to report: "We are shipping lots of fish." Later in June, however, Ayer wrote to P. R. Wadsworth saying: "The fishing is about over. There was a comparatively small catch, due to the fact of the fine wages offered by the work on the Scenic Highway," a state highway construction project.[24]

No figures exist in state records for the numbers of fish caught commercially on Mille Lacs Lake in 1920, since the state was no longer involved in marketing the fish. Harry Ayer made arrangements to ship the fish for band members, but he may have had some difficulty in disposing of the catch. George W. Larson of Minneapolis wrote to Ayer on June 2, stating that the sales prospects were not encouraging. Fish companies and large retail dealers offered only thirteen to fifteen cents a pound for walleye and eight to nine cents a pound for pickerel. That price would not pay for the gas to haul the fish by truck from Mille Lacs. Larson planned to keep out of the fish business until bass season.[25]

Ayer explained the changes in the fishing operation to Wadsworth in early October. He wrote that in 1919 the state of Minnesota bought walleye from the Indians at five cents a pound in Wahkon, deducting seven percent shrinkage. Ayer hauled the fish by truck 16.5 miles and received one cent a pound for his trouble. In 1920, because of the new state ruling, private parties handled the fish. Ayer purchased the fish from the Indians at his store at seven cents a pound and made no deduction for shrinkage. Although Ayer's letter is illegible in many places it appears he purchased fewer than five thousand pounds of fish. This low figure was partly due to the ruling eliminating the use of nets and partly because work on the state highway was more profitable than fishing.[26]

Also in this letter Ayer denied charges that he had told band members they could continue to use nets because he wanted to buy the fish himself. He did tell some people they could net for their own use: "I had understood from Mr. Dickens [superintendent of the Red Lake Agency] that Indians could take fish from their own waters in any manner for their own consumption." Band members continued to use nets in fishing for their own use, resulting in complaints. One woman lost her net to the game warden, who gave it to Ayer, who returned it to the woman. In any case, Ayer stated that he continued to buy fish caught with hook and line throughout the season and he had a perfect right to do so under the state ruling.

It is not clear whether commercial fishing of any significance occurred at Mille Lacs after 1920. A 1922 report noted that the state fisheries program, which continued almost entirely at Red Lake, had purchased 2,669 pounds of tullibees at Mille Lacs, but no information was given about those who caught these fish. In 1921 the law authorizing the Game and Fish Department to remove nongame fish from Minnesota lakes was changed to allow fishing of certain species in lakes smaller than two hundred square miles. The law now stated more precisely that (italics added to show changes) "no fish, *except carp, buffalo-fish, sheepshead, tullibees, bullheads, dogfish, burbot, suckers, and goldeyes*, shall be taken under the provisions of this act from any lake of less area than two hundred square miles."[27]

The provision Carlos Avery had used as the basis for his compromise order allowing commercial angling for walleye in 1919 continued to be on the books until 1945. The fact that the state fisheries program did not resume may simply have been due to Avery's fear of the controversy that occurred in 1920. In any case, since the state no longer marketed fish caught at Mille Lacs, no profits would accrue to the Game and Fish Department's revolving fund.[28]

The end of commercial fishing in Mille Lacs Lake was not based on any knowledge that fish populations were being depleted. It would certainly have been difficult to find actual scientific evidence that commercial fishing was harming Mille Lacs Lake. In the history of game and fish management in Minnesota little attempt had been made to study fish populations or the effect of commercial or sports fishing on them. Anecdotal evidence was usually offered in arguing for tightening or loosening regulations. One example was the often-cited fish mortality that occurred on a regular basis in a variety of large lakes in Minnesota, including Mille Lacs Lake. On August 21, 1906, the lawyers Fosters and Burns of Milaca wrote to the commission saying that the shores of Mille Lacs Lake were littered with dead fish. They believed this circumstance would seriously diminish the lake's stock. As noted earlier Carlos Avery wrote in May 1920 that some had concluded the die-off indicated that the lake was overcrowded, though he professed not to know whether this was the case.[29]

Finally in 1921 the Game and Fish Department attempted to find a scientific answer to what was causing the die-off and what impact it should have on resource management for the lake. The commission induced Barry J. Anson, scientific assistant with the US Fisheries biological laboratory in Fairport, Iowa, to investigate "the cause of the mortality of fishes in certain Minnesota lakes," specifically Mille Lacs Lake, Leech Lake, and Lake Bemidji, all of which suffered mysterious kills during which thousands of fish would wash up on the shore. Anson visited Mille Lacs Lake in August 1921 to gather information. His report was published in *Fins, Feathers and Fur* in December 1921.[30]

Although no such kills occurred during Anson's visit, the scientist was able to examine the remains from a July die-off along a five-hundred-foot section of Carnelian Beach; the kill occurred during a period of extremely warm, calm weather. Anson estimated that on one day in July 650,000 pounds of whitefish had washed up on the shores of the entire lake.

Anson concluded that "the annual mortality represents a natural condition since it is of regular occurrence and could not be the result of pollution." Most of the fish affected were accustomed to cold water, including walleye, whitefish, and tullibees. Anson hypothesized that the rapid warming of the lake waters in June and July would cause cold-water fish to move to depths where the quantity of oxygen must have been small and made smaller by "the enormous numbers of fishes in the deeper parts of the lake." All evidence pointed to the cause of fish deaths being "the result of lowered dissolved oxygen content, occasioned by the want of the natural mechanical means for the introduction of oxygen."

Based on these findings Anson offered recommendations about fish management in these lakes. He noted that Minnesota lakes were opened to commercial fishing in 1917 and allowed to remain open through 1919. In 1920 the lakes were open to commercial fishing by hook and line only, while in 1921 all forms of commercial fishing were prohibited. During 1917, 1918, and 1919 the maximum annual catch of all species in Mille Lacs Lake was 71,000 pounds. Pike, suckers, yellow perch, and pickerel formed the bulk of the catch, and fishing was done by residents only and did not involve commercial companies.

Based on these facts Anson advised permitting commercial fishing, especially "since the above-mentioned maximum annual catch is approximately but one-tenth of the loss, in pounds, of one day during the warm period of the present year. The resulting gain on the part of the state would, obviously, be considerable." Anson concluded by saying that decisions about whether to permit commercial fishing on these and other lakes should be made on a case-by-case basis, "closing or opening particular ones as deemed wise, rather than to attempt to cover all, and essentially different, cases by blanket legislation."

The state apparently found it difficult to follow this advice, in part because of continuing fears about harms commercial fishing posed to sports fishing. These concerns dominated public opinion and governmental action following the uproar in 1920. Carlos Avery, who had been in favor of commercial fishing and more sympathetic to the band members' point of view than other state officials, was soon forced to acknowledge that the practice could not continue. While he wrote in 1920 that "Commercial fishing is a legitimate activity and one which should be carefully fostered so as to perpetuate an exceedingly important and valuable food product" and that it was important as an aid in reducing the population of carp, he was less sanguine in 1922. Avery wrote that "commercial fishing is constantly the source of some controversy, and owing to the fact of the great interest and use of the waters of the state for angling purposes, the sale of all game fish from inland waters suitable for angling must inevitably be discontinued." Avery was not reappointed to his position in 1924, possibly because of his support for some degree of commercial fishing.[31]

In the years that followed pressure against various form of commercial fishing continued. Eventually the program allowing net fishing for rough fish on inland lakes was discontinued. In 1940 Commissioner of Conservation W. L. Strunk wrote that "a considerable number of abuses sprang up and the natural result was that the people of the state were cheated," though he did not specify what those abuses were. However, he noted that if the proper legislation were enacted commercial fishing in international waters could continue.[32]

Of all the state's inland lakes, only in relation to Red Lake did state officials tacitly follow Barry J. Anson's recommendation that each be dealt with on a case-by-case-basis. Here also there was pressure to stop commercial fishing. In 1922 S. A. Selvog, superintendent at Red Lake, noted that some had called for ending the state fisheries program on the grounds that "Red Lake may become depleted and thereby the angling interests interfered with." He noted evidence to the contrary and called for the program to continue.[33]

Authorization for continuing the state fishery at Red Lake was based on the 1919 law. However, in 1929 the legislature specifically authorized fish to be taken and sold from Upper and Lower Red Lakes. The same legislature created Red Lake Game Preserve, including areas outside Red Lake Indian Reservation, and provided for management (including sale) of game and fish resources in the region. Also that year, the Red Lake Fishery Association was incorporated by the Red Lake Band, providing, as Marvin F. Boussu put it, "the instrument by which the Indian commercial fishery began to develop" into a prosperous industry that continued for many years after. Political pressure prevented anything similar from occurring at Mille Lacs.[34]

CHAPTER 25

One Parcel at a Time

By the early 1920s the federal government had largely ceased its efforts to persuade Mille Lacs band members to go to White Earth and would soon, after many years, issue allotments on the reservation at Mille Lacs. However, in some places on the reservation individuals continued to harass and, when possible, remove Mille Lacs band members, one at a time, from parcels of land, one parcel at a time. In 1920 band member Tom Hill wrote to President Warren G. Harding to report on attempts to remove Chief Wadena and eight families from the land they continued to occupy at Cove and request help. In August 1919 George and Alice Hyser had posted a notice on the land that Wadena and the other families occupied in lot 1 of section 16 of 42–26, stating that all persons would have to remove all their improvements "preparatory to fencing said property by order of the owners." A letter from a local man, William Lufkins, stated "the Indian claims that he has lived there all his life time hence the sacredness and the reluctance to move from said place."[1]

Agent P. R. Wadsworth of White Earth apparently believed no one was urging Wadena to move from the land and that once the lands at Isle and Vineland had been allotted the problem would be solved. Band member Tom Hill wrote another letter to Washington in October 1921:

> We are afraid of our lord and we would not tell you anything that
> wasn't true. This is all the truth we are telling you, about what
> the white men are doing to us, when they tore down our houses.
> They are treating us mean in every way. They won't let us kill ducks,
> deer, fish, partridges and everything else, even trees, where we get
> our fire, how are we to live? We beg of you in Washington, to help
> us. I will tell you of some of our times, back before the white man
> settled here and after everything went well, but they came they
> burned down, Nay gwa nay be [Negwanebi]—Wah den ah [Wadena],
> homes when they came. We chi wa gwab—they also set fire to his

house, his women folks were beaten, there were only women home when the white man came. And now its our turn. They tore down our homes Aug. 4, 1921. That makes four times now they've acted so mean. Harry Schockley was the leader this time.

This account summarized many years of village burnings, including what happened in 1901 with Negwanebi and 1911 with Wadena. Now the village at Cove had been attacked. No other details have been found about this incident, but Harry Schockley was the sheriff who burned down Wadena's village in 1911.[2]

The Indian Agency made no attempt to purchase the land on which Wadena lived. In 1923 a suit was filed in Mille Lacs County Court to remove Wadena and others living there, though in a communication with the White Earth agent the lawyers for the landowner, Guy C. Johnson, stated that their client's first choice was to have the people moved off the land in a "humane and paternal" way, preferably during warm weather. Superintendent P. R. Wadsworth, writing to the commissioner of Indian Affairs, noted that Wadena's band had lived on the land for many years. He recommended that they be represented by an attorney "so that full justice may be given them in this matter." He suggested that while it might be that band members had no rights to the land, perhaps "adverse possession rights of the Indians should be regarded." Wadsworth later wrote to the attorneys that he did not think Johnson had any title to the land; had it been different he would have so advised the Indians. He had requested the US attorney represent the Indians in the case.[3]

Despite Wadsworth's conclusions, a lawyer in Washington provided a memorandum to the effect that all "Mille Lac Indian land titles have been extinguished and the only tracts to which the Indian can lay claim are some that have been purchased for their use. This tract is not in the list of purchased lands." Section 16 was state school land, and the defendant, Guy C. Johnson, held title through a school land certificate. The commissioner of Indian Affairs reported this conclusion, stating that it did not appear the Indians had any right to remain on the land "unless such rights have been acquired through adverse possession." The office was prohibited from employing counsel at the expense of the government under US statutes.[4]

Wadsworth, now better informed about the history of Wadena and the others in relation to the property, responded on July 2. He learned that Wadena had been living on the land for thirteen years—that is, approximately since he was burned out of the village on Mozomonie Point in 1911. Others had been living there longer. Wadena's parents lived on the land "years ago," and Wadena "was raised on the land." Corroboration for this statement comes from the 1902 "Schedule of Improvements," in which it is recorded that Noodin, Kegwedosay's widow, lived on this very same plot of ground. It is not known if Noodin herself was still alive when Wadena returned to the site in 1911.[5]

No possibility of an "adverse possession" claim was suggested on July 18, when the chief clerk of the Indian Office responded. He reviewed familiar history about Indian title to the Mille Lacs Reservation being extinguished and the band's Court of Claims case, and stated that since "they have had their day in Court" the only tracts to which they could lay claim were the tracts purchased for allotment. He concluded, "Chief Wadena has no right on the land that the United States can recognize or defend, and you should so inform him." This response eloquently summarized the entire previous history of federal policy toward the Mille Lacs Band.[6]

Wadena and the other band members received minimal representation when the case was argued in the Mille Lacs County district court. A default judgment was entered in favor of Johnson, and the county sheriff was ordered to remove the defendants. It is unclear what actions the sheriff took, but probably they were less drastic than those of his predecessor in 1911. The sheriff reported only a twelve-dollar fee for removing the defendants on July 27, 1923.

Wadena was not through fighting for the land in South Harbor Township. On March 18, 1924, he wrote to the commissioner of Indian Affairs about his claims. In a letter that opened with a summary of the treaties of 1855 and 1864 he recounted the village burnings of the past:

> I was removed by force on land that I had been residing on for thirty years, known as the land that was set apart for the Chief mentioned above of Mille Lacs Lake. I am the remaining Chief known as Chief Wadena of the Mille Lacs Band, which there is only about ten families left. After this removal by force, we were then again ordered to move to another piece of land lying along-side of the Mille Lacs Lake, where we are now located.
>
> In 1923 of last year, we were again ordered to vacate the land we are now residing on. I am asking you, if you will be so kind to see into this matter, that we will get a home where we can be

comfortable and call our own. I hope as soon as you get my letter and will take this matter up at once, let us know what is to become of us in regards of our land rights.[7]

Neither Wadena nor anyone else was ever able to obtain allotments in South Harbor Township, where band members had lived for generations. Still, it appears that he and other band members continued to live on the land. In fact, Johnson did nothing to develop his land. His lawyers reported in October 1924 that "some Indians, presumably the defendants in this action, are again squatting on this land," and in a petition in 1926 the lawyers stated that the defendants were still living on the land. They requested another court order for removal, which the judge issued on June 22, 1926. Whether further action was taken by the sheriff is unclear. In the 1930s the land was forfeited to the state for failure to pay taxes and interest. Wadena died in May 1935; band members have continued to live on portions of this land up to the present day.[8]

Not all Mille Lacs band members survived into old age to lend their will in preserving the reservation. In one case, in June 1925, Tom Wind (Mayzhuckegwonabe), a band member from Pine County, married to Mary Pendegayaush (Wahbooze), whose family lived on an allotment in the area of Vineland, died in an altercation with a Mille Lacs County sheriff's deputy. Wind and his brother John were accused of causing a disturbance in the area of Wigwam Bay. The deputy sheriff, Si Lund, and a constable, Bruce Milton, attempted to arrest the brothers, who resisted. Lund shot and killed Tom Wind. The *Mille Lacs Messenger*, published in Isle, reported that Lund had meant only to "inflict a superficial wound," but, because he was "firing in the uncertain light of the automobile headlights," his aim "was too good." The newspaper insisted that Lund had no choice.[9]

CHAPTER 26

A Fraction of What They Had Been Promised

The actual allotment of lands to Mille Lacs band members finally took place in 1925. Allotments in the Vineland area were concentrated in sections 17, 20, 27, and 28 of 43–27, the northern portion of Kathio Township, and varied between 5 and 7.5 acres each. A much smaller number were made for band members in 42–25, though they were all for 7.5 acres. Allotments were also issued for band members living off the reservation in Pine County.

In all it was a fraction of the Mille Lacs Reservation, a fraction of what would have been set aside under plans in 1882 and 1883, a fraction of what would have been allotted to band members had the promises of the Nelson Act and those made by Henry Rice in 1889 been carried out, a fraction of what the Mille Lacs people consistently claimed as their just heritage.

In the 1920s and 1930s federal officials began again to purchase lands for the use of the Mille Lacs Band on and off the reservation at Mille Lacs. This program of land purchase came under the Wheeler–Howard Act of June 1934, known as the Indian Reorganization Act (IRA). The act had many purposes carried out by federal officials throughout the country. As indicated by its very name, the government aided Indians to reorganize tribal governments. The various Ojibwe bands in Minnesota, except for Red Lake, were treated under the general umbrella of the Minnesota Chippewa Tribe (MCT). In the case of the Mille Lacs Reservation, in October 1938 the MCT granted a charter defining the various smaller groups making up the Mille Lacs Band and the structure and powers of its constituent parts. The charter defined the Mille Lacs Band to include tribal members previously listed on tribal rolls for the non-removal Mille Lacs Band, groups on the Mille Lacs Reservation; as well as villages at Big Sandy Lake; East Lake, which was north of Mille Lacs near Rice Lake in Aitken County; and Danbury, Wisconsin, which included band members living in

Pine County, Minnesota. Under the charter all of these people were considered to be members of the Mille Lacs Band even though not, technically speaking, residents of the 1855 Mille Lacs Reservation. All of these band members were entitled to representation on the band's tribal council, its "governing body."[1]

The federal program for the purchase of additional lands for band members' use began even before the Mille Lacs Band had received its MCT charter. In 1936 officials consulted with tribal leaders and members about desirable lands. Late that year officials advertised in local newspapers their interest in purchasing land throughout the reservation in areas adjacent to previous allotments and purchased lands. They wrote to landowners on the reservation from Isle on the east to Kathio Township on the west, as well as to landowners in other areas off the reservation.

Most of these letters began like this one to a Minneapolis landowner in December 1936: "The Federal Government is planning to purchase a few tracts of land in the vicinity of Mille Lacs Lake, in Mille Lacs County, Minnesota. The land so purchased will be owned by the Federal Government in trust for the use of the Mille Lacs Band of Chippewa Indians." Such letters then stated the understanding that the person addressed owned a parcel of land in that area and inquired: "Will you kindly advise whether this property is for sale and if so will you please advise the price you are asking for it?" If the landowner was interested in selling, the land field agent in Minneapolis, A. L. Hook, or his assistant, Rex Barnes, stated, federal officials would appraise the property to determine whether the owner's offer was reasonable. "Option forms" would then be forwarded to the landowner, leading to the purchase of the land by the federal government.[2]

News of the federal program to buy lands owned by white people at Mille Lacs, in locations in or near the reservation, spread more widely in late 1936. Paradoxically, articles in the *Mille Lacs Messenger* described the land purchase as an attempt to establish an "Indian Colony." On December 24, 1936, the newspaper reported that officials had proposed to buy an entire section of land—either section 22 or section 27 of T43–N25, five miles north of Isle—and establish a colony of 150 Indian families who would come from the area of Leech Lake. The source of this information was said to have been an unnamed "government man" who called on property owners. The article raised questions about "what the Indians would live on after they were gathered up and deposited on the reservation." According to the article the information had caused "a feeling of unrest" in Isle, though "many people wanted more information before they were willing to express approval." Concluding with more accurate information, the article stated that the project at Isle, like a related one to buy land for the Indians at Vineland, was intended to provide "the red men with space for gardens and small fields so they might be able to contribute more toward their own support."

In early January Hazel Carlson of the Isle American Legion Auxiliary wrote to Hook to request accurate information about the project. She repeated the rumor about the Indians from Leech Lake, adding that she had heard that Indians were to be moved from Danbury, Wisconsin, the closest town to the Pine County members of the Mille Lacs Band. Also, she'd heard that the land was to be used "to move the Indians we have here on to farm."[3]

Hook responded to explain the project as conveyed in the letters he wrote to landowners, stating that the land was for the benefit of the Indians then living at Isle, to provide land for homes, with enough space for gardens, and wood for fuel. No Indians would be moved from other places. On the same day the *Mille Lacs Messenger* reported that information was lacking on the subject of the "Indian colony," repeating several of the rumors, a separate article stated that the Isle American Legion and Auxiliary had appointed a committee to investigate the "Colony," including, among others, Hazel Carlson. The committee was already circulating a petition protesting the "proposed move." The group hoped that Isle citizens "would join in opposition to having such a colony so near the village."

A day after that, Henry Paulsen, an Isle businessman associated with the Mille Lacs Timber Company, wrote directly to the Department of Interior in Washington, DC, to protest the apparent plan to purchase land along the lakeshore north of Isle, or at any other point along the lake other than what band members currently occupied: "We are opposed to have Indians at so many different locations within the same locality." He stated: "White people in general as well as white girls have been molested by the Indians around our village here for many years past; we are coming to a stand where we will take a stand against any new Indian reservation or grant being made in this vicinity." He concluded by suggesting that all the Indians at Isle should be moved to the west side of the lake, "where there is a considerable amount of land already located for them."

On January 29 Hook answered Paulsen's letter, stating that he attributed the unfavorable attitude of those in Isle to unfounded rumors. It was clear from the protest letters that the program had been "grossly misrepresented." He explained the goals of the land purchases to aid the band members already living at Isle and added that the suggestion to move the Indians to the other side of the lake was "impractical": "This group of Indians have for a long time made their homes in their present location and land has been allocated there for their use. In the many years that they have occupied their present homes, it is only natural that a sentimental attachment to their location has resulted. We should not fail to consider the human aspect of this matter and realize that these people are citizens of Minnesota, and that the solution of their social and economic problems is in large measure the responsibility of the respective communities where they live." He hoped the citizens of Isle would "see fit to reverse their attitude on this question and cooperate with us in a program for the rehabilitation of this group of people, which we feel . . . assured will be of ultimate benefit to the entire community."[4]

While complaints continued from white people in Isle, A. L. Hook began to receive offers to sell land from other areas around the lake. Even longtime opponents of the Mille Lacs Band's presence, such as Andrew P. Jorgenson, who owned land parcels near the outlet of the Rum River and at the south end of Wigwam Bay, were now willing to sell to the government.[5]

The next day, February 11, the *Mille Lacs Messenger* published two items on the topic, one a short note reporting on Hook's response to Paulsen, the other an editorial entitled "Indian Rehabilitation." The newspaper agreed that rumor was the root of the problem. No one in Isle would "oppose the plan to rehabilitate the Indians now at Mille Lacs," but "nearly everybody will oppose any plan which would add to our troubles by shipping in a lot of Indians without first making dependable long-term arrangements for taking care of them." Rumor may have been the cause of the opposition in the first place, but federal officials were at fault for not publicizing their plan from the beginning.[6]

A subsequent report in the newspaper referred to the government's plan as a rehabilitation program, rather than a colony, though public protests continued. To counter the resistance, Hook spoke to the March 18 meeting of the Isle Civic and Commerce Association, at the Isle Café. In the prepared text of his remarks, he began by explaining the purposes of the Indian Reorganization Act in relation to the loss of land in the settlement era. Hook stated: "We maintain that the Indian has lost his birthright, his way of living, and that he has never been repaid." The IRA "may be considered as a new deal for the Indian and a recognition of the injustice which he has suffered." Land acquisition—purchasing "such lands as may be required to rehabilitate the various Indian groups on a self-sustaining basis"—was an important purpose of the act. Hook noted that the previous allotment system—based on individual ownership of land—had caused a decrease in Indians' landholdings, while in communities where the allotment system was never introduced, such as Red Lake in Minnesota and the Menominee Reservation in Wisconsin, the tribes "are at present supporting the Indian group by a proper utilization of the economic assets" on the respective reservations.[7]

As for what the federal government meant to do in relation to the Indians living at Isle, Hook discredited the many rumors and assured the gathered white citizens and businessmen that there was no intention to bring in Indians from other places to live there. Whatever was done would be purely for the benefit of the Mille Lacs band members already living in the community northeast of the town of Isle, where, as noted, they had purchased a small piece of land as early as 1914, and where the federal government purchased more land in the years after that. The purpose of the federal program was "rehabilitation," to make it possible for each family to have a garden and adequate fuel, that is, timber, to heat their homes and the ability to "make rice," as they had always done. In addition to purchasing suitable land for communities to live on, the government would acquire "wild rice fields" or "suitable locations along wild rice lakes which will serve . . . as camp sites during the ricing season."

In conclusion Hook counted on members of community organizations, such as the American Legion, the Legion Auxiliary, the parent teacher association, women's clubs, and other groups, to help "the Indians become useful citizens of the community" through "united civic action."

Reporting on Hook's presentation, the *Mille Lacs Messenger* mentioned discussion that took place at the end of the meeting. A man from Minneapolis who had built "an expensive lake-shore home north of Isle" stated that "his investment would be depreciated by several thousand dollars if an 'Indian colony' were set up around him." In response Hook reportedly said that "Indians were profitable neighbors for resorts, since they provided an added attraction for tourists," a statement that caused some controversy as, apparently, "Local resort men could not see it this way."[8]

Despite federal officials' best efforts, the idea that they were planning "an Indian colony" at Isle had a resurgence after Hook's speech. On the front page of the *Mille Lacs Messenger* on April 29 it was reported that Isle businessmen were planning another meeting to protest the "Indian colony." The businessmen did not want any Indians moved to the lakeshore "and they don't want valuable property in the district depreciated by having the Indians moved in alongside"—which they believed was the federal government's intention. The newspaper stated that there was no objection to buying more land for the Indians at Isle; the "sore point" was where, exactly, the land was to be bought. The men at Isle were convinced that the government plan was to place the colony on the lakeshore, five miles north of Isle. The men had "for years looked forward to the building up of this area as a resort region" and saw the government plan as "the death of all their hopes." They wanted the colony to be somewhere else, and "almost anywhere else will do."[9]

Despite lack of evidence that the businessmen at Isle were right about what the government intended to do, the protests continued. However, on May 6 the *Mille Lacs Messenger* appeared to contradict the fears of potential resort owners with a photograph of an Ojibwe bark house attached to the following caption:

> Getting Ready for the Tourists
> Chippewa Indians at Mille Lacs are preparing for the summer season by manufacturing a stock of trinkets to sell the tourists. The above view shows an Indian woman making miniature canoes of birch bark.
> Soon these picturesque bark huts will appear beside the highways and red men will bargain with white over the price of a few souvenirs of the Mille Lacs visit. [10]

In the same issue, the newspaper commented, ironically, on a report that the death rate for Indians in the country was decreasing, despite the "white man's gifts" of disease and alcohol. Instead, the Indian population was increasing at a faster rate than any other racial group. The newspaper stated: "Life moves in cycles. In another hundred years the Indians [will have] taken over our country, and the rest of us will be on reservations."

Because of the protests, the program to buy any land for band members living anywhere near Isle were put on hold. Writing to the superintendent of the Chippewa Agency at Cass Lake, A. L. Hook explained:

> Our proposed land acquisition at Isle was blocked because of political pressures exerted by the white citizens of Isle, Minnesota. The matter was taken up with members of the Minnesota Congressional delegation and protests were forwarded to the Office of Indian Affairs. The opposition was so strenuous as to intimidate prospective

land owners with whom we attempted to negotiate; in fact, it completely blocked our program for the time. Since we were unable to accomplish any results, it was deemed advisable to drop the matter rather than carry on a controversy from which we could not hope to profit under existing conditions.[11]

Work continued on land purchases in other areas of the reservation and other locations inhabited by band members, as well as ricing sites throughout the region. One goal was to buy several parcels of land on what archaeologist Jacob Brower had called Sagutchu Point but which was later named after Shaboshkung.

Among other landowners was Henry W. Haverstock, who owned tract 4 of section 16 in T43–R27, at the base of Sagutchu Point. Haverstock was considering selling but appeared puzzled as to why local band members were interested in the property at all. He wrote to Hook:

> You realize that the Indians are scattered along the road for quite a distance and seem to congregate along the lake from the outlet of the Rum River along the lake to the North. That particular area on Mille Lacs Lake consists of the Indian point and my Point and seems to have some historical or religious fascination for the Indians which is probably because of the fact that there were Indian settlements on both places for a long time which is evidenced by the graves located near the clearings, and the Indians seem to feel that they own my property as well as the Indian Point.

Federal officials also contacted Millie M. Weide, who with her late husband had owned 90.5 acres just north of Haverstock's property. She seemed eager to sell the land on what she simply called "the Point" to the federal government for use of Mille Lacs band members. Since her husband's death in 1924 she came to the property only in the summer, to stay in the substantial log cabin, one of several structures there. She seemed to have a sympathetic attitude toward band members, noting that her husband had allowed them to tap the considerable number of maple trees on the property, which now factored into the property's value. From Santa Monica, California, Weide wrote in December 1936: "I know the Indians up there love the 'Point' and would like to see them get it. There would be wood enough to burn for many years and a good income could be made from the sale of maple sugar." Maude Kegg, who in several bilingual books recorded many details of Ojibwe life in the region of Mille Lacs, told of her own experiences going to the sugaring place, or Iskigamiziganing, on this point, which, she noted, was also known as Kegg's Point. In stories echoing Noodinens's account, Kegg recalled her eagerness when her family packed up their horse-drawn wagon to go to the woods and take part in the joyful round of activities during sugaring season.[12]

Federal officials hoped to buy both properties on the point. One reason for the interest in parcels with maple trees was made clear in a letter from A. L. Hook regarding similar land farther south, in which he noted that Harry Ayer had "for a number of years held a sort of monopoly on the production of maple sugar which he gathers from his own land and from other lands he purchases." Areas with sugar bush on them "should be of value to the Indians if the land were in their control."[13]

In some cases federal officials arranged to reacquire land originally bought by band members but which had been tax forfeited because the federal government had never put the land in trust. In other cases land previously allotted to band members—such as acreage near Vineland inherited by Joe Eagle from his father, Migizi—was purchased by the federal government and put in trust for the benefit of the entire Mille Lacs Band.

These land purchases came at a time when protections for Native harvesting of wild rice were added to state law. In 1939 the Minnesota legislature amended earlier laws protecting wild rice to allow only Indians to harvest wild rice in the state. The change highlighted the traditional role of Indian people in relation to wild rice, noting that

> From time immemorial the wild rice crop of the waters of the state of Minnesota has been a vital factor to the sustenance and the continued existence of the Indian race in Minnesota. The great present market demand for this wild rice, the recent development of careless, wasteful and despoiling methods of harvesting together with water conditions of the past few years, have resulted in an emergency, requiring immediate stringent methods of control and regulation of the wild rice crop. The traditional methods of the Indian in such harvesting are not destructive.
>
> On the other hand, the despoliation of the rice fields as now progressing under commercial harvesting methods will result in imminent danger of starvation and misery to large bands of said Indians. They are in danger, therefor, of becoming relief charges upon the state and the counties, many of which are over burdened

with relief loads now. It is further true that many of the reservation lands which were ceded in trust for the said Indians have never been sold and others are reverting because of non-payment by the purchasers. It is therefore the declared purpose of this act to meet said emergency and to discharge in part a moral obligation to said Indians of Minnesota by strictly regulating the wild rice harvesting upon all public waters of the state.

To accomplish this purpose the law granted "to the said Indians the exclusive right to harvest the wild rice crop upon all public waters within the original boundaries of the White Earth, Leach [sic] Lake, Nett Lake, Vermillion, Grand Portage, Fondulac [sic] and Mille Lacs Reservations."[14]

Another part of the law protected the rights of Native harvesters, stating that harvesting wild rice would be limited to "persons . . . of Indian blood, or residents of the reservation upon which said wild rice grain is taken." As the Minnesota commissioner of conservation George A. Selke would note in 1957, "There are a considerable number of white people on the reservations and they, under the law, have the right to be licensed for wild rice harvesting." The law, with its reference to the Mille Lacs Reservation, remains part of the Minnesota Statutes today.[15]

TABLE 10

Allotments on the Mille Lacs Reservation, 1925

TOWNSHIP, RANGE	SECTION	ACRES
T42, R25	1	111.21
Total T42, R25		**111.21**
T43, R27	17	155.54
T43, R27	20	135
T43, R27	27	64.25
T43, R27	28	227.85
T43, R27	29	162.5
Total T43, R27		**745.14**
Total		**856.35**

Source: Mille Lacs Band of Ojibwe, Department of Natural Resources

In the end the total land purchased for Mille Lacs band members under Indian Reorganization Act programs was only a few thousand acres, a fraction more than what had been bought starting in 1914. Perhaps the greatest legacy of IRA programs was the establishment of a system of self-government, which would prove useful to the band in the decades that followed. Early on the band created a tribal council elected by band members. The council was consulted by the federal government when it purchased land for the tribe, supplementing the earlier allotments and sites for ricing. In later years the band instituted a system of government based on the separation of powers also found in the US government, including executive, legislative, and judicial branches.

We Are at an Indian Reservation

On the back of a postcard depicting a road along the shore of Mille Lacs Lake near Onamia and bearing an Onamia postmark, a couple named Carl and Alice wrote to a relative in a town in southwestern Minnesota on September 3, 1942:

> Dear Ma:
>   We are at an Indian Reservation. It warmed up nice. Hope to go fishing tomorrow,
> Love
> Carl & Alice[1]

Despite the fears among local whites expressed more than twenty years before, there were still fish to catch in Mille Lacs Lake. There was also still an Indian reservation there and, as predicted, the Native presence turned out to be an attraction, one from which several white entrepreneurs profited, such as Harry Ayer, who carried on his trading post and his other activities while overseeing band members or serving the federal government as an unofficial agent on the Mille Lacs Reservation. The federal government found Ayer to be helpful, but band members may have considered his double role to be somewhat paternalistic. Sherman Holbert, another white entrepreneur, developed a tourist destination called Fort Mille Lacs, where visitors were entertained by band members who enacted something of Ojibwe culture and history.[2]

In the later years of the twentieth century the presence of the Indian reservation at Mille Lacs was common knowledge for the public in Minnesota, mentioned frequently in newspaper articles about Mille Lacs that named band members and described their activities. When white tourists and fishermen drove up and down Highway 169 they saw band members selling their crafts along the road and in the Ayer trading post.

In contrast to previous years, newspapers began to publish sympathetic stories about band members. In the fall of 1932 the *Minneapolis Star* reported that a sixteen-year-old girl named Batiste Gahbow, a resident of "the reservation" and a pupil at the "Mille Lacs Indian school" at Onamia, had been enrolled in the 4-H club at Cass Lake in 1930. She had competed with six other members in raising their own hogs. Batiste's hog earned first prize, and she "won a trip to the South St. Paul Junior Livestock show." The pig was sold at auction for twenty-two cents a pound. The purchaser then returned it "dressed for distribution among the Indians of the reservation for winter use." Batiste Gahbow (later Sam) would become known as a beloved guide who interpreted Ojibwe culture to visitors at the Ayer trading post and, eventually, at the Indian museum operated by the Minnesota Historical Society. Her son Arthur Gahbow served as chair of the Mille Lacs Band of Ojibwe in the 1970s and 1980s.[3]

It is hard to imagine what the Mille Lacs Reservation would be like today if things had been different. What would have happened if the negotiators of the 1855 treaty had tried their best to respect the treaty as it was negotiated and written? What would have happened if Henry Rice had made clear from the beginning to everyone who would listen that the Treaty of 1863 protected the right of the Mille Lacs Band to remain on the reservation? The same might be asked of federal officials charged with protecting the interests of Native people across the country. Commissioner George W. Manypenny had established the reservation system—of which the Mille Lacs Indian Reservation was a major example—with the understanding that reservations existed to be permanent homes for tribes, but once he was gone many federal officials were only too willing to treat reservations as fragile entities to be sacrificed for the use of timber interests and to the demands of white settlers.

Ultimately the existence of the Mille Lacs Reservation always depended on the stubbornness of the non-removal, nonremovable Mille Lacs band members. While the 1913 ruling of the US Supreme Court made clear that the band had rights in relation to the reservation, it was widely misunderstood by whites in Minnesota, who disrespected the band, its reservation, and its treaty rights. For decades the State of Minnesota continued to disbelieve in hunting and fishing rights and in the continuing existence of the Mille Lacs Reservation.

Only later, in the last decades of the twentieth century, could the Mille Lacs Band pay its own lawyers to take cases to court to assert its treaty rights. In a 1994 federal court ruling—upheld in 1999 by the US Supreme

Court—the 1837 treaty rights to hunt, fish, and gather were affirmed. It was a landmark decision in the field of Indian law.

As with previous successes for the band, the decision caused festering resentment among some whites and questions about the continuing existence of the band and its reservation. Some state, county, and local government officials insisted that the Mille Lacs Indian Reservation had ceased to exist at some point in the past, based on the debatable proposition that Indian reservations ceased to exist if Indians lost title to the lands in them, regardless of the ways those lands changed hands. Contrary to those beliefs, in recent years the federal Office of the Solicitor General affirmed the continuing existence of the Mille Lacs Reservation.

In a November 2017 lawsuit against Mille Lacs County regarding law-enforcement jurisdiction, the Mille Lacs Band sought a legal judgment on the question of the continuing existence of the reservation. Minnesota Attorney General Keith Ellison lent his support in a legal filing in the case, arguing that the reservation still existed, "a statement that seeks to reverse more than a century of state policy," as a reporter for Minnesota Public Radio stated. While the case was still ongoing, the Minnesota Department of Transportation erected signs on Highway 169, the main north–south artery on the reservation, at the point where the highway entered the reservation boundaries, something that would never have happened at any point in earlier years. Finally, in March 2022 US District Judge Susan Richard Nelson ruled that: "Over the course of more than 160 years, Congress has never clearly expressed an intention to disestablish or diminish the Mille Lacs Reservation. The Court therefore affirms what the Band has maintained for the better part of two centuries—the Mille Lacs Reservation's boundaries remain as they were under Article 2 of the Treaty of 1855."[4]

One reason the Mille Lacs Band was able to wage these battles in court was thanks to tribal gaming and construction of the band's popular casinos at Mille Lacs and Hinckley. After all the years of struggle, band members could help make these places tourist destinations, something suggested more than a hundred years before, though earlier observers would have been hard-pressed to predict exactly how this would happen. More than anything band members could have earned from selling game, furs, maple sugar, rice, or baskets along Highway 169, casino revenue meant they could now pay to develop a tribal infrastructure, including health care facilities, schools, housing for seniors, homes for band members, and tribal businesses. Beyond that, the band was able to support worthy economic investments throughout Minnesota.

One historical contrast will aid in measuring the growth of the band's prosperity in the late twentieth century and in the early twenty-first. As told earlier, band leaders traveled to St. Paul in December 1862 to meet with their Indian agent. While in St. Paul these men were stoned in an attack by German immigrants who assumed they were Dakota. The leaders were also refused rooms in any of the city's hotels. One hundred and sixty years later, in 2013, the Mille Lacs Band purchased two downtown hotels; it was reported that these investments encompassed half of the available hotel rooms in the city.[5]

Despite the Mille Lacs Band's increasing success in the twentieth century, some issues were too difficult to solve. Among them was ownership of the piece of land in lot 22 of section 16, T42–R26, along the shore at Cove that Chief Wadena and others had claimed. Despite the federal and state governments' inability to resolve this question, many family members of those who were on this land in 1920 continued throughout the century to refuse to leave. In 1998 Melvin Pewaush, the grandson of Pewaush, was still living on the land. Like generations before him, he had been taken to court more than once, but he would not leave the land on which his ancestors had lived and where many of them had been buried. In one court filing Melvin Pewaush stated: "The Pewaushes have lived on this land since [the removal in the 1920s]. Before my father Jack Pewaush died he told me to stay here, to keep this land for the Indians. If someone didn't stay the whiteman would take it away. I cannot and will not give it up."

Mille Lacs Leaders in the 1820s to 1880s

Mille Lacs Leaders in the 1820s to 1880s

OJIBWE NAME	VARIATIONS	ENGLISH NAME OR MEANING	LOCATIONS	BIOGRAPHICAL INFORMATION
Ayaabe	Iabay, Iabay-kewenzie	Buck	Mille Lacs	Leader of a small band at Mille Lacs in the 1850s and 1860s; his was one of the first Mille Lacs bands to move to White Earth. His daughter Noodinens provided help to anthropologist Frances Densmore in her work on *Chippewa Customs*. See pages 16–19.
Ayaabens		Little Buck	Pokegama	Leader who sometimes went to Fort Snelling in the 1820s and 1830s to visit the Indian agency. He was a signer of the 1837 treaty there. He also signed the treaties of 1842 and 1854.
Bezhig	Biajig, Bayezhig (One)	Lone Man	Snake River, Pokegama, Mille Lacs	The first chief to ask the Indian agent at Fort Snelling to negotiate peace settlements between the Dakota and Ojibwe. He later moved to Mille Lacs. He signed the treaties of 1837, 1842, and 1854.
Biidadens	Bi-dud, Bedud, Pedud	Rat's Liver or Little Liver; it has been suggested that Biidud means a morsel of liver, in Dakota, based on the word liver, which is *pi*. The *ens* ending, however, is a diminutive in Ojibwe.	Mille Lacs	Son of the leader with the name Wazhashkokon, which means Rat's Liver in Ojibwe. He was a signer of the 1855 and 1863 treaties in Washington.

Mille Lacs Leaders in the 1820s to 1880s (cont.)

OJIBWE NAME	VARIATIONS	ENGLISH NAME OR MEANING	LOCATIONS	BIOGRAPHICAL INFORMATION
Bizhiki	Pizhiki	Buffalo	St. Croix River	A member of the Bear clan, he was the father of Gegwedaash. He signed the treaties of 1837, 1842, and 1855.
Gegwedaash	Kegwaydosh	Attempted by the Wind; The Attempter	Yellow Lake, Mille Lacs	He was the son of Bizhiki. He signed the treaty of 1855. His son Mahjekewis became a band chief in the 1870s along the Snake River.
Kaygwaydosay	Gegwedosay		Mille Lacs	Warrior and leader who attended several treaty negotiations.
Kaykaykash	Kaykayke, Gagaagiw			Leader of a small band that later moved to White Earth. According to oral sources he was captured as a child by the Dakota and lived among them until adulthood.
Maheengaunce	Ma'ingaans	Little Wolf	Mille Lacs	A member of the Ma'iingan or Wolf clan, he was son of Zhooniyaa and married a daughter of Shaboshkung.
Makode	Makoday	Bear's Heart	Mille Lacs	Married to Odahnun, sister of the first Negwanebi.
Manoominikeshiinh		Rice Maker (bird)	St. Croix River, Mille Lacs	A member of the Awause or Bullhead clan, he was married to a daughter of the first chief named Negwanebi. He signed treaties in 1855 and 1863.
Maynwaywayaush				Associated with Sandy Lake and Rice Lake, north of Mille Lacs.
Menogishig	Minogiizhig, Minogishick	Noon Day	Mille Lacs, Gull Lake	A son of Makode, he was converted by the Episcopal mission at Gull Lake and became a missionary who worked with the well-known minister Enmegahbowh (John Johnson). He signed the Treaty of 1863.

Mille Lacs Leaders in the 1820s to 1880s *(cont.)*

OJIBWE NAME	VARIATIONS	ENGLISH NAME OR MEANING	LOCATIONS	BIOGRAPHICAL INFORMATION
Mozomonay	Mozomony, Mozomonie	Plenty of Moose	Snake River	Two leaders had this name. The earliest was a chief on the Snake River who died in the 1830s. The second, at Mille Lacs, was the son of Manoominikeshiinh, a signer of the 1863 treaty in Washington.
Negwanebi	Gichi or Che Negwanebi, Naygownabe		Snake River, Mille Lacs	A member of the Ma'iingan or Wolf clan, he was a son of Ozowondib, known as Yellow Head. He was an early migrant from the Snake River to Mille Lacs. He signed the treaties of 1837 and 1842.
Negwanebi No. 1			Mille Lacs	A member of the Ma'iingan or Wolf clan, he was the son of Manoominikeshiinh.
Negwanebi No. 2	Gotigwaakojiins, Kodequahkojeence		Mille Lacs	Son of Ayshkunish, who was a brother of the first Negwanebi.
Noodin	Nodin, Notin, Chinodinaince, Giche Nodin	Wind, Great Wind	Mille Lacs	Two chiefs had this name. The first, sometimes called Chinodinaince, signed several treaties in the 1830s to the 1840s, until his death, just prior to 1850. The second, sometimes called Giche Noodin, was the son of the early leader Shagobay. He died in a battle with the Dakota along the Mississippi in the early 1850s.
Saycosegay			Mille Lacs, Mississippi, Gull Lake	A son of Bezhig.

Mille Lacs Leaders in the 1820s to 1880s *(cont.)*

OJIBWE NAME	VARIATIONS	ENGLISH NAME OR MEANING	LOCATIONS	BIOGRAPHICAL INFORMATION
Shaboshkung	Zhaaboshkaang	Passes Through from the Underside	Mille Lacs	A member of the Awause or Bullhead clan, he was married to Waywish, short for Waywishegeshigokway, a daughter of the first Negwanebi. He signed the treaties of 1855 and 1863.
Shak'pi / Shagobay	Shagobay, Shakopee, Shák'pi	Six (in Dakota) or Little Six	Snake River	Several leaders and warriors at Mille Lacs and in the St. Croix River region bore this name. One of them signed the treaties of 1837 and 1842.
Wadena	Wadena, Waud-e-naw	Little Hill	Mille Lacs	Son of the first Negwanebi, he was chief for a period after his father's death in the 1850s. A signer of the 1855 treaty in Washington, he was succeeded by his son Wahweyaycumig.
Wadena	Wadena		Mille Lacs	Son of the Mille Lacs warrior Kaygwayosay; born around 1851, died 1935. Married to Nancy; opposed removal throughout the early 1900s.
Wahweyaycumig		Round Earth		Son of the first Negwanebi's son Wadena, he removed to White Earth with some of his band members after 1900.
Wazhashkokon		Rat's Liver, Rat's Heart	Mille Lacs	A signer of the 1837 and 1842 treaties, he appears to have died sometime in the 1840s, to be replaced by his son, Bedud or Biidadens.
Zhooniyaa	Shoneyah	Money or Silver	Pokegama, Snake River, Mille Lacs	A son of the early Snake River chief Mozomonay, he was married to a daughter of Bezhig. He signed the 1837 and 1842 treaties.

Notes

Notes to Introduction

1. Westerman and White, *Mni Sota Makoce*, 36; Lawrence Taliaferro Journal, March 21, 1836, MNHS.
2. Gear to Whipple, September 5, 1862, and Enmegahbowh to James Lloyd Breck, September 6, 1863—both box 3, Whipple Papers, MNHS.
3. Brosius to COIA, November 6, 1901, LROIA 63422–1901; Brosious, *The Urgent Case of the Mille Lac Indians*, 3.
4. White, "The Regional Context of the Removal Order of 1850"; White, "Early Game and Fish Regulation and Enforcement in Minnesota."
5. White, "Ojibwe Settlement and Resource Use in South Harbor Township."
6. White, "Use of the Mississippi River and Its Tributaries between Leech Lake and the Platte River." The ethnographic study is not documented in a report.
7. Menomenekay et al. to Secretary of the Indian Department, December 2, 1867, NAM M234, R.155:659.
8. *Princeton Union*, February 4, 1880.
9. Nichols and Nyholm, *A Concise Dictionary of Minnesota Ojibwe*, 60, 85; *Gidakiiminaan (Our Earth)*.

Notes to Chapter 1: The Mysterious Lake

1. Dorothy Clark Sam, interview by author, December 11, 2014.
2. Minnesota Alliance for Geographic Education, "Lake Mille Lacs: Formation of Landscape & Site Characteristics"; Minnesota Department of Natural Resources, Rum River State Water Trail Map.
3. For more information about the use of the adjacent watersheds by Mille Lacs band members, see White, "Use of the Mississippi River and Its Tributaries between Leech Lake and the Platte River."
4. Westerman and White, *Mni Sota Makoce*, 49, 57–59.
5. Walker, *Lakota Myth*, 130–33.
6. "Iced In!," *Mille Lacs Messenger*, May 14, 2013.

Notes to Chapter 2: People of the Lake

1. For a detailed discussion of the Franquelin map in this and subsequent paragraphs, see Westerman and White, *Mni Sota Makoce*, 49, 57–59.

2. See Westerman and White, *Mni Sota Makoce*, 24.

3. Westerman and White, *Mni Sota Makoce*, 24.

4. Warren, *History of the Ojibwe People*, 104.

5. Warren, *History of the Ojibwe People*, 18, 20, 23, 110–11, 152–53, 165.

6. Warren, *History of the Ojibwe People*, 107–8, 161–62.

7. Deloria, *The Indian Reorganization Act*.

8. Kappler, *Indian Affairs*, 2:250–55; 1825 Prairie du Chien Treaty journal, 28, in "Documents Relating to the Negotiation of Ratified and Unratified Treaties with the Various Indian Tribes," ratified treaty no. 139, NAM T494, R.1, available at https://search.library.wisc.edu/digital/AS7AJRPJY3EX6C8Z; Hickerson, "The Southwestern Chippewa," 19, 29, 94n16; Westerman and White, *Mni Sota Makoce*, 36, 90; Lawrence Taliaferro Journal, March 21, 1836, MNHS.

9. Westerman and White, *Mni Sota Makoce*, 91–92; for an early example of a seasonal treaty, see Cormier, ed., *Jean-Baptiste Perrault marchand voyageur*, 67, 69–75.

10. Lawrence Taliaferro Journal, December 17, 1835, quoted and discussed in Westerman and White, *Mni Sota Makoce*, 90; Lawrence Taliaferro Journal, May 7, September 5, 1827; May 5, 1829; August 7, 1830, MNHS.

11. Those present included members of the Ma'iingan clan Noodin, Negwanebi, and Bezhig, as well as Sha-go-bai [Shagobay] (Little Six) and Wazhashkokon (Rat's Liver or Rat's Heart). The first chief recorded to have been named Monzomonay appears to have died, but his son Zhooniyaa (Silver), who was married to the daughter of Bezhig, was present, along with his father-in-law. White Earth genealogies, 1913–15, M455, Roll 10, Powell Papers, MNHS. Transcriptions of the various numbered families in these genealogies used in this narrative were done by Clara Niiska for her website Maquah.net, now available at archive.org. On Zhooniyaa's marriage, see Powell Papers, M455, Roll 10, Family 77, Individual, 77:1.

12. Satz, *Chippewa Treaty Rights*, 145, 147.

13. Treaty with the Chippewa, July 29, 1837, Kappler, *Indian Affairs*, 2:492–93.

14. For an account of such enduring memories about treaties, see White, "The Myth of the 'Forgotten' Treaty."

15. Treaty with the Sioux, September 27, 1837, Kappler, *Indian Affairs*, 2:493–94; Westerman and White, *Mni Sota Makoce*, 156–57.

16. Lawrence Taliaferro Journal, June 20, 21, 1839, MNHS.

17. Parker, ed., *The Recollections of Philander Prescott*, 171.

18. Taliaferro, "Auto-biography of Maj. Lawrence Taliaferro"; Brunson, *A Western Pioneer*, 2:106–7; Pond, "Indian Warfare"; Lawrence Taliaferro Journal, July 2, 1839, MNHS; Schenck, ed., *The Ojibwe Journals of Edmund F. Ely*.

19. Lawrence Taliaferro Journal, July 21, 1839, MNHS.

20. See White Earth Litigation, "Testimony Taken at Cove," with testimony taken at Mille Lacs in the period from June 6 to July 29, 1914, M455, File 10, Roll 5, Powell Papers, MNHS, hereafter, "1914 Testimony Taken at Cove."

21. Gotigwaakojiins did not recall his mother's name because she died when he was very young: "1914 Testimony Taken at Cove," June 7, 1914, 891–94. Gotigwaakojiins was the son of Ayshkunish, brother of Negwanebi the elder and a woman who was the daughter of Bizheki [Bizhiki?], the Snake River chief:

"1914 Testimony Taken at Cove," 774. Schenck, ed., *The Ojibwe Journals of Edmund F. Ely* 13, July 11, 29, 1839. On Odahnun, see Powell Papers, M455, Roll 10, Family 30, Individual 30:4.

22. "1914 Testimony Taken at Cove," 861, 866, 955–56.

23. Boutwell to David Greene, September 28, 1841, box 3, Northwest Missions Collection, MNHS.

24. Boutwell to David Greene, September 28, 1841, box 3; Boutwell to David Greene, March 8, 1843, box 10—both Northwest Missions Collections, MNHS; Ely to David Greene, September 21, 1843, American Board of Commissioners for Foreign Missions Papers, Houghton Library, Harvard University.

Notes to Chapter 3: Seasons at the Lake

1. "1914 Testimony Taken at Cove," 965–66. Makode's father and mother were Chegahgahsindebay and Nahgahwahbequay: see Powell Papers, M455, Roll 10, Family 86:17, 90:1, also 86:55.

2. *St. Paul Minnesotian*, February 7, 1852.

3. White, "Familiar Faces," 326–50.

4. Here and in the following paragraphs, see Densmore, *Chippewa Customs*, 119–29.

5. Stanchfield, "History of Pioneer Lumbering on the Upper Mississippi."

6. For more on the development of economic opportunities for Native people in nearby settler communities, see Norrgard, *Seasons of Change*, 20–42, and throughout.

Notes to Chapter 4: The Reservation and Its Leaders

1. Treaty with the Chippewa, October 4, 1842, Kappler, *Indian Affairs*, 2:542–44.

2. The topic of the Removal Order of 1850 is discussed in White, "The Regional Context of the Removal Order of 1850."

3. White, "The Regional Context of the Removal Order of 1850," 199–203; Warren, *History of the Ojibwe People*, 23; "1914 Testimony Taken at Cove," 868. Rice Maker's wives and their sister were daughters of Mezegun-ahkewenzie: "1914 Testimony Taken at Cove," 960. For the genealogy of Mun-o-min-e-kay-shein [Manoominikeshiinh] (Rice Maker), see Powell Papers, M455, Roll 10, Family 83, where the chief is listed as 83:3.

4. McClurken, *Fish in the Lakes, Wild Rice, and Game in Abundance*, 201.

5. On Rat's Liver, see McClurken, *Fish in the Lakes, Wild Rice, and Game in Abundance*, 73. For more on his family, see Powell Papers, M455, Roll 10, Family 54, where he is listed with his wife Che goke, 54:3. His son Be dud is listed (54:20), with his wife Way nay nube, though there was some confusion in this family tree with another, younger Be dud, who had a different wife. On Shaboshkung, see Powell Papers, M455, Roll 10, Family 78, Individual 78:7.

6. *Annual Report of the Commissioner of Indian Affairs* (1855), 18; Prucha, *The Great Father* 1:326.

7. "Interview between the Comr. of Indian Affairs and Delegation of Chippewas," February 15, 1855, 3, in Ratified Treaty 287, NAM T494, R.5 (February 28, 1855).

8. "Interview between the Comr. of Indian Affairs and Delegation of Chippewas," February 15, 1855, 5.

9. "Interview between the Comr. of Indian Affairs and Delegation of Chippewas," February 15, 1855, 6.

10. "[Second] Interview between the Commissioner of Indian Affairs and the Chippewa Delegates [at night]," February 15, 1855, in Ratified Treaty 287, NAM T494, R.5 (February 28, 1855).

11. "Interview between the Commissioner of Indian Affairs and the Pillager and Winnepic band of Chippewas on Saturday morning, Feb. 17, 1855"; interview with "Mississippi Band of Chippewas, Saturday, 2½ o'clock Feby 17, 1855"; and interview with "Pillagers &c, Saturday night, Feb. 17, 1855"—all in Ratified Treaty 287, NAM T494, R.5 (February 28, 1855).

12. Interview with "Mississippi Band Chippewa Band, Monday, Feb. 19 10 o'clock A.M.," 1, in Ratified Treaty 287, NAM T494, R.5 (February 28, 1855); McClurken, *Fish in the Lakes, Wild Rice, and Game in Abundance*, 94.

13. Interview with "Mississippi Band, Monday evening, Feby. 19, 1855, 9 1/4 o'clock"; interview with "Mississippi Band, Tuesday, Feb. 20, 1855, 2:00 pm," 1–3—both in Ratified Treaty 287, NAM T494, R.5 (February 28, 1855). Clement Beaulieu is mentioned at the bottom of page 3 of the February 20 interview.

14. Interview with "Miss. Band of Chipp., Thursday, March 8, 11 o'clock," 3, 7, in Ratified Treaty 287, NAM T494, R.5 (February 28, 1855).

15. Treaty with the Chippewa, February 22, 1855, Kappler, *Indian Affairs*, 2:685–90.

16. "Chippewa Indians in Minnesota."

17. Schedule of Improvements, May 27, 1902, CCF–White Earth 46578-09-175.2.

18. Nequenebe to Ramsey, April 1, 1852, NAM M842, R.4.

19. Here and below, see Hamilton to Stewart, March 9, 1855, in Willis A. Gorman, Governor's Archives, MNHS.

20. McClurken, *Fish in the Lakes, Wild Rice, and Game in Abundance*, 282–87.

21. 1861 Mississippi Chippewa Annuity Roll, NAM M390, R.3.

Notes to Chapter 5: Permanent Home

1. Here and below, see Rice to Manypenny, February 7, 1856, NAM M234, R.151.

2. Here and below, Manypenny to Huebschmann, May 9, 1856, NAM M1166, R.3.

3. Huebschmann to Manypenny, Morrison, August 12, 1856, NAM M234, R.151.

4. Herriman to Huebschmann, July 2, 1856, NAM M1166, R.3:587; Herriman to Huebschmann, September 27, 1856, Annual Report of Chippewa Agency, in *Annual Report of the Commissioner of Indian Affairs* (1856), 48. On the

grasshoppers and wild rice crop, see also W. McAboy to Manypenny, August 30, 1856, NAM M234, R.151.

5. Herriman to Huebschmann, September 27, 1856, Annual Report of Chippewa Agency, in *Annual Report of the Commissioner of Indian Affairs* (1856), 49.

6. McAboy to Manypenny, August 30, 1856, NAM M234, R.151.

7. McAboy to Manypenny, August 30, 1856, NAM M234, R.151; *St. Paul (Financial Real Estate and Railroad) Advertiser*, March 7, 1857. The road from Crow Wing to Mille Lacs is mentioned in a petition of Mille Lacs chiefs, enclosed with E. Steele Peake to COIA, December 21, 1861, NAM M234, R.152.

8. *St. Paul Weekly Minnesotian*, April 18, 1857; *Minnesota Republican* (Minneapolis and St. Anthony), May 28, 1858.

9. Herriman, Northern Superintendency Annual Report, in *Annual Report of the Commissioner of Indian Affairs* (1857), 55; J. W. Lynde, annual report, September 15, 1859, in *Annual Report of the Commissioner of Indian Affairs* (1859), 71.

10. Cullen to Charles E. Mix, October 10, 1860, NAM M234, R.152; Kappler, *Indian Affairs*, 2:685–90.

11. E. Steele Peake to COIA enclosing petition, December 21, 1861, NAM M234, R.152:267–69.

12. Clark Thompson, Northern Superintendency, Annual Report, October 30, 1861, and Lucius C. Walker, Chippewa Agency, Annual Report, September 25, 1861—both in *Annual Report of the Commissioner of Indian Affairs* (1861), 71, 82, 83, 84.

13. Walker, Chippewa Agency, Annual Report, September 25, 1861, in *Annual Report of the Commissioner of Indian Affairs* (1861), 83.

14. Northern Superintendency, Annual Report, in *Annual Report of the Commissioner of Indian Affairs* (1857), 56.

15. Enmegahbowh to Henry Whipple, August 25, 1862, box 3, Whipple Papers, MNHS; Treuer, *Assassination of Hole in the Day*, 131–33.

16. Gear to Whipple, September 5, 1862, and Enmegahbowh to James Lloyd Breck, September 6, 1863—both box 3, Whipple Papers, MNHS. The September 3 letter is reprinted in the Annual Report of the Northern Superintendency, in *Annual Report of the Commissioner of Indian Affairs* (1862), 79; also in an article by Clark W. Thompson, "History of the Chippewa Troubles," in the *St. Paul Daily Press*, October 2, 1862.

17. Enmegahbowh to James Lloyd Breck, September 6, 1862, box 3, Whipple Papers, MNHS.

18. *Annual Report of the Commissioner of Indian Affairs* (1862), 17.

19. Peake to Whipple, September 10, 1862, box 3, Whipple Papers, MNHS.

20. Gear to Whipple, September 9, 1862, box 3, Whipple Papers, MNHS.

21. *Princeton Union*, October 8, 1896.

22. Buffalohead and Buffalohead, *Against the Tide of American History*, 53–54.

23. Folwell, *A History of Minnesota*, 2:382; Treaty with the Chippewa of the Mississippi and the Pillager and Lake Winnibigoshish Bands (March 11, 1863), Kappler, *Indian Affairs*, 2:839–42.

24. For a basic account of these events, see Treuer, *Assassination of Hole in the Day*, 123.

25. Minnesota, *General and Special Laws of the State of Minnesota*, 88–91. The state treaty is included in the Annual Report of the Northern Superintendency, in *Annual Report of the Commissioner of Indian Affairs* (1862), 84–85, 86.

Dole wrote in his annual report for 1863: "The treaty negotiated with the Chippewas of the Mississippi, under authority of the legislature of Minnesota, was not ratified. In lieu thereof, a treaty was negotiated on the 11th of March last, and afterwards ratified with amendments, to which the Indians readily assented": *Annual Report of the Commissioner of Indian Affairs* (1863), 30–31. More on the state treaty can be found in the letter of Ramsey, Cooper, and Hatch to legislature in the *St. Paul Pioneer and Democrat*, September 19, 1862, and in "The Indian War," *St. Paul Pioneer*, October 5, 1862; and Folwell, *A History of Minnesota*, 2:378.

26. Enmegahbowh to Breck, October 3, 1862, box 3, Whipple Papers, MNHS; Folwell, *A History of Minnesota*, 2:380.

27. Morris, ed., *Old Rail Fence Corners*, 302–6; Board of Commissioners, *Minnesota in the Civil and Indian Wars*.

28. Wedll and Johnson, "The Impact of the Dakota Conflict on the Chippewas of the Mississippi."

29. *St. Paul Pioneer Press*, June 16, 1889, October 3, 1897.

30. Shaboshkung carte de visite, Minnesota Historical Photo Collectors Group, *Joel E. Whitney, Minnesota's Leading Pioneer Photographer*.

31. Enmegahbowh to Breck, October 3, 1862, box 3, Whipple Papers, MNHS.

32. Richard Chute, Minnesota Adjutant General's Office, to Dole, September 26, 1862, in NAM M234, R.153; Dole to Ramsey, September 14, 1862, in *St. Paul Daily Press*, October 2, 1862.

33. Morrill to Thompson, September 16, 1862, enclosed with Thompson to Dole, September 27, 1862, NAM M234, R.153, also reprinted in *St. Paul Daily Press*, October 2, 1862; Johnson addition to letter from Bad Boy to Dole, October 15, 1862, NAM M234, R.153.

34. Thompson to Foster, October 17, 1862, enclosed with Thompson to Dole, October 17, 1862; Thompson to Dole, December 10, 1863—both NAM M234, R.153; see 1862 Mississippi Chippewa Annuity Roll, MNHS M390, R.3; Gear to Whipple, December 8, 1862, box 3, Whipple Papers, MNHS; Ratified Treaty 322, Treaty Journal, February 25, 1863, 1, 3, NAM T494, R.6, hereafter, 1863 Treaty Journal; Usher to Thompson, November 26, 1862, and Thompson to Foster, December 11, 1853, enclosed with Thompson to Dole, December 15, 1862, NAM M234, R.153; Dole to Thompson, December 23, 1862, NAM M21 R.69:456.

35. Usher to Thompson, December 24, 1862, NAM M606, R.4:119.

36. Usher to Chippewa chiefs, December 24, 1862, NAM M606, R.4:157.

37. *St. Paul Daily Union*, December 23, 1862.

38. Foster to Usher, January 26, 1863; see also Thompson to Foster, January 26, 1863—both NAM M234, R.153.

39. Whipple to Dole, January 22, 1863, NAM M234, R.599:812–14, and Whipple Papers, MNHS.

40. Whipple, *Lights and Shadows of a Long Episcopate*, 248–49.

41. Enmegahbowh to Rev. Breck, February 1, 1863, box 3, Whipple Papers, MNHS.

42. Whipple's letter has not been found, though it is mentioned in Rice to Whipple, February 7, 1863, box 3, Whipple Papers, MNHS.

43. Johnson [Enmegahbowh] to Whipple, February 16, 1863, box 3, Whipple Papers, MNHS.

44. Monzomonay (Moose), Te-daw-kaw-mo-say (Walking to and fro), and Way-sa-wa-gwon-aib (Yellow Feather). As noted earlier, Monzomonay was a son of Manoominikeshiinh, born around 1832, who was becoming an important band leader. Te-daw-kaw-mo-say (or other spelling) and Way-sa-wa-gwon-aib may have been there to represent the interests of the relatives of Negwanebi's son Wadena, who appears to have died around 1860. They were both listed in the 1861 annuity roll for that band.

45. Here and below, see 1863 Treaty Journal, February 25.

46. Interviews between the Secretary of War and Chippewas of the Mississippi, 1863 Treaty Journal, February 25, 36–37; February 27, 38, 39.

47. Interview, 1863 Treaty Journal, February 27, 38, 39, 42.

48. Interview, 1863 Treaty Journal, February 27, 45, 47–48.

49. Interview, 1863 Treaty Journal, February 27, 48–49.

50. Interview, 1863 Treaty Journal, February 27, 50.

51. Johnson to Whipple, February 28, 1863, box 3, Whipple Papers, MNHS.

52. Here and below, interview with Mississippi Chippewa, 1863 Treaty Journal, March 5, 59–65.

53. St. Paul Weekly Pioneer and Democrat, March 13, 1863; interview with Mississippi Chippewa, 1863 Treaty Journal, March 6, 71–72.

54. Interview with Mississippi Chippewa, 1863 Treaty Journal, March 6, 70–72.

55. Treaty with the Chippewa of the Mississippi and the Pillager and Lake Winnibigoshish Bands (March 11, 1863), Kappler, Indian Affairs, 2:839–42.

56. Rice to Whipple, March 10, 1863, box 3, Whipple Papers, MNHS.

57. Rice to Whipple, March 18, 1863, box 3, Whipple Papers, MNHS.

58. Rice's Power of Attorney, March 17, 1863, NAM M234, R.153.

59. Treaty with the Chippewa of the Mississippi and the Pillager and Lake Winnibigoshish Bands (March 11, 1863), Kappler, Indian Affairs, 2:839–42.

60. "Interview between Hon. J. P. Usher, Secretary of the Interior and Chippewa Indians," 1863 Treaty Journal, February 25, 27 (also numbered 57).

61. "Submission of the Chippewas," in "News from Washington," New York Times, February 24, 1863.

62. New Orleans Daily Picayune, March 8, 1863.

63. Pittsburgh Gazette, March 19, 1863.

64. Chicago Tribune, March 20, 1863.

65. Winona Daily Republican, March 23, 1863.

66. St. Paul Pioneer, March 27, 1863.

67. Alexander Ramsey, diary, February 10, March 11–14, 25, 1863, MNHS M203, R.39, V.37.

68. Whipple notes, probably from November 1863, filed with printed copy of the 1863 treaty, Whipple Papers, MNHS.

69. Menomenekay et al. to Secretary of the Indian Department, December 2, 1867, NAM M234, R.155:659.

70. Report of interview between COIA and delegation of Mille Lac Chippewas, February 23, 1875, 6–7, NAM M234, R.162:320–28.

71. Johnson to Whipple, March 13, 1863, box 3, Whipple Papers, MNHS.

72. Shaboshkung and Chiefs to Henry Rice, October 12, 1877, Whipple Papers, MNHS.

73. "Chippewa Indians in Minnesota," 164.

Notes to Chapter 6: "They Shall Not Be Compelled to Remove"

1. Here and below, see Johnson to Whipple, May 6, 1863, box 3, Whipple Papers, MNHS.

2. Thompson to Dole, October 28, 1863, NAM M234, R.153.

3. The other chiefs were Zhooneyah or Zhooniyaa, Manoominikeshiinh, Biidadens, Ayaabe, and Gegwedaash, all of whom had been in Washington, as well as Kishkanacut or Kishkanakut, who was a brother of Ayaabe. See petition of Mille Lacs chiefs, November 24, 1863, enclosed with Whipple to Dole, November 24, 1863, NAM M234, R.153. On the family relationship between the two leaders, see Powell Papers, M455, Roll 10, Family 41, for "I ah be ke wen zie," 41:4, and "Kes kah nah kod," 41:10. On the nickname Kwiwisens, and its use in this context, see Kugel, *To Be the Main Leaders of Our People*, 96n73.

4. Morrill to Thompson, January 5, 1864, enclosed with Thompson to Dole, February 1, 1864, NAM M234, R.154.

5. Thompson to Dole, April 19, 1864, NAM M234, R.154.

6. Treaty with the Chippewa, Mississippi, and Pillager and Lake Winnibigoshish Bands (May 7, 1864), Kappler, *Indian Affairs*, 2:862, 863, 865.

7. Johnson to Bartling, December 20, 1865, enclosed with Bartling to Cooley, January 9, 1866, NAM M234, R.155:36–37.

8. Bartling to Cooley, December 22, 1865, NAM M234, R.154:136.

9. Clark to Cooley, February 6, 1866, NAM M234, R.155:89; Clark to Cooley, February 12, 1866, NAM M234, R.155:97.

10. Whipple to COIA, March 19, 1866, NAM M234, R.599:1407–18.

11. Receipt for yoke of oxen, April 7, 1866, R.4, Clark Papers, MNHS; Bean to Whipple, April 9, 1866, box 4, Whipple Papers, MNHS.

12. Bean to Whipple, April 9, 1866, box 4, Whipple Papers, MNHS.

13. A. Norelius to Governor, October 29, 1866, enclosed with Marshall to Secretary of the Interior, November 6, 1866, NAM M234, R.155:307.

14. Marshall to Secretary of the Interior, November 6, 1866, NAM M234, R.155:306; Marshall to Bogy, December 24, 1866, NAM M234, R.155.

15. "A Memorial to Congress for the Removal of the Chippewa Indians," February 11, 1867, NAM M234, R.155:656.

16. Bogy to Bassett, January 8, 1867, NAM M234, Bassett Papers, MNHS.

17. Ruffee to COIA, December 31, 1866, NAM M234, R.155:666; Browning to the President, March 20, 1867, NAM M606, R.7; Treaty with the Chippewa of the Mississippi (March 19, 1867), Kappler, *Indian Affairs*, 2:974–76.

18. Bassett to COIA, March 23, 1867, NAM M234, R.155:444–47; see also Bassett to Taylor, May 9, 1867, NAM M234, R.156:403–4.

19. Bassett to Taylor, May 9, 1867, NAM M234, R.155.

20. Bassett to Taylor, May 9, 1867, NAM M234, R.155.

21. Rice to Whiting, June 19, 1867, NAM M234, R.156.

22. Chiefs to COIA, July 15, 1867, enclosed with Roy to COIA, July 25, 1867, NAM M234, R.155:687.

23. Taylor to Bassett, July 16, 1867, NAM M234, R.156:410–12; Enmegahbowh to Whipple, September 13, 1867, box 5, Whipple Papers, MNHS.

24. Enmegahbowh to Hatch, September 13, 1867, Whipple Papers, MNHS.

25. Enmegahbowh to Whipple, September 16, 1867, enclosed in Whipple to Browning, September 19, 1867, NAM M234, R.155.

26. Whipple to Browning, September 19, 21, 1867, NAM M234, R.155.

27. Enmegahbowh to Whipple, September 23, 1867, and September 25, 1867—both box 5, Whipple Papers, MNHS.

28. Whipple to Browning, September 25, 1867, NAM M234, R.156:287.

29. DuBois to Whipple, September 21, 1867, enclosed with Whipple to Browning, September 25, 1867, NAM M234, R.155.

30. DuBois to Whipple, September 21, 1867, enclosed with Whipple to Browning, September 25, 1867, NAM M234, R.155.

31. DuBois to Whipple, September 29, 1867, enclosed with Whipple to Otto, October 4, 1867, NAM M234, R.155: 733–36.

32. DuBois to Whipple, September 29, 1867, enclosed with Whipple to Otto, October 4, 1867, NAM M234, R.155: 733–36.

33. Whipple to Otto, October 4, 1867, NAM M234, R.155:733–36.

34. Bassett to Whipple, September 30, 1867, box 5, Whipple Papers, MNHS.

35. Browning to Mix, October 12, 1867; here and below, Bassett to Taylor, October 29, 1867—both NAM M234, R.155.

36. Petition from Hartford, MN, April 2, 1867, enclosed with Bassett to Taylor, October 29, 1867, NAM M234, R.155.

37. Melrose petition, n.d., enclosed with Bassett to Taylor, October 29, 1867, NAM M234, R.155.

38. Orrock to Governor, October 8, 1867, enclosed with Bassett to Taylor, October 29, 1867, NAM M234, R.155.

39. Bassett to Taylor, October 29, 1867, NAM M234, R.155.

40. Bassett to Whipple, November 15, 1867, box 5, Whipple Papers, MNHS; Marshall to Whipple, November 23, 1867, box 5, Whipple Papers, MNHS; Marshall to Browning, December 1, 1867, NAM M234, R.155:661–62. Rice was involved with the earlier removal of the Winnebago (Ho-Chunk) in Minnesota and Wisconsin: see McClurken, *Fish in the Lakes, Wild Rice, and Game in Abundance*, 158, 182, 273–74.

41. Roy to Ruffee, November 23, 1867, box 5, Whipple Papers, MNHS;

Menomenekay et al. to Secretary of the Indian Department, December 2, 1867, NAM M234, R.155:659.

42. Menomenekay et al. to Secretary of the Indian Department, December 2, 1867, NAM M234, R.155:659.

43. Whipple to Browning, December 2, 1867, NAM M234, R.155:737–39.

44. Whipple to Browning, December 2, 1867, NAM M234, R.155:737–39.

45. Bassett to Acting COIA, December 13, 1867, NAM M234, R.155:741–45.

46. Bassett to Whipple, December 12, 1867, enclosed with Whipple to Browning, December 17, 1867, NAM M234, R.155.

47. Enmegahbowh to Whipple, January 6, 1868, box 6, Whipple Papers, MNHS.

48. Bassett to Taylor, July 25, 1868, NAM M234, R.156.

49. Enmegahbowh/John Johnson to Whipple, June 20, 1868, box 5, Whipple Papers, MNHS; Minokeshick and chiefs to Whipple, July 20, 1868, NAM M234, R.156.

50. Bassett to Taylor, July 25, 1868, NAM M234, R.156; 1870 Mille Lacs Annuity Roll, US Office of Indian Affairs, Chippewa Annuity Rolls, 1841–1907, MNHS M390, R.3.

51. Peter Roy to COIA, January 19, 1869, NAM M234, R.156.

52. [Peter Roy] to Whipple, June 3, 1868, box 5, Whipple Papers, MNHS.

53. [Peter Roy] to Whipple, June 3, 1868, box 5, Whipple Papers, MNHS.

54. Bassett to Mix, June 30, 1868; Terry to Nichols, August 25, 1868, enclosed with Secretary of War to Secretary of the Interior, September 9, 1868—all NAM M234, R.156.

55. Taylor to Mix, September 20, 1868, NAM M234, R.156:132–34.

56. Taylor to Mix, September 20, 1868, NAM M234, R.156:132–34.

57. Petition, November 14, 1868, NAM M234, R.156:681–83, enclosed with Ramsey enclosures, December 22, 1868, NAM M234, R.157:280–84.

58. Hassler to Parker, October 12, 1869, included in *Annual Report of the Commissioner of Indian Affairs* (1869), 423–25.

59. Wheeler to Ramsey, December 22, 1869, enclosed with Ramsey to COIA, January 1, 1870, NAM M234, R.157:280–84; endorsement on letter from Ramsey, January 8, 1870, NAM M234, R.157.

60. Parker to Ramsey, January 20, 1870, NAM M21, R.94.

61. Ramsey to Parker, January 24, 1870, NAM M234, R.157.

Notes to Chapter 7: Communities at the Lake

1. Clark to Bogy, December 29, 1866, NAM M234, R.155:538. The exact lands selected were: section 16 T43 N R27 W, 195.55 acres; section 21, 233.65 acres; section 22, .5 acres; section 27, lots 1 and 2, 62.65 acres; and the N2 NE3, N2 NW3 of section 28, 160 acres—totaling 652.35 acres.

2. Survey notes for T43–R27, General Description, General Land Office, Stillwater Land District, Taylors Falls Land Office, Records, MNHS.

3. Survey notes for T42–R26, p. 31–32, General Land Office, Stillwater Land District, Taylors Falls Land Office, Records, MNHS.

4. Survey notes for T42–R26, p. 31–32, General Land Office, Stillwater Land District, Taylors Falls Land Office, Records, MNHS.

5. "1914 Testimony Taken at Cove," 875, 878, 890, 960–61.

6. "1914 Testimony Taken at Cove," 861.

7. Schedule of Improvements, May 27, 1902, CCF–White Earth 46578-09-175.2.

8. *Little Falls Transcript*, April 9, 1880.

Notes to Chapter 8: The So-Called Settlers

1. Roberts to Atcheson, May 12, 1870, Special Case 109, NARG 75. "Special Cases" is a collection of correspondence of the Office of Indian Affairs, removed from general correspondence, relating to land disputes. Special Case 109 consists entirely of correspondence concerning the Mille Lacs Indian Reservation.

2. Peltier to Atcheson, June 27, 1870, Special Case 109, NARG 75.

3. Atcheson to Parker, June 30, 1870, Special Case 109, NARG 75.

4. White, "Indian Visits"; here and below, see Atcheson to Parker, June 30, 1870, Special Case 109, NARG 75.

5. Bardwell to COIA, January 9, 1871, Special Case 109, NARG 75.

6. Smith to Parker, March 31, 1871, Special Case 109, NARG 75; *Minneapolis Tribune*, September 5, 1871.

7. Smith to Parker, March 31, 1871, Special Case 109, NARG 75; *Minneapolis Tribune*, September 5, 1871.

8. Smith to Parker, March 31, 1871, Special Case 109, NARG 75.

9. Smith to COIA, May 1, 1871, Special Case 109, NARG 75.

10. Smith to COIA, May 1, 1871, Special Case 109, NARG 75.

11. Smith to Parker, July 17, 1871, Special Case 109, NARG 75.

12. Smith to Clum, September 1, 1871; Drummond to Clum, September 1, 1871—both Special Case 109, NARG 75.

13. Drummond to Clum, September 1, 1871, Special Case 109, NARG 75; *Chicago Tribune*, September 5, 1871; see also *Washington Evening Star*, September 14, 1871; *Minneapolis Tribune*, September 5, 1871.

14. Attorney General to Acting Secretary of the Interior, September 11, 1871; Curtis to COIA, September 21, 1871, and Austin to Commissioner, General Land Office, September 27, 1871—all Special Case 109, NARG 75.

15. Here and below, see Owens and Roos to Commissioner, GLO, September 12, 1871, US General Land Office, Stillwater Land District, Letters Sent, MNHS.

16. Smith to Clum, November 13, 1871, Special Case 109, NARG 75.

17. Smith to Clum, November 13, 1871, Special Case 109, NARG 75.

18. Smith to Clum, November 13, 1871, Special Case 109, NARG 75.

19. Wilder to Smith, November 8, 1872, Special Case 109, NARG 75.

20. Smith to COIA, November 8, 1872, Special Case 109, NARG 75.

21. Jarchow, *Amherst H. Wilder and His Enduring Legacy*, 54–67.

22. Baker to Williamson, July 3, 1876, Special Case 109, NARG 75.

Notes to Chapter 9: The Sabin-Wilder Scheme

1. Jarchow, *Amherst H. Wilder and His Enduring Legacy*, 169n23. On Dwight M. Sabin's career, see *St. Paul Globe*, February 2, 1883; US Congress, *Biographical Directory of the United States Congress*, available online at http://bioguide.congress.gov/scripts/biodisplay.pl?index=s000003.

2. Wilder to Sabin, March 17, 1876, Folsom Papers, MNHS.

3. Wilder to Sabin, March 17, 1876, Folsom Papers, MNHS.

4. Wilder to Sabin, March 17, 1876, Folsom Papers, MNHS.

5. Wilder to Sabin, March 18, 1876, Folsom Papers, MNHS.

6. Joint Resolution, S.F. 339, "Introduced by Mr. Folsom," February 19, 1876, box 4, Folsom Papers, MNHS.

7. Putnam et al. to the Department of Interior, March 23, 1876, and Chadbourne to Folsom, April 10, 1876—both in NAM M234, R.163:331–36. The quotations are from the Chadbourne petition.

8. Here and below, see Frank Folsom to W. H. C. Folsom, April 28, 1876, Folsom Papers, MNHS.

9. Frank Folsom, Declaratory Statement, May 1, 1876, Folsom Papers, MNHS.

10. Owens and Folsom to Folsom, May 9, 1876, Folsom Papers, MNHS; Owens to Commissioner, May 17, 1876, General Land Office, MNHS.

11. Frank Folsom to W. H. C. Folsom, May 9, 17, 1876, Folsom Papers, MNHS.

12. Baxter to Register and Receiver, May 27, 1876, Folsom Papers, MNHS.

13. Frank Folsom to W. H. C. Folsom, June 16, 1876, Folsom Papers, MNHS.

14. Frank Folsom to W. H. C. Folsom, July 22, 27, 1876, Folsom Papers, MNHS.

15. Frank Folsom to W. H. C. Folsom, August 12, 1876, Folsom Papers, MNHS.

16. Chandler to Commissioner, General Land Office, March 1, 1877, Special Case 109, NARG 75; "Mille Lac Indian Reservation in Minnesota," *House Executive Document No. 148*, 48th Congress, 1st Session, April 29, 1884, hereafter, "'Mille Lac Indian Reservation in Minnesota' (1884)"; US Congress, *Biographical Directory of the United States Congress*.

17. Newspaper article, ca. March 1877, Folsom Papers, MNHS.

18. "Mille Lac Indian Reservation in Minnesota" (1884), 13; Sobel, ed., *Biographical Directory of the American Executive Branch*; Taylors Falls Land Office, Receipt, March 23, 1877, Folsom Papers, MNHS.

19. Here and below, see Folsom to Secretary of Interior, March 20, 1877, NAM M234, R.164:231–32.

20. Stowe to Smith, March 8, 1877, NAM M234, R.164:762–65; Chiefs to COIA, April 14, 1877, NAM M234, R.164:494–97.

21. Shaboshkung and Chiefs to Henry Rice, October 12, 1877, box 1, Rice Papers, MNHS.

22. US Congress, *Biographical Directory of the United States Congress*; Sobel, ed., *Biographical Directory of the American Executive Branch*, 302; "Mille Lac Indian Reservation in Minnesota" (1884), 13–14.

23. Folsom to Register and Receiver, June 24, 1878, Folsom Papers, MNHS.

24. Owens and Folsom to Folsom, June 24, 1878, Folsom Papers, MNHS.

25. "Mille Lac Indian Reservation in Minnesota" (1884), 13–14.

26. In "Mille Lac Indian Reservation in Minnesota" (1884), 14, it is reported that the entries amounted to 23,913 acres. For this book, the acreage for the entries of March 12, 1879, were recalculated using the acreage numbers for each piece of land as reported in the Mille Lacs County Assessment Rolls, 1910, for Isle Harbor, South Harbor, and Kathio Townships, on microfilm at the Minnesota Historical Society (MNHS). This process has produced a slightly larger figure, as shown in Tables 7 and 8 (pages 108, 110). See 1910 Mille Lacs County Tax Assessment Rolls for Isle Harbor, Kathio, and South Harbor Townships, Minnesota State Archives, MNHS.

27. *St. Paul Globe*, March 24, 1880.

28. *Princeton Union*, November 16, 1893; George A. Morris Patent, June 7, 1900, Bureau of Land Management, online at https://glorecords.blm.gov/.

29. Wilder to Sabin, March 18, 1876, Folsom Papers, MNHS.

30. *Mille Lacs Band v. United States*, Court of Claims, Docket 30447, David H. Robbins deposition, August 6, 1909, NARG 123, box 2152, hereafter, Robbins deposition.

31. See tract books for the reservation townships in General Land Office records, Tract Books of the United States, Mille Lacs County, T42N, R25W, T42N, R26W, T42N, R27W, T43N, R27W, Bureau of Land Management, Springfield, VA. Scanned copies of these records can be found at https://www.familysearch.org/search/collection/2074276.

32. Mille Lacs County, Tax Judgment Books, 1884–90, in Minnesota State Archives, MNHS.

33. "Mille Lac Indian Reservation in Minnesota" (1884), 14.

34. "Mille Lac Indian Reservation in Minnesota" (1884), 14–15.

35. "Mille Lac Indian Reservation in Minnesota" (1884), 14–15.

36. Taylors Falls Land Office, Receipt, March 25, 1879, and Folsom to Sabin, March 26, 1879—both Folsom Papers, MNHS.

37. "Mille Lac Indian Reservation in Minnesota" (1884), 15; here and paragraphs below, see Capt. C. Williams to Adj. General, August 21, 1879, NAM M234, R.167:973–79.

Notes to Chapter 10: A Deep-Laid Plot

1. Joseph Roberts to Carl Schurz, January 15, 1880, Special Case 109, NARG 75.

2. *St. Paul Globe*, December 27, 1878. A broader view of Walker's role in timber frauds in Minnesota can be found in Plank, "Entrepreneurial Business Ethics in the Era of Land and Timber Acquisition."

3. *St. Paul Globe*, December 28, 1878.

4. *St. Paul Globe*, December 28, 1878.

5. Here and below, see *Princeton Union*, February 4, 1880.

6. *Princeton Union*, February 4, 1880.

7. *Little Falls Transcript*, March 26, 1880.

8. Mille Lacs to Hayes, March 22, 1880, in Special Case 109, NARG 75; here and below, see *Little Falls Transcript*, April 16, 1880.

9. *Little Falls Transcript*, April 9 and 16, 1880.

10. *Little Falls Transcript*, April 16, 1880.

11. Here and below, see *St. Paul Globe*, March 24, 1880.

12. Here and below, see petition, enclosed with Richardson, Houde, and Simmons to Secretary Schurz, May 15, 1880, Special Case 109, NARG 75. See also *Little Falls Transcript*, April 16, 1880.

13. Here and below, see petition, enclosed with Richardson, Houde, and Simmons to Secretary Schurz, May 15, 1880, Special Case 109, NARG 75. See also *Little Falls Transcript*, April 16, 1880.

14. Here and below, see *Little Falls Transcript*, July 23, 1880.

15. Frank Folsom patent for land in T43N, R27W, September 10, 1880, in Bureau of Land Management; Sabin to Folsom, December 1, 1880, Folsom Papers, MNHS.

16. Sabin to Folsom, December 5, 1880, Folsom Papers, MNHS.

17. Sabin to Folsom, December 7, 1880, Folsom Papers, MNHS.

18. Frank Folsom's death on May 21, 1881, is recorded in the *St. Paul Globe*, May 24, 1881; Find a Grave index, Ancestry.com, https://search.ancestry.com/cgi-bin/sse.dll?indiv=1&dbid=60525&h=27484703&tid=&pid=&usePUB=true&_phsrc=rUR399&_phstart=successSource; Folsom, *Fifty Years in the Northwest*, 293.

19. Sobel, ed., *Biographical Directory of the American Executive Branch*, 204, 302; US Congress, *Biographical Directory of the United States Congress*, 1318; *Princeton Union*, December 16, 1880.

20. McFarland to Price, December 30, 1881, Special Case 109, NARG, also in "Mille Lac Indian Reservation in Minnesota" (1884), 9.

21. "Mille Lac Indian Reservation in Minnesota" (1884), 2–10; US Congress, *Biographical Directory of the United States Congress*, 1920.

22. "Mille Lac Indian Reservation in Minnesota" (1884), 7–10.

23. "Mille Lac Indian Reservation in Minnesota" (1884), 10–12.

Notes to Chapter 11: The Mille Lacs Reservation in 1882 and 1883

1. Here and below, see Chapman to Secretary of Interior, August 25, 1882, Special Case 109, NARG 75.

2. "Mille Lac Indian Reservation in Minnesota" (1884), 15–16.

3. "Mille Lac Indian Reservation in Minnesota" (1884), 16.

4. Teller to McFarland, February 13, 1883, NAM M606 R.31:92–93.

5. See Letter of Chiefs, November 10, 1882, Special Case 109, NARG 75.

6. *Official Register of the United States*, 1883, 1:565. Here and below, see Wright to H. Price, June 27, 1883, Special Case 109, NARG 75.

7. Wright's description of the division of labor is the usual prejudiced assessment of Ojibwe men's behavior at times of year when hunting was of less importance and men were not as busy as they generally were during seasons when hunting was a primary source of subsistence.

8. Wright spelled the names of these chiefs Nah-qua-na-be and

Mo-so-ma-na. The spellings given here are those used in the 1881 Mille Lacs
Annuity Roll, MNHS M390, R.5.

Notes to Chapter 12: The First Sabin–Wilder Patents
and the Beginnings of White Settlement

1. Price to Secretary of Interior, July 7, 1883, Special Case 109, NARG 75.

2. Nelson to Teller, July 21, 1883, Special Case 109, NARG 75.

3. On Sabin's election to the US Senate, see St. *Paul Globe*, February 2, 1883;
Act of July 4, 1884, 23 Stat. 76, 89.

4. Ingall to Owens, December 1, 1883, LROIA 22420–1883; Owens to General
Land Office, December 4, 1883, NARG 75. These names were searched for online
at the US Department of the Interior, Bureau of Land Management: https://
glorecords.blm.gov/search/default.aspx.

5. L. F. Hubbard to C. P. Luse, December 22, 1883, LROIA 23545–1883.

6. Luse to Price, January 11, 1884, LROIA 961–1884.

7. Affidavit of O. W. Sylvester, John T. Stilwell, and R. M. Worthington, January 22, 1884, LROIA 2587–1884.

8. Hubbard to Price, February 2, 1884, LROIA 2587–1884, also in Lucius F.
Hubbard, Governor's Archives, MNHS.

9. Price to Hubbard, March 15, 1884, Lucius F. Hubbard, Governor's
Archives, MNHS.

10. Roberts to Wellborn, March 5, 1884, Nelson Papers, MNHS.

11. Joslyn to Speaker of the House, April 28, 1884, in "Mille Lac Indian Reservation in Minnesota" (1884), 1.

12. McFarland to Teller, April 25, 1884, in "Mille Lac Indian Reservation in
Minnesota" (1884), 12.

13. McFarland to Teller, April 25, 1884, in "Mille Lac Indian Reservation in
Minnesota" (1884), 12.

14. Act of July 4, 1884, 23 Stat. 76, 89. A marginal note in US Statutes at Law
refers to 13 Stat., 693, another reference to the Treaty of 1864.

15. Here and below, see Robbins deposition; D. H. Robbins, "Passing of the
Ojibways," *Princeton Union*, May 16, 1907.

16. See selection made by David H. Robbins on May 25, 1883, in section 28,
T43–R27, in the tract book for this township, 104.

17. Robbins deposition; Mille Lacs County, Tax Judgment Books, 1884–90,
Minnesota State Archives, MNHS.

18. Robbins to COIA, May 29, 1884, LROIA 10905–1884. For Robbins's patent,
dated March 7, 1892, see Bureau of Land Management, https://glorecords.blm
.gov/details/patent/default.aspx?accession=MN2260_.350&docClass=STA&sid=
5jyzvraf.43d#patentDetailsTabIndex=1.

19. Jarchow, *Amherst H. Wilder and His Enduring Legacy*, 167–71.

20. Robbins, "Passing of the Ojibways," *Princeton Union*, May 16, 1907.

21. Milton Peden to N. C. McFarland, November 27, 1884, LROIA 23485–1884.

22. Mo-so-mo-ny et al. to Secretary of Interior, March 15, 1885, LROIA

6094–1885; see the Supreme Court case of *U.S. v. Cook*; US Reports: *United States v. Cook*, 86 US (19 Wall.) 591 (1874).

23. G. H. Beaulieu to COIA, August 24, 1885, LROIA 19854–1885.

24. Agent John T. Wallace report, October 26, 1885; J. Wallace, Special Agent, D.O.J. to Attorney General Garland, October 31, 1885—both LROIA 27169–1885.

25. Roberts to Holman, February 9, 1886, LROIA 4778–1886.

26. Chiefs to Hubbard, February 27, 1886, LROIA 7969–1886.

27. Hubbard to COIA, March 4, 1886, LROIA 7969–1886.

28. Sheehan to Atkins, June 14, 1886, LROIA 16267–1886. Robinson Briggs's patent can be viewed at Bureau of Land Management, https://glorecords .blm.gov/details/patent/default.aspx?accession=MN2210__.326&docClass= STA&sid=abj2tawl.41k#patentDetailsTabIndex=1.

Notes to Chapter 13: The Government Breaks No Treaties

1. "Message from the President of the United States Transmitting Communication from the Secretary of Interior, with papers relating to Chippewa Indians in Minnesota," *Senate Executive Document No. 115*, 49th Cong., 2nd Sess., February 28, 1887, hereafter, "Message from the President."

2. Robbins, "Passing of the Ojibways," *Princeton Union*, May 16, 1907.

3. Here and below, see "Message from the President," 27–37.

4. "Message from the President," 33–37.

5. "Message from the President," 18.

6. "Message from the President," 18–19.

Notes to Chapter 14: The White Trespassers

1. Reprinted in *Little Falls Transcript*, November 26, 1886.

2. *Little Falls Transcript*, December 10, 17, 1886.

3. McClellan to Lamar, December 16, 1886, LROIA 33893–1886; Robbins et al. to Sheehan, March 15, 1887, LROIA 7439–1887; *Little Falls Transcript*, March 25, 1887.

4. Tucker to White Earth Agency, March 13, 1887, LROIA 7439–1887.

5. Robbins et al. to Sheehan, March 15, 1887, LROIA 7439–1887.

6. Information on the petition signers' land claims was found in searching for their names at "Land Status Records," Bureau of Land Management, https:// glorecords.blm.gov.

7. Wallace to Attorney General, April 27, 1887, LROIA 11938–1887.

8. Rice to Atkins, January 30, 1888, LROIA 2733–1888.

9. Simmons to Rice, March 1, 1888, LROIA 6356–1888.

Notes to Chapter 15: A Mouthful Here and a Mouthful There

1. *Princeton Union*, May 16, 1907.

2. Folwell, *A History of Minnesota*, 4:219–25, see also 223n31.

3. Folwell, *A History of Minnesota*, 3:184–85; "Report of Investigating

Committees Upon Charges of Bribery in the Senatorial Caucus for United States
Senator for State of Minnesota," [1889], 11.

4. Benjamin Carter et al. to W. D. Washburn, March 30, 1889, LROIA
8393–1889.

5. *St. Paul Pioneer Press*, September 11, 1889.

6. *St. Paul Pioneer Press*, June 14, 15, 16, 17, 1889.

7. The *St. Paul Pioneer Press* stated that the ranch belonged to an R. H. Briggs,
but did not give his brother's name. Robinson P. Briggs obtained land in section
17 of Isle Harbor Township, the current site of Wahkon, while Joshua Briggs's
land was in section 29, directly south of there. As noted earlier, Robinson Briggs's
patent can be found at Bureau of Land Management, https://glorecords.blm.gov/
details/patent/default.aspx?accession=MN2210__.326&docClass=STA&sid=
abj2tawl.41k#patentDetailsTabIndex=1. For Joshua Brigg's patent, see Bureau of
Land Management, https://glorecords.blm.gov/details/patent/default.aspx?
accession=MN2210__.299&docClass=STA&sid=3rlhpk3f.onk#patentDetails
TabIndex=1. See also *Wahkon, Minnesota. Tenth Anniversary*, a publication of the
Wahkon Boosters in 1917, which states that the village of Wahkon included the
region of a hotel started at this location forty years before (around 1877) by
the Briggs brothers.

8. Gardner to Oberly, June 22, 1889, LROIA 16695–1889.

9. "Chippewa Indians in Minnesota," 163–76.

10. "Chippewa Indians in Minnesota," 22, 167–68.

11. "Chippewa Indians in Minnesota," 169.

12. "Chippewa Indians in Minnesota," 171.

13. "Chippewa Indians in Minnesota," 172.

14. "Chippewa Indians in Minnesota," 173.

15. "Chippewa Indians in Minnesota," 174.

16. "Chippewa Indians in Minnesota," 45–46.

17. Robbins, "Passing of the Ojibways," *Princeton Union*, May 16, 1907; Polk,
St. Paul City Directory, 1118, 1375.

18. Rice to Morgan, October 12, 1889, LROIA 29144–1889.

19. "Chippewa Indians in Minnesota," 172–73.

20. "Chippewa Indians in Minnesota," 9.

Notes to Chapter 16: The Aftermath of the Nelson Act

1. Dinwiddie to Ekman, February 19, 1890, LROIA 8304–1890.

2. "Chippewa Indians in Minnesota," 13–27, quotations, 22.

3. Noble to President, January 30, 1890, NAM M606 R.63:150–52, enclosed
in "Chippewa Indians in Minnesota."

4. *Decisions of the Department of the Interior and the General Land Office*, 10:3–9.

5. Richardson to Secretary of Interior, January 22, 1890, LROIA 12874–1890.

6. Richardson to Welsh, February 12, 1890, LROIA 6199–1890.

7. Noble to COIA, March 5, 1890, LROIA 6764–1890.

8. Briggs to Schuler, December 16, 1889; Schuler (name misspelled Shuler) to
COIA, December 19, 1889—both LROIA 36853–1889.

9. Schuler to COIA, March 5, 1890, LROIA 7217–1890.

10. Noble to COIA, March 20, 1890, NAM M606, R.64:95.

11. Cooper to COIA, March 22, 1890, LROIA 9368–1890.

12. Brosious, *The Urgent Case of the Mille Lacs Indians*, 4.

13. Rice to Morgan, July 18, 1890, LROIA 21904–1890.

14. Richardson to Noble, June 27, 1890, LROIA 20033–1890. On Dunn's editorship, see *Princeton Union*.

15. *Princeton Union*, July 17, 1890.

16. Noble to General Land Office, January 9, 1891, LROIA 1561–1891.

17. *Princeton Union*, January 15–July 16, 1891.

18. *Princeton Union*, January 29, 1891.

19. Edward Gottry, letter published in *Princeton Union*, February 5, 1891.

20. *Princeton Union*, February 5, 1891.

21. *Princeton Union*, February 12, 1891.

22. Rice to Morgan, January 21, 1891, LROIA 2969–1891.

23. Rice to Morgan, February 19, 1891, LROIA 7049–1891.

24. Briggs et al. to COIA, February 20, 1891, LROIA 8011–1891; Briggs et al. to Rice, February 23, 1891, LROIA 9208–1891.

25. Rice to Morgan, March 7, 1891, LROIA 9208–1891; *Princeton Union*, April 9, 1891.

26. Rice to Briggs, February 27, 1891, LROIA 9208–1891.

27. Rice to Belt, March 10, 1891, LROIA 9671–1891.

28. *Princeton Union*, March 12, 1891. Wray received a patent for this land in February 1892: see Bureau of Land Management, https://glorecords.blm.gov/details/patent/default.aspx?accession=MN2210__.268&docClass=STA&sid=03jyuucf.tg4#patentDetailsTabIndex=1.

29. *Princeton Union*, April 2, 1891.

30. *Princeton Union*, April 2, 1891.

31. *Princeton Union*, April 9, 1891.

32. Rice to Campbell, April 18, 1891; Rice to Morgan, April 20, 1891—both LROIA 14881–1891.

33. *Princeton Union*, April 23, 30, May 7, 14, 1891.

34. *Princeton Union*, May 7, 14, 1891.

35. *Princeton Union*, May 21, June 4, 11, 1891.

36. *Princeton Union*, June 4, 11, July 2, 1891.

37. "Discontented Reds," newspaper article sent to Schuler, September 8, 1891, LROIA 33172–1891.

38. *St. Paul Globe* article reprinted in *Princeton Union*, August 27, 1891.

Notes to Chapter 17: The Seasonal Round in the 1890s

1. *Princeton Union*, August 27, 1891.

2. *Princeton Union*, on death, February 14, 1907; see also March 2, 1899, August 22, 1918; on drunkenness, February 25, 1892; on theft, October 27, 1892; on fires, May 21, 1891; mosquitoes quote, June 16, 1892.

3. *Princeton Union*, July 16, 1891; Merriam to Morgan, July 17, 1891, LROIA 25823–1891.

4. *Princeton Union*, July 23, 1891.

5. *Princeton Union*, August 27, September 10, 1891.

6. *Princeton Union*, July 30, August 6, 1891.

7. *Princeton Union*, August 6, 1891.

8. *Princeton Union*, August 18, 1892.

9. *Princeton Union*, May 17, 31, June 14, 1894.

10. *Princeton Union*, September 1, 1892, September 6, 13, 27, 1894.

11. Hall to Morgan, August 16, 1892, LROIA 30052–1892; *Princeton Union*, July 27, August 3, 10, 1893.

12. Baldwin to COIA, July 24, 1895, LROIA 31596–1895; *Princeton Union*, August 22, 1895.

13. *Princeton Union*, August 13, 1891; see also September 17, 1891.

14. *Princeton Union*, August 27, September 3, 1891.

15. *Princeton Union*, September 7, 1893, February 11, 1897.

16. *Princeton Union*, September 8, 1892.

17. Hall to COIA, October 1, 1891, LROIA 35987–1891; *Princeton Union*, October 1, 1891.

18. Hall to Morgan, October 24, 1891, LROIA 38714–1891.

19. *Princeton Union*, October 15, 22, November 5, 1891.

20. Hall to Morgan, November 12, 1891, LROIA 40881–1891; Schuler to COIA, December 19, 1891, LROIA 45643–1891; *Princeton Union*, November 23, 1893; Monzomonay to President, February 20, 1894, LROIA 8499–1894.

21. *Princeton Union*, April 6, May 12, November 17, 1892, January 14, 21, 1893; *Svenska Amerikanska Posten*, February 28, 1893, Minnesota Works Progress Administration, MNHS.

22. *Princeton Union*, July 26, 1894, April 22, 1897, November 5, 1896.

23. *Princeton Union*, March 18, 1897; Beaulieu to COIA, February 27, 1897, LROIA 51562–1897.

24. *Princeton Union*, February 18, March 7, April 7, 1892.

25. *Princeton Union*, February 18, March 7, April 7, 31, 1892.

26. *Princeton Union*, March 31, April 7, 1892.

27. *Princeton Union*, July 4, 1895.

28. *Princeton Union*, March 11, 1897.

29. *Princeton Union*, March 31, April 7, 1892; Mille Lacs County District Court, Criminal Case File No. 14 (April 1892), MNHS.

30. *Princeton Union*, April 20, 1893. For the men's land locations and patents, see Enos Jones Patent, May 5, 1899, and Gilbert O. Jahr Patent, February 24, 1898—both at Bureau of Land Management.

31. Harvey M. Bennett's patent is available at Bureau of Land Management, https://glorecords.blm.gov/details/patent/default.aspx?accession=MN2080__.407&docClass=STA&sid=ydvmyvjw.rtw#patentDetailsTabIndex=1.

32. *Princeton Union*, March 22, 1894. The earliest recorded settler named Haggberg in this area was John Haggberg, who obtained title to land in sections 1

and 12 of Isle Harbor Township, adjacent to present-day Isle. See his patent at Bureau of Land Management, https://glorecords.blm.gov/details/patent/default .aspx?accession=MN2210__.300&docClass=STA&sid=quin21i5.lmb#patent DetailsTabIndex=1.

33. Shaywoub and Kecheshaywahbekito were both members of Monzo-monay's band, according to the 1882 Mille Lacs Annuity Roll. A "Shaywahbeketo (Keg)" was credited with having made improvements on three parcels of land in 1902: see Table 9 (page 126). *Princeton Union*, March 29, 1894.

34. *Princeton Union*, April 12, 1894.

35. *Princeton Union*, March 26, April 23, 1896; Wahweyaycumig to Gus Beau-lieu, April 5, 1897, LROIA 13575–1897.

36. Beaulieu to Browning, April 8, 1897, LROIA 13575–1897.

37. *Princeton Union*, April 19, 26, 1894.

38. *Princeton Union*, on log drives, April 21, 1892; on Wadena, June 18, Decem-ber 3, 1891; on Tucker, October 13, 1892; on gardens, August 24, 1893.

39. *Princeton Union*, Trask stories, June 18, July 2, November 12, 1891; on noise and liquor, June 16, 23, 1892.

40. *Princeton Union*, July 18, 1895.

41. *Princeton Union*, August 15, 1895.

Notes to Chapter 18: Land Claims

1. *Princeton Union*, September 10, 1891.

2. *Princeton Union*, September 10, 24, 1891; see Noble's decision of September 3, 1891, in Noble to Commissioner of the General Land Office, September 9, 1891, in *Decisions of the Department of the Interior and General Land Office*, 13:230–36.

3. *Princeton Union*, September 17, 1891.

4. *Princeton Union*, September 24, 1891.

5. In re: Annie M. Warren, Appeal "Before the United States Land Office," May 9, 1892, Warren Papers, MNHS.

6. Gottry to Warren, January 16, 1894, Warren Papers, MNHS.

7. Noble to Commissioner of the General Land Office, April 22, 1892, in *Decisions of the Department of the Interior and the General Land Office*, 14:497–98; *Princeton Union*, May 5, 1892.

8. *Princeton Union*, May 12, 1892.

9. *Princeton Union*, November 17, 1892.

10. *Princeton Union*, December 29, 1892, December 14, 1893; Joint Resolution For the protection of those parties who have heretofore been allowed to make entries for lands within the former Mille Lac Indian Reservation in Minnesota, 28 Stat. 576, December 19, 1893.

11. *Princeton Union*, December 21, 1893.

12. *Princeton Union*, June 4, 1896; Annie M. Warren Patent, November 4, 1899, Bureau of Land Management.

13. *Princeton Union*, May 28, 1896.

14. *Princeton Union*, May 28, 1896.

15. *Princeton Union*, May 19, 1898; Joint Resolution Declaring the lands within the former Mille Lac Indian Reservation, in Minnesota, to be subject to entry under the land laws of the United States, 30 Stat. 784, May 27, 1898.

16. Robbins deposition, 6; *Princeton Union*, July 28, 1892, January 2, 1896; McClurken, *Fish in the Lakes, Wild Rice, and Game in Abundance*, 434.

17. Decision of Secretary of Interior in case of Ma-gee-see v. Johnson, July 5, 1900, LROIA 40374–1901.

18. Decision of Secretary of Interior in case of Ma-gee-see v. Johnson, July 5, 1900, LROIA 40374–1901.

19. Me-gee-see Patent, October 1, 1907, Bureau of Land Management.

20. *Princeton Union*, August 15, 1901.

21. William Wallace Patents, October 6, 1894, and April 22, 1901, Bureau of Land Management.

22. Gogee to COIA, June 6, 1901, LROIA, 30901–1901.

Notes to Chapter 19: The Burning of Villages

1. *Princeton Union*, October 29, 1891.

2. For this and other locations at Mille Lacs, see Brower and Bushnell, *Memoirs of Explorations in the Basin of the Mississippi*, vol. 3, *Mille Lacs*; Brower, *Memoirs of Explorations in the Basin of the Mississippi*, vol. 4, *Kathio*. See also Brower, Mille Lacs Journal, 1900, Brower Papers, MNHS, hereafter, Brower, Journal. On Monzomonay's death, see *Princeton Union*, October 8, 1896.

3. Brower, Journal, May 22, 1900.

4. Brower, Journal, May 20, 1900. "Sagutchu" is possibly from zaagajiwe, "come out over a hill": Nichols and Nyholm, *A Concise Dictionary of Minnesota Ojibwe*, 122.

5. Brower, Journal, May 19, 1900.

6. Brower, Journal, May 30, 1900.

7. Brower, Journal, May 22, 30, 1900.

8. Brower, Journal, May 23, 1900.

9. *Mille Lacs Band v. United States*, Court of Claims, Docket 30447, Naygwounaybe deposition, August 4, 1909, NARG 123, box 2152.

10. Charles Malone Patent, July 17, 1894, Bureau of Land Management.

11. Brower, *Memoirs of Explorations in the Basin of the Mississippi*, vol. 4, *Kathio*, 105, referred to the Negwanebi incident as taking place on the Gim-i-nissing (Chiminising) River, a name he also applied to present-day Isle Bay. In an earlier journal he noted about this location that "Ojibway Indians now occupy the site of the ancient village along the river bank where they have bark houses, small cornfields, and patches of ground fenced in": see Brower, Journal, May 23, 1900. Quote from *Princeton Union*, May 30, 1901. No reference was found in General Land Office records to a Pete Kenedy obtaining land in this area.

12. *Princeton Union*, May 16, June 13, 1901; *Mille Lacs County Times*, May 30, 1901.

13. *Princeton Union*, June 20, 1901.

14. During the third and fourth weeks of June 1901 logs were being moved through Shakopee and Onamia Lakes and down the Rum River: see *Princeton Union*, June 20, 27, 1901.

15. Megesee [Migizi] to Secretary of Interior, June 7, 1901, LROIA 31221–1901.

16. MacComas to COIA, July 22, 1901, LROIA 40374–1901.

17. Brosius to COIA, November 8, 1901, LROIA 63422–1901.

18. Brosious, *The Urgent Case of the Mille Lac Indians*, 3.

19. *Mille Lacs Band v. United States*, Court of Claims, Docket 30447, Endaso-giizhig (Ayndusokeshig) deposition, July 30, 1907, 237, NARG 123, box 2152, hereafter, Endaso-giizhig deposition; Schedule of Improvements, May 27, 1902, CCF–White Earth 46578-09-175.2.

20. Robbins deposition, 10–12.

21. Endaso-giizhig deposition, pdf p. 7–8.

22. Fullerton to Saunders, January 27, 1904, Game and Fish Commission, 103.H.9.9B, MNHS.

Notes to Chapter 20: The Court of Claims Case

1. Agreement between the United States and the Mille Lac Chippewa Indians, August 30, 1902, CCF–White Earth 46578-1909-175.2, pt. I.

2. A description of the functions of the Court of Claims, though with no discussion of its role in relation to Indian tribes and treaties, can be found in Crane, "Jurisdiction of the United States Court of Claims," 161–77.

3. "An Act For the relief of the Mille Lac band of Chippewa Indians in the State of Minnesota, and for other purposes," 35 Stat. 619, February 2, 1909. For references to the earlier legislation, see *Congressional Record*, March 30, 1906, p. 4517, April 3, 1906, p. 4710.

4. "Big Money for Reds," *Princeton Union*, June 1, 1911; *Mille Lac Band of Chippewas v. The United States*, May 6, 1912, in *Cases Decided in the Court of Claims of the United States for the Term of 1911–12*, 440, hereafter, 1912 Court of Claims Decision.

5. 1912 Court of Claims Decision, 443, 446, 448.

6. 1912 Court of Claims Decision, 453, 454, 455.

7. *United States v. Mille Lac Band of Chippewa Indians*, 229 U.S. 498 (1913); McClurken, *Fish in the Lakes, Wild Rice, and Game in Abundance*, 438–39.

8. McClurken, *Fish in the Lakes, Wild Rice, and Game in Abundance*, 438–39.

Notes to Chapter 21: More Burned Villages

1. C. B. Miller to COIA, August 19, 1910, CCF–White Earth 68171-10-175.2.

2. Hall to Howard, September 13, 1910, LROIA 68171–1910, 175.2.

3. Information on the construction of this train line and the early history of Wahkon is found in *Wahkon, Minnesota Tenth Anniversary*, a publication of the Wahkon Boosters in 1917.

4. Foster, *Izatys: Where Nature Reigns*, 10.

5. *Mille Lacs Band v. United States*, Court of Claims, Docket 30447, Beewash deposition, August 5, 1909, 367–68, NARG 123, box 2152.

6. Mille Lacs County District Court, Civil Case File No. 2248 (1910–11), MNHS.

7. *Princeton Union*, March 23, 30, 1911.

8. *Princeton Union*, April 6, 1911.

9. Mille Lacs County District Court, Civil Case File No. 2248.

10. Mille Lacs County District Court, Civil Case File No. 2248.

11. *Princeton Union*, May 11, 1911.

12. Here and below, see *St. Paul Pioneer Press*, October 29, 1911.

13. *Mille Lacs County Times*, June 15, 1911.

14. *Princeton Union*, June 15, 1911.

Notes to Chapter 22: Setting the Stage for Allotments

1. An Act Making appropriations for current and contingent expenses of the Bureau of Indian Affairs, etc., August 1, 1914, 38 Stat. 582.

2. McLaughlin to COIA, September 6, 1917, McLaughlin Papers, Assumption Abbey, Richardton, ND; J. H. Hinton to COIA, July 13, 1917, CCF–White Earth 68933-1917, 155; McClurken, *Fish in the Lakes, Wild Rice, and Game in Abundance*, 439.

3. Here and two paragraphs below, see James McLaughlin, Notebook, 1914–17, r17, v31, p1, 59–60, McLaughlin Papers, Assumption Abbey, Richardton, ND.

4. Sam to COIA, January 31, 1920; Sam et al. to (unknown), February 19, 1920—both CCF–White Earth 10012-1920, 155.

5. McLaughlin, Notebook, r17, v31, p1, 59–60, McLaughlin Papers, Assumption Abbey, Richardton, ND.

6. McLaughlin, Notebook, r17, v31, p28–29, McLaughlin Papers, Assumption Abbey, Richardton, ND.

7. James McLaughlin to Secretary of Interior, November 12, 1917, r9, McLaughlin Papers, Assumption Abbey, Richardton, ND.

8. James McLaughlin to Secretary of Interior, November 12, 1917, r9, McLaughlin Papers, Assumption Abbey, Richardton, ND.

9. Robbins to Schall, January 4, 1916, CCF–White Earth 3591-16.

10. Chief Wadena to COIA, April 28, 1917, CCF–White Earth 68933-1917, 155.

11. Hinton to COIA, July 13, 1917, CCF–White Earth 68933-1917; McLaughlin to Secretary of Interior, November 12, 1917, r9, McLaughlin Papers, Assumption Abbey, Richardton, ND.

Notes to Chapter 23: Lake Fishing

1. Chrislock, *Watchdog of Loyalty*, 52, 68, 89, 206–8.

2. Chrislock, *Watchdog of Loyalty*, 206; *Fins, Feathers and Fur* (December 1917): 1–2.

3. Wicklander to GFD, January 6, 1918, Game and Fish Department (hereafter, GFD), 103.F.9.1B, MNHS.

4. A Todd Co. Farmer to GFD, June 20, 1918, GFD, 103.F.8.12F, MNHS.

5. Brown to Avery, March 26, 1919, reply March 28, 1919, GFD, 103.F.9.1B, MNHS.

6. White, *Familiar Faces*, 282.

7. Berg to Avery, March 19, 1919, reply April 9, 1919, GFD, 103.F.9.1B; Musick to GFD, April 7, 1919, reply April 9, 1919, GFD, 103.F.12.8F, MNHS.

8. Box 1, Ayer Papers, MNHS; GFD, 103.H.10.4F; Ayer to Avery, March 4, 1919, GFD, 103.F.9.1B, MNHS.

9. Enclosed in Ayer to Avery, March 4, 1919, GFD, 103.F.9.1B: Hanson to Avery, March 14, 1919, GFD, 103.F.12.9B; Commissioner to Anderson, March 25, 1919, GFD, 103.F.9.1B, MNHS.

10. Minnesota, Session Laws, 1919, ch. 341, p. 365; *Minnesota Statutes*, 1923, ch. 32, sec. 5604–9, p. 770.

11. Minnesota, Session Laws, 1919, ch. 400, sec. 73, p. 440–41.

12. Barnes to Commissioner, April 28, 1919, reply April 30, 1919, GFD, 103.F.9.1(B), MNHS; GFD, *Biennial Report*, 1920, 39.

13. *Duluth News Tribune*, May 22, 1919, copy in Hostetter to Ayer, May 22, 1919, box 1, Ayer Papers, MNHS.

14. GFD, *Biennial Report*, 1920, 38.

Notes to Chapter 24: New and Continuing Opposition to the Mille Lacs Band

1. C. V. Peel, special agent at White Earth, to Harry Ayer, November 7, 1919, box 1, Ayer Papers, MNHS.

2. Here and below, see Ayer to Wadsworth, April 4, 1920, CCF–White Earth 71577-19, 134.

3. According to the inflation calculator at https://www.usinflationcalculator.com, this amount was equivalent to $5,634.79 in 2020.

4. Oredson to Ayer, November 18, 1919, CCF–White Earth 71577-19, 134.

5. Wadsworth to COIA, May 12, 1920, CCF–White Earth 71577-19, 134.

6. Humason to Game and Fish Commission, March 15, 1920, GFD, 103.F.6.5B, MNHS.

7. Peter W. Evans to Carlos Avery, March 16, 1920, GFD, 103.F.8.12F, MNHS.

8. Dinwiddie to Avery, March 15, March 30, 1920, enclosed with Commissioner to H. C. Boeck, April 6, 1920, GFD, 103.F.8.13B, MNHS.

9. D. E. Emmons to GFD, April 7, 1920, GFD, 103.F.8.12F, MNHS.

10. Enclosed with Humason to GFD, March 15, 1920, GFD, 103.F.6.5B; Avery to Dinwiddie, March 18, April 7, 1920, enclosed with Commissioner to Boeck, April 6, 1920, GFD, 103.F.8.13B; Avery to Evans, March 29, 1920, enclosed with Evans to Avery, March 16, 1920; Avery to Humason, April 7, 1920, enclosed with Emmons to GFD, April 7, 1920—both GFD, 103.F.8.12F, MNHS.

11. Here and below, see J. F. Woodhead to Carlos Avery, May 5, 1920, GFD, 103.F.8.13B, MNHS.

12. Swanson to Avery, May 10, 1920, copy in Ayer papers, MNHS.

13. Hamer to Avery, May 6, 1920; Commissioner to Hamer, May 10, 1920—both GFD, 103.F.6.5B, MNHS.

14. J. F. Woodhead to Carlos Avery, May 11, 1920, GFD, 103.F.8.13B, MNHS.

15. Commissioner to E. E. Dinwiddie and Commissioner to D. H. Emmons, May 15, 1920—both GFD, 102.F.8.12F, MNHS.

16. Wadsworth to Avery, May 18, 1920, Ayer papers, MNHS.

17. Minnesota, Session Laws, 1919, ch. 400, sec. 73, p. 441.

18. *Wahkon Enterprise*, May 20, 1920.

19. Avery to Wadsworth, May 20, 1920, box 2, Ayer Papers, MNHS.

20. Avery to Ayer, May 22, 1920, box 2, Ayer Papers, MNHS.

21. Avery to Cardle, May 27, 1920; Emmons to Avery, May 31, 1920—both in box 2, Ayer Papers, MNHS; GFD, 103.F.8.13B; GFD, 103.H.13.6F, MNHS.

22. Cardle to Avery telegram; Commissioner to Cardle, June 1, 1920—both GFD, 103.F.8.13B; June 2, 1920, GFD, 103.F.8.12F, MNHS.

23. Ayer to Avery, May 31, 1920; Avery to Ayer, June 2, 1920; P. R. Wadsworth to Ayer, June 25, 1920—all in box 2, Ayer Papers, MNHS.

24. Ayer to Swanson, June 6, 1920; Ayer to Wadsworth, June 1920—both in box 2, Ayer Papers, MNHS.

25. Larson to Ayer, June 2, 1920, box 2, Ayer Papers, MNHS.

26. [October 15, 1920?], box 2, Ayer Papers, MNHS.

27. GFD, *Biennial Report*, 1922, 66.

28. *Minnesota Statutes*, 1941, ch. 101.07, p. 847; 1945, ch. 101, p. 891.

29. Enclosed with W. M. Humason, Vineland, to GFD, March 15, 1920, GFD, 103.F.6.5B, MNHS.

30. *Fins, Feathers and Fur* 28 (December 1921): 3–5.

31. GFD, *Biennial Report*, 1920, 34; GFD, *Biennial Report*, 1922, 54; Swanson and Swanson, *Carlos Avery*, 9.

32. *Fins, Feathers and Fur* 1, no. 3 (December 1940): 1.

33. GFD, *Biennial Report*, 1922, 64–65.

34. Minnesota, Session Laws, 1929, ch. 84, 258, p. 85, 299; Boussu, "A Review of the Indian Commercial Fishery at Red Lakes," 3.

Notes to Chapter 25: One Parcel at a Time

1. Hill to Harding, May 3, 1920, CCF–Consolidated Chippewa 37704-1920; Hyser notice on property, August 31, 1919; and Lufkins to Merritt, August 26, 1919, CCF–White Earth, NARA-DC, RG75—both CCF–White Earth 74280-19-308.2.

2. Wadsworth to COIA, May 11, 1920, CCF–White Earth 74280-19-308.2; Hill to Merritt, October 24, 1921, CCF–White Earth 87124-1921, 155.

3. Ueland and Ueland to P. R. Wadsworth, May 23, 1923, CCF–Consolidated

Chippewa 37704-1923, 155; Wadsworth to COIA, May 24, 1923; Wadsworth to Ueland and Ueland, May 26, 1923—both CCF–Consolidated Chippewa 37704-1923.

4. Burke to Wadsworth, June 12, 1923, CCF–Consolidated Chippewa 33704-1923, 155.

5. P. R. Wadsworth to COIA, July 2, 1923, CCF–CCF–Consolidated Chippewa 33704-1923, 155.

6. Hauke to Wadsworth, July 18, 1923, CCF–Consolidated Chippewa 37704-1923, 155.

7. Wadena to COIA, March 18, 1924, CCF–White Earth 37704-1923, 155.

8. Wooster to Campbell, April 23, 1924; Merrit to Wadena, April 25, 1924—both CCF–Consolidated Chippewa 37704-1923, 155; White, "Ojibwe Settlement and Resource Use in South Harbor Township."

9. Probate files for Mary Wind/Wahbooze and Tom Wind/Mayzhuckegwon-abe, in Mille Lacs Probate Records, Consolidated Chippewa, NARG 75; *Minneapolis Journal*, June 14, 1935, p. 16; *Mille Lacs Messenger*, June 13, 1935.

Notes to Chapter 26: A Fraction of What They Had Been Promised

1. Charter of Organization of the Mille Lacs Band of Chippewa, October 8, 1938, box 542, Mille Lacs Band Charter of Organization, NARA-KC, RG 75.

2. A. L. Hook, by Rex H. Barnes, to H. W. Haverstock, December 2, 1936, Mille Lacs General Correspondence, Consolidated Chippewa Agency, container 542, NARA-KC.

3. Hazel Carlson to A. L. Hook, January 3, 1937, Consolidated Chippewa, box 542, Mille Lacs General Correspondence, NARA-KC, RG 75.

4. A. L. Hook to Henry Paulsen, January 29, 1937, Consolidated Chippewa, box 542, Mille Lacs General Correspondence, NARA-KC, RG 75.

5. A. P. Jorgenson to A. L. Hook, February 10, 1937; Jacob Munnell to A. L. Hook, March 29, 1938, box 543, Misc. Rice Sites; Hook to Jorgenson, June 30, 1939, box 543, Tract 8—all Consolidated Chippewa, box 542, Mille Lacs General Correspondence, NARA-KC, RG 75.

6. *Mille Lacs Messenger*, February 11, 1937.

7. *Mille Lacs Messenger*, February 25, 1937; here and below, "Remarks for meeting at Isle, Minn., March 18, 1937," Consolidated Chippewa, box 542, Mille Lacs General Correspondence, NARA-KC, RG 75.

8. *Mille Lacs Messenger*, March 25, 1937.

9. *Mille Lacs Messenger*, April 29, 1937.

10. *Mille Lacs Messenger*, May 6, 1937.

11. A. L. Hook to Louis Balsam, November 30, 1937, Consolidated Chippewa, box 542, Mille Lacs General Correspondence, NARA-KC, RG 75.

12. Henry W. Haverstock to Mark L. Burns, March 2, 1939, Mille Lacs Expandable Land Acquisition Project, box 544, Tracts 64, 65, NARA-KC, RG 25; Millie M. Weide to Rex H. Barnes, December 8, 1936, Consolidated Chippewa, box 544, Tract 64, 65, NARA-KC, RG 25; Kegg, *Gabekanaansing*, 1–13; see also Kegg, *Portage Lake*.

13. A. L. Hook to Louis Balsam, January 11, 1938, Consolidated Chippewa, box 542, Mille Lacs General Correspondence, NARA-KC, RG 75.

14. Minnesota, Session Laws, 1939, ch. 231, H.F. 1100.

15. See section 2, Minnesota, Session Laws, ch. 231, H.F. 1100; Selke to Pinkle, March 20, 1957, Minnesota Conservation Department, "Wild Rice Meetings" file, 104.K.19.13 (B), MNHS; *Minnesota Statutes*, 2018, 84.10, online at https://www .revisor.mn.gov/statutes/cite/84.10.

Notes to Epilogue: We Are at an Indian Reservation

1. Carl and Alice to Anna Schnyders, September 3, 1942, postcard in author's possession.

2. On Harry Ayer and the trading post, see White, *We Are at Home*, 122–24. See also transcript of interview with Sherman Holbert by Bruce White and Elisse Aune, September 28, 2004.

3. *Minneapolis Star*, November 26, 1932; Minneapolis *Star Tribune*, December 29, 1981; White, *We Are at Home*, 131.

4. "Ellison: Mille Lacs Band Still Has 61k-acre Reservation," mprnews.org, February 21, 2020; Kirsti Marohn, "Judge Affirms that 61,000-acre Mille Lacs Reservation Still Exists. What Does That Mean?," mprnews.org, March 10, 2022.

5. Minneapolis *Star Tribune*, March 11, 2013.

Sources

Archival Sources

ancestry.com.

Assumption Abbey. Archives. Richardton, ND.
>   McLaughlin, Major James, Papers. Available on microfilm at the Minnesota Historical Society.

Bureau of Land Management. Springfield, VA.
>   Land Patents. Scans of these can be found online at the BLM website, https://glorecords.blm.gov/search/default.aspx.
>   Tract Books of the United States. Mille Lacs County. T42N, R25W; T42N, R26W; T42N, R27W; T43N, R27W. Scanned copies of these records can be found at https://www.familysearch.org/search/collection/2074276.

Houghton Library, Harvard University. Cambridge, MA.
>   American Board of Commissioners for Foreign Missions Papers.

(MNHS) Minnesota Historical Society. St. Paul.
>   Ayer, Harry D., and Family Papers.
>   Bassett, Joel, Papers.
>   Brower, Jacob, Papers.
>   Carte de visite (Shaboshkung).
>   Clark, Edwin, Papers.
>   Death certificates (Aitkin County).
>   Folsom, William H. C., Papers.
>   Game and Fish Commission.
>   Governor's Archives.
>>   Gorman, Willis A.
>>   Hubbard, Lucius F.
>   Mille Lacs County Archives.
>>   Assessment Rolls, 1910.
>>   District Court. Civil and Criminal Case Files.
>>   Tax Judgment Books.
>   Minnesota Works Progress Administration Papers.
>   Nelson, Knute, Papers.
>   Northwest Missions Collection.

Powell, Ransom J., Papers.
    Transcriptions of genealogies available at http://web.archive.org/
        web/20110104040703/http://www.maquah.net/genealogy/Powell/
        index.html, accessed May 12, 2024.
Rice, Henry M., Papers.
Swanson, Hilding, Papers.
Taliaferro, Lawrence, Journal.
Warren, George H., and Family Papers.
Whipple, Henry B., Papers.
US General Land Office. Stillwater Land District. Taylors Falls Land Office.
    Records.
(MNHS M390) US Office of Indian Affairs. Annuity Rolls.
National Archives. Washington, DC.
    (NARG) Record Group 75.
        (CCF) Central Consolidated Files.
        (LROIA) Letters Received of the Office of Indian Affairs. Some of the same
            series found in the microfilm editions such as NAM M234, available at
            the Minnesota Historical Society.
        NAM M21. Letters Sent of the Office of Indian Affairs.
        NAM M234. Letters Received of the Office of Indian Affairs.
        NAM M606. Letters Sent. Indian Division. Office of the Secretary of
            Interior.
        NAM M842. Records of the Minnesota Superintendency. Available at the
            Minnesota Historical Society.
        NAM T494. Ratified Treaties.
        Special Case 109. Papers relating to the Mille Lacs Reservation.
    (NARG) Record Group 123.
        Court of Claims. *Mille Lacs Band of Chippewa Indians in the State of Minne-
            sota v. The United States.* Docket 30447. Box 2152.

Government Documents

Annual Reports of the Commissioners of Indian Affairs (COIA).
    1855, 1856, 1857, 1859, 1860, 1862, 1863, 1869. Washington, DC:
    US Government Printing Office.
Board of Commissioners. *Minnesota in the Civil and Indian Wars 1861–1865.*
    Vol. 2. St. Paul: State of Minnesota, 1893.
Cases Decided in the Court of Claims of the United States for the Term of 1911–12.
    Washington, DC: US Court of Claims, 1913.
"Chippewa Indians in Minnesota." House Executive Document No. 247, 51st
    Cong., 1st Sess. (March 6, 1890).
*Decisions of the Department of the Interior and the General Land Office in Cases
    Relating to the Public Lands.* Vols. 10 (1890), 12, 13 (1892), 14 (1892). Wash-
    ington, DC: US Government Printing Office.

"Message from the President of the United States Transmitting Communication from the Secretary of Interior, with papers relating to Chippewa Indians in Minnesota." Senate Executive Document No. 115, 49th Cong., 2nd Sess. (February 28, 1887).

"Mille Lac Indian Reservation in Minnesota." House Executive Document No. 148, 48th Cong., 1st Sess. (April 28, 1884).

Minnesota. *General and Special Laws of the State of Minnesota, Extra Session.* St. Paul, MN: Wm. R. Marshall, state printer, 1862.

Minnesota Session Laws. 1939.

"Report of Investigating Committees Upon Charges of Bribery in the Senatorial Caucus for United States Senator for State of Minnesota." n.p, [1889].

Supplement to Mason's Minnesota Statutes 1927. 1940.

United States Statutes at Large. Vols. 23, 28, 35, 38.

Published and Unpublished Sources

Boussu, Marvin F. "A Review of the Indian Commercial Fishery at Red Lakes, Minnesota." US Department of Interior, Fish and Wildlife Service, Bureau of Commercial Fisheries, 1966.

Brosious, S. M. *The Urgent Case of the Mille Lac Indians.* Philadelphia: Indian Rights Association, 1901.

Brower, Jacob. *Memoirs of Explorations in the Basin of the Mississippi: Kathio.* St. Paul: H. L. Collins Company, 1901.

Brower, Jacob, and Bushnell, D. I., Jr. *Memoirs of Explorations in the Basin of the Mississippi: Mille Lac.* St. Paul, MN: H. L. Collins Company, 1900.

Brunson, Alfred. *A Western Pioneer.* Cincinnati: Hitchcock and Walden; New York: Phillips and Hunt, 1879.

Buffalohead, Roger, and Priscilla Buffalohead. *Against the Tide of American History: The Story of the Mille Lacs Anishinabe.* Cass Lake: Minnesota Chippewa Tribe, 1985.

Chrislock, Carl H. *Watchdog of Loyalty: The Minnesota Commission of Public Safety During World War I.* St. Paul: Minnesota Historical Society Press, 1991.

Cloud Cartographics, Inc. *1995 Mille Lacs County Atlas and Platbook.*

Cormier, Louis P., ed. *Jean-Baptiste Perrault marchand voyageur parti de Montréal le 28e de mai 1783.* Montreal: Boréal Express, 1978.

Crane, Judson A. "Jurisdiction of the United States Court of Claims." *Harvard Law Review* 34, no. 2 (December 1920): 161–77.

Deloria, Vine, Jr. *The Indian Reorganization Act: Congresses and Bills.* Norman: University of Oklahoma Press, 2002.

Densmore, Frances. *Chippewa Customs.* 1929. Reprint, St. Paul: Minnesota Historical Society Press, 1979.

Folsom, William H. C. *Fifty Years in the Northwest.* St. Paul, MN: Pioneer Press Company, 1888.

Folwell, William Watts. *A History of Minnesota.* Vol. 2. St. Paul: Minnesota Historical Society, 1924.

———. *A History of Minnesota*. Vol. 3. St. Paul: Minnesota Historical Society, 1926.

———. *A History of Minnesota*. Vol. 4. St. Paul: Minnesota Historical Society, 1930.

Foster, Haelsia Sperry. *Izatys: Where Nature Reigns*. Milaca, MN: Mille Lacs Investment and Improvement Company, 1914.

Gidakiiminaan (Our Earth): An Anishinaabe Atlas of the 1836 (Upper Michigan), 1837, and 1842 Treaty Ceded Territories. Odanah, WI: Great Lakes Indian Fish and Wildlife Commission, 2007.

Hickerson, Harold. "The Southwestern Chippewa: An Ethnohistorical Study." *Memoirs of the American Anthropological Association No. 92*. Menasha, WI: American Anthropological Association, 1962.

Jarchow, Merrill E. *Amherst H. Wilder and His Enduring Legacy to St. Paul*. St. Paul, MN: Amherst H. Wilder Foundation, 1981.

Kappler, Charles J. *Indian Affairs: Laws and Treaties*. Vol. 2. Washington, DC: US Government Printing Office, 1904.

Kegg, Maude. *Gabekanaansing / At the End of the Trail: Memories of Chippewa Childhood in Minnesota*. Edited and transcribed by John Nichols. Occasional Publications in Anthropology, Linguistic Series 4. Greeley: University of Northern Colorado, Museum of Anthropology, 1978.

———. *Portage Lake: Memories of an Ojibwe Childhood*. Edited by John Nichols. Edmonton: University of Alberta Press, 1991.

Kugel, Rebecca. *To Be the Main Leaders of Our People: A History of Minnesota Ojibwe Politics, 1825–1898*. East Lansing: Michigan State University Press, 1998.

McClurken, James, comp. *Fish in the Lakes, Wild Rice, and Game in Abundance: Testimony on Behalf of Mille Lacs Ojibwe Hunting and Fishing Rights*. East Lansing: Michigan State University Press, 2000.

Minnesota Alliance for Geographic Education. "Lake Mille Lacs: Formation of Landscape & Site Characteristics." Accessed September 26, 2019.

Minnesota Department of Natural Resources. Rum River State Water Trail Map. 2016.

Minnesota Historical Photo Collectors Group, comp. *Joel E. Whitney, Minnesota's Leading Pioneer Photographer, Catalog of Cartes de Visite*. St. Paul, MN: The group, 2001.

Morris, Lucy Leavenworth Wilder, ed. *Old Rail Fence Corners: The A.B.C.'s of Minnesota History*. Austin, MN: F. H. McCulloch Printing, 1914.

Nichols, John D., and Earl Nyholm. *A Concise Dictionary of Minnesota Ojibwe*. Minneapolis: University of Minnesota Press, 1995.

Norrgard, Chantal. *Seasons of Change: Labor, Treaty Rights, and Ojibwe Nationhood*. Chapel Hill: University of North Carolina Press, 2014.

Parker, Donald Dean, ed. *The Recollections of Philander Prescott, Frontiersman of the Old Northwest, 1819–1862*. Lincoln: University of Nebraska Press, 1966.

Plank, Tami K. "Entrepreneurial Business Ethics in the Era of Land and Timber Acquisition: A Minnesota Case Study." MA thesis, St. Cloud State University, 2008.

Polk, R. L. *St. Paul City Directory*. St. Paul, MN: R. L. Polk & Co, 1888–89.

Pond, Samuel W. "Indian Warfare." *Collections of the Minnesota Historical Society* 3 (1880): 132–33.

Prucha, Francis Paul. *The Great Father: The United States Government and the American Indians*. Lincoln and London: University of Nebraska Press, 1984.

Satz, Ronald. *Chippewa Treaty Rights: The Reserved Rights of Wisconsin's Chippewa Indians in Historical Perspective*. Wisconsin Academy of Sciences, Arts and Letters, *Transactions* 79, no. 1 (1991).

Schenck, Theresa M., ed. *The Ojibwe Journals of Edmund F. Ely, 1833–1849*. Lincoln and London: University of Nebraska Press, 2012.

Sobel, Robert, ed. *Biographical Directory of the United States Executive Branch, 1774–1977*. Westport, CT: Greenwood Press, 1977.

Stanchfield, Daniel. "History of Pioneer Lumbering on the Upper Mississippi and Its Tributaries with Biographic Sketches." *Collections of the Minnesota Historical Society* 9 (1901): 331–32.

Swanson, Evadene Burris, and Gustav A. Swanson. *Carlos Avery, 1868–1930*. Hutchinson, MN: McLeod County Historical Society, 1993.

Taliaferro, Lawrence. "Auto-biography of Maj. Lawrence Taliaferro." *Collections of the Minnesota Historical Society* 6 (1894): 225.

Treuer, Anton. *The Assassination of Hole in the Day*. St. Paul: Minnesota Historical Society Press, 2011.

US Congress. *Biographical Directory of the United States Congress, 1774–1989*. Bicentennial Ed. Washington, DC: US Government Printing Office 1989.

Wahkon Boosters. *Wahkon, Minnesota. Tenth Anniversary*. Privately printed, 1917.

Walker, James R. *Lakota Myth*. Lincoln and London: University of Nebraska Press, 1983.

Warner, Mary E. *A Big Hearted Paleface Man: Nathan Richardson and the History of Morrison County, Minnesota*. Little Falls, MN: Morrison County Historical Society, 2006.

Warren, William W. *History of the Ojibway People*. 2nd Edition. 1885. Reprint, St. Paul: Minnesota Historical Society Press, 2009.

Wedll, Don, and Tadd M. Johnson. "The Impact of the Dakota Conflict on the Chippewas of the Mississippi." Draft report, 2004.

Westerman, Gwen, and Bruce White. *Mni Sota Makoce: The Land of the Dakota*. St. Paul: Minnesota Historical Society Press, 2012.

Whipple, Henry B. *Lights and Shadows of a Long Episcopate*. New York and London: Macmillan Company, 1899.

White, Bruce. "Early Game and Fish Regulation and Enforcement in Minnesota, 1858–1920." Research report prepared for the Mille Lacs Band of Ojibwe, 1995.

———. "Familiar Faces: Densmore's Minnesota Photographs." In *Travels with Frances Densmore: Her Life, Work, and Legacy in Native American Studies*, edited by Joan M. Jensen and Michelle Wick Patterson, 326–50. Lincoln and London: University of Nebraska Press, 2015.

———. "Familiar Faces: The Photographic Record of the Minnesota Anishinaabeg." PhD diss., University of Minnesota, 1994.

———. "Indian Visits: Stereotypes of Minnesota's Native People." *Minnesota History* 53 (1992): 99–111.

———. Interview with Dorothy Clark Sam, 2014.

———. "The Myth of the Forgotten Treaty: Traditions about the St. Peters Treaty of 1837." In *The State We're In: Reflections on Minnesota History*, edited by Annette Atkins and Deborah L. Miller. St. Paul: Minnesota Historical Society Press, 2010.

———. "Ojibwe Settlement and Resource Use in South Harbor Township, Mille Lacs County: A Preliminary Report." Prepared for the Lake Onamia/Trunk Highway 169 Data Recovery Project, Loucks & Associates, Inc., for the Minnesota Department of Transportation, 1998.

———. "The Regional Context of the Removal Order of 1850," in *Fish in the Lakes, Wild Rice, and Game in Abundance: Testimony on Behalf of Mille Lacs Ojibwe Hunting and Fishing Rights*, compiled by James McClurken, 141–328. East Lansing: Michigan State University Press, 2000.

———. "Use of the Mississippi River and Its Tributaries between Leech Lake and the Platte River by the Mille Lacs Band of Ojibwe and Related Communities." Report prepared for the Mille Lacs Band of Ojibwe and the US Army Corps of Engineers as part of the Reservoir Operating Plan Evaluation (ROPE) study, 2008.

———. *We Are at Home: Pictures of the Ojibwe People*. St. Paul: Minnesota Historical Society Press, 2007.

White, Helen, and Bruce White. "Fort Snelling in 1838 and 1839: An Ethnographic and Historical Study." Report prepared on contract with the Minnesota Historical Society, Historic Sites Department, 1998.

Newspapers

Available on microfilm at the Minnesota Historical Society:

Little Falls Transcript
Mille Lacs County Times (Milaca)
Mille Lacs Messenger
Minneapolis Tribune
Minnesota Republican
Princeton Union
St. Anthony Express
St. Cloud Daily Times

St. Paul Advertiser
St. Paul Daily Press
St. Paul Daily Union
St. Paul Globe
St. Paul Pioneer and Democrat
St. Paul Pioneer Press
St. Paul Weekly Minnesotian
Svenska Amerikanske Posten

Available online at newspapers.com:

Chicago Tribune
Cincinnati Enquirer
Miami (OK) Daily News
New Orleans Daily Picayune
New York Times

Pittsburgh Gazette
Rochester (NY) Democrat and Chronicle
Santa Cruz Evening News
Washington Evening Star
Winona Daily Republican

Index

Page numbers in *italics* refer to images.

Bruce White has dedicated more than four decades to researching Native history in Minnesota and North America. His books include *We Are at Home: Pictures of the Ojibwe People* and, with Gwen Westerman, *Mni Sota Makoce: The Land of the Dakota*. He has authored historical and ethnographic expert reports used in court cases testing treaties and the application of laws relating to Native people. His report in the 1994 Mille Lacs hunting and fishing case was quoted by Sandra Day O'Connor in her 1999 majority opinion upholding the rights of the Mille Lacs Band to hunt and fish and gather in the ceded area of the Treaty of 1837. He lives in St. Paul, Minnesota.